In honor of
Oindrila Mukherjee
On the occasion of tenure

2017

Writing
Liberal Arts & Sciences

GRAND VALLEY
STATE UNIVERSITY
UNIVERSITY LIBRARIES

Folktales from India

The Pantheon Fairy Tale and Folklore Library

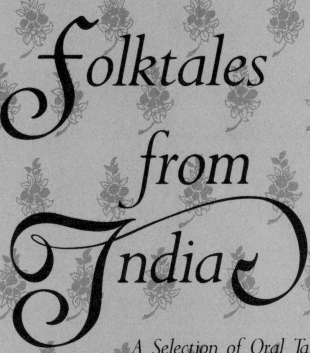

Folktales from India

A Selection of Oral Tales
from Twenty-two Languages

Selected and edited by A. K. Ramanujan

Pantheon Books ~ New York

Permissions acknowledgments may be found on pages 347–348.

Library of Congress Cataloging-in-Publication Data

Folktales from India : a selection of oral tales from twenty-two languages /
selected and edited by A. K. Ramanujan.
p.   cm. — (Pantheon fairy tale and folklore library)
Includes bibliographical references.
ISBN 0-394-55479-5
1. Tales—India.   2. Oral tradition—India.
I. Ramanujan, A. K., 1929–
II. Series: Pantheon fairy tale and folklore library.
GR305.F64   1991
398.2'0954—dc20   91-52624

Book Design by Fearn Cutler
Illustrations by Jenny Vandeventer

Manufactured in the United States of America
First Edition

This book is
for
Carolyn and Alan Dundes

Contents

Preface

This book of Indian oral tales, selected and translated from twenty-two languages, covers most of the regions of India. It is called *Folktales* FROM *India*, not OF *India*, for no selection can truly "represent" the multiple and changing lives of Indian tales. It presents instead examples of favorite narratives from the subcontinent. With few exceptions, each of these tales, though chosen from a teller in one language and region, is also told with variations in other regions. Every tale here is only one telling, held down in writing for the nonce till you or someone else reads it, brings it to life, and changes it by retelling it. These stories were handed down to me, and in selecting, arranging, and adapting, I've inevitably reworked them somewhat. So, consider me the latest teller and yourself the latest listener, who in turn will retell the tale. Like a proverb, a story gains meaning in context; in the context of this book, the meanings are made between us now. A folktale is a poetic text that carries some of its cultural contexts within it; it is also a traveling metaphor that finds a new meaning with each new telling. I have arranged the tales in cycles as I would arrange a book of poems, so that they are in dialogue with each other and together create a world through point and counterpoint.

Nothing can reproduce the original telling of a tale. These were all translated by different hands at different times and places, and I have retold them—making slight changes in some, and more than slight changes in others where the language was fulsome, cumbersome, or simply outdated. I have kept close to the narrative line, omitted no detail or motif, and tried to keep the design of the plot intact. I have not mixed episodes from different variants to make them more dramatic or artistic than they already are.

I have taken care to include only tales from actual tellers, rather than literary texts. About a quarter of these tales were personally collected or recollected; some have never been published before, certainly not in an English translation. Many of the others were chosen from late-nineteenth-century sources: some of the finest oral folktale collections were compiled then, and published in journals like *The Indian Antiquary, The Journal of the Royal Asiatic Society of Bengal*, and *North Indian Notes and Queries*. Civil servants, their wives and daughters, foreign missionaries, as well as many Indian scholars, took part in this enterprise. Indeed, more than two thousand tales were collected, translated, and published during this time; they are old, yet are told and retold today.

While the Introduction discusses the importance of oral traditions for any study of India, one should bear in mind that these tales are meant to be read for pleasure first, to be experienced as aesthetic objects. As an old Chinese proverb tells us: "Birds do not sing because they have answers; birds sing because they have songs." The songs of course have territories, species, contexts, and functions.

In making this book, not only am I indebted to countless tellers all over India—beginning with my own grandmother—but to collectors, scholars, editors, and index makers from different parts of the world for over a century. Wendy Wolf initiated this project through Susan Bergholz five years ago; Barbara Stoler Miller's and Wendy Doniger's delight in the tales has been an inspiration; Yoji Yamaguchi's courtesy, editorial skills, and gentle reminders have helped me finish and shape the book. I heard and collected folktales long before I thought about books: meeting Edwin Kirkland in 1956 in a small South Indian town made me aware of folklore as a field. Half a lifetime of friendship with Carolyn and Alan Dundes (whom I met the very first month after I arrived in America) has been a continuous pleasure and a continuing education. Colleagues in the Department of South Asian Languages at the University of Chicago, grants from the American Institute of Indian Studies, and the riches of the Regenstein Library have all contributed towards this book. I thank them all.

A. K. Ramanujan
University of Chicago
July 1991

Introduction

Anyone studying the culture of India needs to study not only its written classics but its oral traditions, of which folklore is an important part. Folklore pervades childhoods, families, and communities as the symbolic language of the nonliterate parts of the people and the culture. Even in a large modern city like Madras, Bombay, or Calcutta, even in Western-style nuclear families with their well-planned 2.2 children, folklore—proverbs, lullabies, folk medicine, folktales—is only a suburb away, a cousin or a grandmother away. Authentic folk theater flourishes in the back streets of a city like Madras; festivals, with all their attendant folk performances, like that for the elephant-faced god Ganapathi in Bombay, are major annual events. When a friend of mine, a professor of Kannada in a big city college, said to me, "How can you collect folklore in a big city these days?" I asked him to assign his class of urban students an exercise: to write down from memory a folktale they had heard and never read. That evening, my friend sought me out excitedly to show me a sheaf of forty tales that his students had transcribed.

Wherever people live, folklore grows; new jokes, proverbs (like the new campus proverb "To xerox is to know"), rhymes, tales, and songs circulate in the oral tradition. Chain letters and Murphy's laws circulate on paper and graffiti on latrine walls. Verbal folklore, in the sense of a largely oral tradition with specific genres (such as proverb, riddle, lullaby, tale, ballad, prose narrative, song), nonverbal modes (such as dances, games, floor or wall designs, artifacts from toys to outdoor clay horses in villages), and composite performing arts (such as street magic and street theater, which combine prose, verse, song, dance, various local objects, costume, etc.)—all of these expressive folk forms weave in and out of every aspect of city, village, and small-town life. Both public culture and domestic culture cannot be fully understood without a knowledge of the folk idiom. Every kind of Indian cultural practice, every

In writing this introduction, I have used materials from my earlier writings, especially: (1) *Who Needs Folklore? The Relevance of Oral Traditions to South Asian Studies*, the First Rama Wattumull Distinguished Lecture on India, sponsored by the Center for South Asian Studies in March 1988 and published by them as number 1 of their South Asia Occasional Papers Series, University of Hawaii at Manoa; (2) "Telling Tales," *Daedalus*, Fall 1989.

Indian cultural performance, whether it is the classical epic and theater or modern film and political rhetoric, is indebted to oral traditions and folk forms. What we separate as art, economics, and religion appear intermeshed as aspects of the same performance. The aesthetics, ethos, and worldview of a person are shaped in childhood and throughout early life, and reinforced later, by these verbal and nonverbal environments. In a largely nonliterate culture, everyone—whether poor or rich, high caste or low, professor, pundit, or ignoramus, engineer or street hawker—everyone has inside him a large non-literate subcontinent.

In a South Indian folktale, also told elsewhere, one dark night an old woman was searching intently for something in the street. A passer-by asked her, "Have you lost something?"

She answered, "Yes, I've lost my keys. I've been looking for them all evening."

"Where did you lose them?"

"I don't know. Maybe inside the house."

"Then why are you looking for them here?"

"Because it's dark in there. I don't have oil in my lamps. I can see much better here under the streetlights."

Until recently many studies of Indian civilization have been conducted on that principle: look for it under the light, in Sanskrit, in written texts, in what we think are well-lit public spaces of the culture, in places we already know. There we have, of course, found precious things. Without carrying the parable too far, in a book like this, we may say we are now moving indoors, into the expressive culture of the household, to look for our keys. As it often happens, we may not find the keys we are looking for and may have to make new ones, but we will find all sorts of other things we never knew we had lost, or ever even had.

❧ *Indian Regional Languages*[1]

Whoever speaks of "Indian" or "India," as we are doing in the title of this book, must hasten to add that India contains many Indias. Over a hundred

---

[1] Somewhat arbitrarily, I've confined myself to the languages of India, excluding those of Pakistan, Bangladesh, Nepal, and Sri Lanka. Neither the languages (e.g., Bengali, Punjabi, Urdu, Tamil) nor cultural expressions like folklore respect such political boundaries. The tales in this book have cognates in all these South Asian countries.

languages, ten major script systems and several minor ones, many old religions with innumerable sects and cults, racial mixtures over millennia, a variety of landscapes and climates and so on have contributed to an incredibly complex braiding of traditions and countertraditions. It has been said more than once that whatever you can truly say about India, you can also say the exact opposite with equal truthfulness.

Nothing exemplifies the variety of the Indian scene better than the languages. In the 1961 census, 1,652 mother tongues were recorded with the names of speech varieties that the speakers said they spoke. Linguists have classified these speech varieties, or dialects, and subsumed them under 105 or so languages, which belong to four language families.[2] Of these 105 or so languages, 90 are spoken by less than 5 percent of the entire population; 65 belong to small tribes. To these should be added Sanskrit, the father tongue, the language of religious texts, literary classics, and native sciences—and also the English of colonial and postcolonial India, a widely used second language. Fifteen of the languages are written, read, and spoken by 95 percent of the people of India, and each of them is spoken by several million people.

The literatures of these fifteen languages,[3] some of which have long histories, are just beginning to be taught and translated in the West. Literature in a language such as Tamil goes back two thousand years, and in several others such as Bengali and Gujerati, at least eight hundred years. In addition to these written literatures there are oral traditions—riddles, proverbs, songs, ballads, tales, epics, and so on—in each of the 1,600-odd dialects or mother tongues that we have classified under the 105 languages. Indeed, one way of defining

[2] The four language families are Indo-Aryan, Dravidian, Tibeto-Burman, and Austro-Asiatic.

[3] The fifteen literary languages are Assamese, Bengali, Gujerati, Hindi, Kashmiri, Marathi, Oriya, Punjabi, Sanskrit, Sindhi, Urdu, Kannada, Malayalam, Tamil, and Telugu. The first eleven belong to the Indo-Aryan branch of the Indo-European family of languages; the remaining four are the major Dravidian literary languages. (Kashmiri is sometimes classified under Dardic or Indo-Iranian.) In this book, languages with small numbers of speakers like the Austro-Asiatic Santali and Didayi, Dravidian ones like Tulu, Kota, and Gondi, and Indo-Aryan ones like Konkani and Rajasthani are also represented. Till recently they were not written languages (though Tulu did begin to get written a few centuries ago). The following table indicates the number of people who speak each, according to the 1971 census:

Assamese	9 million
Bengali	45 million in India, 70 million in Bangladesh, and 4 million in adjoining areas
Didayi or Gta	a negligible number
Gondi	2 million
Gujerati	26 million
Hindi	163 million in India as a first language

verbal folklore for India is to say it is the literature of the dialects, those mother tongues of village, street, kitchen, tribal hut, and wayside tea shop. This is the wide base of the Indian pyramid on which all other Indian literatures rest.

Students of Indian civilization have valued and attended only to the top of the pyramid. Traditionally, Indians have made a distinction between *marga*, "the high road," and *desi*, "the byway, the country road," in their discussion of the arts. In American anthropology, Robert Redfield, the Chicago anthropologist who influenced the study of India in the 1950s and 1960s, said, "In a civilization, there is a great tradition of the reflective many and there is a little tradition of the largely unreflective many."[4] The "Great Tradition," said to be carried by Sanskrit, is seen as pan-Indian, prestigious, ancient, authorized by texts. The "Little Tradition," or really the "Little Traditions" in the plural, are seen as local, mostly oral, and carried by the illiterate (liberals would call them nonliterate)—the anonymous "unreflective many." Redfield himself and Milton Singer later modified these notions, and others have been critical of them. They were seminal at one time, especially because they urged anthropologists not to ignore the "texts" of a culture in favor of "fieldwork."

Now we need a new emphasis, a larger view regarding the "texts" them-

Kannada	25 million
Kashmiri	2.4 million
Konkani	1.5 million
Kota	less than 1,000
Malayalam	22 million
Marathi	42 million
Oriya	20 million
Punjabi	30 million
Rajasthani	20 million (often considered a dialect of Hindi)
Sanskrit	not a spoken mother tongue
Santali	4 million
Sindhi	1.7 million in India, 8 million in Pakistan
Tamil	40 million
Telugu	47 million
Tulu	1.2 million
Urdu	28 million in India, 10 million in Pakistan

Eleven languages have home states; Hindi is spoken in six states; Sindhi and Urdu are nonstate languages. In each state, in addition to the major language, several other languages are spoken by minorities. For instance, Telugu is spoken by 86 percent of Andhra Pradesh, and the rest speak one or more of nine languages, for example, Tamil, Urdu, Kannada, and Punjabi. Rates of literacy vary according to region, language, religion, and gender.

[4] Robert Redfield, *The Little Community and Peasant Society and Culture* (Chicago: University of Chicago Press, 1960), p. 41.

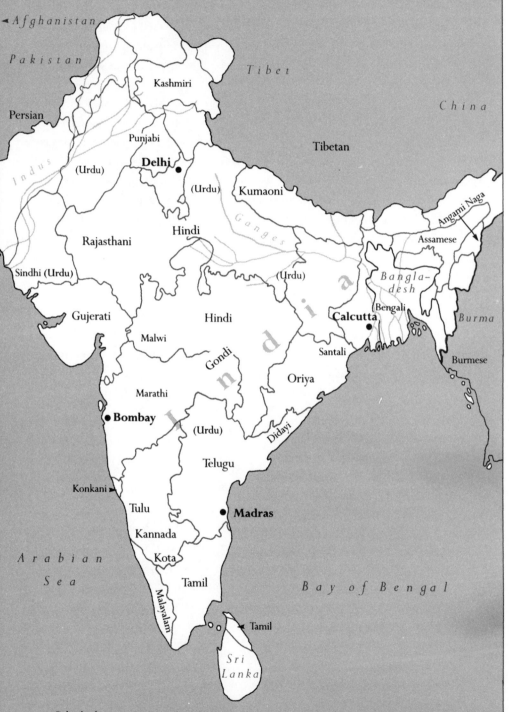

Twenty-two Languages of India

Afghanistan

Pakistan

Tibet

China

Kashmiri

Persian

Indus

Punjabi

Tibetan

(Urdu)

Delhi

(Urdu)

Kumaoni

Ganges

Angami Naga

Hindi

Rajasthani

Assamese

Sindhi (Urdu)

(Urdu)

Bangla-desh

Gujerati

Hindi

Bengali

Calcutta

India

Burma

Malwi

Gondi

Santali

Burmese

Marathi

Oriya

Bombay

(Urdu)

Didayi

Konkani

Telugu

Arabian Sea

Tulu

Kannada

Madras

Kota

Tamil

Bay of Bengal

Malayalam

Tamil

Sri Lanka

Only the languages represented in this book are included here. Locations of the languages are approximate. Many of them are spoken in more than one region. For a more detailed map, see Joseph E. Schwartzberg's *A Historical Atlas of South Asia* (Chicago: University of Chicago Press, 1978), p. 100.

selves. Written and hallowed texts are not the only kinds of texts in a culture like India's. Oral traditions of every kind produce texts. "Cultural performances" of every kind, whether they are plays, rituals, or games, contain texts, written and oral. In a sense, every cultural performance is a text in itself.

When we look at texts this way, we need to modify terms such as "Great Tradition" and "Little Traditions," and to see all these cultural performances as a transitive series, a "scale of forms" responding to one another, engaged in continuous and dynamic dialogic relations. Past and present, what's "pan-Indian" and what's local, the written and the oral, the verbal and the nonverbal—all these are engaged in reworking and redefining relevant others. What are distinguished as "the classical," "the folk," and "the popular," as different modes in Indian culture, will be seen as part of an interacting continuum. Texts, then, are also contexts and pretexts for other texts. In our studies now, we are beginning to recognize and place folk texts in this ever-present network of intertextuality. For folk texts are pervasive, behind, under, and around all the texts of the society and in all its strata, not merely among the rural and the nonliterate. City and village, factory and kitchen, Hindu, Buddhist, and Jaina, Christian and Muslim, every caste and class, the crumbling almanac no less than the runaway computer—all are permeated by oral traditions, tales, jokes, beliefs, and rules of thumb not yet found in books.

~ Interactive Pan-Indian Systems

In the view being developed here, even what's called the Great Tradition is not singular but plural—it is a set of interactive pan-Indian systems like Brahminism, Buddhism, and Jainism, with Tantra and Bhakti interacting variously with these. To be comprehensive, we should add Islam, Zoroastrianism, Christianity, and modernity itself as the other active systems that participate in this give-and-take.[5] Folklore participates in all these systems. For instance, the oral tales in this book are drawn from several communities, and some have literary analogues in Hindu, Buddhist, Jaina, and Islamic as well as Christian texts.

Let us examine briefly the idea that Great Traditions are pan-Indian and

[5] A. K. Ramanujan, "Where Mirrors Are Windows: An Anthology of Reflections on Indian Literatures," *History of Religions*, February 1989.

Little Traditions are not. Sanskrit and Prakrit, though they have a pan-Indian distribution, still originate in particular regions; Sanskrit itself, though trans-local and apparently ageographic, has varieties of pronunciation that can be identified as Bengali, Malayali, or Banarasi.[6] Nor are the so-called Little Traditions necessarily or usually confined to small localities or dialects. Proverbs, riddles, and stories and tunes, motifs, and genres of songs and dances are not confined to a region, even though they may be embodied in the nonliterate dialects and may seem to be enclosed in those mythic entities called self-sufficient village communities. It is well known that such folklore items, like many other sorts of items in cultural exchange, are autotelic: that is, they travel by themselves without (often) any movement of populations. A proverb, a riddle, a joke, a story, a remedy, or a recipe travels every time it is told. It crosses linguistic boundaries any time a bilingual person tells it or hears it.

The languages and regions in India have, therefore, a large stock of shared folk materials. Collections can be made of proverbs, riddles, and tales common to widely separated and distant regions of the subcontinent. Yet these shared items may carry different meanings in different regions and uses. For instance, the proverb "It's dark under the lamp" has been collected in Kannada and in Kashmiri, at two ends of the Indian subcontinent. In Kannada, it means (among other things) that a virtuous man, like a lighted lamp, may have dark, shadowy places, hidden vices. In Kashmiri, I'm told, "It's dark under the lamp" has a political meaning (among others): that a beneficent king may have evil henchmen. This kind of variation in meaning is characteristic of cultural forms. The signifiers, whether they are images or characters or episodes, or even so-called structures and archetypes, may be the same in different periods and regions, but the signification goes on changing. You cannot predict meanings from forms, for the meaning of a sign is culturally and contextually assigned. A sign requires an assignment.

Not only do folklore items—arising and current in apparently narrow, incommunicable corners and very localized dialects—travel within the country or culture area; they are also part of an international network. Archer Taylor's *English Riddles*[7] gives us current English riddles and centuries-old written variants, as well as variants from Africa, India, and the New World. One can collect today, as I know from experience, oral tales from village tellers in

---

[6] Frits J. Stahl, *Nambudiri Neda Recitation* (The Hague: Mouton, 1961).

[7] Archer Taylor, *English Riddles from Oral Tradition* (Berkeley: University of California Press, 1951).

South India that are similar, motif for motif, to the tales we know in the English-speaking world as the Greek *Oedipus* or Shakespeare's *King Lear*.[8]

In a story told about Aristotle in Europe, and about an Indian philosopher in India, the philosopher meets a village carpenter who has a beautiful old knife and asks him, "How long have you had this knife?" The carpenter answers, "Oh, the knife has been in our family for generations. We have changed the handle a few times and the blade a few times, but it is the same knife." Similarly, in a folktale that goes on changing from teller to teller, the structure of the tale may remain constant while all the cultural details change. Parts of different tales are combined to make a new tale which expresses a new aesthetic and moral form characteristic of the culture. When the same tale is told again in a different time or place, it may come to say fresh and appropriate things, often without any change in the story line. Any fixity, any reconstructed archetype, is a fiction, a label, a convenience.

~ Contexts

Tales are told in different contexts and function in a variety of ways. To contextualize a tale fully, we need to know the teller, when, where, and to whom he or she told the tale, what he or she and the listeners thought of the tale, how the listeners responded when they heard it, and other such details. We need to bring also to this kind of ethnography of narrative a sense of where the tale fits in other texts and performances of the culture, what is considered significant, how it makes meanings, what's taboo and what's not, and the place of tellers in the community—not merely the facts of the telling but the feelings, the meanings, and the meaning-making. In the following pages and in the Notes, I shall suggest a few general contexts without going into too much detail.

~ ~ ~

Who tells these tales? There are professional and nonprofessional tellers. By and large, I have chosen tales told by nonprofessional household tellers. In South India, for instance, singers and tellers travel from place to place, their performances being engaged by families or organizations. Mostly, these are tellers of epic stories from the *Ramayana* and the *Mahabharata*, or of stories of

[8] See "Mother Marries Son," "Adventures of a Disobedient Son," "Prince Sabar," and "Hanchi."

gods from the Puranas (encyclopedias of Hindu mythology). In villages, there are bardic troupes that perform epics about caste heroes, or local gods and saints.[9] The bard will intersperse his recitation—which may be performed serially for hours for several nights—with shorter tales and anecdotes as well as poems and songs, just as he will introduce references to current politics. Thus ancient tales and epics are given contemporary relevance.

Domestic tellers tell tales like the ones in this book to children. In families like mine, they were mealtime rather than bedtime stories. An aunt or grandmother would bring together all the children of the house, especially if it was a joint family, and feed them all at once in a circle, mixing the food in a large plate and handing out morsels to each child in turn. Tales would be told to keep the children's attention and to make them eat more. I've also heard tales from the cooks in the house, who were usually widows working for a living in a family of the same caste and speaking the same language. Servants from another class would also tell stories, bringing us in contact with another caste and class. In other families, grandfathers and other senior male figures were the tellers; they didn't tell stories in their kitchen but in the outer parts of the house, and they would have audiences of children from other families as well. We don't know very much how the selection of tales differed or whether the same tale told by a grandfather and a grandmother would be different in detail and outcome. I shall say more about what I call women-centered tales and how they differ from male-centered tales—though both kinds are told by women. A talented person's repertoire would consist of twenty or thirty stories, not much more—and most of them would be what the person had heard in childhood rather than later in life. The largest number I've collected myself from a single teller is twenty-three. Most tellers knew much fewer tales, even if they told them well. They would have a mix of stories about animals, jesters, men, women, fools, wise men, different castes and occupations such as weavers and shepherds and certainly Brahmans—I've modeled my sections on just such a range. As in this book, my tellers told stories associatively—if a dream was mentioned in one tale, it might lead to another about dreams.

Folktales are told not only to make children eat more or put them to sleep. They are often told to keep adults awake: when farmers gather to watch crops all night or graze cows or sheep all day, or when workers slice areca nuts

[9] See Stuart Blackburn et al., eds., *Oral Epics in India* (Berkeley: University of California Press, 1989).

(which have to be processed within a short time after they are harvested) or roll *bidis* (cheap local cigarettes) in a factory. Like work songs, these tales beguile the time and ease the monotony of long labor by engaging fantasy. While doing so, they also carry subliminal, often subversive, meanings.

Tales, like proverbs, are also enlisted to make a point, to find precedent and authority—in political speeches, religious discourses, and legal discussions. For instance, "A Feast in a Dream" was told during a village council meeting (*pancayat*) by a man of the Meo community. The story itself features a Meo outwitting two Muslims. The relations within the story became a metaphor for the relations between the teller and others in the real community. Thus, stories are metaphors in search of a context, waiting to be told and given new relevance.

Special ritual tales, or *vratakathas*, are told as part of a calendrical ritual, and their telling in that context has ritual efficacy. It is believed that both tellers and listeners receive benefits, as depicted in tales like "A Story in Search of an Audience" and "Brother's Day." Very often, an ordinary tale may acquire this status by being told in such a context.[10]

❧ ❧ ❧

How old are the stories? The antiquity of these domestic tales is as amazing as their spread. When I told the story of "The Monkey and the Crocodile" to an archaeologist friend of mine, John Carswell, his face lit up—he was carrying in his briefcase a potsherd from his recent dig in Mantai in Sri Lanka, and the potsherd pictured a monkey sitting on the back of a crocodile. The story was also a Buddhist story, and the first mention in a Hindu text is in the *Pancatantra* (Sanskrit, fifth century). The Brahmana texts, supposed to be dull esoteric texts about ritual detail, carry tales current today.[11] In a learned commentary on an Upanishad, the great Indian philosopher Sankara tells the story "Crossing a River, Losing a Self." This story, which I heard in childhood, was obviously known to Sankara in the seventh century as well, and he uses it as a parable for ignorance of self.[12]

[10] For more details regarding such contexts, see "Two Realms of Kannada Folklore," in Stuart Blackburn and A. K. Ramanujan, *Another Harmony: New Essays on South Asian Folklore* (Berkeley: University of California Press, 1986).

[11] Wendy Doniger O'Flaherty, *Tales of Sex and Violence: Folklore, Sacrifice, and Danger in the Jaiminiya Brahmana* (Chicago: University of Chicago Press, 1985).

[12] *The Brhadaranyaka Upanishad, with the Commentary of Sankaracarya*, trans. Swami Madhavananda (Calcutta: Adraita Ashrama, 1965), p. 120.

The eleventh-century *Kathasaritsagara* contains stories that are to be found in the *Arabian Nights*, in Boccaccio, and in Shakespeare (e.g., the stories of *All's Well That Ends Well* and *Cymbeline*) and also in the current repertoire of village women in Karnataka. My grandmother, who was in her sixties when I was a boy fifty years ago, told me stories that she had heard from her grandmother. S. M. Natesa Sastri, who came from the same part of Tamil Nadu (Trichinopoly), heard the same tales in his childhood and published them in Tamil and in English in the 1870s. This kind of corroboration inspires trust in many of these early recordings. Practically every one of the tales collected in the nineteenth century is confirmed in my conversations with present-day Indians who know the regional languages. Thus, these centuries-old tales are current: variants and parallels are being generated to this day by tellers in households all over the country. In Kannada, in addition to my collections, I know of over three thousand tales collected by fellow folklorists in the last twenty-five years. And they have parallels in other parts of the subcontinent, as we can verify by leafing through recent collections.

~ The Tales in This Book

In choosing and arranging the tales for this book, I have taken into account the major languages, the authentic collections available in English over the past century, the oral narratives listed and classified in the international indexes, as well as the favorite genres and themes that appear again and again in many regions. I have excluded myths (sacred narratives), legends (narratives believed to be true about historical persons and places), and stories known only in written texts. I have also, by and large, excluded narratives sung and performed by bards in public places—though some of the tales in this book (e.g., "Adventures of a Disobedient Son") are told at home as well as by bards. So, here there are no selections chosen directly from Sanskrit sources like the *Pancatantra*, the *Kathasaritsagara*, or the Pali *Jatakas* and Hindu or Jaina Puranas; if a tale from one of these texts, say the *Pancatantra*, is known to occur in the oral tradition (e.g., "The Tiger-Makers"), I have acknowledged it. I have included parables told by Ramakrishna, a religious teacher, genius, and saint; he was known to be illiterate and was a treasure house of oral traditions, out of which he created his own.[13]

---

[13] For a lively recent study of religious parables, see Kirin Narayan, *Storytellers, Saints, and Scoundrels: Folk Narrative in Hindu Religious Teaching* (Philadelphia: University of Pennsylvania Press, 1989).

Instead of arranging the tales according to some classificatory scheme (e.g., romantic tales, tales of magic, etc.), I have arranged them in eleven cycles or sessions, each consisting of eight to eleven tales. Each cycle has one or more of the following kinds of tales:

> male-centered tales
> women-centered tales
> tales (usually two contrasted ones) about families
> tales about fate, death, gods, demons, ghosts, and such
> humorous tales or tales about a jester or clever person
> tales about animals
> stories about stories

Thus, we will encounter similar themes in point and counterpoint several times, often expressing contradictory attitudes (e.g., about fate or sibling bonds), so that tale becomes relevant to tale; they interpenetrate and interpret each other, and together create a world. This is a small sample of a hundred-odd narratives out of some three thousand that I happened to have looked at. I have tried to make the sample represent not all the types of tales but the contrasts and patterns, the variety and the glimpses of coherence, that I experience in the vast body of Indian folktales, making this book of selections a metonymy, a part that speaks of and for something larger than itself. In the following pages, I shall comment on each of the kinds of tales listed above.

᠊ᢦ *Male-Centered Tales*　In these tales a hero is featured prominently and moves out of the parental family in search of adventures. These are like initiatory scenarios for young men who leave the parental family and start a family of their own. As in "Adventures of a Disobedient Son," the hero may start out with a sense of rivalry with his father, kill or master an ogre (a father figure!), win princesses from different worlds, befriend animals (often a bird of the air, a fish or crocodile of the waters, ants of the earth), undertake tasks in which these animals (or the women) help him, and then return victorious to receive recognition, a princess, a kingdom—or at least half of one. Women are no more than pawns or prizes or helpers in his life's game. His antagonists tend to be male, though a stepmother or ogress might also want to get rid of him.[14] The story usually ends with a wedding.

[14] See "Raja Vikram and the Princess of China" and "Adventures of a Disobedient Son."

~ *Women-Centered Tales*   If quests and tasks are part of the life-story of the hero in a male-centered tale, a different focus makes itself felt in women-centered tales. Saving, rescuing, or reviving a man, often solving riddles on his behalf, becomes the life-task of the heroine. In such tales, women predominate and men are wimps, ruled by mothers, mistresses, or wives. In a tale like "The Clever Daughter-in-Law," the heroine outwits a weak nobody of a husband and a mean mother-in-law, as well as male robbers and the village goddess. (Note that in such a tale even the deity is female.) The antagonists are usually women—co-wives, sisters-in-law, stepmothers.[15] Sometimes a male—a father, a brother, or a guru—may desire the heroine inappropriately and turn into her enemy. Her chief helpers also tend to be women.[16] In family tales like those of brothers and sisters, the patterns are reversed: sisters and brothers help each other, or desire each other so much that they become enemies.

Women-centered tales, told by women about women and often to younger women, tend to have a certain pattern: in contrast to the male-centered tale, marriage begins rather than ends the story; a separation ensues, and then a rescue of the male by the female. In "Prince Sabar," the princess is banished by her Lear-like father, gains the love of a prince through her own efforts, but loses him through the jealousy of wicked sisters, and regains him after healing his wounds. She has to earn him all over again through suffering and service. In "The Dead Prince and the Talking Doll," he is already dead. The heroine tends his dead body for twelve years, and at the last minute nearly loses him to a younger, athletic rival who usurps her place. The motif-cluster of the Black and White Brides, the usurping surrogate who takes the heroine's place even after she has won her prince, occurs again and again—a witness perhaps to a recurrent female fear that her husband is not always hers to keep and can be lured away by conniving younger rivals. In "Teja and Teji," a kind of Cinderella story, Teji is supplanted by her stepsister, though not for long.

Several of the women's tales feature a woman—a mother, a wife, or a daughter—who is needed to solve the riddles that her men cannot answer: Birbal's daughter in the Akbar and Birbal stories, the wife in "In Another

---

[15] See "The Kite's Daughter," "A Flowering Tree," "Teja and Teji."
[16] See "Hanchi," "A Flowering Tree," "The Princess Whose Father Wanted to Marry Her." For a discussion of European (Danish) women's tales, see Bengt Holbek, *The Interpretation of Fairy Tales: Danish Folklore in a European Perspective* (Helsinki: Suomalainen Tiedeakatemia, 1987).

Country" and "A Hair's-Breadth Escape." In "The Wife Who Refused to Be Beaten," the woman marries a stupid man who thinks it's masculine to beat his wife with his shoe, prevents him from doing so, and proceeds to rescue him from a wicked woman who cheats him at dice, takes all his money, and throws him into debtor's jail. Such tales are reported very early in collections like the *Kathasaritsagara*. These women are true cousins of the feisty heroines in Shakespeare's comedies that owe their plots to Italian novellas, which in turn are related to tales in the *Arabian Nights* and the *Kathasaritsagara*. The women in these tales contrast sharply with a woman like Sita in the epics, who represents the ideal of the chaste, unquestioning wife who follows her husband like a shadow and suffers all the way. They are analogues of the Dark Goddess in Hindu myth: when the gods are unable to destroy the buffalo demon, they resort to a female figure who has all their power and in addition has the wiles to seduce and outwit the demon.

~ *Tales About Families*   Family relations of every kind, especially intergender relations, are the subject of many tales. Sisters, brothers, brother-sister pairs, sisters-in-law, sons-in-law, mothers-in-law, couples, co-wives, mothers and sons, and fathers and daughters appear in all their complex interrelations. Not only bonds of affection but rivalry, incest, betrayal, and cruelty are explored in these family tales.

Psychologists such as Freud and Jung have attended mostly to myths; but folktales are a potent source of psychoanalytic insights, for they concentrate on close family ties and childhood fantasies.[17] For instance, ambivalence towards parents is expressed in a number of symbolic ways. Mothers are split into good mothers who die and metamorphose into turtles or fruit-bearing trees for their orphaned children, and wicked stepmothers who starve and beat them and sell them down the river, as in "Teja and Teji." Fathers can be either good royal fathers who send their children out on quests and helpful sages who aid them in their journeys, or ogres and faraway kings who refuse to part with their daughters till they have put the young man through his paces in terrible ordeals. Forbidden feelings of incest on the part of fathers and mothers towards their children, or of brothers and sisters towards their siblings, are faced and unpacked with all their implications (see "Sona and Rupa" and "Mother Marries Son"). As these tales are usually told to children

[17] For bibliography and discussion, see Alan Dundas, "The Psychological Study of Folklore in the United States, 1880–1980," *Southern Folklore*, vol. 48 (1991), pp. 97–120.

in the context of the family, they are part of the child's psychological education in facing forbidden feelings and finding a narrative that will articulate and contain if not resolve them—for the tellers as well as their young listeners.

The stories of animal husbands and their disenchantment through the efforts of a wife are, I think, symbolic of the way a woman may see her relations with men: domesticating the wild animal, or bringing him from a state of death to life ("The Dead Prince and the Talking Doll"). "Shall I Show You My Real Face?" depicts a son-in-law who arrives from nowhere and marries a girl from a good family and terrorizes her; the brothers have to rescue her, scare and degrade him, literally make him eat shit, and finally bury him in a backyard well. Such episodes express a deep distrust of marrying strangers and foreigners. The power games and realpolitik of a joint family where women from different statuses and families are married to brothers (or, as co-wives, to the same man) and have to live together in one patrilocal household are pictured vividly in many of these tales (e.g., "The Kite's Daughter," "The Ogress Queen"). In "The Serpent Mother," the youngest daughter-in-law has no supportive family of her own and finds it in a nest of serpents under the ground who shower her with gold and affection—a wonderful fantasy of a secret subterranean family for the orphan in us all.

~ *Tales About Fate, Gods, Demons, and Such*   Another difference between oral tales and the official mythology, in Hindu as well as other religions, is the way the supernatural is treated. In Hindu mythology, the gods do not sweat or blink, nor do their feet touch the ground. In the tales, the gods have bodies. They smell, pee, and shit. The goddesses menstruate. In "The Clever Daughter-in-Law," the goddess craves the spicy gourd *talada* that the daughter-in-law eats and will not share with her; she is so covetous that she sulks and puts her hand on her mouth. The daughter-in-law is not respectful to her, either: she threatens to beat her with a broom (in one variant, to fart in her face) if she doesn't behave herself. In another tale, a Brahman swallows Bidatha, the god of fate who allots people's fortunes, and chases off Saraswati and Lakshmi, the goddesses of learning and of good fortune, with his stick, lashing out at them with his tongue as well.

Many different views of fate are made possible by the tales. In some ("Killed by a Tiger," "Mother Marries Son"), fate is inexorable; when you try to escape it, you run into it head-on. In others ("Outwitting Fate"), a clever man or woman manipulates it, turning the very terms of destiny to the victim's advantage. A number of tales show how a faithful servant or mother or sister overhears a conversation between birds or Fate muttering to herself (Fate in the women's tales is a woman) and proceeds to avert the preordained disasters like the thorns that are waiting in the victim's food or the tree that is about to fall on him—as in "Brother's Day" and "Untold Stories." Such tales give the lie to the stereotype that "peasants," "illiterate folk," or "Orientals" are fatalists who passively accept their destiny.

Notions of karma (actions in one's past lives determining the present) rarely play any part in these tales as they do in Indian epics like the *Mahabharata*. In fact, the tales rarely concern themselves with more than one life—except to make fun of it, as in "Living Like a Pig." But folktales do not confine themselves to one monolithic point of view. Therefore we do have a thoughtful tale such as "Other Lives," in which a Brahman experiences several lives as an untouchable and as a king, and is amazed when a character from a past life enters his present one. But such tales are exceptions.

I have often juxtaposed these various points of view. "The Lord of Death," which is a somber view of the way death takes many beguiling and deadly forms to finish off people, is placed next to "The Shepherd's Ghost," the comedy of a fool who imagines he is already dead when he is not.

Other supernatural figures such as demons are terrifying beings with extraordinary powers in Hindu mythology. In the tales they are gullible creatures whose powers can be exploited by a barber with a mirror, who are scared to death of a shrew with a broom or driven wild by a piper who plays so badly out of tune that it grates on their sensitive ears.

~ *Humorous Tales*   Indian literatures are customarily presented as solemn, spiritual, and humorless. Folktales are an excellent corrective to such a stereotype. I have included a large number of humorous tales and anecdotes in this book, tales that invert and subvert the hierarchies. Just as the women-centered tales counter and complement the attitudes of the male-centered tales, comic tales, tales of jesters and fools, display the underbelly of the novellas and the romantic tales. For instance, the serious tales have various magic objects, bowls that produce food and animals that drop gold with their dung. The comic ones feature rogues who rip off gullible customers by selling them pseudo-magic objects, such as the bear that drops silver rupees in "The Village Rogue." In tales of magic, a metaphor is literalized as in a dream: the word for menstruation in languages such as Tamil and Sanskrit is the same as that for flowering, so the girl in "A Flowering Tree" literally becomes a gorgeous tree that bears flowers. But the same process of literalization becomes a comic resource[18] when the king angrily asks the jester Tenali Rama never to show his face to him again and the next day Rama appears with a pot over his face, or when a woman asks him to describe how the city of Lanka was burned and he sets fire to her house and says, "Like this." He then calls it the *yathartha* or realistic *Ramayana*.

Figures of power like kings, the law, Brahmans and gurus, gods and goddesses, sons-in-law and mothers-in-law, tigers, demons, and robbers are all shown to be stupid, easily outwitted, and all too flawed. Jesters like Tenali Rama take on the Brahmans, laugh at the goddesses, poke fun at their kings, and puncture their vanities. Mere barbers or housewives control demons or cut off their noses or give them tasks they cannot manage. Even erudition, magic, and science lead to suicidal creations when the learned ones won't listen to common sense, as in "The Tiger-Makers." The logic of law and careful inquiry, asking who is truly responsible for a crime, leads to the most absurd results in the Kingdom of Fools.

≁ *Animal Tales*　Animal tales are among the most ancient. They occur in the Buddhist *Jatakas* and in the *Pancatantra*. (The latter text was translated widely via Arabic, Persian, and Latin, and reached Europe early.) These tales are greatly enjoyed by children, enter their stock repertoires through primers, and express their powerlessness regarding adults. They are usually about small animals like themselves who outwit their oppressors.

The most striking characteristic of these didactic fables is their persistent political nature. The nature of power, the qualities of leadership, mother wit and cunning as the weapons of the weak, subversion, betrayal, and con games are regular themes. Here too, the powerful tigers, crocodiles, and black snakes do not win: a dove manages a whole chain of helpers to bring an elephant to its knees, and a small crow gets the king's servants to crush a big bad serpent. Some, of course, reflect the way of the world where the tiger or wolf gobbles up the lamb.

---

[18] See the insightful pages by David Shulman on Tenali Rama in *The King and the Clown in South Indian Myth and Poetry* (Princeton, N. J.: Princeton University Press, 1985), chap. 4.

~ *Stories About Stories*   The repertoire of fiction includes metafiction, or fiction about fiction, where the tellers reflect on tales and tellings in the form of tales. We have a number of such stories about stories, and they tell us much regarding the way the culture thinks about folktales. The very first one, "Tell It to the Walls," speaks of an old woman's need to tell her story to someone; otherwise she gets ill. In "The Barber's Secret," the barber has to tell the secret at least to a tree, and the tree cannot keep the secret either. In a variant of the tale, the barber gets fatter and fatter till he tells the secret to his wife, who in turn gets fat. She tells it to a hole in the earth and covers it up; a tree grows from it, and the flute or drumstick made from the tree broadcasts the secret. The old woman and the barber tell their stories, their secrets, only to lighten themselves, not to enlighten others. Nothing is said about the woman's cruel family being converted, becoming kinder; only she has changed, unburdened of her sorrows. Such a notion of catharsis is not part of Indian classical poetics.

Note also how emotions have weight: the characters are literally, not metaphorically, "burdened," "heavy-hearted" or "light-hearted." Tales and dreams, as we said earlier, take metaphors literally. Such literalization is not merely a literary device. It implies the sense that emotions and thoughts are substances. Material and nonmaterial things are part of a continuum of "gross" (*sthula*) and "subtle" (*suksma*) substance, allowing transformations. One may become the other.

Stories and words not only have weight; they also have wills and rages, and they can take different shapes and exact revenge against a person who doesn't tell them and release them into the world—as in "Untold Stories." Such stories tell you why tales have to be told. They have an existence of their own, a secondary objectivity, like other cultural artifacts. They are part of what the philosopher Karl Popper calls the Third World, or World 3: neither subject nor object, but a third realm that depends on and enters into the construction of subjects and objects. Cultural forms (such as stories) make people what they are as much as people make culture. They are there before any particular teller tells them; they hate it when they are not passed on to others, for they can come into being again and again only in that act of translation. A book such as this is motivated by such a need. If you know a tale, you owe it not only to others but to the tale itself to tell it; otherwise it suffocates, as in "Untold Stories." Traditions have to be kept in good repair, transmitted, or else, beware, such tales seem to say, things will happen to you. You can't hoard them.

Furthermore, stories are part of a more pervasive process in society. The tales demonstrate over and over again that daughters (and sons), wealth, knowledge, and food must circulate. These are *danas*, or gifts, that in accordance with their nature must be given and received. Stories are no different. Communities and generations depend on such exchanges and transfers.

In two of the tales connected with women's rituals, a person tries to tell a ritual tale to someone who doesn't want to hear it. In "A Story in Search of an Audience," the teller goes from relative to relative within her family, from street to street in the town, till she finds a listener in an unborn child in a poor woman's womb, bringing the child many miraculous powers. In "What Happens When You Really Listen," the power of a story like the *Ramayana* is suggested through the transformation of a uncultured dolt. When he really listens to the epic tale of Rama, he becomes part of it. The barrier between reality and fiction is broken.

~ ~ ~

Let me close this introduction with a mention of one or two other aspects of the folktale. Special phrases found only in folktales, such as "Once upon a time" (in Kannada, *ondanondu kaladalli*), or "In a certain town" (*ore oru urle* in Tamil), mark the beginning of tales. They turn the key for our entry into a tale-world and a tale-time, and let us cross a threshold into another kind of space.

In many languages folktales have characteristic endings. In Assamese, a tale often ends with the sentence "We had to send our clothes to the washerman, so we came home." In Telugu they say, "The story went to Kanchi, and we came home." (Kanchi is a famous temple city.) In Kannada they say, "They are there, we are here." These closures break any identification with the characters, separate our world from those of the stories, emphasize their fictive nature, their artifice and fantasy. Furthermore, when my favorite tellers tell a story, there are no adjectives at all describing inner or outer features (as there are in bardic tellings)—that is, there is no editorializing, no telling us what to feel. The story tells itself.

Folklore, contrary to romantic notions of its spontaneity or naturalness, is formal. It makes visible its forms. Identification and disidentification (of the listeners with their characters) have their triggers in the tales and happen at different stages of a tale or a performance—not unlike the process by which a person is possessed or dispossessed in the course of a possession ritual. The charming closing sentence in an Oriya tale says very well what I wish to say about breaking the link with the fictive world, a world that seems quite real while it lasts, though it is not. At the end of a romantic king-and-queen story, the Oriya teller says, "I saw the prince the other day in the market, but he wouldn't talk to me."

Folktales from India

Tell It to the Walls

~ *Tamil* ~~

A poor widow lived with her two sons and two daughters-in-law. All four of them scolded and ill-treated her all day. She had no one to whom she could turn and tell her woes. As she kept all her woes to herself, she grew fatter and fatter. Her sons and daughters-in-law now found *that* a matter for ridicule. They mocked at her for growing fatter by the day and asked her to eat less.

One day, when everyone in the house had gone out somewhere, she wandered away from home in sheer misery and found herself walking outside town. There she saw a deserted old house. It was in ruins and had no roof. She went in and suddenly felt lonelier and more miserable than ever; she found she couldn't bear to keep her miseries to herself any longer. She had to tell someone.

So she told all her tales of grievance against her first son to the wall in front of her. As she finished, the wall collapsed under the weight of her woes and crashed to the ground in a heap. Her body grew lighter as well.

Then she turned to the second wall and told it all her grievances against her first son's wife. Down came that wall, and she grew lighter still. She brought down the third wall with her tales against her second son, and the remaining fourth wall, too, with her complaints against her second daughter-in-law.

Standing in the ruins, with bricks and rubble all around her, she felt lighter in mood and lighter in body as well. She looked at herself and found she had actually lost all the weight she had gained in her wretchedness.

Then she went home.

Untold Stories

᷈ Gondi ᷈ ᷈

A Gond peasant kept a farmhand who worked for him in the fields. One day they went together to a distant village to visit the Gond's son and his wife. On the way they stopped at a little hut by the roadside. After they had eaten their supper, the farmhand said, "Tell me a story." But the Gond was tired and went to sleep. His servant lay awake. He knew that his master had four stories, which he was too lazy to tell.

When the Gond was fast asleep, the stories came out of his belly, sat on his body, and began to talk to each other. They were angry. "This Gond," they said, "knows us very well from childhood, but he will never tell anybody about us. Why should we go on living uselessly in his belly? Let's kill him and go to live with someone else." The farmhand pretended to be asleep, but he listened carefully to everything they said.

The first story said, "When the Gond reaches his son's house and sits down to eat his supper, I'll turn his first mouthful of food into sharp needles, and when he swallows them they'll kill him."

The second story said, "If he escapes that, I'll become a great tree by the roadside. I'll fall on him as he passes by and kill him that way."

The third story said, "If that doesn't work, I'll be a snake and run up his leg and bite him."

The fourth said, "If that doesn't work, I'll bring a great wave of water as he is crossing the river and wash him away."

The next morning the Gond and his servant reached his son's house. His son and daughter-in-law welcomed him and prepared food and set it before him. But as the Gond raised his first mouthful to his lips, his servant knocked it out of his hand, saying, "There's an insect in the food." When they looked, they saw that all the rice had turned into needles.

The next day the Gond and his servant set out on their return journey. There was a great tree leaning across the road, and the servant said, "Let's run past that tree." As they ran past it, the tree fell with a mighty crash, and they just escaped. A little later, they saw a snake by the road, and the servant quickly killed it with his stick. After that they came to the river and as they were crossing, a great wave came rushing down, but the servant dragged the Gond to safety.

They sat down on the bank to rest, and the Gond said, "You have saved my life four times. You know something I don't. How did you know what was going to happen?" The farmhand said, "If I tell you I'll turn into a stone." The Gond said, "How can a man turn into a stone? Come on, tell me." So the servant said, "Very well, I'll tell you. But when I turn into a stone, take your daughter-in-law's child and throw it against me, and I'll become a man again."

So the servant told his story and was turned into a stone, but the Gond left him there and went home. After some time, his daughter-in-law heard about it, and she went all by herself and threw her child against the stone, and the servant came to life again.

But the Gond refused to have him in his house and dismissed him. That's why few people in this region trust a Gond. They even have a saying: "No one can rely on a Gond, a woman, or a dream."

Gopal Bhar the Star-Counter

~ Bengali ~~

One day, the Nawab sent word to Maharaja Krishnachandra that he wanted the whole earth measured, from side to side and from end to end, and that he would greatly appreciate it if the Maharaja would take it upon himself to count the stars in the sky as well. The Maharaja was astounded and said, "I don't want to seem uncooperative, but you have commanded me to do the impossible."

And the Nawab said, "But do it you will."

So the Maharaja fell into a brown study and brooded over how he might fulfill the demands of the Nawab.

It was not long before Gopal Bhar passed by, and seeing the Maharaja in such a state of despair, he tugged gently at the ends of his mustache and said, "Maharaj, what is this I see? If you have troubles, you need only tell your Gopal, and all will be well."

The king was not so easily consoled. He said, "No, Gopal, this is a problem even you cannot solve. The Nawab has commanded me to measure the earth, from side to side and from end to end. And as if that were not enough, he wants me to count the stars in the sky as well."

Gopal was not dismayed. He said, "Ha, Maharaj, nothing could be easier. Appoint me your official Earth-Measurer and Star-Counter, and set your mind at rest. And when I am through, I shall myself go to the Nawab with the results. Only one favor: ask the Nawab for one year to finish the job and a million rupees for operating expenses. In one year's time, I'll bring him the results."

The Maharaja was greatly pleased and relieved, since if the job were not done it would be Gopal's head that would come off and not his own. He did as Gopal had asked.

So Gopal passed a very pleasant year, spending the million rupees on the most delightful women and the most delicious food in the kingdom, as well as on palaces and elephants and jewels and other things of that type. He spent, in fact, such a pleasant year that at its end he went to the Maharaja again, jingling the four nickel coins and two coppers that remained of the million rupees, and assuming a worried frown, said, "Maharaj, the task is more difficult than I had anticipated. I've made an excellent start, and the results are promising. But I'll need another year's time. And incidentally, another million rupees. Operating expenses."

The Maharaja reluctantly petitioned the Nawab, and the Nawab reluctantly granted the extra year and the second million rupees. And Gopal passed his year even more pleasantly than the first, since now he had some experience in these matters.

Exactly one year later to the hour, Gopal came dragging himself up the road to the Nawab's palace. With him were fifteen bullock carts, crammed to creaking with the finest thread, tangled and jumbled and matted and flattened down, and five very fat woolly sheep. He led this odd procession through the gates of the palace and into the court of the Nawab, made a deep and graceful bow, and said, "Excellency, it has been done as you ordered. I have measured the earth from end to end and from side to side, and I have counted the stars in the sky."

"Excellent. And now give me the figures. The exact figures."

"Figures, Majesty? Figures were not in the agreement. I've done as you have commanded. The earth is as wide as the thread in the first seven bullock carts is long, and it is as long as the thread in the other eight is long. There are, furthermore, just as many stars in the sky as there are hairs on these five sheep. It took me a long time to find sheep with just the right number of hairs."

The Nawab could only say, "Impossible! I cannot measure that thread or count those hairs. Still, you have lived up to your end of the bargain. Here's your reward: a million rupees."

And Gopal lived in ease for some little time.

Bopoluchi

~ *Punjabi* ~ ~

A number of young girls were drawing water at the village well and telling each other their fantasies of when and whom and how they would marry.

One of them said, "My uncle will come loaded with wedding presents and dress me in brocade, and I'll get married in a palace."

Another said, "My uncle is coming soon with a camel-load of sweets."

The third said, "Oh, my uncle will be here in no time in a golden carriage filled with jewels."

Bopoluchi was the prettiest of them all and she looked sad— she was an orphan and had no one in the world to arrange a marriage for her or give her a dowry. Still, not to be outdone by the others, she said, "And my uncle will bring me dresses, sweets, and jewels in golden plates."

A robber, disguised as a peddler selling perfumes to country women, happened to be sitting near the well. He heard what Bopoluchi said. He was so struck by her beauty and spirit that he decided to marry her himself. So the very next day, he disguised himself as a rich farmer and came to Bopoluchi's hut with trays full of silken dresses, sweets, and rare jewels—things he had looted and put away.

Bopoluchi could hardly believe her eyes, for it was just as she had fantasied.

The robber even said he was her uncle, her father's long-lost brother, and had come home to arrange his niece's wedding with one of his sons.

Bopoluchi couldn't believe her ears, but she believed him and was ecstatic. She packed up her few belongings and set off with the robber.

But as they went along the road, a crow in a tree croaked:

> *Bopoluchi, beware!*
> *Smell the danger in the air!*
> *It's no uncle that relieves you*
> *But a robber who deceives you!*

"Uncle," said Bopoluchi, "that crow croaks in a funny way. What does it say?"

"Nothing," said the robber. "All the crows in this country croak like that."

A little farther on, they met a peacock which, as soon as it caught sight of the pretty girl, began to scream:

> *Bopoluchi, beware!*
> *Smell the danger in the air!*
> *It's no uncle that relieves you*
> *But a robber who deceives you!*

"Uncle," said the girl, "that peacock screams in a funny way. What does it say?"

"Oh, nothing," said the robber. "All the peacocks scream like that in this country."

Then a jackal slunk across the road and began to howl:

> Bopoluchi, beware!
> Smell the danger in the air!
> It's no uncle that relieves you
> But a robber who deceives you!

"Uncle," said Bopoluchi, "that jackal howls in such a funny way. What does it say?"

"Oh, nothing," said the robber. "All the jackals howl like that in this country."

So Bopoluchi traveled with him many miles till they reached the robber's house. Once they were inside, he locked the door and told her who he was and how he wanted to marry her himself. She wept and wailed, but the pitiless robber left her with his ancient crone of a mother and went out to make arrangements for the marriage feast.

Now Bopoluchi had long, beautiful hair that reached down to her ankles, but the mother of the robber was so old she didn't have a hair on her head.

"Daughter," said the old hag, as she was getting the bridal clothes ready, "how did you manage to get such beautiful hair?"

"Well," replied Bopoluchi, "my mother had a way of making it grow by pounding my head in the big mortar for husking rice. At every stroke of the pestle, my hair grew longer and longer. It's a method that never fails."

"Maybe it will work for me, too, and make my hair grow," said the old woman, who had always wanted long hair and never had very much.

"Maybe it will. Why don't we try it?" said Bopoluchi.

So the old mother put her head in the mortar, and Bopoluchi pounded away with such force that the old woman died.

Then Bopoluchi dressed the dead body in the scarlet bridal dress, seated it on the bridal chair, drew the veil over its face, and put the spinning-wheel in front of it, so that when the robber came home he might think it was his bride. Then she put on the old woman's clothes, picked up her few belongings, and stepped out of the house as quickly as possible.

On her way home, the robber saw her hurrying by. He had stolen a millstone to grind the grain for the feast. She was scared he would recognize her, but he didn't. He thought she was some old woman hobbling along. So Bopoluchi reached home safely.

When the robber came home and saw the figure in the bridal dress sitting in the bridal chair spinning, he thought it was Bopoluchi. He called her to help him with the millstone, but she didn't answer. He called again, but she still didn't answer. After calling a few more times, he flew into a rage and threw the millstone at her head. The figure toppled over, and when he came close, it wasn't Bopoluchi at all but his own old mother with her head bashed in. The robber wept and cried aloud and beat his breast because he thought he had killed his own mother. Soon it became clear to him that Bopoluchi was no longer around and had run away. He was wild with rage and ran out to bring her back, wherever she was.

When she reached home, Bopoluchi knew that the robber would certainly come after her. Every night she begged her neighbors to let her sleep in a different house, leaving her own little bed in her own little house empty. But she couldn't do this forever, as she soon came to the end of friends who would let her sleep in their houses. So she decided to brave it out and sleep in her own bed, with a sharp billhook next to her. Sure enough, in the middle of the night four men crept in, and each seizing a leg of the bed, lifted it up and walked off. The robber himself held the leg close behind her head. Bopoluchi was wide awake, but she pretended to be fast asleep until they came to a deserted spot and the thieves were off their guard. Then she whipped out the billhook and in a flash cut off the heads of the two thieves at the foot of the bed. Turning around quickly, she cut off the head of the third thief, but the robber himself ran away in a fright and scrambled up a nearby tree like a wild cat before she could get at him.

Bopoluchi cried out to him, brandishing her billhook, "Come down, if you are a man, and fight it out!"

But the robber would not come down. So Bopoluchi gathered all the sticks she could find, piled them around the tree, and set fire to them. The tree caught fire, and the robber, stifled by the smoke, tried to jump down and broke his neck.

After that, Bopoluchi went to the robber's house and carried off all the gold and silver, jewels, and clothes that were hidden there. She had them brought home to her village in silver and gold platters, on camels and donkeys. She was now so rich she could marry anyone she pleased.

The Jasmine Prince

~ *Tamil* ~ ~

There was once a king who was called the Jasmine Prince because the scent of jasmines would waft from him for miles whenever he laughed. But for that to happen, he had to laugh naturally, all by himself. If someone else tickled him or forced him to laugh, there would be no scent of jasmines.

The Jasmine Prince ruled a small kingdom and paid tribute to a king greater than himself, who had heard of this extraordinary power to produce the scent of jasmines by merely laughing. The great king wanted to see how it happened and to experience it himself, so he invited the Jasmine Prince to his court and asked him to laugh. But the prince couldn't laugh to order. He tried and tried, but he just couldn't bring himself to laugh. The great king was furious. "He is defying orders. He is trying to insult us," he thought, and clapped him in jail till he produced some laughter.

Right in front of the prison house lived a cripple in a hut. The queen of the realm had fallen in love with this cripple and would visit him at night. From his window, the Jasmine Prince watched her come and go. "But that's not my business," he thought, and behaved as if he had seen nothing. One night, the queen was late. The cripple was furious when she arrived at last, and he beat her up. He pounded her with his arm-stumps and kicked her with his lame leg. The queen patiently endured all this battering and didn't say a thing. She took out the royal dishes that she had brought for him and lovingly served him. After a while the cripple, regretting his brutal treatment of the queen, asked softly, "Aren't you angry that I beat you up?" She replied, "Oh no! It was delightful. I felt great, as if I had seen all fourteen worlds at once!"

Now, right next to the veranda where they were talking to each other, a poor washerman was cowering in a corner in the cold. He had lost his donkey and had searched for it in vain for four or five days. He had despaired of ever finding the animal. But when he heard the queen say what she did, he thought, "If this lady has seen all fourteen worlds, surely she will have seen my donkey somewhere." So he called out to her, "Lady, did you see my donkey anywhere?"

At this the Jasmine Prince, who had been listening from his window, could not keep from laughing. He let out peal after peal of laughter into the night, and at once the air for miles around was filled with the fragrance of jasmines. The dawn was still some hours away, but the prison guards ran to the great king and told him of the laughter and the burst of fragrance. Without even waiting for dawn, the king had the Jasmine Prince brought to his palace and said to him, "When I asked you to laugh for me the other day, you couldn't. But now, what on earth made you laugh in the middle of the night?"

The prince tried hard to hold back the reason for his laughter, but the king insisted, so the prince told him the truth. When the king had heard everything, he issued two orders. One was to send the Jasmine Prince back to his capital with all due honors. The other was to throw his queen at once into the limekiln.

Sona and Rupa

≁ *Malwi, a Rajasthani Hindi dialect of Madhya Pradesh* ≁≁

One evening a prince was returning home on his black mare after a hunt, and took the mare to drink from a stream. As he watched it drink, he saw, along with his own and his mare's reflection, several strands of gold and silver hair floating on the water. Obviously, lovely women with hair of gold and hair of silver had bathed somewhere nearby, upstream. He bent down and picked up the hair. The more he looked at it, the more he thought of the beauty of women with such hair and was infatuated with the images in his head. He tucked the hair into the folds of his turban, mounted his mare, and went home to his palace.

It was time for dinner, but the prince did not appear. Everyone looked for him, but he was nowhere to be found. The queen mother sent servants into every room and every corner. One of the servant women went into the storeroom to fetch some sugar. The prince was lying there, face down, on the floor. She was about to cry out when the prince said to her, "Don't tell anyone or you'll die." But as they say, a woman and the wind cannot hold a secret. She whispered it to the queen, and the queen came to the storeroom loudly scolding her servant: "Why haven't you swept this place, you lazybones?" Then, as if her eyes had just lighted on the prince on the floor, she cried out, "Look who's here! O Son, what's the matter? Why are you lying in the dust? What has made you so miserable? If anyone has insulted you, I'll have his tongue cut out. If anyone has raised his hand against you, I'll have his hand chopped off. Tell me what's troubling you. And get up, for God's sake."

The prince sat up, took out the gold and silver hair from his turban, and holding it up to the queen, said, "I want to marry the girls who have such gold and silver for hair."

The queen said, "That's nothing. We'll find those girls, wherever they are."

"But I must have just those girls whose hair matches this."

"Surely, my son, you'll have them," said the queen. But she felt dizzy and stumbled as she walked out of the storeroom.

Messengers were dispatched all over the capital. The town crier called out in the streets that all the young women of the city should walk next morning in the palace yard with their heads uncovered.

Next morning, there was a long parade of women before the palace. The prince watched them for hours, but he couldn't see any woman whose hair matched what he had in his hand.

Suddenly his eye fell on two girls, with hair of gold and hair of silver, sitting in the courtyard of the women's quarters of the palace. He called out to his mother the queen, and pointed them out to her. The queen was stunned but somehow found the words to say, "O God! They are your sisters, Sona and Rupa."

The prince's face fell. But he wouldn't give up his wish. He said, "Marry them I must, whoever they are. If I can't, I'll leave the country."

The king came down and tried to talk him out of it. Relatives, elders, and ministers talked to him. The queen begged him with folded hands to change his mind. But the prince wanted what he wanted.

So they made arrangements for the wedding. A grand pavilion was raised on green bamboo poles with a vast canopy of silk and canvas. The news traveled from ear to mouth and from mouth to ear till it reached Sona and

Rupa. They were speechless with horror. Their faces went dark and their eyes filled with tears.

Now, on the bank of the river where they bathed grew a sandalwood tree that the two princesses had watered and tended since they were small. It had grown with them. It was now tall and full-grown.

On the wedding day, Sona and Rupa climbed the sandalwood tree and hid in its branches. As the time for the rites grew near, the palace servants looked for them and found them sitting on a high branch. The servants begged them to get down, but they wouldn't. The king himself came to the tree and said:

> *Come down, come down,*
> *My daughters, Sona and Rupa.*
> *The wedding hour has come.*

Sona and Rupa said:

> *O Father, we called you Father.*
> *How can we call you Father-in-Law?*
> *Higher, higher, O sandalwood tree!*

And the tree grew taller and took them higher.

The whole family gathered there and called them, but they wouldn't come down. With each call, the tree grew taller and took them higher still.

Finally, the prince himself came there and called out:

> *Come down, come down,*
> *My sisters, Sona and Rupa.*
> *Our wedding hour is near.*

But they replied:

> *O Brother, we called you Brother.*
> *How can we call you Husband now?*
> *Higher, higher still, O sandal tree!*

All at once, clouds gathered. The skies thundered. The tree suddenly split open and took them inside. Before the family's eyes, Sona and Rupa vanished deep within the tree.

Brother's Day

~ Rajasthani ~ ~

Once there was a brother whose sister was married and lived far away. He said to his mother, "Mother, I want to go visit my sister on Brother's Day and see her dressed in new clothes. Many other men are going to see their sisters and I too want to go."

The mother said, "My son, you are still a child and your sister lives very far from here. How will you go? On that road there are lions and wild animals. They'll scare you. How will you go?"

But he replied, "No, Ma, I want to go." The mother prepared a bundle with a long skirt and a wrap for her daughter, and a turban and a shirt for her daughter's husband. She gave the bundle to her son and said, "Go safely and see your sister dressed in new clothes for Brother's Day."

The youth started out. On the way, he met an enormous tree. The tree said, "Brother, I'm going to fall on you." He said, "Don't fall now. I'm on my way to see my sister dressed in new clothes for Brother's Day. You may fall on me when I come back."

Continuing on his way, he met a river, which said, "I'm going to wash you away." He said, "Brother River, don't wash me away now. I'm going to see my sister dressed in new clothes on Brother's Day. After I've done that, I'll return. Then you may wash me away."

Next he met a snake. The snake said, "I'm going to bite you." He said, "Don't bite me now. I'm on my way to see my sister dressed in new clothes for Brother's Day. After I've done that, I'll return. Then you may bite me."

Then he met a lion, and it said, "Brother, I'm going to eat you." He said to the lion, "Don't eat me now. I'm going to see my sister dressed in new clothes on Brother's Day. When I return, you may eat me."

At last he came to his sister's village, and there he found his sister sitting at the spinning wheel. Their eyes met, but she did not get up because just then her thread broke. (It is believed that if you greet a guest when your thread is broken, harm will come to that guest.)

But the brother did not know why she did not get up to greet him at once, and he thought to himself, "Oh, I've come so far to meet my sister but she, my own sister, doesn't speak to me." He quickly turned to leave, but she joined her thread in a hurry and said, "Oh Brother, where are you going? I was only protecting you. I couldn't greet you with a broken thread."

The brother and sister joyfully greeted one another, and she went hurrying to the neighbor woman's house.

"Oh, neighbor lady, my brother has come and brought me gifts of clothes for Brother's Day. What should I do?"

The neighbor was not a kind woman. She said, "You slut, plaster the courtyard with oil and put butter on the fire to boil." So the sister quickly filled a big pot with butter and put it on the fire to boil, and began to spread oil around the courtyard. But the butter didn't boil and the oil didn't dry.

She hurried to another neighbor and said, "Oh auntie, my brother has come to give me clothing for Brother's Day. I asked the other auntie what to do and she said to plaster the courtyard with oil and put butter on the fire to boil, but the oil won't dry and the butter won't boil."

This neighbor woman was kind and said, "I'll tell you what to do. Take yellow clay and cow dung and plaster the courtyard with these. Put rice in water to cook. When it is cooked, serve it to your brother with butter and a lot of sugar."

She came back to her house, plastered the courtyard with yellow clay and cow dung, cooked the rice in water, and put lots of butter and sugar on it. Then she fed her brother sugar-rice.

One day passed, then two, then four, and the brother said, "Sister, I'll go now." When she heard that she thought, "I'll make some round cakes for my brother. I'll shape them and send them home with him. My father and my mother can eat some of them and my brother will have them to eat on the road. I won't pack ordinary bread. I'll pack nice round cakes."

Next day, she got up in the middle of the night and began to grind some wheat. She had just begun to grind it when a black snake fell into the flour grinder. The snake got ground up, and she didn't know it because it was night and very dark. She made all the flour into round cakes and packed them in a cloth. At dawn she bade farewell to her brother. She gave him the bundle of cakes and said, "Go, Brother, go safely."

She had kept a few of the cakes, only two or three, for her children. After her brother left the children began to pester her: "Hey, Ma, you gave him something all wrapped up. Now give us some too."

She said, "I gave all the cakes to your uncle." But her children didn't believe her words and would not stop pestering her for the sweets. So she took two cakes and broke them into halves, one half for each of the four children. She had just begun to hand them out when she saw that black snake's bones were scattered throughout the cakes. They were sticking out. She cried out, "Oh no, at this very moment my brother may be eating this and dying." And she ran to the kind neighbor woman and pleaded, "Auntie, please watch my house and take care of my children. At this very moment my brother may be eating those cakes and dying."

The neighbor woman agreed, and the sister went running after her brother through the jungle. Twenty-four miles this way, twenty-four miles that way, she ran through forty-eight miles of jungle. As she ran she called, "Oh Brother, stand still, stop!"

At last she came near; the brother heard his sister coming. He recognized her voice and thought, "Why has my sister come running after me? I've taken nothing of hers. Why is she calling me?" When he saw her, the sister said, "Brother, you've not eaten the food, you've not eaten it, have you?"

He said, "See, Sister, this is the way you wrapped the round cakes and they are still wrapped the same way. I haven't touched them. They're still in my bag." She cried, "Oh my brother, a black snake's bones are ground up in them. When I broke one, they were sticking out." He threw down the packet of cakes and went back with his sister to her house.

The sister kept him with her for nearly a week. Then her brother said to her, "How much can you protect me? As soon as I left our village, I met an enormous tree which said, 'I'll fall on you.' After that I met a river which said, 'I'll wash you away.' Then I met a snake and it said, 'I'll bite you.' After that I met a lion and it said, 'I'll eat you.' How can you protect me?"

His sister took her necklace to give to the river; she took a cup of milk for the snake and a goat kid to feed to the lion. She took five toy pebbles to please the enormous tree. Then she ran to her neighbor once more and said, "Oh auntie, please watch my house and look after my children. I'll accompany my brother to my parent's home, and then I'll return."

Then the brother and sister went into the dangerous jungle together. The sister saved her brother from the lion, the snake, the river, and the tree by offering them the things she had brought for them.

After they had walked for a long time, she became thirsty. Her brother said, "Sister, I'll climb that tree and look around. Wherever I see herons circling in the air, below them I'll find water." He climbed a tree and did see some herons circling over a place at some distance in the woods. He said, "Sister, there is surely some water over there. Herons don't circle unless there's water below. You wait for me in the shade and I'll go and bring back some water."

While he was gone, the sister saw Mother Fate wandering in the forest, and heard her saying to herself, "I'm making a cover for the heart of the only son." The sister called out to her, "Old woman, mother, what are you doing?"

She answered, "I'm making a cover for the heart of the only son." At once the sister understood from this that her brother was going to die.

"What can I do, mother?" she pleaded.

Mother Fate told her, "After Holi and after Divali, on Brother's Day, tell the story and worship your brother. Worship him, but on Brother's Day curse him. By these curses your brother will be saved."

Right then and there the sister began to curse her brother: "May my brother's bones be gathered! May my brother die!" She did not stop even when her brother came back. He was shocked to hear her cursing him and thought, "What will happen now?"

They continued on their way and reached their home. There they found that arrangements were under way for the brother's wedding. The sister said, "You are fixing his engagement. Fix mine also." This was a crazy thing to say, as she was already married. The brother said, "My sister used to be good and smart. What's happening to her now?"

It was time for the pre-wedding ceremony, and the groom was seated on a special stool. His sister said, "Why is he sitting there all by himself? Let me sit there also." The others thought this weird, but the brother said, "Let her alone. Do as she asks. Let her also sit on the wooden stool."

When the groom was rubbed with oil and turmeric to make him fair and handsome, the sister cried, "Rub it on me also. Rub it on me also." The brother said, "She has gone crazy. Let her be."

When he was called to eat special meals at the homes of friends and relatives she said, "I will go too." And thus she did everything that the brother did.

When it was time for the groom's departure from the village on horseback (grooms must go to their brides' villages for the wedding ritual), she insisted on riding the horse with him, and he said, "Let her be. Let her sit with me."

When the brother was going to strike the wooden marriage emblem over the bride's doorway with his sword, his sister said, "Me too!" And when he sat with his bride to worship the gods, she sat with him. The brother said, "She has gone crazy. She must do whatever I do."

When it was time for the couple to take the marriage rounds around the sacred fire, completing the ritual, she also took them. When the wedding party returned to the groom's home with the new bride, the sister went too.

Then when the bride and the groom were going inside to sleep, the sister said, "I'll sleep near them." The brother said, "Let her sleep here." So they stretched a curtain between the bridal bed and the side of the room where the sister slept on the floor.

The new husband and wife fell asleep. But in the middle of the night the snake came there, slithering towards the sleeping couple. How could the sister sleep when she was waiting for her brother's enemy? She spotted the snake, struck it, cut it into three pieces, and hid the pieces under a shield. Then she went to sleep in peace.

The next morning when the others woke, she was still asleep. The brother said, "My sister is asleep. I'll say farewell to my guests now. She is crazy and who knows what she will do when she wakes up?" But his mother protested, saying to her son, "No, she is not crazy. It's not like her to sleep like this. From her birth, she has been a light sleeper. Wake her up now, while your guests are still here, or else you'll have to call them back."

They woke her and the sister said, "Gather the whole village. Let everyone know why I left my children at home with my neighbor, how I followed my brother, leaving home and family—all because of my brother's enemy, that snake, who came here on his wedding night."

And she lifted the shield and showed everyone the snake which she had cut into three pieces.

She then explained everything: "Brother, when we were in the jungle I met Mother Fate and she said, 'I'm making a cover for the heart of the only son,' and told me to worship my brother on Brother's Day, after Holi and after Divali. Brothers should give long skirts and wraps to their sisters, and sisters should curse their brothers. May my brother's bones be gathered! May my brother die!"

May he live long.

The Brahman
Who Swallowed a God

~ *Bengali* ~ ~

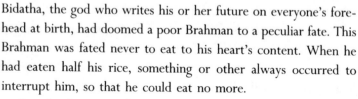

Bidatha, the god who writes his or her future on everyone's fore-head at birth, had doomed a poor Brahman to a peculiar fate. This Brahman was fated never to eat to his heart's content. When he had eaten half his rice, something or other always occurred to interrupt him, so that he could eat no more.

One day he received an invitation to the raja's house. He was delighted and said to his wife, "Half my rice is all I can ever eat. Never once in my whole life has my hunger been satisfied. Today I've by some good luck received this invitation to the raja's house. But how am I to go? My clothes are torn and dirty, and if I go like this, most likely the gatekeeper will turn me away." His wife said, "I'll repair and clean your clothes. Then you can go." And when she had provided him with decent clothes, he set out for the raja's house.

There, though he was late and it was evening, he was royally received. As he viewed the dishes spread out before him, the old Brahman was delighted. He thought, "Whatever happens, today I'll eat my fill." He then sat down and began eating. Now, it happened that a little earthen pot was hanging from a beam of the roof. Just as the Brahman had half finished his dinner, the pot broke and the pieces fell into his food. He immediately stopped eating, took his ritual sip of water to close the meal, got up, washed his hands and mouth, and went to the raja. The raja welcomed him respectfully and asked, "*Thakur,* are you fully satisfied?" The Brahman answered, "Maharaj, your servants were very good to me and served me all I wanted. My own fate is to blame that I couldn't eat my fill." "Why?" said the raja. "What happened?" "Maharaj, while I was eating, a little earthen pot fell from the ceiling and spoiled my rice," said the Brahman. The raja was very angry when he heard this and gave his servants a scolding. Then he said to the Brahman, "Sir, you stay with me tonight. Tomorrow, I'll have fresh food made and serve it to you with my own hands." So the Brahman stayed in the raja's house that night.

Next day, the raja supervised the cooking himself, even prepared some of the dishes with his own hands, and served the Brahman. In the great room where he was served, there was nothing that could spoil the meal. The Brahman looked around, rejoiced at the raja's hospitality, and sat down to eat. But when he was halfway through his dinner, Bidatha saw that he must be stopped, and yet he could not see any way of doing it. So he himself took the form of a golden frog, came to the edge of the Brahman's plantain leaf, and tumbled into his food.

The Brahman was too busy to notice anything. He ate up his rice, frog and all. Dinner over, the raja asked him, "How is it now, *thakur*? Were you satisfied today?" The Brahman answered, "Maharaj, I've never dined so well in all my life." Saying this, he took his leave, received gifts and money from the good raja, and set off for home.

That evening on his way home, while he was walking through a jungle, he suddenly heard a voice: "Brahman, let me go! Brahman, let me go!" The Brahman looked all around him, but he could see nobody. Again he heard the voice: "Brahman, let me go!" Then he said, "Who are you?" The answer came: "I'm Bidatha, I'm Bidatha!" The Brahman asked again, "Where are you?" Bidatha answered, "Inside your stomach. You've swallowed me." "Impossible!" said the Brahman. "Yes," said Bidatha, "in the form of a frog, I tumbled into your food, and you ate me up." "Ah, nothing could be better," replied the Brahman. "You've bothered me all my life, you rascal. I won't let you go! I'll rather close up my throat." Bidatha, in great fear, said again, "Brahman, let me go! I'm stifled in here!" But the Brahman hurried home quickly, and when he arrived, said to his wife, "Give me a hookah, and you hold a stick ready in your hand." His wife did so at once, and the Brahman sat down and smoked the hookah for a long time contentedly, taking great care not to set Bidatha free. The god was further stifled by the smoke, but the Brahman quite ignored all his cries for help.

Meanwhile, there was a terrible commotion in the three worlds. Without Bidatha to regulate matters, the universe was on the verge of a collapse. Then the gods assembled in council decided that one of them must be sent to the Brahman. But who? They all agreed that the goddess Lakshmi would be the right one to go. She said, "If I go to that Brahman, I shall never come back." But they all prayed and begged, so she agreed and went to the Brahman's house. When the Brahman learned that it was Lakshmi, the goddess of wealth and fortune, at his door, he put his upper cloth around his neck as a mark of respect, gave her a seat, and asked her what, in the name of wonder, had brought her to a poor man's house. "*Thakur*," said the goddess, "you've taken Bidatha a prisoner. Let him go, or the universe will be ruined." "Give me the stick," said the Brahman to his wife, "and I'll show you what I think of this goddess of good fortune. From the day I was born, she has shunned me, I've had nothing but bad luck, and here she comes to my house, this Lakshmi!" When she heard this, the goddess vanished, trembling with fear. No one had ever talked to her like that before in all the ages. She told the gods what had happened, and, after another huddle, the gods sent Saraswati, the goddess of learning.

When Saraswati reached his house and called out, "Brahman, are you in? Brahman, are you in?" the Brahman saluted her with great respect and said, "Mother, great goddess, what do you want in a poor man's house?" "*Thakur*, the universe is fast coming apart. Let Bidatha go." The Brahman burst into a great rage and cried, "Wife, give me the stick! I'll teach this goddess of learning. She didn't give me even the first letters of the alphabet. Saraswati comes to my house now, does she?" Hearing this, the goddess got up in a hurry and fled, stumbling.

Finally, the great god Siva himself undertook the mission. Now the Brahman was a Saiva, a devout worshipper of Siva, so devout that he would not even touch water without doing *puja* to Siva. Therefore, as soon as the god came, he and his wife gave him water to wash his feet, offered him *bel* leaves, holy grass, flowers, rice, and sandalwood, and did *puja* to him. Siva then sat down and said to the Brahman, "Brahman, let Bidatha go." The Brahman said, "As you have come personally, O great Siva, of course I must let him go. But what am I to do? I've suffered hardships from the day I was born, thanks to this Bidatha. He is the cause of it all." Then the great god said, "Do not trouble yourself. I'll take you, body and soul, to heaven." When he heard that, the Brahman relaxed his throat and opened his mouth, and Bidatha jumped out. Then Siva took the Brahman and his wife with him to his special heaven.

One Man's Virtue

~ *Oriya* ~ ~

 Only Brahmans lived in a certain village, and they were all very pious. They lived very simple lives, offered their morning and evening prayers regularly, performed every ritual prescribed for them, knew the Vedas by heart and lived accordingly. Like all Vedic Brahmans, they tended a holy fire in the middle of their huts and never allowed it to go out.

In one such family, one night, the youngest daughter-in-law felt the need to go out and pee. It was very dark, and she was afraid of going out in the dark. So she made water over the embers of the holy fire in the middle of the hut. In the morning, when the family woke up, they found an ingot of pure gold in the embers.

Everyone was astonished. The head of the family, an old and wise Brahman, said at once, "Someone has done something wrong. How else would there be a bar of gold in a Brahman fireplace?" He lined up the whole family and questioned them all till the youngest daughter-in-law confessed to what she had done the previous night. He warned her not to do it again and told everyone not to follow her example. He arranged for someone to escort her at night if she needed to go.

The news of this miracle traveled through the village. And slowly at first, and then more and more often, bars of gold began to appear in the ritual fires of various Brahman families. Many of them became rich and began to build big houses for themselves, to wear silk and muslin, to give big dowries with their daughters. The village was no longer the same.

But one family continued to be poor. They lived in a hut, almost the only hut left in town, at the edge of the village. The wife quarreled with her husband every day. "Why don't you let me go at least once in the ritual fireplace?" she pleaded. "We won't be poor any more. We'll have a morsel to eat and a piece of cloth for each of us. Please let me. Just once. One bar of gold will last us a long time." She nagged, she wheedled, she used all her wiles. She was desperate. It would be so easy, but her rigid husband wouldn't let her do it. When she nagged him one day more than he could bear, he burst out, "Do you know why this whole Brahman village is still held together?"

"Why? Because you won't let me pee in the fire and you want to keep us poor when everyone else is rich? Is that why?" mocked the exasperated wife.

"Precisely. We are holding the whole community together by what we are. If we also do what all of them do, or even if we leave this place, it will go to pieces," said the Brahman.

The wife thought this was sheer conceit. "We, by being poor, are keeping all these rich neighbors alive? What notions you have of yourself!"

The Brahman said, "I'll show you the truth of what I say. Pack up everything and let's move to the next village. You'll see what happens."

And they packed up everything and moved to the next village.

Within a week, quarrels arose among the Brahmans. Each accused the other of wanting to buy up his place, his land. The greedier ones ordered their wives and daughters and daughters-in-law to make more and more water in the ritual fireplaces, till the fires almost went out. One day, in greed and anger, one family set fire to another. The hurt family retaliated with more fire. The fires spread, and house after house was burned down till there was nothing left of the village.

When the news reached him, the Brahman who had moved away said to his wife, "You didn't believe me. One's virtue guards not only oneself but everyone around."

A Crow's Revenge

~ *Kannada* ~ ~

In the branches of a big banyan tree, a crow family built a nest and lived in it. A black snake would crawl through its hollow trunk and eat the crow chicks as soon as they were hatched. After this had happened many times, the crow wife couldn't take it any longer. She said to the crow, "We've lost all our chicks to this awful snake, who just waits for me to hatch them and gobbles them all up. We are utterly helpless. Let's move out of this tree." But the crow liked the tree, had grown used to it, and he said, "We must find a way to kill this enemy of ours."

"How can we? We are mere crows. He is such a big snake."

"There must be ways. I may be small and weak, but I have cunning friends. This time, I'll not let this pass."

So he went to his friend the jackal, who heard his case and advised him: "We'll take care of this villain. Go to that lake, where the king and his queens bathe and swim. Pick up a necklace or a jewel, fly away with it, and put it in the snake's hole."

The crow at once flew off to the lake and waited for the king's party to arrive, undress, take off their gold chains and pearl necklaces, and get into the water. Then when they were busy enjoying themselves, he picked up a necklace and flew away. The king's servants saw this, and quickly picked up their spears and sticks and pursued the crow.

The crow went straight to the snake's hole under the tree and dropped the necklace in it. The king's servants dug up the hole, found the black snake, beat it to death, picked up their queen's necklace, and went their way.

The crow and his family were left in peace.

A Story in Search of an Audience

∼ *Telugu* ∼ ∼

Once on the day of *rathasaptami*, the seventh day of the month of Magha, when they take the temple chariot in procession through the streets, an old lady took a ritual bath from head to toe and performed a *puja*.

She had to tell someone the story of the sun god on that Sunday in the month of Magha: that was part of her observance of the day's ritual. So she took a handful of rice colored yellow with turmeric and set out to find someone to whom she could give the sanctified rice and tell the story. But everyone she met was in too much of a hurry.

Her sons were hurrying to the court of the local king. It was already getting late, and they didn't want the king to scold them. When her sons refused to listen to her story, she went in search of her grandsons. It was time for them to go to school, and they didn't want to listen to the old woman's story. When she went to her daughter-in-law, she said she was too busy because she had to attend to her baby.

The old woman then went out of the house to the women who were washing clothes on the riverbank and asked them to lend their ears to her story for the Sundays in the month of Magha. As they had just finished their morning's work and were in a hurry to get home, they too refused. Wherever she went, whomsoever she approached, she couldn't find a single listener. Brahmans, woodcutters, basket weavers, washermen, potters—not one of them was willing to set a few minutes aside to listen to her story.

As a consequence, all these people who refused to listen to her story for the Sundays of Magha suffered. Her sons were punished at court; her daughter-in-law soon found that her baby was deathly ill; her grandsons were beaten by their teacher at school; the women at the river were roundly abused by their mothers-in-law; the Brahman could find no one to feed him that day; for some inexplicable reason, splinters went into the basket maker's fingers; and, try as they would, not a pot would come out right on the potters' wheels that day.

The old woman didn't know any of this. She was sad that she could find no one to listen to her story, but she was patient. She finally went to the back streets and found a pregnant woman of the salt-seller caste who said she would listen to the woman's story but that she was terribly hungry. The poor woman said she had to have some *payasam* first. She wanted it made with milk and sugar and a full measure of rice because she was very, very hungry. The old woman went home, made a full measure of the sweet pudding, and brought it to the pregnant woman. The woman was very happy and ate it all. But before the old woman could begin the story, she was fast asleep. While she slept like this, without a thought in the world, the old woman just waited, the ritual rice in her hand. Suddenly she heard the child in the womb of the pregnant woman say to her, "Why don't you tell *me* the story? I will listen to it. Put the grains of rice in my mother's navel and tell me the story."

The old woman was delighted. She carefully filled the sleeping woman's navel with the ritual rice. Then she told the round belly in front of her and the baby within it her story for the Sundays in the month of Magha. After she finished her story, she sang a lullaby that said, "Wherever you go, deserted villages will become prosperous towns, cotton seeds will become pearls, dry trees will be covered with fruit, even old cows will give milk, barren women will have children, lost jewels will be found, and dead men will come back to life. O baby, you'll have such powers as will make a king's heart glad."

By the time she had finished her story and her song, the salt-seller woman woke up from her sleep. She was now willing to hear the story. But the old woman said, "The baby in your womb listened to my story and it will have a good life. Send me word when your child is born and let me know whether it's a boy or a girl." And then she went home.

A few weeks later, the old woman got news that the poor salt-seller woman was delivered of a girl. The old woman hastened to the salt-sellers' street with a sari and a small beaked cup with castor oil and medicines, all the things that one gives to a newborn baby. With the sari, she made a hammock for the baby, tied the hammock to a branch of a tree in the nearby forest, put the baby in it, and asked the trees to rock it like a cradle and begged the birds to sing the lullaby. Now the child's mother was free to go about her business during the day and earn her living while the trees and the birds looked after her baby. The old woman then went home.

Around that time, the king of the country happened to pass through the forest. He heard the songs of the birds and the wailing of a small child. He was curious and looked around till he found the hammock tied to a branch and the birds singing a lullaby all around it. The birds said to the king, "This little girl is your wife and our mother. Take her home with you, and marry her when she grows up."

So he put the child in a palanquin and took her along with him. When they passed through a deserted village, it became a beautiful, bustling town. On their way, they rested in a cotton field, and all the cotton seeds became pearls. In the poor villages they passed, old cows began to give milk and dry trees sprouted green leaves and were soon covered with fruit. And in his palace, the king's first wife, who had been barren all this while, was blessed with a child that year.

The salt-seller's baby grew into a little girl and soon into a young woman, bringing year after year new riches to the kingdom. At an appropriate time, the king married her.

As you can imagine, the older wife was not at all pleased and was mad with jealousy at the attention given to the beautiful young queen who had come from nowhere into the palace.

One day, in a fit of jealousy, she gathered all the precious jewels in the palace, put them in a box, and had it thrown into the sea. Some time later, fishermen caught an enormous fish, brought it to the palace, and presented it to the older queen. She turned up her nose at it, complained of its stench, and sent it scornfully to the younger queen, who was so delighted with it that she personally supervised its cooking. When the cooks cut it open, they found the box of jewels that the older queen had cast into the sea. The king came to hear of it, and he at once remembered the lullaby the birds had sung that listed all the wonderful things this young woman would bring about. He had seen with his own eyes that most of these things had come to pass. Deserted villages had turned to beautiful towns, cotton seeds had turned to pearls, old cows had flowed with milk, and dry trees had borne fruit. And now a lost chest of jewels had been miraculously recovered. Only one thing was left. He meant to test the last of his young queen's powers—the power to give life to the dead. So he dined in his young queen's quarters and then he moved to his older wife's bedchamber, where he secretly took poison and fell dead.

The elder wife was distraught and sent for the younger one to come and join her in committing *sati* on the husband's pyre. While the body was being made ready for the cremation, the young queen prepared herself to join her husband in death. While she was doing so, a Brahman came to her and asked for water to wash his feet. He also asked the young queen to wash her own feet. Then he asked for a drink of water, and asked her to drink some water herself. He told her to make arrangements for him to have a bath from head to toe and for her to do the same. He asked for sandalwood paste for his body, and asked her to smear turmeric on hers. After that he took some *kumkum* (vermilion) and made a caste-mark on his forehead, and asked her to wear a dot of *kumkum* on hers. Then he asked to be fed a meal, and asked her to eat too. After that he asked for betel nut and betel leaf to mark the end of the meal and the ritual, and asked her to take betel nuts and betel leaf for herself. Thus he made her do everything he himself as a Brahman would do. All the while, the young queen was grieving and in a hurry to go to the cremation ground where her husband's body was waiting to be cremated. But the Brahman did not let her leave till she had done all that he said she should do. At the end of it all, she asked him who he was. He said he was Adinarayana, the sun god about whom the old woman had told her the story when she was still in the womb, even before she was born. He gave her some rice colored with turmeric and told her to sprinkle it on her husband's body. Then he vanished.

The young queen rushed to the cremation ground with the rice in her hand. Everyone was waiting for her. She walked up quickly to the king's body and threw the rice on it. He woke up at once on his bed of firewood as if on a bed where he had fallen asleep. When he and everyone else asked how he had been revived so miraculously, she told them all that she had received these magical powers only by virtue of hearing the story for the Sundays of Maghamasa even before she was born.

The king was astonished and said, "If merely listening to that story can do such things, how much more effective would it be if people actually performed the ritual the story celebrates!" Then he ordered arrangements to be made for his wives to perform the ritual (*vrata*). The same ritual that the queens performed that Sunday is followed to this day by the upper castes in this wicked age of Kali.

The Clay Mother-in-Law

~ *Tamil* ~ ~

Once upon a time, there was a very docile daughter-in-law. She was obedient to her husband's mother and waited upon her slightest wish. The old woman kept up her dignity as a mother-in-law, saying very little and often merely nodding her commands. Every morning, the daughter-in-law would come to the old woman and ask her how many measures of rice she should cook for that day. The old woman would ponder the problem seriously and then hold up her hand. On some days the hand would show two outstretched fingers, on other days it would show three, according to her fancy. The daughter-in-law would take the order silently and go into the kitchen to cook two measures of rice, or three, as the wrinkled hand commanded.

One day the old woman fell ill and passed away. The young daughter-in-law wept her eyes out. She could not see her way about the little house and she missed her mother-in-law's daily instructions. Who was there now to tell her how much she should cook for the day? She was in a perpetual funk, unable to make any decisions. Her husband was at first pleased with his wife's devotion to his mother, but he soon tired of answering her eternal questions about measures of rice.

He thought of a way out of all this bother. He went to the nearest potter and ordered a clay image of his mother, as large as life. He gave special instructions to the potter to make one hand show two fingers and the other three. In a few days the clay mother-in-law was painted, dressed, and ready for use. The husband brought it home and planted it in a prominent place near the kitchen. The young wife was delighted at the return of her lost mother-in-law. It seemed to be the end of her troubles, and she could begin the day properly now. Whenever she was in doubt about measures of rice, she would look out of the kitchen and take orders. If she happened to see the two-fingered hand first, she would cook two measures for the day; if she caught a glimpse of the three-fingered hand, that day the rice-pot would overflow with boiled rice. She was happy with the clay mother-in-law, and her husband was happy with the happiness of his wife.

Things went on smoothly for a while, till one day the husband became aware that his rice-bags were being emptied every few weeks, though there were only two people in the house. He asked his wife, and she told him her daily procedure: she asked her mother-in-law every morning and followed her instructions. Her husband was furious: "Two or three measures of rice every day for just the two of us? Ridiculous! We aren't eating all of it, are we? When my mother was alive, you used to cook the same two measures and all three of us would have our bellies bursting!" She replied in a low voice, "We are not two, but three. You've forgotten Mother. As usual, I give her dinner before I eat. On many days, I've very little left for myself. If you don't mind my saying so, Mother eats more rice than she used to."

The husband couldn't believe his ears. What was this wild tale of a mud mother-in-law eating up whole bags of rice? He flew into a rage and beat up his wife. Then he threw her out, and her clay mother-in-law with her.

But the truth was this: twice every day, the young wife, according to custom, would spread a leaf before her mother-in-law and serve all the dishes one by one. But as soon as she went into the kitchen, the neighbor's wife would come in quietly through a cunningly made hole in the wall, steal all the food, and vanish the way she came. This way, she didn't have to cook at all. The poor fool of a daughter-in-law believed all along that her mother-in-law had dined off her leaf as usual. Her innocence had now landed her in the streets.

She was miserable. She took the effigy of her beloved mother-in-law in her arms and walked into the night, afraid of the dark, crying, praying, cursing her fate. She walked and walked and soon came to the woods outside the town. She clutched her mother-in-law closer to her bosom and shivered in the terrifying dark. Every little sound scared the poor young woman, who had rarely before stepped out of her house. She somehow climbed a tree and tied herself to a branch with her sari, clinging all the while to her mother-in-law. As she sat there trembling, she heard loud footfalls. Burly mustached men, with burning torches in their hands, were parting the bushes and coming towards her tree. From their dress and their murderous looks, she guessed they were thieves. They came right under the tree where she was hiding. Tired after a busy day, they lowered their burdens from their backs and sat down to share the loot. In the light of the torches, they seemed like devils to her. The poor woman began to shake with fear and lost her grip on the clay mother-in-law. Down it fell, with a great big crash, right on the gang of thieves under the tree.

The thieves panicked and took to their heels, and fled in all directions before they knew what had hit them. Meanwhile the young wife had fainted from sheer terror, and she lay unconscious among the branches till dawn.

When day dawned and she woke up as from a nightmare, the first thing she saw on the forest floor was her clay mother-in-law, broken in three pieces, surrounded by countless treasures and a few burnt-out torches. After making sure there was no one around, she carefully climbed down from her perch and gathered up the pieces of her clay mother-in-law. She thanked her for saving her life and for bringing her an undreamed-of treasure.

A few hours later, when she made her way back, the furious husband saw his wife at his door, with a broken clay effigy in one arm and a heavy bundle in the other. He scolded her first for coming back, but soon learned of the precious bundle she had brought. He dragged her inside the house and heard her story in all its detail. His eyes popped out as he saw the rubies and gold in the bundle. He put them aside safely, and with her help he went back to the tree in the forest, bundled up the remaining loot, and brought home secretly a treasure worth a kingdom.

As he spread the treasures on the floor and sorted them out, he wanted to know how much it all amounted to. He sent his wife to the neighbor's house to borrow a big measuring vessel, warning her not to breathe a word about what they were going to measure.

The neighbor woman was curious to know what these poor people had that day to measure in such a big vessel, but the young wife wouldn't tell her anything. So the neighbor stuck a piece of tamarind at the bottom of the measuring vessel before she lent it to the young woman. When the measuring vessel was returned later, the neighbor woman and her husband were aston- ished to see a brilliant gem stuck to the tamarind at the bottom. They wondered, speculated, and thought of all the possible ways in which their neighbors, penniless till yesterday, could have amassed such wealth, enough to be measured in measuring vessels. It was a mystery, and the woman grilled the young wife with questions at the very next opportunity. That innocent told her in whispers ("Don't tell anyone," she said every now and then), pouring out her breathless tale of her adventures in the night—how she had been driven out, how frightened she was, how she had stayed in a tree with her mother-in-law, and all the rest of it. She ended by saying it was all her mother-in-law's doing that they now had all this wealth.

The clever neighbor knew better than to believe this nonsense about the dead mother-in-law. Her husband thought that here was a shortcut to fortune. He too had a big clay doll made, put it in his wife's arms, took her into the jungle, and left her there. He told her he would never take her back into his house unless she brought her husband as much wealth as their neighbor's stupid wife had brought hers.

Now, this woman was confident of her plans and had worked out her strategy carefully. As expected, the same thieves came there with torches in hand to share the day's loot. As soon as they untied their bundles, the woman in the tree threw down her doll on them. There was a big crash. At once, the thieves took to their heels, but they didn't go far this time. They were suspicious. They had been taken unawares the first time; but now they wanted to see what this crash was all about. They hid behind some trees and watched. They saw a woman get down from the tree and begin robbing them of their ill-won riches. With shouts of anger, they closed in on her, scolded her for scaring them out of their treasure the other night, and before she could say anything, beat her till she was blue and faint, and left her tied up to the tree.

Her husband found her the next day, nearly gone mad with fear, very much worse for the night's treasure-hunt, but not a penny richer.

The Clever Daughter-in-Law

~ *Kannada* ~ ~

There was a mother-in-law who was a terrible tyrant. She gave her daughter-in-law no freedom. She saw to it that the young woman did all the housework, cleaned the cowshed, and carried water from the well. By this time it would already be evening. Mother and son would then eat by themselves, and give the daughter-in-law leftovers and stale rice. If the young woman so much as breathed a complaint, the mother-in-law would pick up a broomstick and rain blows on her head. If she wept, the old woman would let loose a barrage of abuse: "You slut, you hussy, you want to wash away our house in your tears and bring bad luck, you daughter of a whore," and so on. The son was meek and kept his mouth shut.

In their back yard, a snake-gourd plant grew and thrived; long gourds swung from it. Everyone's mouth watered when they saw the gourds. In season, the mother-in-law would make a big potful of delicious snake-gourd *talada*. She and her son would eat most of it and give the daughter-in-law their leavings. Once, after several days of this semistarvation, the young woman was seized with a craving to eat a full meal of the delicious snake-gourd *talada*.

That day, the daughter-in-law came home in a hurry with her garbage basket and called to her mother-in-law.

"Why are you howling like a vixen?" shrieked the old woman. "What's the matter with you?"

"I ran into Big Auntie's husband. He says Auntie isn't well and wants to see you. She is seriously ill and holding on to her life only to see you, he said. He wanted me tell you that."

"*Ayyo*, my sister is dying. O Sister, what happened to you?" cried the mother-in-law, beating her breast. "Come in now, I'm sautéeing the *talada*. You take care of it. I'll go and see my sister," she said, and left the house.

The daughter-in-law was quite excited. She made some more *talada*. She cooked all sorts of other dishes and served her husband a big meal. Then she poured all the *talada* into a big vessel, took it on her hip, and went out as if she was going to get water for the house. She went straight to the temple of Kali, the Black Goddess, entered it, and closed the door behind her. There was no one there. She sat there and ate the entire potful of *talada*. The goddess, who was looking on, was astonished at the speed of her eating and the quantity she consumed. In her amazement, she put her right hand on her mouth. The daughter-in-law didn't notice any of this but continued to eat to her heart's content. When she was done, she belched a big belch of utter satisfaction, picked up the empty vessel, and went to the pond to wash it.

When she came home with a pot of water, the main door of her house was closed. Her mother-in-law had returned. She tapped on the door, which was soon opened by her angry mother-in-law. Sparks were flying from her eyes. She had a stick in her hand and rained blows on the young woman's back and waist till she fell to the ground, crying pitifully. "You daughter of a whore, how long have you waited to cheat me like this? You've gobbled up a potful of *talada* like a buffalo, you dirty slut!" screamed the woman and rained some more blows. When the husband came home, he too joined in the punishment.

Meanwhile, the whole town was buzzing with the news that the image of Kali in the temple now had its hand on its mouth. People from other towns also came to see this miracle, and they all had their own interpretation. Everyone was scared that this was a bad sign. Something terrible was going to happen to the village, they thought, and shuddered.

"Someone has polluted the Goddess. That's why she has shut her mouth with her hand. She is angry. There won't be any more rain. No children will be born in this village any more," they said, terror-stricken. Worship and rituals were performed all over the village. They arranged festivals and sacrificed goats. But nothing seemed to please the Goddess. So the village elders sent the town crier through the area to announce a big reward to anyone who would make the Goddess remove her hand from her mouth. No one came forward.

The daughter-in-law watched all this. One day she came to her mother-in-law and said, "Mother-in-law, tell the elders we'll get the goddess Kali to remove her hand from her mouth. I know how to do it."

The mother-in-law was furious at first. "Look at this fool! She wants me to lose face in the village. She wants to act big as if she was a holy woman. What no one could do, she says she'll do. Fat chance!" she sneered. But the daughter-in-law persisted and finally convinced her that she knew something no one else knew.

On the appointed day, the young woman took her tamarind broomstick and the garbage basket full of rubbish and went to the temple. She shut everyone out and closed the door behind her. She put down the basket in front of the Black Goddess and, brandishing her broomstick, challenged Kali: "You jealous female! What's it to you if I ate my snake-gourd *talada?* Why do your eyes burn? If you'd only asked me, I'd have given you some. May your face burn, may your cheeks swell and explode, may your eyes sink in and go blind! Will you take your hand off your mouth now or shall I beat you with my broomstick? Now!"

There was no answer. The daughter-in-law was furious; she looked like Kali the Black Goddess herself. She went up to the image and gave Kali's face several whacks with her broomstick. Kali whimpered and cried "*Ayyo!*" and removed her hand from her mouth. The image now looked as it had always looked. "That's better!" muttered the daughter-in-law. She picked up her basket and broom and came home with the news that she had managed to get Kali to take her hand off her mouth.

The whole village was agog with the news. They ran to the temple to see for themselves, and they couldn't believe their own eyes. They praised the daughter-in-law as the greatest of chaste wives, a *pativrate*, whose virtue had given her miraculous powers. They gave her a big reward and many gifts.

Now the mother-in-law was terrified by this incident. She felt that her daughter-in-law had strange powers and would take revenge against her for the terrible things she had done to her all those years. The young woman knew some kind of magic, and who knew what she might do?

On a dark new-moon day, at dead of night, mother and son whispered to each other. She said to him, "Son, this one frightened even Kali, the Mother Goddess, and made her take her hand off her mouth. She won't let us go unharmed. We have beaten her, starved her, given her every kind of trouble. She'll take revenge. She'll finish us off. What shall we do?"

"I can't think of anything. You tell me," said the cowardly son.

The mother said, "She's asleep now. We'll wrap her up in her mat, take her to the fields, and burn her in the pit there. Then I'll get you a beautiful new bride."

"All right, let's do it right now," said he, and they both gagged the young wife quickly and rolled her in her bedclothes and mat. She knew they were going to do something awful to her, but she mustered her courage and lay still. They carried her to the pit in the field outside the village and hid her behind a bush while they went looking for twigs and firewood. As soon as they left, she rolled around and loosened the mat, slid out of it, pulled off the string around her hands, and took the gag from her mouth. She found a log nearby, which she wrapped in her bedclothes and mat. Then she walked a short distance away, climbed a banyan tree, and hid herself in its branches.

Mother and son came hurrying back. They spread twigs and branches all around the bundle in the mat, put more firewood over it, covered it with dry straw, and lighted it. The fire burned with leaping flames as they watched it. When the knots in the branches crackled and burst, they said, "The bones, the bones are splitting." When the log inside caught fire, a large knot cracked in the flames and went off like a gunshot. They were satisfied that the skull had now exploded as it does in a cremation. It was long past midnight, and they went home.

The daughter-in-law crouched hidden in the branches. That same night, four robbers came there to sit under the tree and divide up their loot. They had just broken into a rich man's mansion and plundered jewels, gold, and cash. As they sat down, they saw a fire burning a distance away, so one of them climbed the tree to see if there was anyone near the fire. He came right up to the branch where the young woman was perched. When he saw someone sitting there, he said softly, "Who's there?" She boldly put out her hand, gently shut his mouth, and whispered, "Ssh! Not so loud. I'm a celestial. I'm looking for a good, handsome man. I'll marry you and make you rich beyond your dreams. Just be quiet!"

The robber couldn't believe what was happening to him. He thought he had reached heaven and seen the Great White Elephant descend from the sky. He took her hand and said, "Are you for real?" She said, "Hmm." Then she slowly pulled out her little bag of betel leaf and betel nut, gave him some, and put some into her own mouth. He came closer to kiss her. She turned away, saying, "Look, we're not married yet. But you can put your betel leaf into my mouth with your tongue. When I've eaten from your mouth, I'll be as good as your wedded wife. All right?"

Beside himself with joy, he put out his tongue with the chewed betel leaf on it and brought it close to her mouth. She at once closed her teeth powerfully on his tongue and bit it off. Screaming with unbearable pain, he lost his grip and fell down. The robbers below ran helter-skelter in panic. The man who had lost his tongue could only babble and blabber and spit blood, making noises like "*Ba ba bababa . . .*" as he too ran after his companions. His noises scared them even more and they fled faster, with him squealing behind.

When it was light, the daughter-in-law cautiously climbed down the tree and saw to her amazement the gold, jewels, and money under the tree! She quickly bundled it all up and went straight home. When she tapped on the door, calling out, "Mother-in-law, mother-in-law, please open the door!" the old woman opened the door hesitantly, her face blanched with fear. There in front of her was her smiling daughter-in-law. The mother-in-law fainted at the sight. The young woman carried her into the hall, sprinkled cool water on her face, and revived her. The husband just stood there, not knowing what to think.

When she came to and opened her eyes, the mother-in-law asked, "How did you . . . ? How is it you are . . . ?"

The daughter-in-law briskly replied, "After you cremated me, messengers from Yama, the god of death, took me to him. His eyes were shooting flames like the eyes of our Kali, our village goddess. As soon as he saw me, He said, 'Send this one back. Her mother-in-law is a sinner. Bring *her* here and put the Iron Crow to work on her, to tear her to pieces with its beak. Dip her in cauldrons of boiling oil.' He ranted on like that about you. I fell at his feet and begged him, 'Don't do this to my mother-in-law. She is really a very fine woman. Give me whatever punishment you wish, but please spare my mother-in-law.' He was pleased, he even smiled, and said, 'You can go now. We'll do as you say. But if your mother-in-law ever gives you any trouble, we'll drag her here. My messengers will always be watching.' Then he gave me all this gold and jewelry and money and sent me home. People say bad things about the god of death, but he was so good to me."

The mother-in-law embraced her daughter-in-law with fear and trembling in her heart.

"*Ayyo!* You're really the angel of this house. You've saved me from the jaws of death's messengers. From now on, I'll do as you say. Just forgive everything I've done to you. Will you, my darling daughter-in-law?" she said, touching the young woman's chin tenderly.

The daughter-in-law was now the boss in the house. Her mother-in-law and her husband followed her wishes, and everyone was happy.

The Barber and the Brahman Demon

~ Bengali ~ ~

In the district of Burdwan, there lived a barber who was very idle. He would do no work and devoted his time to preening himself with an old mirror and a broken comb. His old mother rebuked him all day for this, but it didn't touch him. At last, one day in a fit of anger, she struck him with her broom. The young barber felt humiliated by this and left home, determined never to return till he had amassed some wealth. He walked far till he reached a forest and thought of praying to the gods for help. But as he entered the forest, he met with a *brahmarakshasa*, a demon who was once a Brahman, dancing wildly. He was terrified but he kept his wits about him. So he mustered all his courage and began to dance too, keeping time with the demon. After a while, he asked the demon, "Why are you dancing? What has made you so happy?"

The demon laughed and said, "I was waiting for your question because I knew you were a fool and didn't know the reason. It's simply because I want to feast on your delicate flesh. That's why. Now tell me, why are *you* dancing?"

"I have a far better reason," returned the barber. "Our king's son is very ill. The doctors have recommended for his cure the heart's blood of one hundred and one *brahmarakshasas*. His Majesty has proclaimed by beat of drum that he'll give away half his kingdom and one of his beautiful daughters to anyone who gets the medicine. I have, with great trouble, captured one hundred *brahmarakshasas* and now, with you, I make up the full quota of one hundred and one. I have already seized your soul, and you are in my pocket." So saying, he took out his pocket mirror and held it before the *brahmarakshasa's* eyes. The terrified demon found his image in the glass. He could see it there in the clear moonlight and thought himself actually captured. He trembled and prayed to the barber to release him. The barber would not agree at first, but the demon promised him wealth worth the ransom of seven kings. Pretending to yield unwillingly, the barber said, "But where is this wealth you promise, and who will carry it and me to my house at this hour in the dead of night?"

"The treasure is under that tree behind you," said the *brahmarakshasa*. "I'll show it to you and I'll carry you with it to your house in an instant. As you know, we demons, we have special powers."

Saying this, he uprooted the tree and brought out seven golden jars full of precious stones. The barber was dazzled by all that wealth, but he cunningly concealed his true feelings and boldly ordered the demon to carry the jars and himself at once to his house. The demon obeyed, and the barber was carried home with all the wealth. The demon then begged for his release, but the barber didn't wish to part with his services so soon. So he asked him to cut the paddy of his field and bring the crop home. The poor demon believed himself still in the barber's clutches and so consented to reap the grain.

As he was cutting the paddy, a brother demon happened to pass that way. He asked the *brahmarakshasa* what he was doing. The first demon told him how he had accidentally fallen into the hands of a shrewd man and had no way of escaping his clutches unless he did what he was told. So he was reaping the man's rice crop. The second demon laughed and said, "Have you gone mad, my friend? We demons are superior to men and much more powerful. How can any man have any power over us? Can you show me the house of this man?"

"I can," replied the first demon, "but only from a distance. I dare not go near it till I've cut all this paddy." Then he showed him the way to the barber's house.

Meanwhile, the barber was celebrating his newfound wealth. He had bought a big fish for the party, but unfortunately a cat had entered the kitchen through a broken window and had eaten up most of it. The barber's wife was very angry and wanted to kill the animal. When she went after it, the cat escaped through the same window by which it had entered. Knowing the ways of cats, she expected it to return, so she stood there waiting with a fish knife in her hand. Now the second *brahmarakshasa* tiptoed like a thief towards the house and wanted to take a peek at his friend's captor. So he slowly thrust his bushy head through the broken window. The angry wife, who was waiting there for the naughty cat, brought down her sharp knife on the intruding demon and made a clean slash through his long nose, cutting off the tip. In pain and fright, the demon ran away, ashamed of showing his friend a face minus a nose.

The first demon patiently reaped all the grain and came back to the barber for his release. The wily barber showed him the back of the mirror. The *brahmarakshasa* looked at it anxiously and was relieved not to find his image in it. So he fetched a deep sigh and went his way, dancing with a light heart.

Why the Fish Laughed

~ *Kashmiri* ~ ~

As a fisherwoman passed by the palace hawking her fish, the queen appeared at one of the windows and beckoned her to come near and show her what she had. At that moment a very big fish jumped about in the bottom of the basket.

"Is it a male or a female?" asked the queen. "I'd like to buy a female fish."

On hearing this, the fish laughed aloud.

"It's a male," replied the fisherwoman, and continued on her rounds.

The queen returned to her room in a great rage. When the king came to see her that evening, he could tell that something was wrong.

"What's the matter?" he asked. "Are you not well?"

"I'm quite well, thank you. But I'm very much annoyed at the strange behavior of a fish. A woman showed me one today, and when I asked whether it was male or female, the fish laughed most rudely."

"A fish laugh? Impossible! You must be dreaming."

"I'm not a fool. I saw it with my own eyes and heard it laugh with my own ears."

"That's very strange. All right, I'll make the necessary inquiries."

The next morning, the king told his *wazir* (minister) what his wife had told him and ordered the *wazir* to investigate the matter and be ready with a satisfactory answer within six months, on pain of death.

The *wazir* promised to do his best, though he didn't know where to begin. For the next five months he labored tirelessly to find a reason for the laughter of the fish. He went everywhere and consulted everyone—the wise and the learned, the people skilled in magic and trickery, they were all consulted.

Nobody could explain the mystery of the laughing fish. So he returned brokenhearted to his house and began to arrange his affairs, sure now that he was going to die. He was well enough acquainted with the king's ways to know that His Majesty would not go back on his threat. Among other things, he advised his son to travel for a time, until the king's anger had cooled off somewhat.

The young fellow, who was both clever and handsome, started off and went wherever his legs and his kismet would take him. After a few days, he fell in with an old farmer who was on his way back to his village from a journey. The young man found him pleasant and asked if he might go with him. The old farmer agreed, and they walked along together. The day was hot, and the way was long and weary.

"Don't you think it would be much more pleasant if we could carry one another sometimes?" said the young man.

"What a fool this man is!" thought the old man.

A little later, they passed through a field of grain ready for the sickle and waving in the breeze, looking like a sea of gold.

"Is this eaten or not?" asked the young man.

The old man didn't know what to say, and said, "I don't know."

After a little while, the two travelers came to a big village, where the young man handed his companion a pocket knife, and said, "Take this, friend, and get two horses with it. But please bring it back. It's very precious."

The old man was half amused and half angry. He pushed away the knife, muttering that his friend was either mad or trying to play the fool. The young man pretended not to notice his reply and remained silent for a long time,

till they reached a city a short distance from the old farmer's village. They walked about the bazaar and went to the mosque, but nobody greeted them or invited them to come in and rest.

"What a large cemetery!" exclaimed the young man.

"What does the fellow mean," thought the old farmer, "calling this city full of people a cemetery?"

On leaving the city their way led through a cemetery where some people were praying beside a grave and distributing *chapatis* (unleavened bread) to passers-by in the name of their beloved dead. They gave some of the bread to the two travelers also, as much as they could eat.

"What a splendid city this is!" said the young man.

"Now the man is surely crazy!" thought the old farmer. "I wonder what he'll do next. He'll be calling the land water, the water land. He'll be speaking of light when it's dark, and of darkness when it's light." But he kept his thoughts to himself.

Presently they had to wade through a stream. The water was rather deep, so the old farmer took off his shoes and *pajamas* and crossed over. But the young man waded through it with his shoes and *pajamas* on.

"Well, I've never seen such a perfect idiot, in word and deed," said the old man to himself.

Yet he liked the fellow. He seemed cultivated and aristocratic. He would certainly amuse his wife and daughter. So he invited him home for a visit.

The young man thanked him and then asked, "But let me ask, if you please, if the beam of your house is strong."

The old farmer mumbled something and went home to tell his family, laughing to himself. When he was alone with them, he said, "This young man has come with me a long way, and I've asked him to stay with us. But the fellow is such a fool that I can't make anything of what he says or does. He wants to know if the beam of this house is all right. The man must be mad!"

Now, the farmer's daughter was a very sharp and wise girl. She said to him, "This man, whoever he is, is no fool. He only wishes to know if you can afford to entertain him."

"Oh, of course," said the farmer, "I see. Well, perhaps you can help me to solve some of his other mysteries. While we were walking together, he asked whether we should not carry one another. He thought it would be a pleasanter mode of travel."

"Certainly," said the girl. "He meant that one of you should tell the other a story to pass the time."

"Oh yes. Then, when we were passing through a wheatfield, he asked me whether it was eaten or not."

"And didn't you know what he meant, Father? He simply wished to know if the owner of the field was in debt or not. If he was in debt, then the produce of the field was as good as eaten. That is, it would all go to his creditors."

"Yes, yes, of course. Then, on entering a village, he asked me to take his pocket knife and get two horses with it, and bring back the knife to him."

"Are not two stout sticks as good as two horses for helping one along the road? He only asked you to cut a couple of sticks and be careful not to lose the knife."

"I see," said the farmer. "While we were walking through the city, we did not see anyone we knew, and not a soul gave us a scrap of anything to eat, till we reached the cemetery. There, some people called us and thrust *chapatis* into our hands. So my friend called the city a cemetery and the cemetery a city."

"Look, Father, inhospitable people are worse than the dead, and a city full of them is a dead place. But in the cemetery, which is crowded with the dead, you were greeted by kind people who gave you bread."

"True, quite true," said the astonished farmer. "But then, just now, when we were crossing the stream, he waded across without taking off even his shoes."

"I admire his wisdom," said the daughter. "I've often thought how stupid people were to get into that swiftly flowing stream and walk over those sharp stones with bare feet. The slightest stumble and they would fall and get wet from head to foot. This friend of yours is a very wise man. I would like to see him and talk to him."

"Very well, I'll go find him and bring him in."

"Tell him, Father, that our beams are strong enough, and then he will come in. I'll send on ahead a present for the man, to show that we can afford a guest."

Then she called a servant and sent him to the young man with a present of a dish of porridge, twelve *chapatis*, and a jar of milk with the following message: "Friend, the moon is full, twelve months make a year, and the sea is overflowing with water."

On his way, the bearer of this present and message met his little son who, seeing what was in the basket, begged his father to give him some of the food. The foolish man gave him a lot of the porridge, a *chapati*, and some milk. When he saw the young man, he gave him the present and the message.

"Give your mistress my greetings," he replied. "And tell her that the moon is new, that I can find only eleven months in the year, and that the sea is by no means full."

Not understanding the meaning of these words, the servant repeated them word for word to his mistress; and thus his theft was discovered, and he was punished. After a little while, the young man appeared with the old farmer. He was treated royally, as if he were the son of a great man, though the farmer knew nothing of his origins. In the course of the conversation, he told them everything—about the fish's laughter, his father's threatened execution, and his own exile—and asked their advice about what he should do.

"The laughter of the fish," said the girl, "which seems to have been the cause of all this trouble, indicates that there is a man in the women's quarters of the palace, and the king doesn't know anything about it."

"Great! That's great!" exclaimed the *wazir's* son. "There's yet time for me to return and to save my father from a shameful and unjust death."

The following day he rushed back to his own country, taking with him the farmer's daughter. When he arrived, he ran to the palace and told his father what he had heard. The poor *wazir*, now almost dead from the expectation of death, was carried at once to the king in a palanquin. He repeated to the king what his son had said.

"A man in the queen's quarters! Never!" said the king.

"But it must be so, Your Majesty," replied the *wazir*, "and to prove the truth of what I've just heard, I propose a test. Please call together all the female attendants in your palace and order them to jump over a large pit, specially dug for this purpose. The man will at once betray his sex by the way he jumps."

The king had the pit dug and ordered all the female servants of the palace to try to jump over it. All of them tried, but only one succeeded. That one was found to be a man!

Thus was the queen satisfied and the faithful old *wazir* saved.

Soon after that, the *wazir's* son married the old farmer's daughter. And it was a most happy marriage.

A *Parrot* Called Hiraman

~ *Bengali* ~ ~

A birdcatcher and his wife were always in want. One day his wife said to him, "I'll tell you why we are poor. It's because you sell every bird you catch. If we ate some of these birds, we might have better luck. That's what they say. So let's cook and eat whatever birds you catch today." The birdcatcher agreed.

So the two of them went birdcatching, with their limed rods and nets, but on that day they caught nothing till sundown. Then, just as they were returning home, they caught a beautiful gem-green parrot called a *hiraman*, a native of the Molucca Islands.

The birdcatcher's wife took the terrified bird in her hands and felt it all over and said, "This is such a tiny bird. It would hardly be a mouthful. There is no use killing it." The *hiraman* said, "Mother, do not kill me. Take me to the king and sell me. He'll give you a lot of money." The couple were taken aback on hearing the parrot speak, and when they recovered from their astonishment, asked the bird what price they should set. The *hiraman* answered, "Leave that to me. When the king asks my price, just say, 'The bird will tell you its own price,' and then I'll mention a large sum."

So the birdcatcher took the bird to the palace the next day and offered it for sale. The king, delighted by the beauty of the bird green as an emerald, asked him what he would take for it. The man said, "His Highness may kindly ask the bird. It will tell you." "What! Can the bird speak?" said the king, and turned to the bird half in jest and asked, "Well, *hiraman*, what is your price?" The *hiraman* said, "Please Your Majesty, my price is ten thousand rupees. Do not think the price is too high. Count out the money to this man. I'll be of great service to Your Majesty." The king laughed and said, "Of what service can you be to me, little bird?" "Your Majesty will see that in due time," said the *hiraman*. The king, amazed by the way the bird talked to him, ordered his treasurer to count out the sum of ten thousand rupees to the birdcatcher.

The king had six queens, but he was so taken up with the bird that he almost forgot their existence. His days and nights were spent in the company not of the queens but of this bird. The *hiraman* not only replied intelligently to every question but recited to him the names of the three hundred and thirty million gods of the Hindu pantheon, the hearing of which is itself an act of piety.

The queens felt quite neglected by the king, became jealous of the bird, and decided to kill it. It was some time before they got an opportunity, as the bird was the king's inseparable companion. One day the king went out hunting and was away for two days. The six queens thought this was their chance to put an end to the bird, and said to one another, "We'll go and ask the bird which of us is the ugliest of all in its eyes, and whoever is judged by the bird to be the ugliest shall strangle it." Then they went into the room where the bird was. But before the queens could put any questions, the bird sweetly and piously recited the names of the three hundred and thirty million gods and goddesses. The hearts of the six queens melted into tenderness, and they came away without doing any harm to the bird.

The following day their jealousy and ill-will returned, and they called themselves fools for being so charmed by the bird. So they steeled their hearts against all pity and went there this time determined to kill it at once. "O hiraman," they said, "we hear that you are a very wise bird and your judgments are always right. Please tell us which of us is the prettiest and which the ugliest." The bird, knowing their evil designs, said to them, "How can I answer your question when I'm in a cage? To make a proper judgment, I must look minutely at each one of you, limb by limb, front and behind. If you wish to know what I think, you must first set me free."

At first, the women were afraid to set the bird free lest it should fly away. On second thoughts, they set it free after shutting all the doors and windows of the room. But the clever bird had examined the room already and seen a water passage in one corner through which it could escape. When the queens had repeated their question several times, the bird said, "Ugh! Talk of your beauty! There's more beauty in the little toe of the princess who lives beyond the seven seas and the thirteen rivers than in all six of you." The queens were furious to hear their beauty thus slighted, and they rushed towards the bird to tear it to pieces. But before they could reach it, it escaped through the water passage and took shelter in a woodcutter's hut nearby.

When the king returned home from hunting, he did not find his hiraman on its perch. He asked the queens, and they said they didn't know anything about it. He had the whole palace searched but could not find his bird. He was grief-stricken, and began to say all day, "O my hiraman, O my hiraman!

Where are you?" The ministers even feared for his sanity. They sent out town criers throughout the kingdom to proclaim by beat of drum that anyone who found the king's pet parrot would be rewarded with ten thousand rupees. The woodcutter heard the proclamation and happily brought the bird to the palace and got his reward. The king now heard from the parrot how the queens had tried to kill it. Mad with rage, he banished the six queens to the wilderness where, it was rumored a few days later, the wretched women were all devoured by wild beasts.

After some time, the king said to the parrot, "*Hiraman*, you said that none of the queens had the beauty even of the little toe of the princess who lives beyond the seven seas and the thirteen rivers. Do you know how I can get to her?"

The *hiraman* said, "Of course I do. I can take you to the door of her palace, and if you will do as I tell you, you'll soon have her in your arms. Actually, she is waiting for you, though she doesn't know it."

"I'll do whatever you tell me. Where do I begin?"

"What you need is a *pakshiraj*, a winged horse. If you can get one, you can ride on it and we'll cross the seven seas and thirteen rivers in no time."

"I have, as you know, a large stable of horses. Why don't we go now and see if we have any of the *pakshiraj* breed?"

The king and the *hiraman* went to the royal stables and examined all the horses. The *hiraman* passed by all the fine-looking horses and lighted upon a lean, wretched-looking pony, and said, "That's the horse I want. It is a genuine *pakshiraj*, but it must be fed for six months with the finest grain before it can do what you want it to do." The king put the pony in a stable by itself and personally saw to it that it was fed every day with the finest grain of the kingdom. The pony rapidly changed its appearance and at the end of six months had become a magnificent steed. The *hiraman* looked it over and pronounced it fit for service. Then the parrot asked the king to order the royal silversmiths to make some *khais*, fried grains of rice, out of silver. The silversmiths worked overtime and made a large quantity of silver *khais*. They were now ready for the aerial journey, when the *hiraman* said to the king, "I must tell you one more thing. Please give the horse only one stroke of the whip at starting. If you give it more than one, we will be stuck midway and never reach the palace. And when we return after capturing the princess, then too you must whip the horse only once. If you whip it more than once, we will come only halfway." The king then mounted the *pakshiraj* with the *hiraman* and the bag of silver *khais*, and gently touched the animal once with his whip. The horse shot through the air with the speed of lightning, passed over many countries, crossed the seven oceans and the thirteen rivers, and landed that very evening at the palace gate of the beautiful princess.

Now, there was a tall tree near the gate. The *hiraman* told the king to put the horse in the stable nearby, and then to climb the tree and hide himself in the branches. Then the bird took the silver *khais*, and with its beak began dropping *khai* after *khai* from the foot of the tree, all through the corridors, right up to the door of the bedroom of the princess of peerless beauty. Then it joined the king on the tree. Some hours after midnight, the princess's maidservant, who slept in the same room, came out for something, opened the door, and found the silver *khais*. Not knowing what they were, she showed them to her mistress, who was so struck by the appearance of the little silver bullets that she too came out and began picking them up. She saw a regular stream of them beginning at her door and going she knew not where. She knew then that something exciting was afoot. She went on picking up the bright shining pieces, and they led her through the corridors till she came to the foot of the tree. At once the king jumped down from the tree (all according to the bird's instructions), caught hold of her, and put her on his horse along with himself. The *hiraman* perched on his shoulder. The king gently touched the horse just once with the whip, and they were whirled through space with

the speed of lightning. But the king was so eager to get home quickly with his new-won prize that he forgot and whipped the horse again as he would any other. At once the horse was grounded outside a dense forest. "Oh, what have you done?" cried the *hiraman*. "Did I not tell you never to whip the horse more than once? You've whipped it twice, and we are done for. We may be stuck here till we die." But what was done was done. The *pakshiraj* had become powerless and the party was stranded far from home. They got down from the horse and found the place utterly deserted. They ate some fruit and slept that night right there on the ground.

Next morning, it just happened that the king of that country came there to hunt. As he pursued a stag which he had pierced with an arrow, he came across the king and the princess. Struck almost blind by her dazzling beauty, he wanted her for himself. He whistled for help, and his attendants flocked around him. He seized the princess and carried her off with him, but not before putting out the king's eyes. The king who had crossed seven seas and thirteen rivers for her sake was left there sightless and alone—yet not alone, for the good *hiraman* was with him.

The princess was taken into the palace of the king, and with her went the pony. When the king came near her, she told him that she was observing a six-month vow of devotion to Siva and that he must not come near her for those six months. She asked this because she knew it took six full months for the *pakshiraj* to recover its strength. Then she pretended to engage in religious ceremonies every day as part of her vow, and the king assigned a separate house for her. She took the *pakshiraj* with her and fed it the choicest grain of the kingdom. But she needed the *hiraman* to help her and thought of a ruse. She ordered her servants to scatter on the roof of her house heaps of rice, wheat, and all sorts of lentils as food for the birds. Thousands of birds came to the roof every day to take part in the feast. The princess looked among the birds every day for the *hiraman*. But the good bird was stuck in the forest. It had to take care of itself as well as the blinded king, and they both lived on fruit from various trees.

The other birds would say to the parrot, "O *hiraman*, you are miserable here in the forest. Why don't you come with us for just a little while to that good lady's feast of grains? She scatters them for the likes of us every day. We go there every morning and eat our fill all day along with thousands of other birds." The shrewd parrot could guess who the pious lady was and why she was throwing this open party for the birds, and decided to go with them one morning. The *hiraman* saw the princess, talked to her about the blinded king, and told her how to cure him of his blindness, and how she could escape. This was the plan: as the six months had nearly gone by, the pony would soon be ready for flight; the king's blindness would be cured if the *hiraman* could bring the fresh excrement of the chicks of *bihangama* birds in the tree outside the gate of the princess's own palace beyond the seven seas and the thirteen rivers.

The very next morning, the *hiraman* started out, reached the spot that night, and waited for morning. At dawn, it waited below the nest of the birds with a leaf in its beak, and gathered the excrement of the chicks. Then it flew back over all the seas and the rivers and applied the precious excrement to the sightless sockets of the king's eyes. The king at once opened his eyes and saw. In a few days the *pakshiraj* was ready and in fine fettle. On the appointed day the princess escaped to the forest on the pony, picked up the king and the *hiraman*, and all three reached the king's capital in no time. The king and princess were soon married in a gorgeous ceremony and lived happily for a long time, with many sons and daughters. The *hiraman* was always with them, reciting the names of the three hundred and thirty million gods of the Hindu pantheon.

A Plague Story
~ Bengali ~ ~

Once a terrible bubonic plague broke out in Asia and wiped out millions of people. The pious king of Bharat summoned all the old and wise priests of the realm to find ways to arrest the sweeping plague. He said to the assembled priests, "The plague has come very near the borders of my kingdom. Tell me what I should do to save my people." The priests conferred for a long time, and their spokesman said to the king, "My lord, this is a visitation from the great god Siva and so we must appease him by offering worship and prayers throughout the kingdom." The king at once ordered that worship and prayers be offered in every Siva temple and in every home. He paid for it all from his royal coffers.

A week after the priests began their worship, one midnight the great god Siva appeared before the senior priest and said, "What do you want?" The priest's hair stood on end, and he prostrated himself full length on the ground before the great god and stammered, "O Siva, savior of the universe, you know what we want. Save us from the plague advancing towards our kingdom." The god replied, "Done! Your prayers have pleased me. My servant Nandi will guard your country against all evils." And then he vanished.

Early next morning, the happy news was conveyed to the king, who rewarded each of the priests with twenty five milch cows and fifty bags of cowrie shells, and sent them home.

Now Nandi was posted to see that the plague did not enter the kingdom. He watched the borders vigilantly day and night. One night, as he was on his rounds along the frontiers, the grim Plague assumed a body and a shape, and appeared before him, threatening to enter the kingdom. Nandi, with his trident lifted high, shouted at him, "Get out of my sight, you villain. One step more and you'll be finished." The hideous figure would not give way so easily, and there was a monstrous scuffle between the two giant figures. It went on for days. Several hills were demolished and great trees were uprooted as the giant bodies dashed against them. At last a truce was made, and they came to terms. It was agreed that the Plague would stay only for a day in the capital and take only one man as its victim.

But the next evening, a great hue and cry was raised in the city, for it was reported that not one or two but a hundred men had died of plague. The king sent at once for the priests and asked for an explanation. They hastened anxiously to Nandi and asked him the reason. Nandi flew into a rage and ran out in search of the Plague. He met him on the dusty floor of a ruined house. He caught him by the neck and thundered, "Scoundrel! You have broken your promise. You've taken not one but a hundred victims. You'll pay for this." Even from under Nandi's grip, the Plague let out a peal of laughter and said, "Brother, I've not broken my promise. Don't be angry with me. I did actually take only one man as I promised, but the other ninety-nine died out of fear. What could I do? These people had a simple fever and a little swelling of the glands, and they mistook them for signs of my approach and they died of fear. I had nothing to do with it." Nandi loosened his iron grip and let the Plague go.

The Monkey
and the Crocodile

~ *Kannada; Tamil* ~ ~

On the banks of the Ganges, a monkey lived in a rose-apple tree. The rose-apples were delicious and plentiful. While he was eating them with obvious relish one day, a crocodile came out of the river, and the monkey threw down a few rose-apples and said, "These are the best rose-apples in the world. They taste like nectar." The crocodile chomped on them and found them truly wonderful. The monkey and crocodile became friends, and the crocodile took to visiting the monkey every day to eat the fruit of that wonderful tree and to talk in its shade.

One day the crocodile went home and took some of the fruit to his wife. "These are wonderful. They taste like nectar. Where did you get them?" asked the wife.

He said, "From a tree on the banks of the Ganges."

"But you can't climb the tree. Did you pick them up from the sands?"

"No, I've a new friend who lives in the tree, a monkey. He throws them down for me and we talk."

"Oh, that's why you've been coming home late! A monkey that lives on such fruit must have such sweet flesh. His heart must taste like heaven. I'd love to eat it," said the crocodile wife.

The crocodile didn't like the turn the conversation was taking. "How can you talk like that? He's my friend! He's like a brother-in-law to you."

But the wife sulked and said, "I want his heart. Why are you so taken with this monkey? Is it a he or a she? Bring me his heart, or hers, which is even better. Or else I'll starve myself to death."

The crocodile tried his best to talk her out of her jealousy and ill-will, but he couldn't. He agreed to bring the monkey home on his back for a meal, as it were.

Next day, he invited the monkey to go home with him. "My wife has heard so much about you. She loved the rose-apples. She wants you to come home with me. If you come down from the tree and sit on my back, I'll take you there."

The monkey said, "You are a crocodile and live in the water. I can't even swim. I'll drown and die."

"Oh no, I'll take you carefully on my back. We don't live in the water. We live on a dry, sunny island in the middle of the river. Come with me. You'll enjoy it."

The monkey was persuaded and came down. He brought handfuls of rose-apples for the crocodile's wife. As the crocodile swam through the river, he felt terribly guilty. His conscience wouldn't allow him to take his friend home and let his wife make a meal of his heart, without at least telling him what he was doing. So he said, "I haven't been quite straight with you. My wife sent me today to bring you home because she wants to eat your heart. That's what she wants, and I couldn't go against her wishes."

"Oh, is that what she wants? My heart! Why didn't you tell me this before? I would have been happy to bring it down and give it to your wife," said the monkey.

"What do you mean?" asked the crocodile.

"I don't carry my heart around with me. I usually leave it in the tree when I come down. Let's go back and I'll give it to you."

The crocodile turned around and swam back to the bank. The monkey quickly jumped off his back and clambered up the tree to safety.

What Happens
When You Really Listen

~ *Telugu* ~ ~

A villager who had no sense of culture and no interest in it was married to a woman who was very cultured. She tried various ways of cultivating his taste for the higher things of life, but he just wasn't interested.

Once a great reciter of that grand epic, the *Ramayana*, came to the village. Every evening he would sing, recite, and explain the verses of the epic. The whole village went to this one-man performance as if it were a rare feast.

The woman who was married to the uncultured dolt tried to interest him in the performance. She nagged him and forced him to go and listen. This time, he grumbled as usual but decided to humor her. So he went in the evening and sat at the back. It was an all-night performance and he just couldn't keep awake. He slept through the night. Early in the morning, when a canto was over and the reciter sang the closing verses for the day, sweets were distributed according to custom. Someone put a few sweets into the mouth of the sleeping man. He woke up soon after and went home. His wife was delighted that her husband had stayed through the night and asked him eagerly how he had enjoyed the *Ramayana*. He said, "It was very sweet." The wife was happy to hear it.

The next day his wife again insisted on his listening to the epic. So he went to the enclosure where the reciter was performing, sat against a wall, and before long fell fast asleep. The place was crowded, and a young boy sat on his shoulder and made himself comfortable and listened open-mouthed to the fascinating story. In the morning, when the night's portion of the story came to an end, everyone got up and so did the husband. The boy had got off earlier, but the man felt aches and pains from the weight he had borne all night. When he went home and his wife asked him eagerly how it was, he said, "It got heavier and heavier by morning." The wife said, "That's the way that story is." She was happy that her husband was at last beginning to feel the emotions and the greatness of the epic.

On the third day, he sat at the edge of the crowd and was so sleepy that he lay down on the floor and even snored. Early in the morning, a dog came that way and pissed into his mouth a little before he woke up and went home. When his wife asked him how it was, he moved his mouth this way and that, made a face, and said, "Terrible. It was so salty." His wife knew something was wrong, asked him what exactly had happened, and didn't let up till he finally told her how he had been sleeping through the performance every night.

On the fourth day, his wife went with him. She sat him down in the very first row and told him sternly that he should keep awake no matter what happened. So he sat dutifully in the front row and began to listen. Very soon, he was caught up in the adventures and the characters of the great epic story. On that day, the reciter was enchanting the audience with the story of Hanuman the monkey and how he had to leap across the ocean to take Rama's signet ring to Sita, the abducted wife of Rama. When Hanuman was making his leap, the signet ring slipped from his hand and fell into the ocean. Hanuman didn't know what to do. He had to get the ring back quickly and take it to Sita in the demon's kingdom. While he was wringing his hands, the husband, who was listening with rapt attention in the first row, said, "Hanuman, don't worry. I'll get it for you." Then he jumped up and dived into the ocean, found the ring in the ocean floor, and brought it back and gave it to Hanuman.

Everyone was astonished. They thought this man was someone special, really blessed by Rama and Hanuman. Ever since, he has been respected in the village as a wise elder, and he has also behaved like one. That's what happens when you really listen to a story, especially the *Ramayana*.

Tenali Rama

~ *Kannada; Tamil; Telugu* ~ ~

Tenali Rama (Krishna) was a jester at the court of Krishnadevaraya, king of Vijayanagara in South India in the sixteenth century, just as Gopal Bhar was the jester of Bengal and Birbal the jester of Moghul North India. Scores of stories are told about him all over South India, in Telugu, Tamil, and Kannada. Children's books, comics, and even a television serial have been created around this legendary jester.

How Tenali Rama Became a Jester

In a South Indian village called Tenali there lived a clever Brahman boy. His name was Rama. Once, a wandering *sannyasi* was impressed with the boy's looks and clever ways. So he taught him a chant and told him, "If you go to the goddess Kali's temple one night and recite these words three million times, she will appear before you with all her thousand faces and give you what you ask for—if you don't let her scare you."

Rama waited for an auspicious day, went to the Kali temple outside his village, and did as he was told. As he finished his three-millionth chant, the goddess did appear before him with her thousand faces and two hands. When the boy looked at her horrific appearance, he wasn't frightened. He fell into a fit of laughter. No one had ever dared to laugh in the presence of this fearsome goddess. Offended, she asked him, "You little scalawag, why are you laughing at me?"

He answered, "O Mother, we mortals have enough trouble wiping our noses when we catch a cold, though we have two hands and only one nose. If you, with your thousand faces, should catch a cold, how would you manage with just two hands for all those thousand runny noses?"

The goddess was furious. She said, "Because you laughed at me, you'll make a living only by laughter. You'll be a *vikatakavi*, a jester."

"Oh, a *vi-ka-ta-ka-vi*! That's terrific! It's a palindrome. It reads *vi-ka-ta-ka-vi* whether you read it from right to left or from left to right," replied Rama.

The goddess was pleased by Rama's cleverness that saw a joke even in a curse. She at once relented and said, "You'll be a *vikatakavi*, but you will be jester to a king." And she vanished.

Soon after that, Tenali Rama began to make a living as jester to the king of Vijayanagara.

 ## Tenali Rama's Ramayana

A courtesan once invited Tenali Rama to recite the story of the *Ramayana*. He began the story by saying, "Rama and Sita went to the forest," and stopped there. He said nothing more. The courtesan waited and waited and finally asked, "Then what happened?" "Don't be impatient," said Tenali Rama. "They're still walking in the forest."

At another time, he was angered by a similar request from another arrogant courtesan. "I'll really make you experience the *Ramayana*, just as it happened," he said, and continued: "In the *Ramayana*, Hanuman the monkey set fire to the city of Lanka, just like this!" And he set fire to the courtesan's house.

Two Sisters

~ *Santali* ~ ~

A Santal had two daughters. Once they had spread some paddy on a flat stone to dry in the sun and were resting under a tree. A crow flew in from somewhere and perched on that tree. It had a ripe fruit in its beak. The girls looked at the fruit and wanted it. At that moment the crow chanced to drop the fruit. The girls picked it up and ate it. It smelled and tasted wonderful. They asked the crow where they could get such fruit. The crow asked them to follow it, and they did.

The crow flew over hills and jungles. The girls followed its flight. Whenever they were tired and sat down to rest, the crow too would rest on a branch. After many days, they arrived in a dense jungle. In the middle of it stood the tree with the miraculous fruit. The two sisters plucked and ate all the fruit they could lay their hands on. Then the elder sister was thirsty and asked the younger one to make a leaf-cup and bring some water from the nearby hill stream. While the younger sister was gone, a tiger appeared from nowhere, pounced on the elder sister, and devoured her. As she was dying, she cried and sang a song:

> *My darling sister, what a bad moment I chose*
> *to send you for water!*
> *Now I'll never see you again, never, never,*
> *not till I'm born again!*

The wind carried the wailing song as the younger sister returned with water in the leaf-cup. She found only a tuft of torn hair and a skull where her sister once had been. Then she heard the tiger growl from the bushes nearby, and she quickly climbed a tree. There she sat among the branches for seven days and seven nights without food and water. One day, two cowherd boys passed that way, saw the girl in the tree, and persuaded her to come down. One of them married her, and they raised a family together.

The seasons came and went. When it rained, a snake-gourd plant sprouted out of the skull of the dead sister, and the tuft of hair grew into a bamboo bush with lovely nodes on its stems. In time, the snake gourds grew ripe and dried up. The bamboo bush grew large and became a grove. The two cowherds brought their cattle to graze in that area. One day, they cut a bamboo stem to make a flute and a dried-up snake gourd to make a *kendra*, a stringed instrument. Whenever they played the flute and the *kendra*, the tune of the wailing song that the sister had sung before she died seemed to burst forth from the instruments. Although no one else knew what it was, the younger sister could tell that her sister's spirit was somewhere around. She knew that her dear sister couldn't tear herself away from her even after death.

The unmarried cowherd also had made himself a flute and a *kendra*. After a time, he was surprised to see that someone seemed to be tidying his hut whenever he was away. The floor was swept clean and the kitchen things were washed and stacked. He couldn't understand what was happening.

He mentioned this mystery to his cowherd friend and his wife. One day the wife waited for them to go to the forest with their cattle and hid behind a tree outside their friend's hut. Oh, was she surprised when she saw a young woman come out of his *kendra* as soon as the place was deserted and begin to tidy up things! She could see that it was none other than her elder sister, returned from the dead. She rushed in and embraced her and cried, "Don't you ever go away and leave me again!"

When the friends returned, they too rejoiced at their reunion. The bachelor married the elder sister. And the families lived happily next to each other, bringing up sons, grandsons, and great-grandsons.

Sukhu and Dukhu

≈ *Bengali* ≈ ≈

A man had two wives and had a daughter by each of them. Dukhu was the daughter of the elder wife and Sukhu was the daughter of the younger. The man loved his younger wife and her daughter Sukhu more than the older wife and her daughter Dukhu.

The daughters' natures were just like their mothers'. Sukhu was as lazy and ill-tempered as Dukhu was active and lovable. Furthermore, Sukhu and her mother hated the other two and treated them badly anytime they had the chance.

The man took ill, and died in spite of every kind of treatment. The younger wife inherited all his property, and she drove Dukhu and her mother out of the house.

Dukhu and her mother found an empty hut outside town and occupied it. They made a living by spinning thread.

One day when Dukhu was spinning outside her hut, the wind blew hard and carried away her wad of cotton. She ran after it but couldn't catch up with it. When she began to cry in desperation, she heard a voice in the wind, "Don't cry, Dukhu, come with me. I'll give you all the cotton you want."

So she followed the wind.

On the way, she met a cow, which spoke to her: "Not so fast, Dukhu. My shed is covered with dung. Wash it clean for me, and I'll help you later." Dukhu drew water from the well and got herself a broom and washed the cowshed clean as clean could be.

The wind was waiting for her to finish. As soon as she finished, she went with the wind again. They came to a plantain tree, which stopped her and said, "Where are you going, Dukhu? Can't you stop a minute and pull down all these creepers from my body so that I can stand up straight? It's hard to stand bent down like this all day and all night. Please."

"I'll be glad to do that," said Dukhu, and she tore down all the creepers that were smothering the tree.

The tree said, "You're a good girl. I'll help you some other time."

"I didn't do anything special, really," said Dukhu and hurried on, for the wind was waiting for her.

Next she met a horse and it said, "Where are you going, Dukhu? This saddle and bridle cut into me. I can't bend down to eat the grass. Will you please take them off for me?"

Dukhu took off the saddle and bridle. The horse was grateful and promised her a gift.

The wind said, as they moved on, "Do you see that palace there? That's where the Mother of the Moon lives. She can give you as much cotton as you want."

With that, he left her there.

Dukhu walked towards the palace. It seemed deserted. She felt afraid and lonely. She stood there in front of it for a while and then decided to go in. Timidly, step by step, she walked through the rooms. Not a mouse stirring, not a living soul anywhere. Suddenly she heard a noise behind a closed door. She went up to it and knocked softly. A voice said, "Come in."

Dukhu pushed the door open and saw an old lady working at a wheel. She was luminous as if the moon was specially shining on her.

Dukhu bowed to her, touched her feet and said, "Granny, the wind blew away all my cotton. If I don't spin, my mother and I will starve. Will you give me some cotton?"

"I'll give you something better than cotton," said the old Mother of the Moon, "if you are deserving. Do you see that pond out there? Go to that pond and dip in it twice. Only twice, not three times, remember."

So Dukhu walked out of the palace and went to the pond and took a dip. When she rose out of the water, she had been changed into someone very beautiful. When she took a second dip, she was covered with silks, pearls, and gems. Her sari was muslin, and she had gold necklaces so heavy that they weighed her down. She couldn't believe what was happening to her.

When she ran back to the palace, the old woman said, "Child, I know you are hungry. Go to the next room. I've food there for you."

The next room had food of every kind, the best rice, the finest curries, sweets beyond her dreams. After eating her fill, she went back to the old woman, who said, "I want to give you something more," and showed her three caskets, each bigger than the next. "Choose one," she said. Dukhu chose the smallest one and said good-bye to the old woman and left the palace.

As she retraced her steps, she met the horse, the plantain tree, and the cow. Each wanted to give her a gift to take home with her. The horse gave her a young colt of the finest *pakshiraj* breed; the tree gave her a bunch of plantains yellow as gold and a pot full of old gold coins called mohurs; and the cow gave her a tawny calf whose udders would never be dry.

Dukhu thanked them all for their wonderful gifts, seated herself on the colt with the pot of gold and the plantains, and found her way home, with the calf walking close behind her.

Her mother, meanwhile, had made herself sick with anxiety, not knowing where Dukhu had gone and when she would come back. She was beside herself with joy when she heard Dukhu's voice call out, "Mother, where are you? Look what I've got!"

When the mother had recovered from her shock of joy, she couldn't believe her eyes. The muslins, the jewels, the gold coins, the plantains, the horse, and the calf—she looked at every one of them over and over. She was speechless.

After a while she found her voice and asked her daughter how she came by all these fabulous things. Dukhu told her the whole story about the wind, the cow, the tree, the horse, and the old Mother of the Moon, and ended by saying, "That's not all. Here's something else she has given me: this casket!"

She then showed her mother the casket. They thought it would be full of more jewels, pearls, gold, and silver. But when they slowly opened it, out of it stepped a most handsome young man dressed like a prince.

"I've been sent here to marry you," he said to Dukhu, without wasting an extra word.

Soon a date was fixed, kith and kin were invited, and a great gala wedding was celebrated. The only people who did not come to the wedding were Sukhu and her mother.

Now, Dukhu's mother was a good woman. Though she had suddenly come into wealth and status, it hadn't gone to her head. She still wanted to be friends with Sukhu and her mother. So she offered Sukhu some ornaments, as they now had heaps of them. But Sukhu's mother was offended. She put her fist to her cheek and hissed, "Why should Sukhu take your leftovers? She's not going begging for jewels! If God had wanted to give my daughter jewels, he would have kept her father alive. My Sukhu is lovely as she is. She needs no ornaments. Only girls who are ugly as owls need fine saris and necklaces to make them look good."

But she didn't forget to make discreet inquiries to find out how Dukhu had come by her great good fortune. Once she learned where Dukhu had gone and how she found the Mother of the Moon, she said to herself, "I'll show her! She is trying to rub her good luck in my face. I'll make my Sukhu a hundred times richer."

Then she brought Sukhu a spinning-wheel and made her spin in the outer yard where the wind was blowing. "Listen to me carefully, Sukhu, my dear," she said. "The wind will blow away your wad of cotton. Then don't forget to howl and wail till the wind asks you to follow it. Be courteous to anyone you meet on the way. Go wherever the wind takes you till you meet the Mother of the Moon."

"I'll do exactly as you say, Mother," said Sukhu and began to spin.

Soon, as expected, a big wind swept away all her cotton, and she began to howl and cry as if someone in the house had died.

"Don't cry, Sukhu, just for a wad of cotton. Come with me. I'll get you all the cotton you want," said the wind.

Sukhu then followed the wind, just as Dukhu had done earlier. She too met the cow, who asked her to clean its shed. But she tossed her head and said, "Clean your stinking shed? Me? Fat chance! I'm on my way to see the Mother of the Moon."

When she met the tree, she said, "I've better things to do than take your creepers down. I'm in a hurry. I'm going to meet the Mother of the Moon."

She was just as insulting to the horse. "You stupid nag, who do you think I am? Your groom's daughter or something?"

They said nothing, but they were hurt. They bided their time.

It was a long way to the palace, and Sukhu was sick and tired of walking. She arrived at the palace in a foul mood. Forgetting her mother's instructions, she burst into the old woman's room and screamed, "The wind has blown away all my cotton. You'd better give me some at once or else I'll break things! And don't take too long about it."

The old woman didn't raise her voice. She said to the young woman quite gently, "Don't be impatient. I'll give you something far better than cotton. But you must do as I say. Do you see that pond through the window? Go out there and take two dips in it. Only two dips, no more, or you'll be sorry."

Sukhu ran to the pond and jumped into it. And it made her a beauty. She dived into it a second time, and she came up covered with silks and jewels. She was beside herself with joy and couldn't stop looking at herself in the water. Then she thought, "If I take one more dip, I'm sure I'll get much more than Dukhu did. The old woman doesn't want me to have more than she gave Dukhu. That's why she asked me not to take more than two dips. But I'm going to do it." And dip she did, a third time. But when she rose from the water, she was grief-stricken to see that her jewels and finery were gone, her nose had grown long as an elephant's trunk, and her body was covered with blisters and boils.

She ran to the Mother of the Moon, white with rage, shaking her head and fists at her. "Look what you've done to me!" she screamed.

The old woman looked at her from top to toe and said, "You didn't listen to me. You dipped in the pond more than twice, and this is what you get for not listening to me. You've yourself to thank for the mess you're in . . . But I've one more thing to offer you."

Then she showed her the three caskets, each one bigger than the next, and asked the young woman to choose one for herself. Sukhu had eyes only for the largest of them and chose it.

Meanwhile her mother was impatiently pacing to and fro in her yard, worrying about her girl not coming home. "When is she going to be back and when can I feast my eyes on all the jewels?" she cried. Suddenly she heard her daughter's voice from behind the bushes: "Mother!"

The mother ran out to greet her but nearly died of shock when she saw what she saw. Her daughter's nose was as long as an elephant's trunk. Her body was covered with boils, not jewels. "What's happened to you? Sukhu, what's happened to you? Why? What did you do?" she cried in despair.

But Sukhu showed her the casket. "The old crone asked me to choose, and I chose the biggest of them!"

The mother thought, "The old woman must be playing tricks. She has some surprise waiting here. She's going to make up for the way she treated my Sukhu." Anxiously, with beating hearts, they opened the casket, and out came a long black snake, hissing angrily. It pounced on Sukhu and swallowed her whole, as a python swallows a goat.

Her mother went raving mad and died soon after.

One, Two, Three

~ Santali ~ ~

A rich and powerful raja was convinced in his heart that no one in the world was as powerful as he was. But he told no one about it. One day he began to wonder whether others could guess what he was thinking. So he called together all his officers and servants and asked them to tell him what thought was in his heart. Many of them made guesses, but no one could satisfy the raja with his answer.

Then the raja ordered his *dewan* (minister) to find him someone who could guess his thought, and he gave the *dewan* exactly a month's time to find this genius. The *dewan* searched everywhere, but all in vain, and as the month was coming to a close he grew quite desperate. But he had a daughter who cheered him up by saying that she would find the right man on the appointed day. The *dewan* said, "All right, let's see what you can come up with," and gave over the job to his daughter.

When the appointed day arrived, his daughter brought home a simpleton, a shepherd in their employ, and asked her father to take him to the raja. The *dewan* was aghast at his daughter's choice, but the daughter insisted that this stupid shepherd was the answer to all his troubles. The *dewan* saw no alternative and he trusted his daughter, so he took the shepherd to the court.

The court had already assembled and the raja was waiting. The *dewan* presented the shepherd to the raja. When the shepherd lifted his eyes to look at the raja, the raja held up one finger. At this, the shepherd held up two fingers. Then the raja held up three fingers, but at this the fellow shook his head violently and tried to run away. Then the raja laughed and seemed very pleased. He praised the *dewan* for bringing him such a clever man, and gave him a rich reward.

The *dewan* was nonplussed. He couldn't make sense of what had happened, and begged the raja to explain.

"When I held up one finger," said the raja, "I asked him whether I alone was king. By holding up two fingers, he reminded me that there is also God, who is at least as powerful as I am. Then I asked him whether there was any third, and he vehemently denied that there was a third. This man really read my thoughts. I've been thinking that I alone was powerful, but he has reminded me that there is God as well, but no third."

Then they all went their ways. That night, the *dewan* asked the stupid shepherd what he had made of the exchange between him and the raja. The fellow explained: "I've only got three sheep of my own, master. When you took me before the raja, he held up one finger, meaning he wanted one of my sheep. As he is a great raja, I offered to give him two. But when he held up three fingers to show that he wanted all three of my sheep, I thought he was going too far. So I tried to run away."

The Wife
Who Refused to Be Beaten

~ *Kashmiri* ~~

A very rich merchant in the Kashmir valley had a very stupid and ignorant son. He engaged the best teachers in the land for him, yet the fellow learned nothing. He was too idle, too careless, too thickheaded to profit by any instruction. He lolled away his time instead. His father gradually lost hope and began to despise him, though his mother was always making excuses for him.

When the lad had reached a marriageable age, his mother begged the merchant to seek out a suitable bride for him. The merchant, however, was too ashamed and troubled to say or do anything about his stupid son, and had made up his mind never to get him married. But the mother had set her heart on it. Not to have a son married would be a disgrace; it would also be against their custom and religion. So she urged other excuses on his behalf and spoke of how she had noticed now and again extraordinary traits of wisdom and wit in her son. This sort of talk only infuriated the merchant. He finally said to her one day, "Look here, I've heard this many times before, and it's a lot of foolishness. Mothers are blind. But I'll give the fool another chance. Send for him and give him these three *pansas*. Tell him to go to the bazaar and buy something for himself with one *pansa*, to throw another *pansa* into the river, and with the remaining *pansa* to get at least five things—something to eat, something to drink, something to gnaw, something to sow in the garden, and some food for the cow."

The woman did so, and the boy took the three small copper coins and left.

He went to the bazaar and bought a *pansa's* worth of something to eat—that was easy. He then came to the river, and was on the point of throwing a *pansa* into the water when he suddenly realized the absurdity of the whole thing and stopped himself. "What's the good of doing this?" he said aloud. "If I throw the *pansa* into the river I'll have only one left. What can I buy with one *pansa*—to eat and drink and all the other things Mother asks for? And yet if I do not throw this *pansa* away, I'll be acting disobediently."

In the midst of this soliloquy, the daughter of an ironsmith came up, and noticing his distress, asked him what the matter was. He told her all that his mother had asked him to do and that he thought it would be extremely stupid to obey. But what was he to do? He didn't wish to disobey his mother either.

"I'll tell you what to do," she said. "Go and buy a watermelon with one *pansa*, and keep the other in your pocket. Do not throw it into the river. The watermelon contains all the five things you need. Get one and give it to your mother, and she'll be pleased."

The boy did so.

The merchant's wife saw how clever her son was and she was glad. "Look," she said to her husband as soon as he came in, "this is our son's work. Don't you think he's terribly clever?"

When he saw the watermelon, the merchant was surprised, and said, "I don't believe that our son has done this on his own. He would never have had the good sense. Someone has been advising him." And then turning to the boy, he asked, "Who told you to do this?"

The lad replied, "The daughter of an ironsmith."

"You see," said the merchant, "I knew this was not the work of that stupid fellow. On second thought, let him get married. If you agree and he also wishes it, he can marry this ironsmith's daughter who has shown some interest in him and seems to be so very clever."

"Yes, yes," replied the wife quickly, "nothing could be better."

When the merchant visited the ironsmith's hut and saw the young woman who had helped his son, he told her, "I've come to see your parents."

She replied, "My father has gone to buy a ruby for a cowrie, and my mother has gone to sell some words. But they'll be here soon. Please take a seat."

"All right, I'll wait," said the merchant, much perplexed by the young woman's words. "Where did you say your parents had gone?"

"My father has gone to get a cowrie's worth of ruby, that is, he has gone to buy some oil for the lamp. My mother has gone to sell a few words, that is, she has gone to try and arrange a marriage for somebody."

The merchant was struck by the young woman's cleverness, but he said nothing.

Soon after, the ironsmith and his wife returned home. They were astonished to see the great and rich merchant in their little hut. They gave him a most respectful *salaam*, and asked humbly, "Why have you honored our house with your visit?"

He told them he wanted his son to marry their daughter. They were surprised but readily accepted the offer. A day was fixed for the wedding.

The wind carried the news everywhere, and people began to talk about the way the big merchant was getting his son married to a lowborn ironsmith's daughter. Some busybodies talked to the son and tried to prejudice him against

the young woman. They advised him to warn her father that if he continued to sanction the wedding, and if the marriage really took place, he would beat the girl seven times a day with his shoe. They thought this would scare the ironsmith and he would break off the engagement. They added, "Even if he is not scared off and the marriage is celebrated, it will still be a good thing to treat your wife like this. In this way she will learn obedience and never give you any trouble."

The stupid fellow thought this was a splendid plan, and he did go to the ironsmith and behaved exactly as he was told.

The ironsmith, of course, was quite disturbed by this threat. He called his daughter and told her what the merchant's son had said, and begged her to have nothing to do with the man. "It's better never to be married," he said, "than to be married to a man who'll treat you like a horse thief."

The daughter comforted her father. She said, "Don't worry on my account, Father. Obviously, some wicked people have influenced the young man to come and talk to you like this. I won't let it happen. There's always a gap between what a man says he'll do and what he actually does. Don't be afraid. What he says will never come to pass."

On the appointed day, the marriage was celebrated. During the nuptial night, the bridegroom got up at midnight. Thinking that his bride was fast asleep, he picked up a shoe and was about to beat her with it, when she opened her eyes. "Don't do that," she said. "It's a bad omen to quarrel on one's wedding day. If you still feel like beating me tomorrow, you can do it. But let's not quarrel today." The bridegroom found that reasonable, but when on the following night he again lifted his shoe to strike her, she said, "Don't you know it's a bad omen for a husband and wife to disagree during the first week of their marriage? I know you are a wise man and you'll listen to me. Postpone this till the eighth day and then you can beat me all you like." The man agreed, and flung his shoe aside. On the seventh day, the young woman returned to her father's house, according to the custom of all Muslim brides.

"Aha!" said the man's friends when they met him. "So she has got the better of you. What a fool you are! We knew it would be like this."

Meanwhile the merchant's wife had plans for her son. She thought it was time he became independent. Therefore she said to her husband, "Give him some merchandise and let him travel and gain experience."

"Never," the merchant said. "To put money into his hands is like throwing it into the river. He will lose it in no time."

"Never mind," insisted his wife. "He will learn wisdom only this way. Give him some money, and let him visit other countries. If he makes money, he'll learn to value it. If he loses it and becomes a beggar, we may hope that he will value it when he gets it again. Either way, he will profit. Without such experience, he'll never be fit for anything."

The merchant was persuaded. So he gave his son some money and some goods and servants, asked him to be careful, and sent him away. The young merchant set out with all his goods and a great troop of servants. The caravan had not gone very far into the next country when they passed a large garden surrounded by thick high walls. The young merchant wanted to know what kind of a place it was and sent out servants to go and see what was inside. They went and came back and told him that they had seen a grand building in the middle of a beautiful garden. Then the young man himself went in and entered the mansion. There he was greeted by a lovely woman who invited him in to play a game of *nard*, a game played with counters. The woman was an expert gambler. She knew every kind of trick to get her opponent's money. One of her favorite tricks was this: while playing, she kept a cat by her side. She had taught the cat to brush against the lamp at a given signal and put out the light. She always gave the sign when the game was going against her. In this and other ways, she had amassed immense wealth. Now she practiced the cat-trick on the young merchant, who lost time after time. He lost everything—his money, his merchandise, his servants, himself. And then, when he had nothing left, he was thrown into prison. There he was treated harshly and given little food. Often he lifted his voice and prayed to God to take him out of this world of troubles.

One day he saw a man pass by the prison gate. He called him and asked from where he had come. When the man told him that he came from such-and-such a country, the young merchant knew that the stranger had come from his own father's place.

"That's good," said the prisoner. "Will you please do me a great favor? You see I am shut up in this place. I cannot get free until I've paid my debts. Will you please take these two letters, one to my father and the other to my wife? If you'll do this for me, I'll be eternally grateful to you, and I'll reward you when I get back."

The man consented, and took the two letters when he went.

In one letter the young merchant told his father all that had happened. And in the other, for his wife, he told lies, all about how he had made lots of money and would soon return and beat her with his shoe as he had warned her before the wedding.

Now, the man who took the letters could neither read nor write. He delivered the letter meant for the father to the wife, and the one meant for the wife to the father. The father was very happy to read the letter full of good news. But he couldn't understand why it was addressed to his daughter-in-law and not to him, and why his son threatened her with a beating when he returned. When the daughter-in-law read her husband's letter, she was unhappy to hear of his misfortunes, and wondered why he had sent the letter in her father-in-law's name and not in her own. Rather bewildered, she went to her father-in-law. They were both mystified when they compared the two accounts.

The daughter-in-law, being wise and brave, decided to go and see her husband herself and, if possible, get him out of prison. The old merchant approved and sent her with some money.

The young woman disguised herself as a man and quickly reached the place where the lovely temptress lived. She sent word to her that she was the son of a wealthy merchant, and was soon invited to a game of *nard*. The so-called merchant's son agreed, and the game was set for that evening. Meanwhile, the so-called merchant's son bribed the woman's servants with gold and loosened their tongues. They told her, in whispers, of the many tricks their mistress played on her opponents during the game, and especially of the cat-trick. That evening, when the young wife arrived at the mansion for the game, she had a little mouse hidden away in a fold of the sleeve of her tunic.

They began to play the game. The so-called merchant's son was quite good at such games and began to win. The wicked gambling woman couldn't take losses for long and made a sign to her cat. When the cat moved towards the lamp, the so-called merchant's son let her mouse run free. Away scurried the mouse, and away went the cat after it, helter-skelter all over the room.

"Shall we get on with the game?" said the young woman in disguise. As nothing was now in her way, she won that game and then a second and a third and a fourth, till she had not only got back all that her stupid husband had lost, but the grand house, the wicked woman, and her entire entourage of servants.

After putting all her new-gotten treasure into large boxes and loading them on her horses, she went to the prison and released all the prisoners. Her husband came with others to thank her, but he didn't recognize her in her disguise. She, however, seemed to take special notice of him and asked him if he would like to be her *sardar*. He was very pleased and agreed at once to become her headman. She gave him some good fresh clothes. When he changed into them, she arranged to put away his old ragged clothes in a separate box and kept it with her. She entrusted him with all the keys of all the boxes except the box that contained his ragged clothes. That she kept with herself. Everything ready, they left, taking the wicked gambling woman along with them.

As they approached their own country, the so-called merchant's son said to her *sardar*, "I have to go on a little business of my own. You take all these things with you and go straight to the city and keep them carefully in your house. I know your father and I trust you. If I don't come within twenty days, all these things are yours."

Then she went by another route to her own home. Her *sardar* went straight to his home with all the servants and the baggage and the wicked woman. On reaching her own home, the young woman told her father everything and asked him to say nothing of her success to anyone. Then she visited her father-in-law. As soon as her husband saw her, he said, "Where have you been? Do you remember how many times I have to beat you?" And then he proceeded to take off one of his shoes.

"Oh, stop it!" said his parents. "You want to spoil this grand homecoming with such meanness?"

His wife said, "Now I see. I thought you would have gotten some sense into that head of yours after all this suffering. But you haven't. You are the same stupid man you always were. Look here—bring that box to me, that little box. Whose dirty clothes are these? Look at them and remember how the jailers treated you, how they beat you, how little and what bad food they gave you, and what names they called you! Now you tremble. Good! I am the rich merchant's son who set you free. The letter you addressed to your father was brought to me. I read about your troubles and came there disguised as a merchant's son, played with this woman who fooled you, and won back everything you had lost. I even won this woman and all her property as well. There she is. Ask her if she recognizes me."

"Yes, yes," said the woman.

The merchant's son was speechless. The merchant's wife blessed her daughter-in-law. The merchant, who had kept quiet all this while, spoke now with mounting anger and disappointment in his stupid son. He turned to his wife and said, "Now do you believe that your son is a fool? Let his wife keep all these goods and jewels in her care. She is too good for him."

The Ogress Queen

～ *Kashmiri* ～ ～

People tell a story about a king who had seven wives but no children. When he married the first woman, he thought she would bear him a son. When she didn't, he married a second with the same hope. When she too turned out to be barren, he married a third, then a fourth, and then the others. But no son and heir was born to make his heart glad and to sit on the throne after him.

Overwhelmed by grief, he was walking in a neighboring wood one day when he saw a woman of supernatural beauty.

"Where are you going?" she asked.

"I'm very miserable," he said. "I have seven wives but no son and heir to call my own. I came to this wood today hoping to meet some holy man who might bless me with a son."

"And you expect to find such a person here in these lonely woods?" she asked, laughing. "Only I live here. But I can help you. What will you give me if I give you what you wish?"

"Give me a son and you can have half my country."

"I don't want your gold or your country. I want you. Marry me, and you shall have a son and heir."

The king agreed, took the beautiful woman to his palace, and married her that very week.

Very soon after that, all the other wives of the king became pregnant. However, the king's joy did not last long. The beautiful woman whom he had married was really a *rakshasi*, an ogress. She had appeared before the king as a lovely woman only to deceive him and work mischief in his palace. Every night, when the entire royal household was fast asleep, she would rise and go to the stables and pens, and there she would eat an elephant, a horse or two, some sheep, or a camel. Once her hunger for raw meat and thirst for blood were satisfied, she would return to her room and behave as if nothing had happened. At first the king's servants were afraid to tell him they were missing some animals. But when the toll increased and more and more animals were taken every night, they had to go to him. He gave strict orders to protect the palace grounds and appointed guards everywhere. But the animals continued to disappear, and nobody knew how.

One night, the king was pacing in his room, not knowing what to do. His eighth and most beautiful wife said, "What will you give me if I discover the thief?"

"Anything. Everything," said the king.

"Very well, then. You rest now, and I'll show you the real culprits in the morning."

The king was soon fast asleep, and the wicked queen left the bedchamber and went straight to the sheep pens. She killed a sheep, filled an earthen pot with its blood, returned to the palace, went to the bedrooms of the other seven wives of the king, and stained their mouths and clothes with the blood she had brought. Then she went and lay down in the royal bedroom where the king was still sleeping. At dawn, she woke him up and said to him, "You won't believe this, but your other wives, all seven of them, are the true culprits. They eat live animals. They are not human beings; they are all *rakshasis*. Beware of them. You too are in danger. Go now and see if what I say is not true."

The king did so, and when he saw the bloodstained mouths and clothes of his queens, he feared for his life and flew into a rage. He ordered that their eyes be put out at once and that they be thrown down a big dry well outside the city and left there to starve to death. And it was done.

The very next week, one of them gave birth to a son. The starving queens, nearly dead of hunger, couldn't help eating the newborn child for food. When another queen had a son, he too was eaten. As each of the other queens gave birth to a son, that child was devoured in turn. The seventh wife, who was the last to give birth, did not eat her portions of the other wives' children, but kept them till her own son was born. When he was born, she begged them not to kill him but take the portions she had saved. So this child alone was spared.

The baby grew and became a strong and beautiful boy. When he was six years old, the seven women thought they should show him a bit of the outer world. But how? The well was deep, and its sides were perpendicular. At last one of them thought of a way. They stood on each other's heads, and the one who stood on the top of all took the boy with her and put him on the bank at the well's mouth. The little fellow ran here and there and finally to the palace nearby, entered the kitchen, and begged for some food. He got a lot of scraps. He ate some of the food and brought the rest to his mother and the king's other wives.

This continued for some time. He grew bigger and taller. One morning the cook asked him to stay and prepare the dishes for the king. The cook's mother had just died and he had to go and arrange for the cremation of the body. The clever boy promised to do his best, and the cook left. That day the king was particularly pleased with the dishes. Everything was rightly cooked, nicely seasoned, and beautifully served. In the evening the cook returned. The king sent for him and complimented him on the excellent food he had prepared that day and asked him to cook like that every day. The cook was an honest man and confessed that he had been absent most of the day because his mother had died. He told the king that he had hired a boy to do the cooking that day. When he heard this, the king was surprised and commanded the cook to employ the boy regularly in the kitchen. From then on, there was a great difference in the king's meals and the service, and His Majesty was more and more pleased with the boy and sent him many presents. The boy took them and all the food he could carry to his mother and the king's other wives.

On the way to the well each day, he had to pass a fakir, who always blessed him and asked for alms and always received something. Some years had passed this way, and the boy had grown up to be a handsome young man, when one day by chance the wicked queen saw him. She was struck by his good looks. She asked him who he was and where he came from. The boy didn't know whom he was talking to and so told her everything about himself and his mother and the other queens in the well. And from that moment on, the wicked woman began to plot against his life. She pretended to be sick and called in a *hakim*, a local doctor. She bribed him to tell the king that she was mortally ill and that nothing but the milk of a tigress would cure her.

"My love, what's this I hear?" said the king when he went to see his wife. "The *hakim* says you're very ill, and that you should drink the milk of a tigress. But how can we get it? Who will dare milk a tigress?"

"I think I know someone who is brave enough to milk a tigress—the lad who serves the cook in the palace kitchen. He is brave and faithful, and he'll do anything you ask him to do, out of gratitude for all you've done for him."

When the king asked the young man to go and get the milk of a tigress, he readily agreed. When he started out the next day, against all the women's wails and protests, he met the fakir on the way. When the fakir heard of his dangerous errand, he said to the young man, "Don't go. Who are you to take on such derring-do?" But the fellow was determined to win the king's favor and he was also eager for adventure. The fakir finally said, "All right, then follow my advice and you'll succeed. I'll tell you where to go. When you meet the tigress, aim a small arrow at one of her teats. When the arrow strikes her, she will ask you why you shot at her. Then tell her that you didn't mean to kill her, but only to make a bigger hole in her teats so that she could feed her cubs more quickly. Tell her that you pitied the cubs, who looked weak and sickly as if they needed more milk." Then, with the fakir's blessing, he went to the forest to look for the tigress.

The young man soon saw a tigress with cubs, aimed an arrow at one of the teats, and struck it. The tigress angrily asked him why he had attacked her. He replied as the fakir had told him to, and added that the queen was dangerously ill and needed the tigress's milk for her cure. "The queen!" said the tigress. "Let her die! Don't you know she is a *rakshasi?* Keep away from her. She'll kill you and eat you."

"I'm not afraid," said the young man. "Her Majesty is not my enemy."

"Very well, I'll give you some of my milk, but beware of the queen. Look here," said the tigress, taking him to an immense rock, "I'll let a drop of my milk fall on this rock and you'll see what happens." As soon as she did so, the rock split into a thousand pieces! "You see the power of my milk. Yet if that queen were to drink the whole of my milk, it would not have the slightest effect on her. She is a *rakshasi,* I tell you. Go and see for yourself."

The young man returned and gave the milk to the king, who took it to his wife. She drank all of it in one gulp and pretended to be cured. The king was very impressed with the young man and promoted him to a higher position. But the queen was determined to put an end to him and was still plotting. After some days, she pretended to be ill again, and told the king, "I'm getting ill again, but don't worry about me. My grandfather lives in the same jungle as the tigress who gave the young man her milk. He has a special medicine that would cure me. Please ask the brave young man to go and get it for me."

So the young man started out again, and when he passed the fakir, the fakir said to him, "Where are you going?" The young man told him.

"Don't go," said the fakir. "This man is a *rakshasa* and will certainly kill you." But the young man was not to be talked out of it. "You must go? Then go, but listen to me first. When you see the *rakshasa,* call him Grandfather. He will ask you to scratch his back, which you must do—but do it very roughly."

The young man promised, and went. The jungle was fearful and dense and he thought he would never reach the *rakshasa*'s house. At last he saw him, and cried out, "Grandfather, I'm your daughter's son. My mother is ill and she says you have the right medicine for her. She has sent me for it."

"All right," said the *rakshasa*, "I'll give it to you. But first come here and scratch my back. It's itching terribly." The *rakshasa* lied, for his back did not itch. He only wanted to see whether or not the young fellow was the true son of a *rakshasi*. When the young man dug his nails into the old *rakshasa*'s flesh and made as if he would scratch some of it off, the *rakshasa* asked him to stop, gave him the medicine, patted him, and sent him back. When the king gave the medicine to his wife, she was secretly full of rage. But the king was now more pleased with the young man than ever and gave him large gifts.

The wicked queen was now at her wits' end to know what to do with such a lad. She wanted him out of the way but she didn't want the king to know it. The fellow had escaped from the claws of a tigress and the clutches of her grandfather. How did he do it? What could she do to him? Finally she decided to send him to her grandmother, a terrible old *rakshasi* who lived in a house in the woods. "This time, he will not come back," she said to herself, and said to the king, "I've a very valuable comb at my grandmother's place. Could you send the young man to bring it to me? I'll give him a letter to take to my grandmother." The king agreed and the lad started out, passing the fakir's place as usual. When he told him where he was going and showed him the queen's letter, the fakir said, "Let me read it."

When he had read it, he said, "You're going there to be killed. This letter is an order for your death. Listen to this: 'The bearer is my enemy. I cannot rest as long as he is alive. Kill him as soon as this reaches you.'"

The boy shook a little when he heard these terrible words, but he didn't wish to break his promise to the king even if it cost him his life. So the fakir tore up the queen's letter and wrote a new one which said, "This is my son. I want him to meet his great-grandmother. Take care of him and show him a good time." The fakir then gave the new letter to him and said, "Call the woman Grandma, and don't be afraid of her."

The young man walked on and on till he reached the old *rakshasi*'s house. He called her Grandma and gave her the letter. The old hag read the letter and hugged and kissed him, and asked how her granddaughter and her royal husband were doing. She attended to him in all sorts of ways and gave him every valuable thing she could think of. Among other things, she gave him a bar of soap that became a huge mountain when it was thrown to the ground, a jar full of needles that became a hill bristling with thorns when thrown down, and a jar of water that became a wide lake when spilled on the ground. She also showed him various secret things and explained their meaning: seven fine cocks, a spinning wheel, a pigeon, a starling, and a bottle of medicine.

"These seven cocks," she said, "contain the lives of your seven uncles, who are in different parts of the world. No power can hurt them as long as these seven cocks are safe. That's why I keep them here. The spinning wheel contains my life. If it's broken, I'll be broken and will die. Otherwise, I'll live forever. The pigeon contains your grandfather's life, and the starling your mother's. As long as they live, nothing can harm your grandfather or your mother. And this medicine can give sight to the blind."

The young man thanked the *rakshasi* for all the things she had given him and for all the things she had shown him. In the morning, when the *rakshasi* went to bathe in the river, he took the seven cocks and the pigeon and killed them, and dashed the spinning wheel to the ground and broke it to pieces. As he destroyed the birds and the spinning wheel, the *rakshasi*, the *rakshasa*, and their seven sons in different parts of the world perished, making horrible sounds. Then he put the starling in a cage, took it and the precious medicine for restoring sight to the blind, and started back for the king's palace. His first stop was at the well, where he gave the eye medicine to his mother and the other women and restored their eyesight. They all clambered out of the well and went with him to the palace. He asked them to wait in one of the rooms while he went to the king and prepared him for their coming.

"O king," he said, "I've many secrets to reveal. Please hear me. Your wife is a *rakshasi*, and has been plotting against my life because she knows I am the son of one of your wives. You remember the seven queens you threw into a well at her instigation? I am your son by the seventh queen. Your eighth queen, the *rakshasi*, is afraid you'll discover one day soon who I am and that I'll become heir to the throne. She wants me dead. I've just slain her father and mother and seven brothers, and now I'll kill her. Her life is in this starling." Saying this, he twisted the neck of the bird, and the wicked queen died on the spot with a broken neck. And when she died, her original, ghastly *rakshasi* form returned to her as she lay sprawled on the ground. "Now come with me," he said to his father, and took him to his seven queens. "Here are your true wives. There were seven sons born to your house, but six of them died to satisfy the pangs of hunger in that well of death. Only I have survived."

"Oh, what have I done!" cried the king. "I was deceived, I was blind, and I've done terrible things to my innocent wives." And he wept bitterly.

He gave his kingdom into the hands of his only son, who governed it wisely. The young king also conquered the surrounding countries with the help of the magic bar of soap, the needles, and the water that the *rakshasi* had given him. The old king spent the rest of his days happily with his seven good wives.

Killed by a Tiger

~ *Santali* ~~ ~~

On the outskirts of a forest, a brother and sister lived in a small mud hut. As their parents had died long ago, it was the brother's duty to find a suitable bridegroom for his sister. It so happened that once a young man from a distant village came hunting to their forest and got lost. At nightfall he came to their house. They gave him shelter, and the sister fell in love with him, and the two were married. The sister soon left with her new husband for his village, which was far away.

Months later, the brother wanted to visit them. He gathered fruits and tubers for the journey, asked for directions to the distant village from other villagers, and set out. He had to cross several forests, hills, and valleys. He was walking through a forest when it grew dark. Though he was strong and had his bow and arrows and his pickaxe, he was still afraid of tigers and wild animals. As he sat down tired under a *mahul* tree, the tree asked him to come up and rest in its branches. He climbed up, settled in the crook of a big branch, and ate his fruit while night deepened. He could see the tracks of tigers, bears, and snakes under the tree. As he watched, a tiger came and said to the tree, "Come, let us visit the village. A boy is about to be born there. Let us go and see by what means the boy will die." The tree said it couldn't go that night; it had a guest in its house. But would the tiger please come back in the morning and tell the tree about the boy?

The man in the tree was startled when he heard the name of the village where they were going—it was his sister's village. He wondered whether his sister had had a baby. He waited anxiously all night, without a wink of sleep. In the morning, the tiger and the other wild animals returned and told the

tree that the newborn boy would be killed by a tiger, and on his marriage day. They also said that the boy's father was the headman of the village.

Now the brother knew who the boy was, for his sister's husband was the headman. He raced anxiously to the village and found that indeed his sister had given birth to a son in the night. He now knew what the wild animals knew and the parents did not—the time and manner of the boy's death.

As he was visiting his sister for the first time, he was treated royally. When he was about to leave, he made them promise that they would not forget to consult him when it was time for the boy to get married.

Years passed. Leaves and flowers fell many times. The boy grew up to be a big handsome fellow. His parents arranged his marriage to a suitable girl and invited the brother to the wedding. He rushed posthaste to his sister's village, but instead of joining in the feasting and merrymaking, he stayed close to the bridegroom. He had his bow and arrows and pickaxe with him, ready to strike. He kept vigil all night outside the room where his nephew slept. Early in the morning, the nephew went out into the open fields, not heeding his uncle's warning cry. A tiger lay in wait there and pounced on him from the bushes. But the uncle, who had been waiting all these years for this moment, was at the tiger's throat in a flash and hacked it to death.

He then told his nephew and the family about the tiger in the forest and the prophecy he had heard. The sister wept tears of joy and thanked him for saving her son's life.

At that moment, the nephew looked at the dead tiger at their feet and shouted in triumph, "So this is the creature that would have eaten me up!" He kicked the tiger in the head. His kick landed in the tiger's open mouth and his foot struck its fangs. He was wounded and began to bleed. The bleeding would not stop, no matter what they did, and he soon bled to death.

Outwitting Fate

~ Tamil ~ ~

A young Brahman in search of knowledge had heard about a great sage and philosopher who lived in the heart of a dense forest, far from the madness of civilization. So he walked for days through the thorns of the jungle and the menace of wild beasts till he reached the lonely cottage on the bank of a river where the great sage lived. The old sage welcomed the young seeker, accepted him as his disciple, and gave him a place to stay in his hut. The young man served the master and his wife in various ways, did some of the household chores, and learned all he could from the old master.

Now the old man was still youthful, and in his old age his wife became pregnant for the first time. Just when she was eight months into her pregnancy, the sage had a desire to go and visit the source of the holy river by which he lived. As he could not take her with him, he entrusted her to the care of his disciple and another sage's wife.

The old sage's wife was ready to give birth and, at the appropriate time, went into labor. The woman friend stayed with her inside the cottage and the disciple waited outside, anxiously praying that she should safely give birth to a healthy baby.

Now, Hindus believe that Brahma, the Creator, is present at the birth of every child and writes on the newborn infant's forehead his or her future fortunes. He is supposed to arrive just at the moment of birth, just when the child leaves the mother's womb to enter the world. He is, of course, invisible to ordinary mortals. But the young disciple's eyes were not exactly those of any ordinary mortal. His master had given him all kinds of knowledge and various powers. So he was startled to see a person entering, most unceremoniously, the cottage where his master's wife was giving birth.

"Stop right there!" said the disciple angrily. The great god shuddered, for no one so far had ever seen him or stopped him like this in his eternal round of duties. He was astonished, and quite bewildered when he heard the following words of rebuke: "You old Brahman, what do you think you're doing, entering my master's cottage without so much as a by-your-leave? Right in front of me! My teacher's wife is in labor. You can't go in there."

Brahma hastily explained to the young man who he was and what he was about to do. The baby had already begun to leave the womb and he had very little time to waste. When the young man heard who he was, he tied his upper cloth around his waist as a mark of respect before an elder and a god, prostrated himself before Brahma, and begged his pardon.

Brahma was in a hurry. He wanted to go in at once, but the young man would not let him go until he had told him what he meant to write on the forehead of the newborn child. "Son," said Brahma, "even I do not know what my stylus will write on the forehead of the newborn. As the child comes into the world, I place the stylus on its head and it writes the fate of the child according to its good or bad acts in its previous life. You shouldn't stop me here. I have to go in at once."

"Then," said the young man, "on your way out, you must tell me what was written on the forehead of my guru's child."

"All right," said Brahma in a hurry, and went in. In a moment he returned, and the young man asked the god what his stylus had written.

"Son, I'll tell you what it wrote," said Brahma. "But if you tell anyone about it, your head will split into a thousand pieces. The child is a boy. He has a hard life before him. A buffalo and a sack of rice will be his share in life; he'll have to live on it. What can be done?"

"What! O Father of the Gods, this child is the son of a great sage. Is this his fate?" cried the disciple.

"What do I have to do with it? Such are the fruits of a former life. What's sown in the past must be reaped in the present. But remember what I said: if you reveal this secret to anyone, your head will explode in a thousand pieces."

Then Brahma vanished, leaving the young disciple bewildered by what he had heard and pained by the thought of what a hard life awaited his guru's newborn son. But he could tell no one about it. His guru returned from his pilgrimage and was delighted to see his wife and child doing well. And the young disciple forgot his sorrow in the learned company of the old sage.

Three more years passed in deep study, and again the old sage decided to go on a pilgrimage to the sacred source of the Tungabhadra River. Again his wife was pregnant, and he had to leave her in the care of his disciple and a friend's wife. This time, too, Brahma came at the moment of birth. The young man was waiting for him. Brahma was again stopped at the door and promised to tell the young man what his stylus would write on the forehead of the second child. On his way out, the god told the young man, "The child is a girl this time. My stylus has written that she has to earn her living as a prostitute, sell her body every night. Remember what I told you last time: if you tell this to anyone, your head will split into a thousand pieces. Don't forget."

When Brahma left, the young man was still in shock. The daughter of the holiest of men was fated to live the life of a prostitute! He was so deeply hurt by the thought that he couldn't even find the language for it. After turning it over and over in his mind for days, he consoled himself with the thought that fate alone governs human lives.

The old sage returned from his pilgrimage, and the young disciple spent two more years with him. At the end of these years, when the boy was five and the girl two, the disciple himself decided to go on a pilgrimage to the Himalayas. The thought of the growing children and the miserable life that was waiting for them filled him with pain and even anger, though he consoled himself again and again with thoughts of fate.

With his guru's permission, he left the forest hut and his guru's family, and journeyed towards the Himalayas. He visited many towns and learned men, lived with and learned from many sages. He wandered for twenty years, examining the world, understanding human nature, pondering the ways of providence. Then he decided to return to his guru's place on the banks of the river where he had begun his studies.

But when he got there, he found that his guru had died and so had his wife. His heart heavy with sorrow over their passing, he went to the nearest town in search of his guru's children. After a while, he found a coolie with a single buffalo. He at once recognized his guru's son in this poor man. What Brahma's iron pen had written on his forehead had come to pass. The disciple's heart grew heavier. He could hardly bear to see his great guru's son a poor man living off a single buffalo. He followed the poor man to his hut, where he had a family, a wife and two ill-fed children. There was a sack of rice in his house and no more. Each day the family anxiously took out a little of it, husked it, and cooked it. When the sack was empty, with his coolie's savings he was able to get one more sack, that's all. That's how they lived, just as the stylus of Brahma had written.

The disciple started a conversation with the sage's son, calling him by name, and asked, "Do you know me?"

The coolie was astonished to hear his name from the lips of an utter stranger. The disciple introduced himself and explained who he was and begged him to follow his advice. As the disciple was himself middle-aged and looked like a sage, the coolie was impressed. Then the disciple said, "Son, please do as I tell you. As soon as you wake up tomorrow, take your buffalo and sack of rice and sell them in the market for whatever price they'll fetch. Don't think twice about it. Buy whatever you need for a great dinner for you and your family, and finish it all by tomorrow evening. Leave not even a mouthful for the next day. Reserve nothing. With the rest of the money, feed the poor and give gifts to the best Brahmans in town. You'll never regret it. I'm your father's disciple and I'm telling you this for your own welfare. Trust me."

But the coolie couldn't believe him. "What will I do to feed four mouths in this house if I sell it all tomorrow?" he cried. "You Brahmans are always advising poor people like me to give it all to Brahmans. It's all very well for you. You are at the receiving end."

But his wife, who had overheard this conversation, intervened. She said, "This gentleman looks like a wise man, just like your father who was his guru. He must know something we don't. Let's follow his advice for one day and see."

The coolie's doubts broke down when she also supported the holy man. The next day, somewhat anxiously, he sold his buffalo and his sack of rice. What he bought with the money was enough to feed fifty Brahmans morning and evening as well as his own family. So that day he fed people other than his own family for the first time in his life. When he went to bed that night after this unusual day, he couldn't sleep. He got up in the middle of the night and found his father's disciple sleeping on the flat ground outside his hut. The disciple was wakened by the coolie's arrival and asked him what the matter was. The coolie said, "Sir, I've done as you've told me. In a few hours it'll be dawn. What will I do when my wife and children wake up? What will I feed them? I've nothing left, not a pice, not a handful of rice, and no buffalo to give us milk."

The disciple showed him some money he had, enough to buy another buffalo and a sack of rice, asked him to go back to bed, sleep well till morning, and see what happened.

The coolie had bad dreams that night and woke up early. When he went out to wash his face at the well, he looked at the makeshift shed where he used to feed his buffalo some straw the first thing every morning. The thought occurred to him that he didn't have a buffalo to feed this morning. But, to his astonishment, he found another buffalo standing there. He thought, "Fie on poverty! It makes you dream of buffaloes when you have none." It was still dark. So he went in and brought out a lamp to see if the buffalo was real. It was a real beast! And beside it was a sack of rice! His heart leapt with joy and he ran out to tell the holy man, his father's disciple. But when he heard the news, the disciple said with a disgusted air, "My dear man, why do you care so much? Why do you feel so overjoyed? Take the beast and the sack of rice at once, and sell them as you did yesterday. Give your family and the Brahmans another terrific meal."

The coolie obeyed this time without any misgivings. He sold the buffalo and the sack of rice, bought provisions, and again fed his family and fifty Brahmans, keeping nothing back. Thus it went in the house of the sage's son. Every morning he found a buffalo and a sack of rice, which he sold and fed his family and the Brahmans with the money. A month passed. The holy man was now sure that this kind of good life had become an established fact in the life of his guru's son. So one day he said, "When I heard that my great guru's son was living a wretched life, I had to do something about it. I've done what I could. You're now living comfortably. Continue to do what you've been doing. Reserve nothing for yourself. If you do, your happiness will end. If you hoard the money, this good fortune will desert you."

The sage's son had seen with his own eyes and felt with his own hands the good fortune that had come to him, thanks to the holy man's advice. He wholeheartedly agreed to do everything the holy man said, to the last detail.

Then the holy man said, "I've to go do something else now. Tell me where your sister is. She was two years old when I last saw her, twenty years ago. Where is she now?"

The sage's son choked on tears when his sister was mentioned. "Don't ask about her," he said. "She's lost to the world. I'm ashamed of her and don't want even to think of her at this happy time."

The disciple remembered very well what Brahma's iron pen had written on her brow. He said, "Never mind. Just tell me where she is."

"She's in the next village. She is the village prostitute," said the sage's son, finding it hard to say.

Then the holy man took leave of the sage's son after blessing him and his wife and children. He wanted now to find his master's daughter and do something for her. He set out for the village where she lived. He reached her house before nightfall and knocked at her door. The door was opened at once, for no one in her profession ever waited for a second knock. When she looked out, she was surprised to see a holy man at her door.

"Do you know me?" he asked. She did not. He then explained who he was. When she heard that he was her father's disciple, she wept bitterly. Shame at the thought that she, the daughter of a great sage, was now a common prostitute stung her to tears, and she fell at his feet. Then she explained how poverty had brought her to this pass and how miserable she was. He consoled her and said, "Daughter, my heart burns to see how necessity has driven you to this wretched life. But you can do something about it. If you're willing to follow my advice, you can live a different life. Shut your door tonight and say that you'll open it only to someone who brings you a large measure full of pearls of the first water. Do it just for tonight, and I'll talk to you in the morning."

She was disgusted with the life she led, so she readily agreed, in spite of all her doubts, to follow the holy man's advice. She bolted the door. When her customers came and knocked on it, she told them from within that her price had gone up: it was nothing less than a large measure of pearls. Her customers thought she was crazy and they left. The night was coming to a close and she was worried: who was there in the village who could bring her a measure full of the best pearls?

But Brahma's prophecy had to be fulfilled somehow. So, when no mortal came to her that night as a customer, in the small hours of the night Brahma himself assumed the shape of a young man and visited her with a measure full of pearls, and stayed the night with her. She now had a god for a lover.

He left at dawn. The sage's daughter told the holy man that after all a man, a wonderful man, had visited her with a measure full of pearls. The holy man knew his suggestion had worked. He said, "From today on, you're among the purest of women. There are few people in the world who can afford to bring you a measure of pearls every night. So, whoever brought you these pearls last night must continue to bring them to you every night. He'll be your only lover and husband. No one else must ever touch you. Just do as I say. Sell all the pearls he brings you every day and spend all the money you get on feeding the poor. Keep nothing for the next day. Hoard nothing. Give it all away. The day you fail to do this, you'll lose your husband and fall back into your old wretched life. Will you do as I say?"

The sage's daughter happily agreed. The holy man then went to live under a tree near her house to see if his plan would work. He was happy to see that it did.

When he was satisfied with the happy turn of events for his sage's son and daughter, he took leave of her to go on another pilgrimage.

On the day of his departure, he woke up too early. The moon was up. He had heard the crows cawing and mistaken it for the signs of dawn. He got up and began his journey. He had not gone too far when he met a beautiful person walking towards him leading a buffalo; he carried a sack of rice on his head, and a bundle of pearls was slung over his shoulder.

"Who are you, sir, walking like this in the forest?" asked the holy man.

The man with the buffalo threw down the sack at this question and almost wept as he replied, "Look, my head has become almost bald from carrying this sack of rice every night to that coolie's house. I lead this buffalo to that man's shed. Then I dress up and carry these pearls to his sister's house. My iron pen wrote their fates on their foreheads, and thanks to you, you wretched clever man, I have to supply them whatever was promised at their birth. When will you relieve me of these burdens?"

Brahma wept, for it was none other than Brahma himself.

"Not till you grant them a good ordinary life and happiness!" said the holy man. Brahma did exactly that and was relieved of his troubles in these two cases.

Thus were fate and Brahma outwitted.

Four Girls and a King

~ *Punjabi* ~~

A king spent the day sitting on the throne and holding court, but at night he would wander through his capital in disguise looking for adventures.

One evening he saw four girls sitting under a tree in a garden, talking very earnestly to each other. He stopped to listen. The first said, "Of all the tastes, the taste of meat is the best."

The second said, "I don't agree. There's nothing so good as the taste of wine."

"No, no," cried the third, "you are both wrong. The sweetest taste of all is the taste of love."

"Meat and wine and love are sweet all right," said the fourth, "but nothing can equal the taste of telling lies."

The girls were then called home and they left. The king, who had listened to this exchange with great interest, made a mental note of the houses they went to, marked each door with chalk, and returned to his palace.

The next morning he called his *wazir* and said to him, "Send someone to that narrow street next to the garden, and fetch the owners of the four houses which have a round mark of chalk on their doors." The *wazir* went there in person and brought the four men to the court. The king asked them, "All four of you have daughters, don't you?"

"Yes, we have, Your Highness," said they, trembling.

"I'd like to talk to your girls. Bring them here," said the king.

The men objected, fearing some harm to their daughters. "It's not proper for our young unmarried daughters to come to the palace."

The king said, "Your daughters will come to no harm, I assure you. They will be safe and you can bring them without any publicity."

Then he sent four litters with curtains to the four houses, and the four girls were brought to the reception room of the palace. The king summoned them one by one to his presence. To the first he said, "Daughter, what were you talking about last night when you sat with your friends under the tree?"

"I wasn't telling tales against you, Your Highness," she answered.

"I do not mean that. Just tell me what you were saying."

"I merely said that the taste of meat was the most pleasant of tastes."

"Whose daughter are you?" asked the king.

"I'm the daughter of a Bhabra."

"If you are one of the Bhabra tribe, what do you know of the taste of meat? They never touch meat. They are so strict that they even drink water from a vessel through a cloth for fear they might swallow an insect."

"That's quite true. But from my own observation, I think meat must be extremely pleasant. There's a butcher shop near our house. I have noticed that when people buy meat, nothing is wasted or thrown away. It must be quite precious. When they have eaten the meat, the bones are seized upon by the dogs, and they do not leave the bones till they are picked clean as a lancehead. And even after that, the crows come and carry them off. When the crows are done with them, the ants gather and swarm over them. That's why I think that the taste of meat must be very pleasant."

The king was very pleased with her argument and said, "Yes, daughter, meat is indeed very good to eat." Then he sent her away with a handsome present.

The second girl was then brought in and the king asked her, "What were you talking about last night under the tree?"

"I was not talking about you, Your Highness," said the girl.

"That's true, but tell me, what did you actually say?"

"Oh, I said that there was no taste like the taste of wine."

"Whose daughter are you?"

The girl replied, "I'm the daughter of a priest."

"That's a joke. Priests hate the very name of wine. What do you know of the taste of it?"

The girl said, "It's true I never touch wine, but I can easily understand how pleasant it is. I learn my lessons on the top of my father's house. Below there are wineshops. One day I saw two nicely dressed gentlemen who bought wine, sat there, and drank it. When they got up and went away, they staggered about from side to side, and I thought, 'Look at these fellows weaving through the street, knocking against the walls, falling down and getting up at every step. I'm sure they'll never touch that wine again.' But I was mistaken. They came back the very next day and did the same things. That's when I said to myself, 'The taste of wine must be very delicious. Otherwise these men would never have come back for more of it.'"

The king said, "Yes, daughter, you're right. The taste of wine is indeed delicious." And he sent her home with a handsome present.

He then called in the third girl and asked her, "What were you talking about last night under the tree?"

"I wasn't saying anything about you, Your Highness," said the girl.

"I know that. But tell me what you were saying."

"I was saying," she said, "nothing in the world is so sweet as the taste of lovemaking."

"But," said the king, "you are a very young girl! How can you know anything about making love? Whose daughter are you?"

"I'm the daughter of a bard," she replied. "It's true I'm very young, but I have eyes and ears. From what I've seen I guess somehow that lovemaking must be very pleasant. My mother suffered so much when my little brother was born. She didn't even expect to live. Yet very soon after that, she went back to her old ways as a dancing-girl and welcomed her lovers just as before. That's why I think lovemaking must be irresistible."

"You're absolutely right," said the king, and sent her home with a handsome present.

When he asked the fourth girl the same question, "Tell me what you and your friends talked about last evening under the tree," she too said, "It was not about the king."

"Nevertheless, what was it you said?"

"Oh, I said that people who tell lies must like it very much."

"Whose daughter are you?" asked the king.

"I'm the daughter of a farmer," she answered.

"What made you think there's pleasure in telling lies?"

The saucy girl said, "Everybody lies. Oh, you yourself will tell lies someday, if you haven't done so already!"

"How come? What do you mean?"

The girl said, "Give me two *lakhs* of rupees and six months, and I'll prove it to you."

The king was intrigued, and he gave her the money and agreed to wait for six months.

Six months later, he called her to his court and reminded her of their agreement. The girl had meanwhile built a fine mansion with the king's money. It was beautifully furnished with paintings and carvings as well as silk and satin. She said to the king, "Come with me and you shall see God." The king arrived at the mansion that evening with his two ministers.

The girl said, "This place is God's own dwelling-place. But He will reveal himself only to one person at a time, and He will not reveal himself to anyone who is a bastard, born out of wedlock. Now, you may enter one by one."

"All right," said the king. "Let my ministers go in first. I'll go in last."

So the first minister went through the door and found himself in a peaceful and lovely room. As he looked around for God, he said to himself, "This is a lovely place, certainly fit for God. But who knows whether I'll be able to see Him or not? Maybe I'm a bastard, who can tell?" He looked some more and strained his eyes but he couldn't see God anywhere. Then he said to himself, "I can't go out now and tell the others that I didn't see God. They'll think I'm a bastard. So I'll have to tell them I've seen God."

So he went out, and when the king asked him if he had seen God, he answered at once, "Yes, I saw Him as plainly as I see you."

"Really, did you see Him?"

"Really and truly, I did."

"What did He say to you?"

"He asked me not to repeat His words to anyone," answered the minister. Then the king asked the second minister to go in.

The second minister obeyed his king's orders, but as he crossed the threshold, he thought in his heart, "I wonder if I am a bastard?" He was now in the magnificent chamber and stared all around him, but he too did not see God nor any signs of Him. Then he said to himself, "It's quite possible I am really a bastard, for I cannot see God. But how can I admit it and bear the disgrace? I'd better pretend that I've seen God."

When he returned to the king, he said, "I've not only seen God but I've also spoken to Him."

Now it was the king's turn, and he entered the chamber confidently. But he looked and looked all around him and saw no sign of anything like the Almighty. He was very troubled and began to doubt himself. "Both my ministers have obviously seen this God, wherever He is. Obviously they are true sons of their fathers. Is it possible that I, the king, am a bastard and that's why I cannot see God? Admitting to this will lead to confusion of every kind. So I have to say that I have seen Him too."

Having decided this, the king stepped out and joined the rest.

"And now, Your Highness, have you also seen God?" asked the girl who was waiting for his return.

"Yes," he answered firmly, "I have seen God."

"Really?" she asked again.

"Certainly," insisted the king.

The girl asked the same question three times, and all three times the king lied without a blush.

"O king," said the girl, "don't you have a conscience? How could you possibly see God, since God is a spirit?"

Hearing this rebuke, the king suddenly remembered the girl saying that one day he too would lie, and he broke into laughter and confessed that he had not seen God at all. The two ministers, by now shamefaced and alarmed, also confessed the truth. Then the girl said, "O king, we poor people have to tell lies now and then to save our lives, but what did you have to fear? Telling lies, therefore, has its own attractions for many, and to them at least the taste of lying is sweet."

The king was not offended by the trick the girl had played on him. Instead, he was so struck by her wit and confidence that he asked for her hand and married her. She became his confidential adviser in all his affairs, public and private. And she grew in wisdom and her fame spread through many lands.

If It Isn't You,
It Must Be Your Father

~ *Kannada* ~ ~

Once a lamb was drinking water in a mountain stream. A tiger came to drink the water a few yards above him, saw the lamb, and said, "Why are you muddying my stream?"

The lamb said, "How can I muddy your water? I'm down here and you are up there."

"But you did it yesterday," said the tiger.

"I wasn't even here yesterday!"

"Then it must have been your mother."

"My mother has been dead for a while. They took her away."

"Then it must have been your father."

"My father? I don't even know who he is," said the desperate lamb, getting ready to run.

"I don't care. It must be your grandfather or great-grandfather who has been muddying my stream. So I'm going to eat you," said the tiger. And he pounced on the lamb, tore him to pieces, and made a meal of him.

Why Audiences Laugh or Cry

~ *Punjabi* ~ ~

A Muslim preacher was once holding forth in his mosque on sinners and the torments that awaited them in hell. As he carried on, getting more eloquent by the minute, he saw a member of his audience, a poor farmer, weeping. Tears were running down his cheeks.

"Ah, crying for your sins, are you?" said the preacher, very happy with the effect he was having on his audience. "My words have struck home, have they? When I speak of the torments of hell, you remember your sins, don't you?"

"No, no," answered the man, wiping his tears. "I was not thinking of my sins. I was thinking of my old he-goat that got sick and died last year. Such a loss! My old he-goat had a lovely beard just like yours. I've never seen two beards more alike."

Hearing this, the villagers began to laugh, and the preacher took refuge in the Koran.

Akbar and Birbal

~ *Urdu* ~~

Akbar, the great Moghul emperor, had a Hindu raja in his court who played the jester, counselor, wise man, and fool. His name was Birbal. Many stories are told about Birbal's wit, wisdom, and occasional folly. Here are a few.

The Best of Flowers

One day Akbar asked the assembled courtiers, "Which flower is the best flower of all?"

No one could answer.

Finally it was Birbal's turn.

Birbal said, "That flower is the best of all flowers from which the whole world's clothing is made."

Akbar was delighted and accepted the answer.

Make It Shorter

One day Akbar drew a line with his royal hand on the floor of the open court, and commanded, "Make this line shorter, but don't by any means erase any part of it."

Everyone was stumped by this puzzle.

When it was Raja Birbal's turn, he at once drew a longer line next to the first one. He didn't touch the first line.

Everyone in the court saw it and said, "That's true, the first line is shorter."

Bring Me Four

One day Akbar said to Birbal, "Bring me four individuals: one, a modest person; two, a shameless person; three, a coward; four, a heroic person."

Next day Birbal brought a woman and had her stand before the emperor. Akbar said, "I asked for four people, and you have brought only one. Where are the others?"

Birbal said, "Refuge of the World, this one woman has the qualities of all four kinds of persons."

Akbar asked him, "How so?"

Birbal replied, "When she stays in her in-laws' house, out of modesty she doesn't even open her mouth. And when she sings obscene insult-songs at a marriage, her father and brothers and husband and in-laws and caste-people all sit and listen, but she's not ashamed. When she sits with her husband at night, she won't even go alone into the storeroom and she says, "I'm afraid to go." But then, if she takes a fancy to someone, she goes fearlessly to meet her lover at midnight, in the dark, all alone, with no weapon, and she is not at all afraid of robbers or evil spirits."

Hearing this, Akbar said, "You speak truly," and gave Birbal a reward.

 ## Sons-in-Law

One day, when Akbar and Birbal were out hunting, the emperor pointed to a crooked tree and said, "Why is that tree crooked?" Birbal answered, "That tree is crooked because it is the son-in-law of all the trees in the forest." "Why do you say that?" asked Akbar. Birbal quoted a proverb: "A dog's tail and a son-in-law are always crooked." Akbar asked, "Is my son-in-law also crooked?" "Of course, Your Majesty!" said Birbal. "Then have him crucified," said Akbar.

A few days later, Birbal had three crosses made—one of gold, one of silver, and one of iron. When Akbar saw them, he asked, "Why have you made three crosses?"

Birbal answered, "Your Majesty, one of them is for you, one is for me, and one is for Your Majesty's son-in-law."

"And why are we to be executed?" asked Akbar.

"Because," said Birbal, "we are all the sons-in-law of someone." Akbar laughed and said, "Well then, let my son-in-law go."

The Night-Blind Son-in-Law

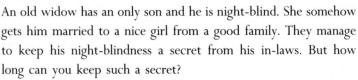

~ *Kannada* ~~

An old widow has an only son and he is night-blind. She somehow gets him married to a nice girl from a good family. They manage to keep his night-blindness a secret from his in-laws. But how long can you keep such a secret?

He is invited to visit his in-laws for the first time to celebrate Dipavali, the festival of lights. His mother is nervous about the visit and warns him, "Be careful. You can't see a thing after dark. So don't move around too much after nightfall. Travel only during the day and stay there only one night."

He wants to reach his in-laws' place before it gets dark, so he walks as fast as his legs will take him. But by the time he reaches the outskirts of the village, it is already evening, and his vision is getting quite dim. He remembers what his mother said and finds a place to sit down. Unfortunately, the place he chooses happens to be a garbage dump for his in-laws' household. Just then, his mother-in-law comes there with the day's garbage and dumps it—right on his head, as she doesn't see him at first. When he is startled, she recognizes him. She is shocked. It is none other than her own esteemed son-in-law! New sons-in-law should be treated like gods, and what has she gone and done? She is terribly embarrassed by what she has done, covers her face with her sari, and runs back home. On the way she meets her ten-year-old son driving a buffalo home and says to him urgently, "Son, look here. Your brother-in-law has arrived, but for some reason he's sitting in our garbage dump. Maybe he had to relieve himself. I didn't see him sitting there and I emptied my garbage on his head. He must be angry. Run now and bring him home, gently. He likes you."

The boy also likes his new brother-in-law. He runs all the way, calling, "Brother-in-law, where are you?" He finds him still sitting in the garbage.

"Why are you sitting there? Come, let's go home," he says, taking him by the hand. The son-in-law, though night-blind, is quite smart. He says, "I wasn't just sitting there, kid. I was wondering how many cartloads of manure your garbage would make. You've enough there for an acre or two." Then he affectionately puts his hand on the boy's shoulder and goes with him. When he sees the buffaloes looming darkly towards him, he jumps and says, "Woy! What's that?"

The boy says, "These are our buffaloes. I had taken them out to graze."

"Oh, they look big and healthy," says the son-in-law, holding on to the tail of one of the animals and letting himself be led by it. As they are going along, the buffalo comes close to a *hagevu*, an open grain-pit. The son-in-law tumbles right into it. The boy says, "What's the matter? Can't you see very well or what?"

"Oh no, I can see very well. I just wanted to see how deep your grain-pit is. I'm getting one made at my place. Now give me a hand. There, that's a good boy," says the son-in-law, clambering back to firm land. For the rest of the way, he keeps close to a wall, groping along its length. The boy asks him, "Brother-in-law, why are you walking along the wall, holding on to it? Are your eyes no good?"

"*Che, che!* What are you saying? I'm just measuring how long your outer wall is. I'm just curious."

Just when he reaches the outer door, he stumbles against the ram that is standing there and the ram butts him quite savagely. As he falls down, the boy gives the ram a blow, gives his brother-in-law a hand, and asks, "Didn't you see the ram standing there?"

"Oh, I saw him all right. I liked his looks and thought of giving him a rubdown. But look what the beast did! Why have you taught him to butt strangers like that?"

It is night already and they all sit down to the night meal on the floor, with burnished plates set on little wooden platforms. The mother-in-law herself comes to serve them the various dishes, as this is a special occasion. As she is a well-to-do woman, she has all sorts of silver rings on her toes and anklets on her legs, and bangles and bracelets on her hands. All these ornaments make noise and her footsteps can be heard. The son-in-law is scared that the ram has come into the room somehow and will butt him again. Before he knows it, he has gotten hold of the wooden piece under his plate and swings it at what he thinks is the ram in front of him. It hits his mother-in-law, and she

flees to the kitchen in a panic. She thinks her son-in-law is furious at her for
unloading all that garbage on his head earlier that evening. Others think he
is angry because he really wants to have his own wife serve him, not his
mother-in-law. Then his wife herself comes and serves the rest of the dishes.

After the meal, everyone goes to bed. He and his wife are sleeping in a
little room. His younger in-laws sleep in the verandah. In the middle of the
night, he feels like getting up to go and pee. He gets up somehow, and

remembering what he can of the layout of the place, he cautiously gropes
along, goes to the urinal, and tries to retrace his steps. But he loses his way
to the little room and instead strays into the room where his mother-in-law
and father-in-law are sleeping. He puts his hand out and gropes for his wife's
form. His hands touch his mother-in-law's feet. She is startled awake and
cries out, "Who's that?"

He says, "It's me, it's me."

She says, "Why did you come here, at this hour?"

By now he has realized his mistake and says, "Oh, really nothing. I'm sorry
I hit you with that wooden piece when you were serving me food. I wanted
to come and touch your feet and ask your forgiveness, that's all. I did wrong.
Please forgive me."

She feels acutely embarrassed by her son-in-law's words, and says, "It's all
right. Please go back to your room and go to sleep."

He doesn't let go of her feet. He keeps saying, "Just forgive me, forgive
me."

By this time, his wife is awake and listening to the goings-on. She thinks, "He went out to pee and now he's gone to my mother's bedroom and is asking forgiveness. What will the neighbors think?"

And she gets up and comes to her mother's bed and says to him, "Come back, let's talk about it in the morning, let's go to sleep." She drags him out by the hand and leads him back to her bed.

The night soon comes to an end, and it dawns. He gets up early and says he is in a hurry. He has to go back to his village, as he has lots of work waiting for him. He bids good-bye to his wife and to his in-laws and begins his homeward journey, happy and proud that he got through it all with not one of them suspecting he is blind as a mole.

Shall I Show You My Real Face?

~ Tamil ~ ~

A fierce tiger had somehow acquired the art of changing his form, and he wanted very much to marry a Brahman wife. Though he liked his meat and couldn't live without it, he loved the smell and taste of food cooked by Brahmans, even though it was vegetarian. So, one day, he took on the shape of a learned young Brahman who could recite the *Ramayana* and went to the door of a Brahman family. The family invited him in with great respect and fed him great meals of rice and curried vegetables and mango pickles and yoghurt. The tiger didn't take long to express his interest in marrying the daughter of the family. The family admired the learned Brahman's voice and his knowledge of Sanskrit, and they were delighted. The wedding was arranged quickly, as the son-in-law seemed to be in a hurry and didn't have any family of his own to invite. A few days later, the son-in-law said he should return to his home beyond the jungle and asked permission to take his new bride with him.

The old Brahman father readily agreed and said, "Son-in-law, sir, you are her husband and she is all yours. We have brought her up lovingly. Sending her away is like sending her into the wilderness, but I know you'll take good care of her." The son-in-law left the very next day. His mother-in-law prepared all sorts of sweets and cakes for her daughter's and her new husband's journey. To ward off any lurking demons, she put a couple of *neem* leaves in each bundle of food and in the hair of her innocent daughter, as she blessed the young couple and tearfully bade them farewell.

On the way, everything went well and they had a pleasant journey. But anytime the girl wanted to sit down near a pond or under a tree to rest, the son-in-law would get angry and say, "Will you be quiet and come along, or shall I show you my real face?"

Though she didn't understand what he was saying, she rightly felt the menace in his voice and manner. So she went meekly along till she came to another pond or tree and felt like resting, and he said again, "Will you be quiet and come with me, or shall I show you my real face?"

After hearing this for a while, and not particularly liking the change that was coming over her husband as they entered deep into the woods, she said to him, "All right, show me your real face!"

As soon as she said that, the husband was transformed. Four legs, black stripes all over a long yellow body, and a whiskered tiger's face confronted her. This was a tiger and not a man! And it said, "Your husband is a tiger. Never forget it. We'll reach home very soon. I'll bring you everything you need, vegetables, rice, spices, and some meat for myself. Cook and keep house for me. But don't you disobey me, ever!"

They lived together as husband and wife in a proper house in the middle of a jungle, and she even had a son, who was a tiger cub. But she was miserable. She hadn't bargained for a life with a mean man-eating tiger, nor for the meat and entrails he brought home. As she was crying all alone in the house one day, a crow happened to come down to peck at some grains of rice. He noticed the crying girl and asked her what the matter was. The girl told the crow her story and asked it if it would take a letter for her. The crow said, "Yes, anything to help you."

The girl brought out a palmyra leaf and wrote a letter with an iron nail describing her misery in the woods and begging her brothers to come and rescue her. She tied this palmyra leaf to the neck of the crow, which flew to the village and landed in front of her brothers. They noticed the leaf around its neck, untied it, and read the letter. There were three of them and they set out at once, guided by the crow.

As they entered the jungle, they saw a stray donkey. The youngest fellow, who was a bit lame, was also quite playful. He wanted to take the donkey along. His brothers argued over it for a while, but the youngest brother took the animal along anyway. Further on, they saw a big black ant, the biting kind, and the middle brother took it along in a coconut shell. Nearby there was also a big palmyra tree lying on the ground, and the eldest took it with him. It might come in handy when they fought the tiger, he thought.

It was already noon, and they had nothing to eat. So they sat near a pond and drank up practically all the water. When they were about to leave, they found a washerman's vat, round as a fat man's belly, and they took that along with them.

They soon reached their sister's house, and the sister welcomed them.

"I'm so glad you've come," she said, "but the tiger will be here any minute. Go hide in the loft, and when he goes out again, we'll plan the next thing to do."

She helped them get up into the loft, which they did with their belongings, the ant, the donkey, the palmyra trunk, and the washerman's vat. When the tiger returned, he sniffed all around and said, "I smell human smells!"

His wife said, "Of course, what do you expect? You married a human girl!"

"I know your smell. This is different," he said. He was hungry and wanted to be fed the Brahman food she had made for him. Just as she served him rice on a banana leaf, the lame youngest brother in the loft whispered, "I need to pee. I can't hold it any longer." The eldest said, "Then go, but don't make any noise." And he did, and his piss fell right onto the rice on the tiger's leaf.

"What's that?" said the tiger, suspiciously.

"Oh, that? I left some ghee in a pot in the loft and it must have toppled over," said the wife.

After a little while, the youngest brother said, "I've got to shit. What shall I do?"

The eldest brother said, "All right, go ahead."

And the youngest brother did, and it fell right onto the tiger's leaf. The tiger roared, "What's this? It looks like shit!"

His wife said, "Don't say ugly things when you're eating. That's just some mashed lentils I cooked and put up in the loft. Some cat or something is playing up there."

The tiger ate it all up, thinking it was some kind of *tovaiyal*—lentils cooked, mashed, and spiced.

Suddenly he heard a big voice say from the loft, "Tiger, your time is up. I'm your brother-in-law up here. I want to eat you up."

The tiger, taken aback, looked up and said, "Where are you?"

"Up here! Hear me roar!" said the eldest, while the youngest put the ant into the donkey's anus. When the ant bit the donkey in that tender place, the donkey began to bray in the loudest possible voice. The tiger was terrified. "Is that your voice? Show me your leg!" he said.

The eldest brother showed him the palmyra trunk, brandishing it from the loft. The tiger said, "*Abba!* I've never seen such a leg!"

Taking advantage of the tiger's fright, the middle brother said, "Look at my belly! Big enough to hold you!" and showed him the washerman's vat.

The tiger shuddered and took to his heels, saying, "Such a voice, such a stout leg, such a huge belly, I've never seen anything like it!"

And he fled for his life.

It was dark by that time, and they wanted to return home while the tiger was still in a state of terror. So they quickly ate what little food was left and prepared to leave. The tiger cub was asleep. They wanted to get rid of it, so they cut it in two pieces and suspended them over the hearth, with a hot plate on the stove. And they made haste and ran, the three brothers and their sister, towards home.

The sister had bolted the front door of the house from inside, and they had left from the back door. As the pieces of the slain tiger cub began to drip blood over the hearth and onto the hot plate, it hissed and sputtered. When the tiger cautiously returned that night, found the front door locked, and heard the hiss and the sputter on the hot plate, he thought his wife was making *dosai*, pancakes.

"So you've locked the door and you're making *dosai* for your brother! Let's see," he said, tiptoeing around to the back of the house. As he entered, what did he see but his dear tiger cub sliced in two and hung over the hearth, his wife gone, and with her everything that was valuable in the house. For the tiger had collected all the finery from the travelers he had attacked and killed—rings and necklaces and silks and such.

The tiger grieved over the cruel death of his son and was furious at the treachery of his wife. He vowed revenge. He swore he would get her back and tear her to pieces as she had torn his son.

But how? He used the one magic trick he knew and assumed the shape of the Brahman husband and made his way to his father-in-law's village. His wife and brothers-in-law saw him from a distance and were ready for him. As he came to the door, her parents welcomed him. The brothers-in-law also scurried here and there, serving him, bringing rice and vegetables and molasses for the feast. The tiger Brahman was very pleased with the hospitable welcome. He didn't see any brother-in-law who looked huge and terrifying and had a big harsh voice. The family were all small-boned and had soft voices.

Meanwhile, the eldest brother had spread some twigs and grass across the mouth of a disused well behind the house, and spread a fine silken mat over it. It is customary in such households to give the son-in-law an oil massage and a hot bath before dinner, and so his three brothers-in-law requested the tiger Brahman to take his seat on the lovely mat for the massage and the bath. As soon as he sat on it, the mat, and the twigs and the grass under it, gave way and sank under him. And down fell the tiger son-in-law into the well with a great crash. They filled the well with stones and rubbish, and that finished off the tiger.

~ ~~

This story is told to explain the Tamil proverb *"Summa irukkiya, svarupatte kattattuma?"* (Literally, "Will you be quiet, or shall I show you my original shape?")

A Malcontent Cured

~ Kashmiri ~ ~

One day a dissatisfied fellow was sitting under a walnut tree, and his eyes fell on a great pumpkin growing nearby.

"O God," said the malcontent, "how foolish You are to give such small nuts to this big tree and such immense fruit to this thin plant! Now if pumpkins were growing on this big tree and nuts on the pumpkin plant, I'd have admired Your wisdom!"

Even as he finished saying this, a walnut fell down on the man's head and startled him.

"O God," he continued, "You are right after all. If the pumpkin had fallen on me from such a height, I would surely have been killed. Great is Your wisdom and Your goodness."

The Kite's Daughter

~ *Assamese* ~ ~

A rich potter had no sons. His wife bore him only daughters. When his wife became pregnant again, he told her, "You'd better not give birth to a daughter this time. If you do, I'll sell you to the Gypsies."

When she was about to give birth, the potter's wife went to her mother's house, as it was the custom. Unfortunately, this time too she brought forth a daughter.

This made her tremble with fear, and before her husband could ever hear of it she wrapped the child in a sari, put it in a pot, covered it with another cloth, and set it afloat in the river. As it drifted down the river, a washerman who was washing clothes on the bank saw the pot, became curious, swam towards it, and brought it to the shore. When he uncovered it, he was a bit dismayed to see the little baby in it. Just as he was wondering how he would present it to his wife, a big kite pounced on the baby and flew away with it to her nest on a banyan tree. The kite had taken one look at the baby and felt great love for it. The child looked lovely to her, and she wanted to bring it up.

She then built a large nest high up in the branches and made the baby comfortable in it. Whenever she saw anything in the human world that seemed good for the child, she would swoop down on it and bring it to the child. Food, clothes, toys—she provided the baby everything. The baby grew up into a pretty little girl.

One day, while she was looking for a dress for her child, the kite spied the princess of the realm bathing in a special place in the river. She had left her clothes and jewelry on the bank. So the kite's daughter now had royal clothes. She soon had brushes, combs, mirrors, vermilion pots and oil cups and whatnot.

The little girl grew up into a charming young woman. And she stayed in the tree which was her home. One day the kite said to her, "Child, you are now a grown young woman and I'm anxious about your being alone here. I have to make long journeys sometimes. So let me tell you what you can do. If you are ever in danger, just sing this song:

> *O wind*
> *That shakes the leaves*
> *Of this banyan tree,*
> *Bring me my mother,*
> *Bring me my mother, my kite!*

And wherever I am, I'll hear it and come home at once."

One warm day, a merchant sat down under the tree to rest from his journey and the heat of day. The forest was still and there was no sign of any other human being. But suddenly a long hair floated down and fell on his lap. It was silken and very long, seven cubits long. The merchant was surprised and looked up at the tree. There he saw a beautiful girl combing her hair very comfortably on a branch. The merchant, almost gasping with surprise now, said to her, "Who are you? Are you a human being or are you a goddess? Or are you an evil spirit? What are you?"

The poor girl had never before seen a man, though she had heard of them from her kite mother. At the first sight of a man, she was scared and didn't know how to answer him. So she sang as she had been taught:

> *O wind*
> *That shakes the leaves*
> *Of this banyan tree,*
> *Bring me my mother,*
> *Bring me my mother, my kite!*

And the kite appeared at once and asked her, "Child, what's the matter?" In reply, her daughter could only point to the man standing under the tree. The kite looked at him and like any mother sized him up quickly. She thought, "If this man is as good as he looks, he would make a very good husband for my girl."

Then the kite went and perched beside the handsome young merchant and told him the whole history of the girl. He said, "I'm blessed with the goods of this world. I have seven wives already. If you don't mind that, I'll make your daughter my wife and I promise I'll love her and look after her. She'll never want for anything. Never will she have a moment's trouble."

The kite was pleased with this straightforward and honorable answer. She thought for a moment and she agreed. She had some trouble, however, in persuading her daughter to leave her and go with the merchant. But she did, and then brought her down dressed in bridal clothes that she had collected towards this auspicious day, and gave her in marriage to the merchant. She begged him with tears in her eyes to look after her dear daughter. Then she whispered in the girl's ear that she could summon her with her song whenever she wanted.

The merchant took his bride home. He loved her and lavished every attention on her. His other seven wives were extremely jealous. They were afraid he would forget them, now that he had this beauty for his youngest wife. So all seven wives did their best to give her a bad time.

One day, they all came to her and said, "You think you're a cut above us, don't you? We have to cook and clean and do all the household chores while you eat and sleep. Go into the kitchen and cook for us today."

The poor girl had never cooked anything in her life. When she was left alone in the kitchen, she began to cry helplessly. Then she suddenly remembered her mother kite, went out into the orchard behind the house, and sang her mother's song. And the kite, true to her word, appeared at once and asked her, "Why did you call me? Why are you crying?"

When she heard about her daughter's trouble, she said, "Is that all? That's nothing we can't take care of. I'll show you how to cook. Fill a cooking pot with water and throw a grain of rice into it. In another pot of water, throw a few vegetables. Set both pots on the stove and put some firewood under them. Then do nothing else, and leave the kitchen. When you come back, you'll find as much rice and vegetables as anybody can eat. It'll be inexhaustible and you can feed the whole household. And the cooking will be delicious. You'll see."

The kite then flew away. The daughter did exactly as she was told and had a wonderful meal ready in no time at all. The seven wives sat down to their meal. They dug holes under their plates, and when the kite's daughter served them food they threw it into the holes and asked for more. But the food was inexhaustible, and when they tried it they couldn't help loving it in spite of themselves. So the co-wives had to admit defeat.

Another day, they asked her to sweep the cowshed. As she had never done anything like that before, she stood under the banana tree near the shed and sang again to summon her mother:

> *O wind*
> *That shakes the leaves*
> *Of this banana tree,*
> *Bring me my mother,*
> *Bring me my mother, my kite!*

When the kite appeared and heard about her task for the day, she said, "Oh, that's nothing. Take one twig from the broom and wave it gently along the length of the cowshed. And see what happens."

The girl did as her mother told her to, and the cowshed was swept so clean that nobody had ever seen anything so clean before. The merchant was very pleased with her and loved her even more.

The Chait Bihu festival was approaching. The merchant gave five measures of cotton to each of his eight wives and asked them to make him clothes for the occasion. He added that he would like to see who made the best. The seven co-wives set to work at once. They plucked the fibers, separated them from the seed, spun the cotton, and started weaving the cloth. But the eighth wife, who too wanted to do things like them and didn't know how, sat in a corner quite dejected. The co-wives happily said to each other, "Now her game is up. She doesn't know a thing about spinning and weaving. He'll throw her out, that's all."

But that night, she cried and sang in the orchard and summoned her mother, who anxiously asked, "What is it, my dear? Why did you call me this time?" Her daughter told her she needed to weave five measures of cotton and didn't know how. The kite said, "Don't you worry. You'll be able to do it. When I leave, get four bamboo caskets and fill each with some cotton. Seal them and do nothing else. When your husband asks for his clothes on the day of the festival, hand him the four caskets."

The kite's daughter did as she was told by her mother. Her co-wives went on weaving with a great deal of show and noise. When they saw her doing nothing, they were beside themselves with joy and said to each other, "This fool doesn't know a thing about spinning and weaving. On Bihu Day, we'll see the fun when our husband asks her for the clothes. Just can't wait!"

On the day of the festival, the seven wives gave their husband seven sets of clothes. The eighth gave him four bamboo caskets. The co-wives laughed gleefully, and even the merchant was a bit angry. He asked her, "What's all this? Where are my clothes?" She said, "Just open the caskets and see."

When the merchant opened the caskets, he found the most divine finery in them. The clothes were woven so fine that those of the others looked like coarse rags in the eyes of the merchant and everyone else. The merchant tore up the clothes made by the seven elder wives and wore most happily for days the clothes given him by the kite's daughter.

In course of time, the seven wives came to know that their co-wife had help from a kite in all the magical things she did. They put their heads together, plotted for days, and came up with a plan to do away with the kite. One of them spied on the kite's daughter and learned the song with which she summoned her mother. Then she sang the song, imitating the girl's voice, and called the kite to the cowshed. As soon as the bird came into the shed, the jealous co-wife beat her to death with a broom and buried her under a heap of cow dung. The kite's daughter didn't suspect a thing. After her mother's death, the girl sang many times for her but the kite never came. She gradually began to suspect that something was wrong, and it dawned on her one day that her co-wives had killed her mother. She was beside herself with grief.

Meanwhile the merchant was preoccupied with his own work and had to leave home on business. Before he left, he ordered his seven wives to look after his youngest wife.

A few weeks after his departure, a tradesman came to the village in a boat to sell combs, mirrors, vermilion, scents and oils, and other such things that womenfolk love to buy. The merchant's seven wives went to him, bought a roomful of his goods, and said that they would give him in return the most beautiful girl he had ever set his eyes on. They described her beauty in such tempting terms that the tradesman was eager for the exchange. Then they tried to persuade their young co-wife to go with them the next time they went to buy all those lovely things. She replied, "No, sisters, I don't want anything. Besides, he, my husband, has asked me not to leave the house and go anywhere." But the co-wives were not about to give up their plan, so they coaxed her and cajoled her till she yielded. They all went to the riverside and took her into the boat to see the tradesman's wares. While she was looking at them, they slipped away and made a signal, at which the boatmen cut the moorings and the tradesman sailed away with the girl.

He took her home and gave' her work to do. His house was on the bank of the river, and the girl had to sit in the hot sun and look after the drying fish. There she would sit all day and sing a sad song:

> *My mother was a potter's wife.*
>> *She let me drift along the river.*
> *My mother was a kite who brought me up.*
>> *A merchant prince was my husband then,*
> *And my seven co-wives sold me to a fisherman.*
>> *Here I sit, a guardian now of drying fish.*

One day, the merchant happened to pass by along the river in his boat. He was returning home from his long journey. He heard the song and recognized the voice, and asked his boatmen to stop the boat. To his great delight, it was his own wife who was singing the sad song! So he went up to her and asked her how she came to be where she was, and she told him everything. He took her home in his boat. When they reached home, he put her in a box with breathing-holes and took it into his bedroom with all his other boxes. Then he called his seven wives and asked them about the eighth wife, and they replied almost in a chorus that she had gone to her mother's house quite some time ago and had not come back. The merchant said, "I'm afraid you've done something to her. I want to see whether you're telling the truth or not. So I'm going to test you."

He ordered his men to dig a deep pit and fill it with thorns. Then he asked them to tie a thread across the whole length of the pit. After that, he asked his wives to cross the pit walking on the thread. "If you're innocent, nothing will happen to you. If you're guilty, you'll fall in and die."

They tried in vain to talk him out of it, but they were forced to take the test. One by one they attempted to cross the pit on the thread, and six of them fell into the pit of thorns. Each time, the thread gave way and was replaced by another. Only the seventh wife succeeded in going across to the other side. It turned out that she was not really guilty. She had been busy cooking in the kitchen all along and had had no part in the plot to lure the kite's daughter into the tradesman's boat. The thread did not give way even though she crawled across it seven times.

The merchant then had his six bad wives buried alive in that same pit. Then he lived peacefully and happily with his seventh wife and the kite's daughter.

~ ~~

We came away because we had to send our clothes to the washerman.

A Flowering Tree

~ *Kannada* ~ ~

In a certain town, the king had two daughters and a son. His older daughter was married.

In the same town, there lived an old woman with her two daughters. She did menial jobs to feed and clothe and bring up her children. When the girls had reached puberty, the younger sister said one day, "Sister, I've been thinking of something. It's hard on Mother to work all day for our sakes. I want to help her. I will turn myself into a flowering tree. You can take the flowers and sell them for good money."

Amazed, the older sister asked, "How will you turn into a flowering tree?"

"I'll explain later. You first sweep and clean the entire house. Then take a bath, go to the well, and bring me two pitchers full of water, without touching them with your fingernails," said the younger sister.

The older sister listened to her carefully, swept and wiped and cleaned, took a bath, and brought two pitchers of water as the younger sister had told her.

Right in front of their house stood a tall tree. The sister swept and wiped the ground under it, too. Both girls then went there, and the younger one said, "Sister, I'll sit under this tree and meditate. Then you pour the water from this pitcher all over my body. I'll turn into a flowering tree. Then you pluck as many flowers as you want, but do it without breaking a twig or tearing a leaf. When you're done, pour the water from the other pitcher over me, and I'll become a person again."

The younger sister sat down and meditated on God. The older one poured water from the first pitcher all over her sister. At once, her sister changed into a great flowering tree that seemed to stretch from earth to heaven. The older sister plucked the flowers carefully, without hurting a branch or twig or leaf. After she had enough to fill a basket or two, she emptied the second pitcher of water over the tree—and the tree became a human being again, and the younger sister stood in its place. She shook the water from her hair, and stood up. They both gathered the flowers in baskets and brought them home. The flowers had a wonderful fragrance. They wove them into garlands.

"Where shall I sell them?" asked the elder sister.

"Sister, why not take all of them to the king's palace? They will pay well. Mother is always doing such awful jobs for our sake. Let's pile up some money and surprise her," said the younger one.

So the older sister took the basketful of garlands before the king's palace and hawked her wares, crying, "Flowers, flowers, who wants flowers?"

The princess looked out and said, "Mother, Mother, the flowers smell wonderful. Buy me some."

"All right, call the flower girl," said the queen. They both looked at the flowers, and they were lovely. The queen asked, "How much do you want for these?"

"We are poor people. Give us whatever you wish," said the older sister. They gave her a handful of coins and bought all the garlands.

When the older sister came home with the money, the younger one said, "Sister, Sister, don't tell Mother. Hide it. Don't tell anyone."

They sold flowers like this for five days, and they had five handfuls of coins.

"Shall we show these to Mother?" asked the older sister.

"No, no, she'll get angry and beat us," said the other. The two girls were eager to make money.

One day the king's son saw the flowers. They smelled wonderful. He had never seen such flowers anywhere. "What flowers are these?" he wondered. "Where do they grow, on what kind of tree? Who brings them to the palace?"

He watched the girl who brought the flowers, and one day he followed her home to the old woman's house, but he couldn't find a single flowering tree anywhere. He was quite intrigued. On his way home he tired himself out thinking, "Where on earth do they get such flowers?"

Early the next morning, while it was still dark, the king's son went and hid himself in the tall tree in front of the old woman's house. That day, too, the girls swept and washed the space under the tree. As usual, the younger girl became the flowering tree, and after the older one had gently plucked all the flowers, the tree became a young woman again. The prince saw all this happen before his very eyes.

He came straight home and lay on his bed, face down. His father and mother came to find out what the matter was. He didn't speak a word. The minister's son, his friend, came and asked him, "What happened? Did anyone say anything to hurt you? What do you want? You can tell me."

Then the prince told him, bit by bit, about the girl turning into a flowering tree. "Is that all?" said the minister's son, and reported it all to the king. The king called the minister, and sent for the old woman. She arrived, shaking with fear. She was dressed in old clothes and stood near the door. After much persuasion, she sat down. The king calmed her and softly asked her, "You have two girls at your place. Will you give us one?" The old woman's fear grew worse. "How does the king know about my daughters?" she thought. She found her voice with difficulty and stammered, "All right, master. For a poor woman like me, giving a daughter is not as great a thing, is it, as your asking for one?"

The king at once offered her *tambula*—betel leaf and betel nut—cere-monially on a silver platter, as a symbolic offer of betrothal. She was afraid to touch it. But the king forced it on her and sent her home.

Back home, she picked up a broom and beat her daughters. She scolded them: "You bitches, where have you been? The king is asking after you. Where did you go?"

The poor girls didn't understand what was happening. They stood there crying, "Mother, why are you beating us? Why are you scolding us?"

"Who else can I beat? Where did you go? How did the king hear about you?"

The old woman raged on. The terrified girls slowly confessed to what they had been doing—told her how the younger girl would turn into a flowering tree, how they would sell the flowers and hoard the money, hoping to surprise their mother. They showed her their five handfuls of coins.

"How can you do such things, with an elder like me sitting in the house? What's all this talk about human beings becoming trees? Who ever heard of it? Telling lies, too. Show me how you become a tree."

She screamed and beat them some more. Finally, to pacify her, the younger sister had to demonstrate it all: she became a tree and then returned to her normal human self, right before her mother's eyes.

Next day, the king's men came to the old woman's house and asked her to appear before the king. The old woman went and said, "Your Highness, what do you want of me?"

The king answered, "Tell us when we should set the date for the wedding."

"What can I say, Your Highness? We'll do as you wish," the old woman said, secretly glad by now.

The wedding arrangements began. The family made ritual designs on the wedding floor as large as the sky, and built a wedding canopy as large as the earth. All the relatives arrived. At an auspicious moment, the girl who knew how to become a flowering tree was given in marriage to the prince.

After the nuptial ceremony, the families left the couple alone together in a separate house. But he was aloof, and so was she. Two nights passed. Let him talk to me, thought she. Let her begin, thought he. So both groom and bride were silent.

On the third night, the girl wondered, "He hasn't uttered a word. Why did he marry me?" She asked him, aloud, "Is it for this bliss you married me?"

He answered roughly, "I'll talk to you only if you do what I ask."

"Won't I do as my husband bids me? Tell me what you want."

"You know how to turn into a flowering tree, don't you? Let me see you do it. We can then sleep on flowers, and cover ourselves with them. That would be lovely," he said.

"My lord, I'm not a demon, I'm not a goddess. I'm an ordinary mortal like everyone else. Can a human being ever become a tree?" she said very humbly.

"I don't like all this lying and cheating. The other day I saw you become a beautiful tree. I saw you with my own eyes. If you don't become a tree for me, for whom will you do it?" he chided her.

The bride wiped a tear from her eyes with the end of her sari, and said,

"Don't be angry with me. If you insist so much, I'll do as you say. Bring two pitchers of water."

He brought them. She uttered chants over them. Meanwhile, he shut all the doors and all the windows. She said, "Remember, pluck all the flowers you want, but take care not to break a twig or tear a leaf."

Then she instructed him on how and when to pour the water, while she sat in the middle of the room, meditating on God. The prince poured one pitcherful of water over her. She turned into a flowering tree. The fragrance of the flowers filled the house. He plucked all the flowers he wanted, and then sprinkled water from the second pitcher all over the tree. It became his bride again. She shook her tresses and stood up smiling.

They spread the flowers, covered themselves with them, and went to bed. They did this again and again for several days. Every morning the couple threw out all the withered flowers from their window. The heap of flowers lay there like a hill.

The king's younger daughter saw the heap of withered flowers one day and said to the queen, "Look, Mother, Brother and Sister-in-Law wear and throw away a whole lot of flowers. The flowers they've thrown away are piled up like a hill. And they haven't given me even one."

The queen consoled her: "Don't be upset. We'll get them to give you some."

One day the prince had gone out somewhere. Then the king's daughter (who had meanwhile spied and discovered the secret of the flowers) called all her friends and said, "Let's go to the swings in the *surahonne* grove. We'll take my sister-in-law; she'll turn into a flowering tree. If you all come, I'll give you flowers that smell wonderful."

Then she asked her mother's permission. The queen said, "Of course, do go. Who will say no to such things?"

The daughter then said, "But I can't go alone. Send Sister-in-Law."

"Then get your brother's permission and take her."

The prince came in just then, and his sister asked him, "Brother, Brother! We're all going to the *surahonne* grove to play on our swings. Can Sister-in-Law come along?"

"It's not my wish that's important. Everything depends on Mother," he answered.

So she went back to the queen and complained, "Mother, if I ask Brother, he sends me to you. But you don't really want to send her, so you're giving me excuses. Is your daughter-in-law more important to you than your daughter?"

The queen rebuked her, saying, "Don't be rude. All right, take your sister-in-law with you. Take care of her and bring her back safely by evening."

Reluctantly, the queen sent her daughter-in-law with the girls.

They all went to the *surahonne* grove. They tied their swings to a big tree. Soon everyone was playing merrily on the swings. Abruptly the king's daughter stopped all the games, brought everyone down from the swings, and accosted her brother's wife: "Sister-in-Law, you can become a flowering tree, can't you? Look, no one here has any flowers for her hair."

The sister-in-law replied angrily, "Who told you such nonsense? Am I not another human being like you? Don't talk such crazy stuff."

The king's daughter taunted her, "Oho, I know all about you. My friends have no flowers to wear. I ask my sister-in-law to become a tree and give us some flowers, and look how coy she acts. You don't want to become a tree for us. Do you do that only for your lovers?"

"*Che*, you're awful. My coming here was a mistake," said the sister-in-law sadly, and she agreed to become a tree.

She sent for two pitchers of water, uttered chants over them, instructed the girls on how and when to pour the water, and sat down to meditate. The silly girls didn't listen carefully. They poured the water on her indifferently, here and there. She turned into a tree, but only half a tree.

It was already evening, and it began to rain, with thunder and lightning. In their greed to get the flowers, the girls tore the leaves and broke the branches. They were in a hurry to get home. They poured the second pitcher of water at random and ran away. When the princess changed from a tree to a person again, she had no hands and feet. She had only half a body. She was a wounded carcass.

Somehow in that flurry of rainwater, she crawled and floated into a gutter. There she got stuck in a turning, a long way off from home.

Next morning, seven or eight cotton wagons were coming that way and a driver spotted a half-human thing groaning in the gutter. The first cart-driver said, "See what that noise is about."

The second one said, "Hey, let's get going. It may be the wind, or it may be some ghost, who knows?"

But the last cart-driver stopped his cart and took a look. There lay a shapeless mass, a body. Only the face was a beautiful woman's face. She wasn't wearing anything.

"*Ayyo*, some poor woman," he said in sorrow, and threw his turban cloth over her and carried her to his cart, paying no heed to the dirty banter of his fellows. Soon they came to a town. They stopped their carts there and lowered the Thing onto a ruined pavilion. Before they drove on, the cart-driver said, "Somebody may find you and feed you. You will survive." Then they drove on.

When the king's daughter came home alone, the queen asked her, "Where's your sister-in-law? What will your brother say?" The girl answered casually, "Who knows? Didn't we all find our own way home? Who knows where she went?"

The queen panicked and tried to get the facts out of the girl. "*Ayyo!* You can't say such things. Your brother will be angry. Tell me what happened."

The girl said whatever came to her head. The queen found out nothing. She had a suspicion that her daughter had done something foolish. After waiting several hours, the prince talked to his mother.

"*Amma, amma.*"

"What is it, my son?"

"What has happened to my wife? She went with my sister to play on the swings, and never came back."

"O Rama! I thought she was in your bedroom all this time. Now you're asking me!"

"Oh, something terrible has happened to her," thought the prince. He went and lay down in grief. Five days passed, six days passed, fifteen days passed, but there was no news of his wife. They couldn't find her anywhere.

"Did the stupid girls push her into a tank? Did they throw her down a well? My sister never liked her. What did the foolish girls do?" He asked his parents and the servants. What could they say? They too were worried and full of fear. In disgust and despair, he changed into an ascetic's long robe and went out into the world. He just walked and walked, not caring where he went.

Meanwhile, the girl who was now a Thing somehow reached the town where her husband's elder sister had been given in marriage. Every time the palace servants and maids passed that way to fetch water, they would see her. They would say to each other, "She glows like a king's daughter." Then one of them couldn't stand it any longer and decided to tell the queen.

"*Amma, amma*, she looks very much like your younger brother's wife. Look through the seeing-glass and see for yourself."

The queen looked, and the face did seem strangely familiar. One of the maids suggested, "*Amma*, can I bring her to the palace. Shall I?"

The queen pooh-poohed this: "We'll have to serve her and feed her. Forget it."

The next day again the maids mumbled and moaned, "She's very lovely. She'll be like a lamp in the palace. Can't we bring her here?"

"All right, all right, bring her if you wish. But you'll have to take care of her without neglecting palace work," ordered the queen.

They agreed and brought the Thing to the palace. They bathed her in oils, dressed her well, and sat her down at the palace door. Every day they applied medicines to her wounds and made her well. But they could not make her whole. She still had only half a body.

Now the prince wandered through many lands and ended up outside the gate of his sister's palace. He looked like a crazy man. His beard and whiskers were wild. When the maids were fetching and carrying water, they saw him. They went back to the queen in the palace and said, "*Amma*, someone is sitting outside the gate, and he looks very much like your brother. Look through the seeing-glass and see for yourself."

Grumbling, the queen went to the terrace and looked through the seeing-glass. She was surprised: "Yes, he does look remarkably like my brother. What's happened to him? Has he become a wandering ascetic? Impossible," she thought. She sent her maids down to bring him in. They said to him, "The queen wants to see you."

He brushed them aside. "Why would she want to see me?" he growled.

"No, sir, she really wants to see you. Please come," they insisted and finally persuaded him to come in. The queen took a good look at him and knew it was really her brother.

She ordered the palace servants to heat up whole vats of oil and great vessels of steaming water for his baths. She served him and nursed him, for she knew he was her brother. She served new kinds of dinner each day, and brought him new styles of clothing. But whatever she did, he wouldn't speak a word to his elder sister. He didn't even ask, "Who are you? Where am I?" though by this time, they both knew they were brother and sister.

The queen wondered, "Why doesn't he talk to me when I treat him so royally? What could be the reason? Could it be some witch's or demon's magic?"

After some days, she started sending one or another of her beautiful maids into his bedroom every night. She sent seven maids in seven days. The maids held his hands and caressed his body, and tried to rouse him from his stupor. But he didn't say a word or do a thing.

Finally the maidservants got together and dressed up the Thing that sat at the palace door. With the permission of the disgusted queen, they left it on his bed. He neither looked up nor said anything. But that night, the Thing sat at his feet and pressed and massaged his legs with its stump of an arm. It moaned strangely. He got up once and looked at it. Then he stared at it for a few moments and realized it was really his lost wife. He asked her what had happened. She, who had had no speech all these months, suddenly broke into words. She told him whose daughter she was, whose wife, and what had happened to her.

"What shall we do now?" he asked.

"Nothing much. We can only try. Bring me two pitchers of water, without touching them with your fingernails," she replied.

At once he brought her two pitchers of water without anyone's knowledge. She uttered chants over them and instructed him: "Pour the water from this pitcher over me, and I'll become a tree. Wherever there is a broken branch, set it right. Wherever a leaf is torn, bind it together. Then pour the water from the second pitcher over the tree."

Then she sat down and meditated.

He poured the water on her from the first pitcher. She became a tree. But the branches had been broken, the leaves had been torn. He carefully set each one right and bound them up, and gently poured the water from the second pitcher all over the tree. Now she became a whole human being again. She stood up, shaking the water from her hair, and fell at her husband's feet.

Then she went and woke up the queen, her sister-in-law, and touched her feet also. She told the astonished queen the whole story. The queen wept and embraced her. Then she treated the couple to all kinds of princely food and service and had them sit in the hall like bride and bridegroom for a ritual celebration called *hase*. She kept them in her palace for several weeks, and then sent them home to her father's palace with cartloads of gifts.

The king was overjoyed at the return of his long-lost son and daughter-in-law. He met them at the city gates and took them home on an elephant howdah in a grand ceremonial procession through the city streets. At the palace, they told the king and the queen everything that had happened. Then the king had seven barrels of burning lime poured into a great pit and threw his youngest daughter into it. All the people who saw it said to themselves, "After all, every wrong has its punishment."

A Musical Demon

~ Tamil ~ ~

A very poor Brahman grew sick of being poor and set out on a pilgrimage to Kashi, the holy city. After walking many miles in the sun, he stopped in a shady grove to rest and eat the stale rice he had packed himself for the journey. As he squatted under a tree to answer the call of nature, he was startled by a deep, unearthly voice that said, "Don't." He quickly got up and looked about him for the source of the voice. He could see no one around. He then walked to a nearby pond to rinse his mouth when he again heard the voice say, "Don't!" This time he went ahead and rinsed his mouth, not heeding the warning. But when he unpacked his little packet of rice and sat down to eat, he heard it again: "Don't!" He ignored it and ate his meal, but when he got ready to leave the grove, the voice said, "Don't go!" The Brahman stopped and looked around.

He saw no one. So he called out, "Who are you? Why are you making all these noises?"

"Look up and you'll see me," the voice said from somewhere above. When he looked up, he saw perched on a tree a *brahmarakshasa*, a demon who was once a Brahman.

Then the demon told him its sad story: "In my previous life I was born into a Brahman family and was a great expert in the art of music. I spent my whole life hoarding my knowledge and never shared it or taught it to anyone. That's why I've become a demon. That's God's punishment. If you turn around, you'll see a little temple. In that temple, a piper plays all day in the most atrocious manner, always out of tune. It's torture to me; it's like pouring hot molten lead in my ears. I cannot bear it. Every wrong note goes through me like an arrow. My whole body is sore; it feels like a sieve full of holes drilled by that dreadful noise. If this goes on any longer, I'll go stark mad and do terrible things. Being a demon, I can't even kill myself. I'm bound to this tree. O good Brahman, I beg of you, please transport me somehow to the next grove where I can enjoy some peace. You will also release some of my own powers. You'll earn great merit if you help a poor demon who was once a Brahman like you."

The poor Brahman's heart went out to the demon. But poverty had made him cunning. He replied, "All right, I'm prepared to move you to the next grove, as you wish. But what's in it for me? Will you do something for me in return?"

The demon said, "Of course, I'll do you a good turn. Do this for me now." So the Brahman carried the demon on his back to another grove, far away from the temple, and let him perch on a big tree there. The demon was relieved and happy; he had also recovered some of his own powers through this move. He blessed the Brahman and said, "I know you're poor and feeling wretched. Do as I tell you and you'll never be poor again. I'll now go and possess the princess of Mysore. Her father the king will summon all sorts of magicians to rid her of me, but I won't budge. I'll leave when you arrive. The king will be pleased that you chased away the demon that afflicted his daughter and he will give you enough wealth to last you a lifetime. But I'll do this on one condition: if I go and possess anyone else, you mustn't interfere. If you come anywhere near me then, I'll finish you off."

The Brahman traveled on to Kashi, bathed in the holy river, visited the

temple, and as he was returning home, remembered what the demon had
said. So with great difficulty he reached Mysore and went to stay with an
old woman who took in paying guests. When he asked her casually what was
new in town, she told him: "A demon has possessed our king's daughter and
no magician has been able to drive it out. The king has announced that he
will give lots of money to anyone who drives out the demon who possesses
his daughter."

When the Brahman heard this, he knew at once that his good times had
begun. He went to the palace and sent word to the king that he had the
power to drive the demon away and cure the princess of the affliction. No
one believed that this little Brahman could do anything of the sort. Halfheart-
edly, the king agreed to try the Brahman's methods.

As soon as he was taken to the princess's quarters, he asked everyone to
leave him alone with the patient. Once they left the room, the demon began
to speak through the princess: "I've been waiting for you all these days. I'll
leave now, as I promised. But don't forget what I told you the last time we
met. If you come anywhere near where I'm going now, I'll kill you."

Then, with a great big noise, the demon who was once a Brahman left the
body of the princess and disappeared. Everyone in the palace was overjoyed
to see that the princess was herself again. The king gave the Brahman lots of

money and several villages as part of the reward. Then the Brahman found a suitable bride in town and married, and lived happily with a growing family.

The demon who left the Mysore princess flew straight to Kerala and possessed the princess of Travancore. The king of Travancore tried every method, magical and otherwise, to rid his daughter of the demon that possessed her. It was all in vain. One day, someone told him about the clever Brahman who lived in Mysore and how he had been able to rid the Mysore princess of a similar demon who had possessed her. So he sent a letter to the king of Mysore and said that he would suitably reward the Brahman if he would help rid his daughter of the obstinate demon.

The king of Mysore invited the Brahman to his palace and ordered him to go visit his friend the king of Travancore and see what he could do for the princess there. The Brahman was terrified at the prospect of meeting the demon again. Yet he could not disobey royal orders. Neither could he face the prospect of the demon's murderous wrath by interfering with his present possession. After thinking long and hard, he made the necessary arrangements to take care of his wife and children in case something should happen to him, and journeyed to Travancore. Once he got there, out of sheer terror he malingered and pretended to be sick, and never left his quarters for two whole months. But he couldn't malinger forever. He had to face the task of driving out the demon who was afflicting the princess.

Once he decided to face his mission, he took his courage in both hands, prayed to God to protect him from danger, presented himself at the palace, and asked to be led to the princess's chamber. As soon as the demon saw him, he screamed, "I'll kill you, I'll tear you to pieces! You had no business coming here!" and rushed towards the Brahman with an iron pestle in his hand.

The Brahman had, after all, come there after giving up all hope of surviving this encounter. With the courage born of desperation, he used his wits and said quietly, "Look here, you ugly demon, will you do as I say now and leave at once, or would you like me to bring that piper from the temple? He will gladly play his atrocious music night and day here in this palace."

As soon as he heard the mention of the dreaded piper, the demon who was once a Brahman, that music-loving monster, cried aloud in pain, "No, no! Don't bring him anywhere near me! Here I go!"

And, with a great big noise, he left the princess and disappeared.

The princess of Travancore recovered quickly from the ill effects of that horrible possession. The king was enormously pleased with the Brahman's work and gave him so much money he's still counting it, after taking it in cartloads to Mysore where he happily rejoined his wife and children.

Other Lives

~ *Kashmiri* ~ ~

For many years, a Brahman practiced austerities and offered worship to the gods in order to learn something of what happens to us when we die. At last the gods favored him.

One morning, as he was bathing in the river, his spirit left him and went into the body of an untouchable cobbler's child. The child grew up, learned his father's business, married, and became the father of a big family. Then suddenly he became aware that he was truly a Brahman, so he abandoned everything and went to another country.

Now, just as he reached that country, the king died without an heir. So the ministers and elders resorted to the popular custom of sending an elephant and a hawk around the country to elect a successor. The people would accept as king anyone that the elephant and the hawk acknowledged. Well, wonder of wonders, the stranger, the Brahman in the body of the cobbler, was chosen for the royal office. The elephant bowed before him, and the hawk perched on his right hand, and thus proclaimed him king in the presence of all the people.

A few years later, the cobbler's untouchable wife came to know of his whereabouts and went to join him. Then people began to gossip and ask questions, and soon it became known that the king was a cobbler and that his wife was also lowborn. The people were outraged. Some rioted, some fled, some took to penance, and others burned themselves. Everyone was afraid of being excommunicated. The king too could not bear the shame and the chaos, and threw himself into a fire.

At once his spirit went and reoccupied the corpse of the Brahman that still lay on the riverbank, and went home. When his wife saw him at the door, she said, "You're back already! How quickly you bathed and performed your morning prayers!" The Brahman said nothing. He only looked surprised and wondered: "Can this be what happens when one dies? Did all this really happen? Or did I dream it?"

Just about a week after this a man came into the Brahman's courtyard and begged for food, saying he had eaten nothing for five days. He said he had been running away from his country as fast as he could, because a cobbler had become king and polluted the whole kingdom. All the people, he said, were running away or burning themselves to escape the evil that might befall them. The Brahman gave the man some food, but said nothing. "How can such things be?" he thought. "I've lived as a cobbler and raised a family for years, and then reigned as a king for several years. Just when I was convinced it was a dream, this man arrives at my house and confirms the truth of those happenings. Yet my wife says I've not been absent from the house for very long this morning. I believe her, for she does not look a day older, nor is the place changed in any way. Maybe the soul passes through various stages of existence according to a man's thoughts and words and acts, and in the great Hereafter time is measured differently: in that time, a day is equal to an aeon and an aeon is equal to a day. Maybe."

Living Like a Pig

ᴖ *Telugu* ᴖᴖ

One day, a guru foresaw in a flash of vision what he would be in his next life. So he called his favorite disciple and asked him what he would do for his guru in return for all he had received. The disciple said he would do whatever his guru asked him to do.

Having received this promise, the guru said, "Then this is what I'd like you to do for me. I've just learned that when I die, which will be very soon, I'm going to be reborn as a pig. Do you see that sow eating garbage there in the yard? I'm going to be reborn as the fourth piglet of its next litter. You'll recognize me by a mark on my brow. When that sow has littered, find the fourth piglet with a mark on its brow and, with one stroke of your knife, slaughter it. I'll then be released from a pig's life. Will you do this for me?"

The disciple was sad to hear all this, but he agreed to do as he had promised.

Soon after this conversation, the guru did die. And the sow did have a litter of four little pigs. One day, the disciple sharpened his knife and picked out the fourth little pig, which did indeed have a mark on its brow. Just as he was about to bring down his knife to slit its throat, the little pig suddenly spoke. "Stop! Don't kill me!" it screamed.

Before the disciple could recover from the shock of hearing the little pig speak in a human voice, it said, "Don't kill me. I want to live on as a pig. When I asked you to dispatch me, I didn't know what a pig's life would be like. It's great. Just let me go."

A Heron in the Mouth

~ Bengali ~ ~

A pundit was crossing a field on his way home. He had a fit of coughing and spat on the ground. He was surprised to see that he had spat out a white feather along with his phlegm. He couldn't explain it. He worried about it. He turned it over and over in his mind till he could bear it no longer. As soon as he reached home he called his wife and said to her, "Something is worrying me. I have to tell someone. But if I tell it to you, will you promise not to tell anyone about it?"

"Of course, I won't tell a soul. I promise," said the wife. Then he told her about the white feather he had found in his spit.

But she couldn't keep it to herself. It was very much on her mind. So, as soon as she saw a neighbor, the first thing she said to her was this: "My mind is full of something. Will you promise not to tell anyone if I tell you about it? I promised my husband not to tell anyone about it."

"Of course," said the neighbor. "You know how good I am about keeping secrets. I won't breathe it to a soul. Tell me."

"Are you sure you won't tell anyone?"

"If you are that distrustful, keep it to yourself. When have I betrayed a secret of yours?"

"All right, all right, I'll tell you. I know you're a good friend. When my husband was crossing the field on his way home, do you know what he spat out? He coughed up heron's feathers, lots of them! I don't know what's happening to him. I'm quite worried," said the wife.

"Oh, you shouldn't worry about it. Such things happen. It will pass. But it is a good idea not to tell anyone about it. They'll spread rumors."

But she couldn't wait to tell it to someone. As she hurried home, she looked around for someone to whom she could tell this secret that was bursting out of her. And as soon as she met a friend, she came out with it.

"Promise not to tell anyone. I told the pundit's wife I would keep her secret. Do you know what happened today? The pundit coughed up a whole big heron in the field. I thought pundits were vegetarians. But you never know," she said.

"A whole heron? It's such a big bird! How could he? Strange man! But I'll tell no one, depend on me."

Soon after that, another neighbor heard that several flapping herons had flown out of the pundit's mouth. By the end of the day, the news was all over town that flights of herons and storks and cranes and all sorts of big birds had come flying out of the pundit's mouth. The surrounding villages also heard about it, and villagers hitched bullocks to their carts and made their way to the pundit's village to see this monstrous happening, which might even be a miracle. Birds of all sizes and colors, some even from faraway countries, were coming out of the pundit's mouth and darkening the air, went the rumor.

The poor pundit nearly went mad. He ran away and hid himself in a tree till the news had died out and was replaced by a new rumor.

Tenali Rama's Art

~ Kannada; Tamil; Telugu ~ ~

Once the king wanted paintings on his palace walls, so he commissioned a painter to cover his walls with pictures. The pictures were much admired, but Tenali Rama had questions. Standing before a body drawn in profile, he asked naively, "Where is the other side? Where are the other parts?" The king laughed and replied, "Don't you know that you must imagine them?" "Oh, that's how paintings are done! I understand now," said Tenali Rama.

A few months later, Tenali Rama came to the king and said, "I've been practicing the art of painting night and day for months. I'd love to paint some things on your walls."

The king said, "Wonderful! Why don't you get rid of the old faded paintings and paint new pictures?"

Tenali Rama whitewashed over the old paintings and did new ones of his own in their place. He drew a leg here, an eye there, a finger in another place. He covered the walls with many such body parts, and then invited the king to view his handiwork. The king was both surprised and dismayed by these dismembered limbs on his walls and asked, "What have you done here? Where are the pictures?"

Tenali Rama said, "In paintings, you have to imagine the rest. You haven't yet seen my masterpiece." Then he led him to a blank wall with a few strokes of green on it.

"What's this?" asked the king, somewhat exasperated.

"That's a cow eating grass."

"But where is the cow?" asked the king.

"After eating grass, the cow went home to its shed," said Tenali Rama.

One More Use for Artists

~ *Gujerati* ~ ~

A great raja's daughter was beautiful and talented, and she loved to hunt in the woods on horseback. One day, as she was galloping after a fine buck, she suddenly found herself in a dense forest, all alone. She climbed a tree to see if she could spot her followers anywhere in the distance. As she reached the top branch, she was shocked to see a great forest fire.

She watched the fire lapping up trees and shrubs, closing in with tongues of flame on the nests of birds and the lairs of animals, destroying everything in its way. Herds of deer and other animals ran about in a frenzy of fear, and birds of various colors were suffocated by the thick smoke, screaming and screeching as they fell into the fire.

In the midst of this horrible scene, the princess was deeply moved to see a pair of wild geese trying very hard to save their young ones, their little chicks who didn't even have wings yet. As they tried to carry them here and there, they flew distractedly while the fire came towards them closer and closer. They had very little hope of saving themselves or their young ones. As the fire was about to catch the nest, the old male bird made a last desperate attempt and saved himself by flying to a point of safety, leaving the family behind. The mother goose threw herself as a guard over her little ones, and with all of them screaming wildly, was burned in the flames that closed over them.

The princess watched all this, and as she rode away safely, was both moved and angered by what she had witnessed. "How selfish and unreliable these males are!" she said to herself. "I'm sure they are the same all the world over, whether they are birds or beasts or men. I'll have nothing to do with them ever. I'll never trust them." And she made up her mind then and there never to marry, ever.

Her followers, who had been frantically looking for her, soon caught up with her, and they all went home.

From that day on, the princess wore a serious face, shunned all males, and told her parents that she would never marry anyone. The old parents were very upset over this, and begged of her to tell them what had made her take such a drastic decision. She was silent and gave them no explanations. Soon everybody came to know that the princess was not for marriage, and the number of suitors soon fell off.

One day a well-known artist happened to visit the raja's court and painted some exquisite pictures for the palace. But just as he was getting ready to leave, he caught a glimpse of the princess and wanted to put all that beauty into a painting. So he begged the princess to give him a few sittings, which she reluctantly did. He painted with great pleasure a faithful likeness of her face and figure. And when he finished the painting, instead of giving it to her, he quietly took it with him when he left the city.

He visited next another raja, who was a great lover of paintings, and sold the painting of the princess to him for a large sum of money. The picture was hung up in the raja's great hall where everyone who saw it admired it and talked about it. They were enchanted by the beauty of the princess and wondered who the original could be.

The king's only son and heir had been away hunting all this time and returned home, saw the painting in the hall, and fell madly in love with the image on the canvas without even asking who the original was. When he did ask, nobody knew who or where she was. The lovesick prince lost all pleasure in his daily rounds, shunned company, fell into a gloomy silence, and moped away in his corner of the palace. The father was very unhappy to see his son depressed and soon learned the cause of it. He felt anxious for his son's health and sent messengers in search of the artist. But the artist had long since left the country and gone away to foreign lands, as artists tend to do.

The prince's health and temper grew steadily worse and he was angry with anyone who came near him. One day the old prime minister, a trusted friend of the royal family, happened to arouse him from his gloomy reverie, and the prince was so furious that he at once sentenced him to death. The young prince's word was law in that palace, and the old man had no way of escaping his fate. When the raja heard of it, he summoned the prince and persuaded him to put off the execution for a few days, so that the prime minister might arrange his affairs and transfer his powers to someone else. The old minister was allowed to go home to his family for the time.

Though he didn't wish to talk about it to anyone, his family knew all about the fate that awaited him. His youngest daughter, his favorite in the family, talked to him soothingly, comforted him, and wormed out of him the secret of the prince's rage and sorrow.

Now this young woman was very clever and resourceful. She soon found a way of getting her father out of his difficulty. She went to the young prince, and somehow succeeded in getting an audience. She begged him very hard to spare her father's life for a certain length of time, so that she herself could go abroad and find the original of the wonderful painting that was the cause of all this trouble.

This pleased the prince very much. The young woman's scheme sounded quite plausible. He saw some hope of realizing what was so far only a wisp of a dream. So he relented and withdrew his terrible order, and the old minister returned to his duties in the palace. The raja was very pleased at this turn of events and wished the young daughter of his minister every success.

Now the minister's daughter was herself a good artist. She made a faithful copy of the great artist's painting. She then dressed herself as a man and set out on her travels disguised as a wandering artist. She hardly knew where to go or whom to ask, but she loved her father and was determined to save his life. So she traveled for months in different directions, showed the picture of the princess wherever she halted, and asked everyone she met, but no one could identify the person in the painting. After a year's weary wandering, she arrived at a distant and strange country, and there, to her great joy, everyone who saw the picture knew who the person in the picture was. They all exclaimed at what a true and speaking likeness the painting was of the daughter of their own raja. And they all spoke of her as "The Princess Who Was Determined Never To Marry."

"Never to marry?" asked the minister's daughter. "What's wrong with her? Did something terrible happen?"

"Nobody knows," they said, "not even her parents."

This news damped her enthusiasm somewhat. If the princess had turned against marriage, how was she, a mere stranger, to succeed in getting her married to the prince who was dying for her?

Still, she was a brave girl and was willing to try more than one way of reaching the princess. She rented a house near the palace and opened her studio there. Every day she set up her easel near a large window that looked out on the palace and worked away with her paints and brushes, till the courtiers and finally the king himself wanted to know more about her. One day the raja summoned her to the court to show him her paintings. When he saw them, he liked them a lot, bought some of them, and invited her to do some pictures for the special palace he was building for his only daughter. Meanwhile, the minister's daughter had the opportunity to see the princess several times, and she was now sure the princess was the true original of the painting that had so enthralled the prince and nearly driven him out of his senses.

When the walls in the new palace were ready, the artist began to paint all sorts of lovely designs and figures on them, decorating even the ceilings and arches. The raja and his court came often to see them and to admire her artistry. Each picture was a study in itself, and each had a story that the artist recounted in her own winning manner. All this drew the ladies of the court to these pictures. Some of these women were friends and attendants of the princess. The minister's daughter thought these women, if anyone, would surely know the reason why the princess shunned all males and despised marriage. So she set to work on them and won them over with her art and courtesy till one of them opened up to her. She was a confidante of the princess, and she told the artist the secret story of the princess's adventure in the forest and her disillusionment with all males in nature.

This was all the minister's daughter wanted to know. On one of the walls of the living room, she drew a picture that was just the reverse of what the princess had seen in the forest. It was a wonderful picture that showed the utter fickleness of females and the devotion of a male. She substituted a pair of antelopes for the geese, and in the place of the princess she painted a very handsome young prince, so young, so brave and handsome, that he would win the heart of any woman.

As soon as this picture was ready, the minister's daughter persuaded the friends of the princess to ask her to come and have a look at it. One day, to her great joy, the princess did honor her with a visit. She went from picture to picture and greatly admired the artist's skill. She at last came to the picture of the antelopes and the prince, and she was arrested by it. She stood there for a while lost in thought, and then turned to the artist and said, "What's the story in this picture?"

"O princess," replied the daughter of the prime minister, seizing her chance, "this picture is about something that really happened to the prince of our country. He was out hunting in the forest and he saw this scene in a forest fire, which convinced him of the fickleness of all females and the faithfulness of males. This may not interest you very much, but it concerns us greatly in our country. This incident has brought such a change in the prince's life. Since this happened, he has shunned all women as faithless and refuses to marry anyone. This decision on the part of his son and heir causes our raja great grief and has cast a gloom over the whole court. Nobody knows what to do about it."

"How very strange!" cried the princess, hardly letting the artist finish her story. "Can males then be faithful and females false? I, for one, always believed that males were false and faithless in all of nature. But now I see there are two sides even to that question. After all, I've observed only one instance and made up my mind too quickly. I'll have to rethink the whole question."

"Oh, I'm glad to hear you say so, my princess," said the artist, obviously delighted by this turn, "but how I wish our good prince too would see his mistake as you do yours. But you are not stubborn as he is."

"Someone should point it out to him, I think," said the princess, "and perhaps, like me, he might change his mind. As I have benefitted from an incident in his life, he might profit from one in mine. Please feel free to tell him about my case and see whether it will change his mind."

"Surely I shall, with the greatest pleasure, as soon as I get home," replied the artist, her heart fluttering with joy at this unexpected success.

From that day on, through word of mouth, everyone in the kingdom came to know that the princess had conquered her aversion to marriage and was once again open to offers, and suitors began to crowd the capital. But the princess refused their attentions and seemed displeased with all of them— for a new reason. Her chief pleasure was in looking at the pictures the artist had painted on her new walls and talking to her endlessly about the prince, in whom she had become greatly interested.

The minister's daughter knew what to do. She fanned the flames by telling the princess all sorts of vivid stories about the prince's manliness and virtues. She did it so thoroughly that the princess one day could no longer contain herself and wanted very much to see him. This was the very thing the minister's daughter had hoped for. She readily promised the princess that she would return to her own country and do everything she could to bring the prince back. She would tell him the princess's story and make him eager to see her and talk to her.

Great was the joy of the old prime minister, her father, and the young prince when the minister's daughter returned home and told them everything she had accomplished. The old man hugged her and called her the savior of his life. The young prince loaded her with gifts. The prince didn't waste a day in preparing for his journey. He set out with a grand cavalcade and a magnificent train of followers for the court of the princess's father, and we needn't tell you that the princess accepted him right away as a worthy suitor. The wealth of two kingdoms was poured into the splendor of a gala wedding.

Heron Boy

~ *Tulu* ~ ~

A mother had an only son. When he grew up, they got him married. But there was trouble between husband and wife. The wife wouldn't sleep with her husband, and he wouldn't sleep with her.

One day, he came back home from somewhere and asked his wife to serve him some rice gruel. When she did, he found fault with it and went out to sit by himself. He called for some betel nut. In a huff, she brought it out and slapped it down beside him. As he sat there chewing it, she felt like sitting there next to him and having some too. He gave her some. She took out some betel leaf, but she needed some lime to go with it. She was too shy to ask him for lime. She looked around and saw something that looked like lime oozing down the wall. She wiped it off with her finger, smeared it on the betel leaf, and ate it with the betel nut. Do you know what she ate for lime? The droppings of a paddy heron.

After some days, she felt light-headed, and her stomach was queasy. She was pregnant. Everyone was happy, and they had a grand *bayake* ceremony for her. They gave her all kinds of food to satisfy her *bayake*, or cravings, a blouse, a sari, jewels, and gold. It was really grand. After the *bayake*, the husband and the in-laws sent her to her mother's house, where she gave birth. She gave birth to a heron. She was very much disturbed and said, "Oh God, my brother-in-law's wife gave birth to a baby, my brother's wife gave birth to a baby. But God had to put a heron in my womb!"

Meanwhile they sent word to her husband: "Your wife has given birth." And the mother-in-law came over to see the daughter-in-law and her new baby. When she saw a heron on the mat, she asked, "Where is your baby?"

"Hmm? What, *mami*? You're looking at my baby, there. See?"

"*Ayyo!* That's a bird! After all that, what was born was a heron, a heron that pecks around in the paddy fields? Now what can we do with it? We can't kill it. She went through her pregnancy, she gave birth. Even if the newborn is a heron, we have to take care of the new mother." So she went and got the traditional foods a husband's family provides for a new mother and her child. The young woman ate these. After a month and some days, she went to the temple, as is customary. Ten or fifteen days later, she was brought home for a cradle ceremony. She took the cradle under one arm and the heron under another, and carried them both.

There she stayed, at her husband's house. Some two weeks later, there was a wedding in the village. All her sisters-in-law, the wives of her brothers, went to the wedding. They wouldn't have liked it if she went with this thing. "What should I do?" she thought.

"Why are you so troubled?" said her husband. "That's our fate. God made the child and gave it to us, didn't He? Take it. Let's go. It's time for the wedding."

"Right." So she took the heron and went to the wedding. While she was there with the other neighbors, cooking and cutting up cucumbers, the heron sat next to her. When she put the cucumber slices to one side, he picked out the seeds with his bill and flew to a certain village where there was a big open space. There he planted the seeds and returned home.

Now, the mother didn't know that the heron had gone somewhere and planted those seeds. Sometime later, he went back and pleaded with God to create a big palace for his mother. God appeared before the heron and said He would certainly make a palace for her then and there. And He did. And in a couple of days, it was as if the plants were dancing—the vegetables grew big and ripe.

Then the heron came and said to his mother, "I've made a house for you, Mother. I want you and Father to come with me so I can show you."

"How far is it? You can easily fly there, but how are we to come?" the mother asked.

"I will take you. Father can sit on my right wing and you sit on the left. I'll carry you to the place," the heron said and called his father to go with them.

"But Son, how are we to come?" the father asked, not quite understanding what was happening.

"Don't worry about that, Father. I'll take you. Don't be afraid. Sit on my wing."

"All right." So the mother and the father sat on the wings, father on the right wing and mother on the left. The bird faced north and flew and flew and flew and took them to the house with the vegetable garden.

"This is our house, all for us," he said and showed them around. "See the garden made specially for people who stay in the house," he said, showing his mother the ripe cucumbers and other vegetables. "But Mother, if you give any of the vegetables from this garden to anyone else, I'll have to take my life. It will be the end of me. I'll die. You must not give anything that you see here at your feet to anyone else."

"Yes, child, all right," said the mother.

Then the heron went into the rows of vegetables and hid himself there and waited, thinking, "Let's see who she'll give these to."

About that time, an old woman came bumping along, supporting herself with a stick. She looked at the vegetables in the garden and expressed great pleasure. She spoke to the mother: "*Abba!* whose garden is this, child?"

"It's ours, granny," said the mother.

"How about cutting just one of those cucumbers and giving it to me, child?" asked the old woman.

"Of course," said the mother, and cut one of the cucumbers, which was about this big. "Granny, one thing: my son doesn't like me to give these to anyone. Don't show this to anyone. No one should know. Just take it and go."

"Yes, of course," the old woman said and hid the cucumber in her sari as she carried it away.

But the heron saw it all, even though she hid it in her sari. He saw his mother cut the cucumber and give it to the old woman. At once he flew up and landed at his mother's feet.

"You cut one of my cucumbers. I said you shouldn't give them to anyone. But you did, didn't you? That's the end of me. I'll have to take my life," he said and fell down, rolled over, and died right there at her feet. As the bird stopped breathing, an eighteen-year-old boy appeared in its place and stood in front of her.

The mother exclaimed, "*Ayyo!* Its life is gone. But they decided to give me instead a real flesh-and-blood boy!" and she embraced him.

They are there even now, in that new house, growing vegetables, eating and selling them. That's all there is to it.

The Tiger's Adopted Son
~ *Didayi* ~ ~

An old couple had no children and no land. They were very poor. They went out to the jungle every day, dug roots and tubers, and ate them. They lived that way.

When they were already old, the woman got pregnant. After several months, she gave birth to a child in the tuber patch. She called out to the old man, "Old man, the child is born. What should we do?"

He said, "We have nothing to eat. We have no clothes or anything else. How will we take care of a child?"

She said, "Well, old man, let's leave him here in the tuber patch and go home. Then maybe someone will take care of him."

They agreed and left him in the tuber patch and went home. The child began to cry. A tiger heard the child cry and went to the tuber patch. He picked up the child and took him home. There he fed him and brought him up as his own.

When he grew up, the tiger thought he would go and get a girl for him to marry. He asked the boy, "Do you want me to go and get you a girl?"

The boy said, "As you wish, Father. If you want me to marry, go ahead and find a girl for me."

The tiger went out, waited for a girl to come by, and caught her. On the way back, he couldn't help taking a bite out of her ear. He came home with her and said, "Son, I've brought a girl for you. Go out and take a look at her."

The boy went out and looked. "She's missing part of an ear," he said. He went back to the tiger and said, "Father, I don't want one with half an ear."

The tiger went on bringing back girls in the same way—after biting off a hand, or a nose, or an ear. Finally the boy said, "Father, bring me a good one, a whole one, an undamaged one."

So the tiger went out once more, this time to bring back a whole girl. He grabbed a girl in the middle of her wedding, scaring off the whole wedding party. He brought her back with great care and married her to the boy.

For some time, the boy and the girl lived happily as man and wife. Then one day, the wife was cutting vegetables and cut her hand with the knife. She wiped the blood off with some leaves and threw them away. The tiger smelled those leaves, picked them up, and licking the blood off them, thought, "If their blood is so delicious, how much tastier their meat must be! I'm going to eat them."

Maybe he was thinking all this aloud, or maybe the look in his eyes gave it away, but somehow the boy and the girl realized that he intended to eat them. They ran away that same night. In the morning, the tiger looked, and saw that the children were not there. He searched for them, found their footprints, and went after them.

The boy and the girl, up in a tree, watched silently. As the tiger came after them, the boy slashed at him with a sword and killed him.

Then they went to the girl's village where her parents and brother lived. When his father-in-law and mother-in-law saw them, it made them very happy. They had thought the tiger had taken their daughter and eaten her. The boy and girl stayed and lived there from that day on.

How to Live on Half a Pice

~ *Konkani (from Salsette, Goa)* ~ ~

An old woman had a daughter who was old enough to be married. She was also old enough to help her mother in her daily tasks, but she never did because she was terribly lazy. She lay in bed all morning while her mother got up early and did all the cooking and cleaning. Every morning, her mother would call out to her daughter, "Get up, Bharo, it's morning. The sun has risen and gone as far as the pavilion."

And the daughter would reply, "If the sun has gone to the pavilion, let him. I'll dress my hair without a thread or a comb, and I'll live on one *dambri*. Then she would get up, taking her own sweet time, eat and drink, dress and do her hair.

This went on day after day. One day the king's son happened to pass the old woman's hut. He overheard the old woman say, "Get up, Bharo, it's morning. The sun has gone as far as the pavilion." He also heard Bharo reply, "If the sun has gone as far as the pavilion, let him. I'll dress my hair without a thread or a comb, and I'll live on one *dambri*."

These last words made such an impression on him that he decided to marry Bharo and test her claim that she could live on one little copper coin, the smallest in the realm. He knew it wouldn't be easy to marry a poor woman, he being the prince. So he went and threw himself down in a stall in his father's stables. Everyone in the palace missed him and searched for him everywhere. That evening, the maidservants of the palace came to the stables with bags of gram, chickpeas, to feed the horses. And the prince saw what they did: they ate all the gram and threw the husks to the horses. The prince could not contain his anger. He came out of his hiding-place and said, "Aha! You eat the gram yourselves and throw the husks to the horses. No wonder you're getting fatter and fatter and my horses are getting lean."

The maidservants didn't pay any heed to what the prince said but cried out, "Oh, here you are! Prince, what are you doing here? They are searching the whole country for you, and here you are in the stables."

The prince threatened them with a thrashing if they went and told the king where he was. But the naughty girls didn't care for his threats. They ran to the king, giggling all the way, and asked him, "Your Majesty, shall we tell you one or shall we tell you two?"

The king, anxious about the whereabouts of his missing son, said impatiently, "What do you care? You eat and you cry. I'm thinking of my missing son."

But the maidservants replied, "My lord, if you'll listen, it's good news."

The king said, "You may tell me one or you may tell me two, but whatever it is, say it quickly."

The maidservants told him that they found the prince lying down in the stables when they went to feed the horses. The king at once went to the stables, found the prince, and said to him, "What's the matter with you? Has anyone done anything to hurt you? If anyone has raised his hand against you, I'll cut off his hand. If any one has raised his leg against you, I'll cut off his leg. If anyone has put his evil eye on you, I'll cut out his eye. Just tell me. If you want anything, I'll get it for you."

To which the prince replied, "Nothing is the matter with me. Nobody has lifted his hand or leg against me, or cast the evil eye on me. I want only one thing: I want to marry such and such an old woman's daughter."

"Is that all you want? You'll have your wish. Cheer up, come and eat your dinner."

The prince then left the stables and went with his father, soon himself again. Before he summoned the old woman, the king of course tried to talk the prince out of a possible foolish marriage. He was after all a prince and would one day rule the country; how could he marry a girl who was no better than a beggar? But the prince was stubborn. He even said that he would kill himself if he couldn't marry that girl.

So the king, seeing no way out, sent a messenger to the old woman and summoned her to the palace. She was panic-stricken. She wondered what she had done wrong that the king should summon her. She thought and thought, but she could remember nothing. It was the king's order and she must obey. So she went trembling to the palace. When she bowed low, the king motioned her to a chair, which she modestly refused. She was too poor, had never had a chair, had never sat on one. The king himself held her by the hand and seated her gently on a chair. Then he said, "We want to form an alliance with you. You must give your daughter to our son."

The old woman, when she found her voice, said, "O great raja, you're making fun of me. What's your position and mine? How can it be?"

The king soon convinced her it was no joke and that the prince wanted to marry no one in the world but her daughter Bharo. The old woman could not understand any of this. How can a king ask for a beggar woman's daughter, and that Bharo, too, the lazy good-for-nothing? She said neither yes nor no, but went home, lay down, and covered herself with a quilt. Her daughter Bharo found this quite unusual. Her mother had never taken to her bed like this. So she came to her and asked her if she was not well. The old woman asked her to go away and not bother her. But Bharo insisted on hearing what was the matter, and the old woman finally told her that the king had sent for her and had asked her for her daughter's hand, and she was much troubled, didn't know what to do. Bharo was delighted to hear that the prince had proposed to her, and she roused her mother and told her to go at once to the king and tell him that the proposal was accepted. Unwillingly, the bewildered old woman went back to the king and told him what Bharo had said. The king sent word to the prince, who was happy.

The king made grand preparations for the wedding, and the poor old woman did what little she could do to entertain her poor and low-class relations. But the wedding was a gala affair.

A month or two later, the prince remembered Bharo's saying, "I'll live on a *dambri*." So he wanted to put her to a test at once. He asked his father to build him a ship, as he wanted to trade in foreign lands. The king said there was no need for him to do any business; he was getting old and wanted the prince to take over the reins of the kingdom soon. The prince said he must go at least for a few months and therefore must have a ship. The king yielded and gave orders for a ship to built. He had enough men and enough money. So a ship that would have taken others months to build got completed in days. A captain and a crew of sailors were also employed.

The prince had to buy provisions for the journey. But he bought very little. He asked his wife Bharo to go with him on his voyage. She didn't have a clue as to what was in his mind. She was delighted to go with him anywhere and do anything whatever, for better or worse.

The ship set sail under a good breeze and they sailed for days till they reached a faraway country, where they cast anchor. They stopped there for a day or two. When their provisions were all finished, the prince planned to leave Bharo alone in the ship. He went on land pretending to have some business to do, taking the captain and the crew with him, and disappeared, leaving Bharo alone on the ship. Without her knowledge, he had tied up in her sari half a pice, which was worth no more than three *dambris*.

Then the prince and his crew went home by a land route. A few hours after he had left, Bharo felt hungry. So she went to the ship's storeroom to pick up something to eat, but she found it empty. There was nothing left anywhere in the ship. She had to go without food that day and that night. The next day, when she was wondering what to do, she felt something tied in her sari. She untied the knot and found half a pice, worth three *dambris*. What could she do with half a pice? Just as she was thinking of it, she caught sight of an old fisherman who had come to fish near the ship in his boat. She called out to him and addressed him as "uncle." The old man was surprised to hear someone call him "uncle" from within the ship, and even more surprised to see that it was a young woman who seemed to be quite alone on this big ship. He rowed closer. Bharo threw the half-pice coin to the old man and begged him to get her some parched gram and rice. The old man didn't have the heart to refuse her. He went ashore and bought her half a pice's worth of parched gram and rice, gave it to her, and went about his business. As soon as he was gone, Bharo took the gram and rice and was going to eat it all up eagerly, when, misfortune of misfortunes, it all fell out of her hands into the water. She was about to burst out crying when she saw hundreds of large fish come swimming up and eat all the gram and rice. After eating it, the fish went to the dry shore and threw up heaps and heaps of gold mohurs. The sight of this both amazed and delighted Bharo, who was soon able to collect all the gold coins and fill the ship with them. She starved for another day, but waited for the fisherman to come back to fish. When he did, she gave him one gold mohur, asked him to buy all sorts of food, and gave him another mohur for his trouble. Bharo now had plenty of food and she ate happily all day. The next day, when the old fisherman came back, she went ashore and bought a piece of land with his help. The next day, she bought timber, bricks, stones, and everything one would need to build a large mansion. The old fisherman erected a little hut for her nearby, and she began to supervise the building of a house for herself. With his help, she bought a suit of man's clothes and disguised herself as a man.

In a couple of months, the prince her husband wanted to see how she was faring with her half a pice. So he got himself another ship and came looking for his old ship. When he found it, it was empty. His wife was nowhere to be found. He thought that the poor thing was drowned and dead. Just as he was about to turn back and return to his country, his eye fell on a palatial building on the seashore, nearly finished. He wanted to find out whose it was. He landed and went to the spot, disguised as a workman, and offered his services. The overseer, who was no other than the old fisherman, took him to see Bharo. She was still in a man's disguise and the prince didn't quite know who this person was. But she knew at once who he was, though she didn't let him know. She treated him as a stranger and gave him a job. She didn't have the heart to give him any hard work and so asked him to supervise the building. He was also asked to live at the supposed master's house. When Bharo ordered her servants to serve the prince at her own table, the prince modestly refused to sit and eat with his master. But Bharo insisted on his eating first (as a wife would, according to custom), and this he reluctantly did, a bit nonplussed by the strange ways of this kind master. Soon the house was complete. Bharo then commissioned the old fisherman and the prince to furnish the house. The prince had great taste in furniture, bought the best available, and when it was all arranged under his supervision, the house looked utterly beautiful.

Now Bharo paid all the workmen their wages and discharged them—all except the prince, whom she asked to stay on for a few days more. One day, when they were alone, she asked him to her chamber. Before he came in, she threw off her disguise, put on her best sari and her richest jewels. When the prince came in, he was struck dumb at seeing Bharo, his wife, standing before him. He asked himself, "Am I dreaming? Is this really my wife?" As soon as he could speak, he asked her what all this meant. Bharo then told him how, after he had gone, she had starved for a day, and how she had found the half a pice in her sari without knowing how it got there, how she had given the little coin to the old fisherman and asked him to buy some parched gram and rice, and how just when she was about to eat it, it fell into the water, and how when it fell into the water it was eaten by a large shoal of fish, which soon threw up heaps of gold mohurs on the shore, and how she had collected the gold, and how she had lived comfortably since then and was able to build the large mansion they were now in, and how wonderful his taste was in furnishing it.

Now it was the prince's turn to tell her how he had married her and why, how he had brought her only to leave her alone in that empty ship just to test her. He was now quite happy that she could really do what she had said every morning she would do, that is, "dress her hair without a thread or a comb, and live on one *dambri*."

Then they sold off the mansion, took the cash and the heaps of gold mohurs, and went home, where they lived happily to a ripe old age.

The Magic Bowls

~ *Tamil* ~ ~

A man was poor, and his wife nagged him every day for being such a lazy good-for-nothing. The poor fellow would listen to all her abuse patiently, slip out of the house whenever he could, and stay out till it felt safe to come home.

One day, her anger boiled over. She scraped together whatever stale food remained in her pots, tied it up in a dirty cloth, thrust it into his hand, and sent him packing. "Go somewhere, anywhere, and earn something. And don't you come back till you do!" she said, as she slammed the door.

The man took his bundle of cold rice and trudged out of the village. He walked and walked for miles till he came to place where three roads crossed. A huge banyan tree had grown up there and had lent its shade to weary travelers for many years. The man was tired and his legs ached. He sat down under the tree. He tied his bundle of rice to one of its branches and soon he was fast asleep, his head pillowed on the roots of the banyan.

Now, there were *vanadevatai* living in the banyan tree. These forest spirits sighted the sleeping man below and the bundle of rice on the branch above him. They wanted to taste his dinner. No sooner did they think of it than it was done. What's more, they liked that cold rice very much. They had tasted nectar and all the dishes of heaven, but this was something new. They had never tasted stale rice before. It had a wonderful flavor of its own. What a change from their dull routine of ambrosia and fruit from heaven's trees!

The few handfuls of rice in the poor man's bundle were just enough for a round among the *vanadevatai*. They were pleased and thought they should give their poor sleeping host something in return for the food they had taken away.

When the poor man woke up, he was hungry and looked for his bundle. When he found it, the food was gone. In its place, there were four odd-looking empty bowls. Raging with hunger, he banged the bowls on the ground. At once, several lovely women appeared before him with all sorts of divine dishes in their hands, ready to serve him. He was dumbstruck by the magic of it all, but he was too hungry to be frightened or ask questions. As he fell to, the lovely women served him gently, silently, attended to his slightest gesture, and treated him like a god. Soon he came to believe that he was indeed master of these nymphs. His marvelous dinner over, his heavenly servants disappeared without a trace, leaving the four empty bowls behind them.

Praying gratefully to all the gods, he picked up the empty bowls with great respect. He held them to his bosom and hastened home, big with his story. When she heard it, his wife nearly burst with joy. They placed the magic bowls at the feet of their household gods and looked at them again and again to make sure they were still there. They could not believe their own good fortune. They felt they should use their god-given gift worshipfully, only after offering public prayers to the gods and charity to their neighbors.

Even as the next day dawned, the man was out of the house. He went to every door and invited every family in the village, rich and poor alike. Everyone was skeptical. Some laughed outright. Some thought it was a practical joke, some that the man must be crazy. They quoted a proverb: "The guests of the poor come back home early."

The guests gathered by noon in the small hovel. Many of them had taken the precaution of eating well before they arrived. They came just to see what was happening, and were they surprised!

The poor man and his wife brought forth four odd-looking vessels and very respectfully requested them to bestow upon the guests their gracious gifts. And lo and behold! dozens of lovely women, each lovelier than the next, adorned to the fingertips, rose out of the bowls. In their hands were plates full of the daintiest dishes. Silver platters appeared from nowhere before the bewildered guests, and service began.

As the guests ate, new dishes arrived by the dozen and the heavenly women served them so readily that everyone felt that they forestalled one's slightest wishes. The guests were fed till they were ready to burst. They had trouble getting up and carrying themselves home.

The village buzzed with the news. Everyone talked about it. The poor man, no longer poor, was the rage for months.

Now, there was a rich man in the village who thought no end of himself. He grew envious of the sudden wealth and the growing popularity of his neighbor who till yesterday had been a penniless beggar. He paid a visit to his fellow villager one day and was treated to the miracle of the bowls and the lovely women who rose from them for the mere asking. He quickly made friends with their owner, gave him and his wife gifts, and soon wormed the secret out of them.

"It's so easy," he thought. "There's nothing to it." He hurried home and ordered his best cook to make the most sumptuous dishes at once. Next morning, he traveled in a palanquin, as fast as his bearers could take him, and arrived at the spot where three roads crossed. He carefully arranged a big basket full of the finest dishes that money could command, right under the banyan tree. Then he dismissed his servants till evening, and composed himself as if for sleep. Of course, he wasn't going to sleep. He was too curious to see the forest spirits and what they would do. He lay there for a long time till somehow sleep stole over him. When he woke up, all in a hurry, he saw beside him four odd-looking bowls. And his basket was empty.

He had succeeded. Of course, he had never once doubted he would. After all, he had brought for the spirits in the banyan tree the tastiest, the richest, the most royal of all human dishes. How could they help giving him what he wanted? Here they were, in full view, the magic bowls!

He hurried home, asking his palanquin bearers to go faster. He called his entire household and sent them running with the news and invitations to every family in the village.

People from all corners flocked to his dining hall. Their mouths watered at the memory of the recent banquet. Here was another, and a rich man's, too! Many starved all day to do justice to his hospitality.

The rich man beamed at his guests and motioned them to their seats. Servants brought in the bowls with great ceremony and placed them on a pedestal. His head wrapped in a lace turban, wearing earrings and turquoises, their master stood before the bowls and loudly ordered them to bring forth a divine banquet for everyone assembled.

Hardly had his voice stopped ringing when out came dozens of big burly men. They looked like wrestlers. They had rolls of muscle on their arms, and their looks would have scared the bravest of men. They came out of the bowls and went after the host and his hungry guests. They seized them one by one, whipped out gleaming razors, and with great gusto shaved every head in the hall, shaved them so close that every head was clean and shiny like a bronze bowl. Not a single guest escaped the barbers' banquet, not even the wives. And as the terrified guests crawled out, a muscular fellow at the door held up a large mirror to their faces and forced them to take a good long look at themselves before they left the hall, never to return.

The Four Jogis

~ Santali ~~

Once four jogis, mendicant holy men, were out on a begging expedition and decided to beg from a raja. As they went along they discussed how they should beg of the raja. And while they were discussing it, they saw a field rat and one of them exclaimed, "I know how I shall beg of him. I shall say, 'See, he throws up the earth, scrapety-scrape!'" This did not help the other three, but farther on, some frogs jumped into a pond as they passed by, and one of the others at once said, "I know what I shall say. I shall say, 'Plumpety-plump, down he sat.'" A little later they saw a pig wallowing in the mud, and the third jogi said, "I have it! I shall say, 'Rub away, rub away! Now some more water! Rub away, rub away! I know, my boy, what you are going to do.'" The fourth jogi was still at a loss for what he could say to the raja, but when he came in sight of the raja's city, he exclaimed, "I know what I shall say: 'Highways and byways, what a big city! The bailiff is going his rounds, his rounds.'"

Then they got a man to write down these four forms of address on a sheet of paper and presented it to the raja. The raja took it, read it, but could not make head or tail of it. And when the four jogis saw him looking so puzzled, they were afraid that he would ask them to read it. They took to their heels, for they themselves could not read and were no longer sure what the paper contained.

Now, the raja had a *tehsildar*, a chief officer, who looked after his accounts, and a barber who shaved him every day. That evening after the jogis had run away, the *tehsildar* proposed to the barber that, when shaving the raja the next morning, he should cut the raja's throat and they could then control the kingdom. The barber consented. Not content with this, the *tehsildar* plotted with the palace bailiff that same night to break into the raja's palace and steal his money and jewels. They began to cut a hole through the mud wall of the raja's room, but it so happened that the raja was in it, puzzling over the paper the jogis had put into his hand. He kept reading it over and over again, and just as the *tehsildar* and the bailiff had cut halfway through the wall, they heard the raja saying, "See, he throws up the earth, scrapety-scrape!" At once they concluded that they had been heard and they crouched down. The raja went on: "Plumpety-plump, down he sat." This made them think they had been seen, and the bailiff crept to the door to listen. He heard the raja saying, "Highways and byways, what a big city! The bailiff is going his rounds, his rounds." Then the bailiff felt sure that he had been discovered, and he ran off with the *tehsildar*, without completing their burglary.

The next morning the barber went to shave the raja, and while he was sharpening his razor, the raja began to study the mysterious paper, murmuring, "Rub away, rub away! Now some more water! Rub away, rub away! I know, my boy, what you are going to do!" The barber thought the raja referred to his rubbing the water over his face for shaving, and concluded that the *tehsildar* had revealed the plot. So he threw himself at the raja's feet and confessed everything, swearing that the *tehsildar* and not he was to blame. The raja at once sent for the bailiff to take the *tehsildar* and the barber to prison. When the bailiff came in, he found the raja repeating, "See, he throws up the earth, scrapety-scrape!" He at once concluded that the raja was referring to the burglary, and he fell on his knees and confessed all that had happened. This was news to the raja, and he went and saw the place where the wall had been partly cut through, and then he sent all three guilty men to prison. Then he dispatched messengers to look for the jogis who had been the means of saving his life and property. But the jogis had been so frightened and had run away so far that they were never found.

A Friend in Need

~ *Malayalam* ~ ~

A tortoise in a pond and a fox in a nearby den were good friends.

Once when they were chatting of this and that by the pond, a leopard arrived on the scene. The fox fled in panic. The tortoise, poor thing, couldn't move fast enough to hide or escape. With one leap, the leopard grabbed him with his mouth and settled down under a tree to make a meal of him. But neither his teeth nor his claws could make a dent in the hard shell of the tortoise.

The fox was watching the leopard's struggles from his den and thought of a way to save the tortoise. So he came out, approached the leopard, all courtesy and innocence, and said, "I know an easy way to crack the shell of that tortoise. Just throw him into the water. He will soak in it, and the water will soften the shell in a few minutes. Try it."

The foolish leopard said, "Never thought of it. What a good idea!" and threw the tortoise into the pond. What more could the tortoise have wished for?

Winning a Princess

~ *Tulu* ~ ~

The king of a certain country had three sons. All three were very well educated in the martial arts. One day, an invitation came from the north that there would be a contest in string games and ball games. The youngest prince set out to play. His brothers stopped him. They said, "Don't try to play the string game and break your arms. Don't try to play the ball game and break your legs. They are dangerous. Don't go." But the youngest prince didn't listen. He went to the north. He entered the contests, won in every one of them, and returned with prizes and gold.

Six months later, there was another contest for people who could walk a mile on the ocean. The youngest prince got ready to go. The older brothers stopped him. "Don't try to walk on the ocean and drown in it," they said. But he didn't listen. He went and entered the contest. He walked six paces beyond the required mile. He won the contest and returned with diamond medallions.

Six months later, everyone was stirred up by another announcement. In the capital city of Ramarajya, there was a princess named Kamasandage. Every suitor who tried to win her had failed and was now drawing water for her gardens. Not one had succeeded. When he heard of it, the youngest prince got ready to go and try his hand at winning this impossible princess. The older brothers stopped him. "I'm older than you are. I should be getting married before you. So I'm going," said the eldest brother. The youngest said nothing.

The oldest brother set out for Ramarajya and arrived at Kamasandage's palace. As required, he poured gold into the gold bin, pearls into the pearl bin, coins into the coin bin. He washed his hands and feet at the door. When he went in, the servants of the palace brought him betel leaves to chew. "After you've chewed the betel, go into the hall outside the kitchen and sit on the couch there," said the servants. When the prince did as he was told, the doors closed behind him. As he sat on the couch, he felt drowsy. As he dozed off, four dolls came at him from the four corners of the room and began to slap him left and right on the cheeks. The prince couldn't bear this onslaught.

He broke through the closed door and began to run. Kamasandage's servants caught him, shaved his head, and set him to work in the princess's garden drawing water for her plants.

Six months passed. The first prince did not return. The second prince said, "Let me go and see what's happened to my brother," and he started out for Kamasandage's capital city.

The second brother didn't fare any better and suffered exactly the same fate as the first one. Another six months passed. Neither of the two brothers had returned. So the youngest said, "Let me go see what's happening," and he mounted his horse and rode off.

As the youngest prince was riding through a field, he heard groans and cries from a deep pit by the wayside. "Help me, save me!" cried a strange voice. A gang of cowherd boys had overpowered a demon and thrown him into the pit, which was so deep he couldn't get out. The young prince went to the edge of the pit and said to the demon, "If I help you to get out and save you, you'll surely kill me and eat me up. So I don't think I should do anything about it." The demon cried out in a panic, "No! No! Don't go away. If you save me, I'll help you in all sorts of ways. Anyhow, there are sixteen demons waiting out there on the way. They won't let you go alive. You'll need me." The prince undid his turban into yards and yards of cloth and let it down into the pit. The demon grabbed hold of one end and clambered up to safety.

As soon as he reached level ground the demon cried, "I want water to drink. I'm thirsty." The prince said, "Where can I get you water in this dry field?" The demon suggested, "Tie up your horse to a hair on my leg and you sit on my shoulders while I walk. If you see any water in the distance, tell me." The prince did as he was told, and they moved at incredible speed and covered great distances. The demon asked, "Do you see any water any-where?" "No," said the prince, "I can see only a wisp of smoke." The demon walked some more and asked again, "Do you see any water?" The prince now said, "Yes, I see a pond in the distance." When they came closer, it was really the ocean. The demon set the prince down and said, "Now, you must get me a cartload of flat rice and a cartload of brown sugar." The prince rode down to the nearest market and fetched him a cartload of flat rice and a cartload of sugar. The demon sat on the sand of the seashore, mixed the rice and sugar, and made a meal of it. Then he drank half the ocean and felt happy. His hunger and thirst were quelled.

Then the demon said, "If I come with you as I am, everyone will be scared. No one will come anywhere near you. Let me take the shape of a fly and sit on your shoulder. You mount your horse and ride into town." The prince mounted his horse, and the demon sat on his shoulder as a fly. On the way, the prince bought a bunch of bananas. When he came to a house, he found a number of children playing. He called them and gave each one a banana and asked them, "Whose house is this?" They said, "This is the house where the palace carpenter lives." "Then ask him to come here. I want to see him," said the prince. They said, "He can't come. He is blind." "Then call his wife," said the prince. They ran in and told the wife about the stranger at the door. She came out with her husband, the blind carpenter. He had made the four dolls that guarded Kamasandage's room. After he had made those special dolls for her, she didn't want him to make any more like them and sell them to others, so she had had his eyes plucked out and was maintaining him with a generous pension. The prince asked the carpenter, "How does one get into the palace of Kamasandage?" The carpenter said, "I won't tell you." The prince gave him a thousand rupees to loosen his tongue. "This is nothing. This won't buy me betel leaves for a month," said the carpenter. The prince gave him two thousand rupees. The carpenter said, "This is a pittance. It won't buy me coffee and snacks for a month." The prince gave him five thousand, but the carpenter said, "This won't last me one trip to the market."

When he heard this, the demon resumed his own shape, leaped from the prince's shoulder, and grabbed the carpenter by the neck. The carpenter cried out in pain, "Let me go, let me go! I'll tell you whatever you want." When the demon loosened his grip, the carpenter told the prince the secret of entering Kamasandage's palace. The prince moved on. On the way to the palace, he bought four oranges, a buffalo calf, a piece of coconut, a hen's egg, and a pair of scissors.

At the entrance of Kamasandage's palace, there stood a bin for gold. He poured gold into the gold bin. Then he poured pearls into the pearl bin, coins into the coin bin. Then he washed his hands and feet, went in, and was received by a maid who brought him betel leaves to chew. She said, "After you've chewed the betel, go into the hall next to the kitchen and you can rest on the couch." The prince sat on the couch and placed the four oranges on his head. Hardly had he arranged them when four dolls came at him from the four corners of the room. When they saw the oranges on the prince's head, they picked one each, went back to the corners, and began to eat them.

After they had finished eating, they came back to the prince, affectionately looked for lice in his hair, and put him to sleep.

When it dawned the next day, the maid came in and took him to the next room. She said, "There are seven doors you have to cross to get to Kamasandage's inner quarters. I'll open three of them for you, but you must open the other four yourself." She then opened three of the doors and led him through them.

When the prince opened the fourth door, a huge leopard rushed out to devour him. The prince showed the beast his buffalo calf. The leopard grabbed

the calf with its teeth and took it away to make a meal of it. When the prince opened the fifth door, a huge dog leaped at him with its mouth open. He threw it a big piece of coconut, which the dog caught in its mouth and left the room. When the prince opened the sixth door, he was faced with a hissing cobra, to which he gave an egg. The cobra left him alone. When he opened the seventh door, a big pair of scissors came towards him. The prince put his pair of scissors between the blades of the big one and they fell to the floor together. Relieved, he went into the inner chamber and took a seat.

When no one came to talk to him, he said in a loud voice, "I've heard that Kamasandage is a great princess. Her fame is known to all three worlds. But here in her chamber, there's not a soul to greet a guest or offer him a piece of betel leaf." At once, a maidservant disguised as Kamasandage came in with a plate full of betel leaves and betel nut, gave it to him, and sat down next to him. The prince said, "Where is the spittoon?" The woman got up at once, ran in, and brought him the spittoon. He knew then this wasn't the princess, so he slapped her three times and sent her out.

After a little while, he said again, "Kamasandage's fame is far-flung in all three worlds, but here in her palace there's not a soul to greet a guest." At once, another maidservant dressed as Kamasandage came in and sat next to him. But before she could open her mouth, he said, "This is supposed to be the great Kamasandage's palace. But there seems to be no one here even to sweep the dust on the floor." The woman quickly got up, fetched a broom, swept the floor, put the broom back in its corner, and sat down again next to the prince. He knew then this was not Kamasandage but some maidservant. He slapped her three times and sent her out.

After she had left, Kamasandage's mother came and said to him, "In the next room, there are two beds. They are three yards apart. If you're as much of a hero as you pretend to be, you must bring them close together without ever touching them." Then she left him alone. The prince entered the bedroom. There were two beds there, three yards apart, with a curtain between them. He went and lay down on one of them. On the other lay none other than Princess Kamasandage.

The prince said, "Instead of lying here like a dummy, I could tell a story, if only there was someone to say 'Hmm, hmm.' Who's here to listen to a story?" The demon, who was now a fly perched on the curtain, said, "I'll listen. I'll say 'Hmm, hmm.'" The prince began to tell a story.

"Once a potter, a weaver, a goldsmith, and a Brahman went together on a pilgrimage. At night, they each took turns to stay awake for two hours while the others slept and to keep watch over their belongings. One night while he was keeping vigil, the potter made out of clay a lovely female doll. At the end of his watch, he woke up the weaver and went to sleep. The weaver clothed the doll in a colorful sari and put a blouse on it. When he was ready to sleep, he woke up the goldsmith, who put a wedding *tali* and earrings on the doll. It was the Brahman's turn next to keep watch. He used his powers and breathed life into the doll, by which time it was morning. They all woke up, and each wanted the newly created girl for himself. They got into a big fight over the question of whom she belonged to. Now tell me, O curtain, who is the rightful husband for this girl?"

The curtain said, "Of course the Brahman should marry her." The prince said, "But the Brahman gave her life. He is like a god." Kamasandage was furious. She said, "Can't you see that it's the goldsmith who is the rightful husband?" And in her fury, she tore the curtain. The force with which she tore it caused her bed to move a whole yard towards the other one.

Now the prince said again, "Instead of lying here doing nothing, I could tell another story—if only I had a listener to say 'Hmm, hmm.'" "I'll listen and I'll say 'Hmm, hmm,'" said the demon in the guise of a fly as he moved to perch on Kamasandage's blouse. The prince began to tell a story.

"A king had a daughter and a son. When the daughter was ready to get married, the king found a suitable bridegroom and arranged a wedding. He set the eighteenth day of the next month as the wedding day. The mother of the girl and her brother didn't know anything about this. So the brother and the mother both found her suitable bridegrooms also and set the same date for the wedding. None of them knew what the others were doing.

"The eighteenth day of the next month arrived. Elaborate arrangements were made. Canopies as large as a rice field were put up. Sugarcane plants were tied to the pillars as auspicious markers. Coconut fronds were woven into thatches and formed the warp and woof of the canopies. The walls of the city were plastered and whitewashed till they looked as good as new. Town criers were sent out to announce the wedding all over the city. All the relatives were invited. All the kith and kin came to the wedding. Now three bridegrooms came from three directions with their parties towards the wedding canopy. The girl heard about this confusion. She knew that it couldn't easily be sorted out and would lead to serious quarrels between her three dear kin: her father, mother, and brother. She wanted to save herself the shame and them the fights. So she asked the servants to build a fire with the excuse that everyone would need more light at night. When the firewood was piled high and properly lit, she jumped into the fire and killed herself. The three bridegrooms rushed to the spot. One of them threw himself in the fire and killed himself too. Another buried his head in his hands and sat on the nearby well. The third one ran out to find if some pundit would know how to revive her.

"When he found the pundit, he was about to cook a meal for himself. When the bridegroom came running to him, he asked him to sit down while he cooked for both of them. The bridegroom didn't want any food, but the pundit wouldn't listen. He looked around for something to cook. Just then a young child came crawling towards him. He picked up the child, washed it, cut it up, and cooked its flesh into a terrific curry. Then he threw the bones in a corner. When he invited the bridegroom for the meal, he was horrified and refused. He said he wouldn't be able to eat anything till the child was somehow brought back to life. 'Oh, I was going to do that,' said the pundit, and he went into his back yard, brought back a handful of green leaves, and crushed the juice onto the bones of the slaughtered child. At once the child sat up and began to crawl about as if nothing had ever happened to it. The bridegroom got up, plucked the green leaves from the pundit's hand, rushed back, and squeezed the sap of the leaves onto the dead princess's bones. The princess and the first bridegroom who had perished in the fire came alive and stood up.

"Now," asked the prince, addressing the blouse, "tell me which of these three young men should rightfully marry the princess?"

"The man who brought the leaves and revived her," said the blouse.

"But the man who gave her life is like her father," said the prince.

"Then it is the man who sat on the well," said the blouse.

Kamasandage said impatiently, "Can't you see that the man who jumped into the fire and perished with her is the rightful husband?" In her fury, she tore the blouse in two. She tore it with such force that her bedstead moved a whole yard towards the other one.

The prince said once again, "Instead of sitting here with nothing to do, we could have still another story—if only there was someone to say 'Hmm, hmm.'"

"I will listen and say 'Hmm, hmm,'" said the demon, who now sat on Kamasandage's sari in the form of a fly. The prince began a third story.

"A king's daughter finished her studies with a teacher and was about to leave school. The teacher said, 'What are you going to give me as a parting gift?' She said, 'Anything you ask for.' The teacher made her promise that she would sleep with him on her wedding night. Soon after that, she was betrothed to a nice young man, and on her wedding night she remembered her promise to her teacher. When she told her newlywed husband, he said, 'A promise is a promise. You must go to your teacher.' So she set out in the night for her teacher's house. On her way, she met a robber, who stopped her and asked her to give him all the jewels she was wearing. She said, 'I'm in a hurry. I have to go see someone. If you'll please wait till I get back, I'll give you everything.' The robber trusted her and said, 'All right, I'll wait.' A little later, she ran into a hungry tiger, which wanted to eat her. She said, 'I'm in a hurry. I must go see someone. Can you wait till I get back? Then you can eat me whole.' The tiger, though hungry, said, 'All right, I'll wait for you to return.'

The next thing she met was a snake, which wanted to bite her. She said to the snake, 'I'm in a hurry. I have to go see someone. Can you wait till I return?' The snake agreed. The princess reached her teacher's house and knocked on his door. The teacher opened the door reluctantly, for it was late at night and there were robbers about. He was surprised when he saw the princess and found out why she had come all that way to see him on her wedding night. He said, 'How can I do something like that even if I did ask you to sleep with me then? You have my blessings. Go back to your husband.' She touched his feet, refused all escort, and took the same road back that she had come by. She went straight to the snake and said, 'You can bite me now.' The snake said, 'You brought me luck. Because I looked at your face, I happened upon the eggs of wild hens. I'm full.' Then she looked for the tiger and asked it to devour her. But it said, 'You brought me luck. After meeting you, I found a buffalo calf. I had a terrific meal. You can go now." When she next met the robber and began to take off all her ornaments, he said, 'Wait. After I met you, I ran into a party of rich merchants. You brought me luck. You go home now.' And she returned home to her waiting bridegroom."

"Now, tell me," said the prince, "who is the noblest of them all? The teacher? the husband? the robber? the snake? or the tiger?"

The demon fly on Kamasandage's sari said, "Of course, the teacher." Kamasandage was furious. She shouted, "Can't you see how noble the husband is? He is the best of them!" While she said it, she also tore her sari in her rage. She tore it with such vehemence that her bedstead moved a whole yard and joined the other one.

The prince at once got up and left the room. She called him and sent maids after him, but he wouldn't even turn around and look at her. He vanished into the night. Now Kamasandage became obsessed with thoughts of the prince. She searched for him with her servants all over the place and then went journeying through the kingdom.

One day, when she came to a field planted with sesame, she saw a man guarding the sesame and she had a feeling this was the prince. In order to test him, she gave him a copper and asked him, "Give me a pennyworth of sesame, sesame leaf, sesame twigs, and sesame cake." The man at once plucked a sesame plant and gave it to her. She knew then that this was none other than the prince. She begged him to return with her to her palace. He flew into a rage and slapped her three times. But when she refused to leave him alone, he laughed and went with Kamasandage to her capital city of Ramarajya. Before he did anything else, he released all the captive princes from her garden. Then he married her and ruled the kingdom in great style.

Crossing a River, Losing a Self

~ Kannada; Tamil; Telugu ~ ~

A foolish guru and his twelve idiot disciples were making a pilgrimage, when they had to cross a river. It was evening. They looked at the river, and the guru said, "Stand back. This river is treacherous. She has swallowed up many people. You have to be careful. We must wait till she's asleep." Then he called one of his disciples and asked him to find out if the river was awake or asleep. They had lit a campfire, and the disciple took one of the burning logs to the river, stood a few feet away, and slowly dipped it in the river. At once, the water hissed and smoked. He took fright and fled the riverbank, came panting to his guru, and said, "Swami, this is no time to cross the river. She is fully awake. As soon as I touched her, she hissed like a venomous snake and smoldered with hate. She was about to gobble me up. I somehow escaped and ran for my life." The guru said, "I'm glad you got away. Let's wait till she's asleep. We'll rest in that grove till then."

While they were resting, another disciple said, "My grandfather was a great merchant. He was once crossing this river with his two donkeys laden with sacks of salt. And do you know what this terrible river did? It was summer, and they bathed in the river and washed their donkeys. But when they reached the other shore, they found that the river had eaten up all the salt! Not a stitch was loose and there was not a hole in the sacks, but this rogue of a river somehow had looted every grain of salt. Still, my grandfather was happy that she spared his life and took only his salt. This river is a rogue and a scoundrel. I'm glad we're a mile away from her."

Then they slept awhile and woke up early in the morning, and the guru said, "Try again and see if she is still asleep." The disciple took the same log and carefully dipped it again, and the river didn't hiss this time nor did it smolder. He ran back with the good news and said, "This is the time to cross. Hurry up and get moving, and don't make any noise. The river is fast asleep." So they held each other's hands and cautiously put their feet in the water and, step over step, they crossed the river, trembling with fear lest it should wake up and devour them.

When they had crossed to the other bank, they were about to congratulate themselves when one of them said, "Did all of us cross without any danger? Are we sure? This is a most treacherous river. Let's count how many we are."

And he counted everyone, but forgot to count himself. He began to wail: "Look, we are only twelve! The river has swallowed up one of us." The guru consoled him and asked another man to count. He also counted everyone but himself. Still another counted and came up short. Finally, the guru himself counted each one carefully on his fingers, but he too forgot to count himself and said sadly, "It's true, we're only twelve. One of us is gone!"

They all began to cry and howl over the loss of their friend, though they couldn't tell who was the lost one. And they began to berate the river, calling it every kind of name: "O you rogue, you scoundrel, you murderer of innocents, what have you done? You've eaten our brother and tricked us most cruelly! May you dry up, may you be filled with pits!"

While they were railing and mourning thus, a passer-by asked them why they were in so much distress. They told him how they had lost a man to the river, and count as they would, over and over, they came up with only twelve.

The man saw what the problem was and said, "I'm glad I came this way. I know the arts of magic and know how to bring back the lost man in two minutes. But it will cost you something." At once the guru said, "You are really a godsend. If you'll only bring back our disciple, we'll give you whatever we have." Then they took out all their travel money from the knots in their dhotis and gave it to him.

He took the money and sent them running to get a basketful of cow dung. At once the disciples scurried here and there in town, gathered up the dung, and brought it back. The man asked them to make a long flat line of cow dung, and made them stand in a row in front of it. Then he made them bend down and press their noses in the dung.

"Now," he said, "count the number of dents you've made in the cow dung and tell me how many you are."

They scrambled up and each of them counted, and they all found exactly thirteen nose-marks in the soft cow dung. They were amazed, jumped with joy, and said, "We're thirteen again! All of us are here! One of us was lost and found again, thanks to this magician!"

Prince Sabar

~ Gujerati ~ ~

A great sultan had seven daughters. Though he was very fond of them all, his favorite was the youngest. Naturally, the other six were jealous and hated her.

One day the sultan was in a humorous mood. He summoned his seven daughters to his room and asked them this rather queer question: "Tell me, what's the cause of all your prosperity and happiness? Is it your own kismet or mine? Be honest and tell me exactly what you think."

Without a moment's thought, six of the girls cried out at once, "Of course, Father, there's no doubt that it's your good stars that keep us all happy."

The sultan was pleased, but he was surprised to see that his youngest and best-loved daughter did not join this chorus of voices. She was silent. She even seemed embarrassed when her sisters spoke so loudly. She seemed to have something in her mind which she didn't dare utter.

The sultan was a bit put out by his youngest daughter's silence. "What is it?" he said, raising his voice. "Why are you silent? Surely you don't disagree with your sisters, do you?"

"I'm sorry, Father, I do," she said, with some difficulty. "I don't think your destiny can guide ours. We each have our own separate kismet which brings us good and evil. I'm your daughter and a princess only because of my own good star."

"Oh indeed!" shouted the sultan. "So you owe all your happiness to your own good star? Is this the way you return all the love I've showered on you?

You ungrateful creature, we shall see how your kismet takes care of you from now on." Then he called his guards and said, "Drive this girl away from my palace and never let me see her face again!"

The girl walked out on her own, taking nothing but the clothes she was wearing. The guards followed her, and left her when she reached the outskirts of the town.

Some time after this the sultan had to visit a distant country. He got a beautiful ship ready, and his astrologers found an auspicious day for his journey. On that day, he took leave of all his friends and relatives and his subjects. As he was saying farewell to his daughters, he asked each of them to name something that she would have him bring back from his travels. Each girl named something she would most like to have, and the sultan embarked in his ship with his courtiers and servants to the sound of music.

The sailors unfurled the sails and raised the anchor. The wind was most favorable. But to their surprise the ship stood stock-still, like an obstinate horse. They spent some time trying to find out what was stopping its movement, but everything inside and outside the ship was in fine condition, to a pin, as it should be. The sultan sent for the cleverest astrologers in the city, and they, after much thought and calculation, told him that the ship did not move only because the sultan had neglected to ask one of his nearest of kin what she wanted as a gift. The sultan at once thought of his youngest daughter. He flew into a rage that such a worthless creature should be the cause for this delay. Nevertheless, he dispatched messengers to find the poor girl and ask her what she would have her father bring back from the foreign country.

After much fruitless searching, one of the messengers found her at last in a jungle. She was living as an ascetic devoted to the service of Allah, under the shade of a large tree. When he approached her, she was in the middle of a prayer. He called out to her and somewhat rudely asked her what gift she wanted the king to bring her.

The princess gave him no reply, as she didn't want to interrupt her prayer, but merely said, "*Sabar*," which means "Wait." The messenger, who was in a hurry, took that as an answer and left her at once. He knew the sultan was impatient and the ship was waiting. He hurried to his master and told him that the princess had asked for a thing called "sabar."

"Just like her," growled the sultan. "Sabar! What can the stupid girl mean by it? Just like her to send me such an impudent reply. She'll get what she deserves."

As he was speaking these words, the ship began to move. After that, it sailed smoothly and soon reached its destination.

The sultan landed with all his followers in the new country, stayed there for a few days, and enjoyed himself. Before he returned, he bought every little thing that his six daughters had asked for and stored them all safely in his ship. But no one could find what his youngest daughter had asked for. Wherever they went, they met with the same reply—there was no such thing as "sabar" anywhere on earth. So the sultan said there was no use wasting more time in search of something stupid like that, and they all went on board without it.

But when the anchor was raised and the sails unfurled, the ship wouldn't move. It again stood firm as a rock. The sultan knew this time what the reason was. He flew into a rage again, and sent his servants on shore to ask every passer-by in the streets whether he or she knew where they could buy the mysterious thing called "sabar." The servants wandered all over the city for a whole day in search of this rare thing, and soon people were laughing at them. They were all tired and were about to give it up, at least for the day, when a poor old woman happened to pass by. They put to her, for the last time, the same question they had asked thousands that day. And she replied, "Sabar! Oh yes, I know what that is. It is a stone and I have it in my yard. It has been there ever since I was born, and we've always called it the Sabar Stone. What will you pay for it?"

The servants were so glad their search had come to an end that they said, "Come, let's go see it. We'll give you a hundred pieces of gold for it."

The old woman was more than happy to get so much gold for a worthless stone. She took them readily to her hut and showed them a big rough stone, half-buried in the ground. They gave her the gold, dug up the stone, and carried it back to the ship. As soon as it was inside the ship, it began to sail away, and the sultan reached home a few days later.

A couple of days after his arrival, he sent his daughter the stone by the same messenger who had gone to her earlier. When she saw her father's servant approach her with a heavy burden on his head, she thought her father's heart had softened towards her and that he had now sent her a big present to ask her to come home. But to her grief, the man threw down a huge rough stone at her feet and said gruffly, "Here's the thing, the sabar you asked for. The sultan brought your sisters the best diamonds and rubies he could find. Surely your star must be a very bright one: he has sent you a rough black

stone. Keep it safe, my lady. You may be able to wash your clothes on it."
So saying, he walked away.

The poor girl was hurt by these taunting words. She cried for a while, but as soon as she recovered from her crying fit, she rolled the stone into a corner. She decided to put it to the very use her father's servant had mockingly suggested.

She washed the stone clean and day after day washed her clothes on it. As she scrubbed and rubbed the clothes that had begun to look like rags, she thought of her former life as a princess and wept.

After a few days of this scrubbing, she noticed that the stone was gradually wearing away and getting thinner and thinner. The stone is soft stone, she thought, and forgot about it. But one day, its surface suddenly broke under her hand, and to her great surprise she saw a beautiful fan lying neatly folded in a cavity inside it. She pulled out the fan at once, and not having had any such luxury for a long time, she happily unfolded it and began to fan herself—when, presto! a very handsome, tall, and sprightly young prince appeared before her and seemed to wait for her commands! Confused by this sight, she dropped the fan, and was about to run when the prince caught her by the hand. He tried to calm her by telling her that the fan had the power of summoning him and that his name was Prince Sabar. She had only to wave the fan the way she did, and he would be summoned from wherever he was. However, if she waved it in the opposite way, it would make him return to his father's kingdom at once. The princess was astonished by all this. She picked up the fan and playfully gave it a shake or two, and the prince vanished from her sight. Then, in a flurry of anxiety, she waved it again the right way and brought him back.

They soon grew fond of each other. She carefully put away the fan and kept him close to her. In time, the prince had a large palace built for her and they happily lived together in great comfort. Whenever Prince Sabar wanted to see his parents or his people, he would ask her to wave her fan the opposite way, and he would be immediately transported to his old city. Otherwise, Prince Sabar never left her side.

This happy change in her fortunes was somehow reported to the sultan and his six daughters. The sisters burned with jealousy and the sultan was so mortified that he couldn't even stand anyone mentioning the youngest daughter in his hearing. One day, the six girls paid a visit to their sister, without asking the sultan's permission. She welcomed them. She was very happy to see them and pressed them to stay. But they left very soon, promising to return another day.

After they were gone, Prince Sabar was not very happy about his wife admitting these sisters to her new home. He had heard all about the way her father had treated her and about their jealous ways. He was afraid they might, in their jealousy, do her some harm or somehow try to put an end to her happiness. But the princess was innocent and trustful. She eagerly looked forward to her sisters' visits.

One evening, the prince felt like visiting his parents. The princess waved her fan and away he went. When he was gone, she felt terribly lonely and was about to summon him back when, to her joy, her sisters came to see her. They stayed in her palace till late at night.

She was very happy to see them and was in high spirits. But her sisters didn't feel so happy. Not only did they feel very jealous of her, but they had come prepared to do something that would seriously hurt and maybe even kill Prince Sabar. So while some of them engaged their unsuspecting sister in conversation, the others quietly sneaked into Prince Sabar's bedroom, pulled back the bed sheet, and spread upon the mattress a lot of powdered glass mixed with a particularly malignant poison. Then they spread the sheet over it, got out of the room quickly, and rejoined their sisters, looking more innocent than ever.

Late that night, the six wicked princesses left their sister's palace and went home to their own.

As soon as they were gone, the princess waved her fan and got back her beloved Prince Sabar. It was late. He was tired and sleepy, so he went at once to bed, while the princess stayed behind to say her prayers as she did every night. All at once, she heard Prince Sabar scream, "Help! Oh, help me! I'm pierced on all sides with something, I don't know what! I'm sure it's the work of those wicked sisters of yours. I told you not to let them visit you, but you wouldn't listen. Now I'll soon be dead and you can have all you want of their company. For heaven's sake, wave your fan, and let me go back to my parents."

The princess was bewildered. When she ran to him, she found him covered with powdered glass. He was bleeding all over and was turning a strange blue. She had him removed quickly to another bed and began to pick out the glass splinters. But he roared with pain and cried that he would not stay with her any longer. He forced her to wave her fan, much against her own wishes, and transport him to his own country.

Now the princess was in shock. She wept. She tore her hair and waved her fan again and again to make him come back to her, but he did not come. She cursed herself for trusting her sisters and wept to think that maybe the prince did not come to her because he was already dead.

After a sleepless night, she rose early and disguised herself as a wandering vendor of drugs, the kind who goes through the jungles collecting roots and herbs. Then she left the palace to go in search of her lost lover.

She didn't know where he came from. She wandered from jungle to jungle without finding a trace of Prince Sabar. After many days of this fruitless wandering, she felt so tired and sick that she thought she would die.

One day, when she was resting under some trees on the bank of a river, she looked up and saw a pair of songbirds sitting in the branches. They were, to her surprise, talking like human beings. One of them said, "Oh, did you hear of poor Prince Sabar! He is suffering terribly from powdered glass and poison in his flesh. I wish somebody knew about the healing properties of my excrement. If someone were to apply it all over his body, all the pieces of poisoned glass would come out of his flesh. If it was applied a second time, it would heal all his wounds and make him whole again, with not a scar on his skin."

"Oh, that is all very well, but even if someone were to collect your excrement, how could he cross this great river and go to the other side, where Prince Sabar's palace is?" asked the other bird.

"Easy enough," said the first. "He has only to tear off some of the bark of this very tree we are perching on and make it into a pair of sandals for his feet. Then he would be able to walk on water and cross this river as safely as if it were a road. We can't do it ourselves. I only wish some human being could hear what I'm saying."

After this conversation, the birds flew away. The princess took heart from what she had heard. She now knew what she could do. She got up at once, tore off a long piece of the tree's bark with a knife, fashioned a rough pair of sandals, and tied them to her feet with some fiber. Then she collected as much of the bird's excrement as she could carry in her bag. Swinging it over her shoulders, she entered the rushing river with all sorts of misgivings. As she put out one foot and then another and hesitated whether to go on or withdraw, she suddenly found herself gliding smoothly over the surface of the swiftly flowing water. Before she knew it, she was on the other side of the river and found herself in a strange country.

She had dressed and equipped herself like a *vaid*, an itinerant doctor, so a large crowd soon gathered around her. With a little questioning, she soon

got them to talk about Prince Sabar's condition. They told her the most skillful doctors had been attending him, but he was not any better. He was in great pain, and his family had begun to despair. His father had issued a proclamation calling upon physicians from far and wide to come and try their skill on his dying son.

When she heard this, the princess walked quickly to the palace and sent word that she had the remedies that would cure the prince. She was quickly led to the room where her long-lost lover lay in great pain. He had grown thin and the light in his eyes was dim. She put on a brave face and ordered the servants to bring her a soft white sheet. She laid it on the floor, spread some of the bird's excrement evenly on it, and wrapped it all around the prince's body. Then she put a pillow under his head and stroked him gently till he fell asleep. His parents were surprised and delighted, for the prince had not slept for days.

The princess sat by his bedside and watched him sleep. When he opened his eyes, the look of acute suffering was gone. Months of pain seemed to have been smoothed away. He appeared calm and refreshed.

The princess then removed the sheet from his body. Everyone was shocked to see it covered with hundreds of glass splinters and lots of foul matter. The skin still had a scratched and wounded look. So the princess (to everyone's disgust) applied the excrement once more, and in a few hours the prince was well enough to get up and walk about.

The parents were overjoyed at this miraculous cure. The princess was inwardly beside herself with joy, but she had to pretend and wear a disinterested, clinical look.

The prince's father, the old king, took her of course for a wandering *vaid*. He offered her as much gold as she wanted, but she refused to take anything. Then he offered gifts of land, a house, and other things that would make her rich, but the princess refused them all. She said she accepted nothing for her services, but she would like mementos—the ring from the prince's finger, the dagger he usually wore at his side, and the silk handkerchief he had in his hand. The prince at once gave her the three things she asked for. She put them in her bag and said she was content with what she had got. Then she left the palace.

The miraculous sandals helped her to ford the river, and after a long journey by land she arrived at her own palace. She threw off her disguise, decked herself in her most beautiful clothes, and waved the magic fan to summon the prince to her.

This time he obeyed the fan's summons and came to her. But he was still angry. Not even looking at her, he said, "What do you want of me now? Surely your dear sisters' company ought to be enough for you!"

But the princess pretended not to understand him and said, "Tell me, my dear, tell me everything that happened to you after you forced me to send you away that day. I've been terribly unhappy since then, and none of my sisters have visited me. I decided to have nothing to do with them after what they did to you. I'll never see them again."

This pacified the prince and he told her in detail the story of his illness, how he had suffered the most intense agony for months, and how when he felt close to death a wandering *vaid* had appeared from nowhere and had cured him with foul-smelling excrement. He had succeeded where none of the great doctors had. "I'd give almost anything," he said warmly, "to see that man once more and thank him properly for everything he did for me. He was so gentle, and he had magic in his hands. He completely won my heart with the way he comforted and cured me. But he seemed to have come only to take care of me. And he would accept nothing but my ring, my dagger, and my handkerchief."

After some teasing, the princess slyly produced one by one the ring, the dagger, and the handkerchief, and asked the prince, "Are these the three things you gave the *vaid* who cured you, my love?"

The prince recognized them at once and asked her where she got them and whether she knew the *vaid*. She said, "Of course, I know him very well." Then she showed him the *vaid*'s disguise, the sandals and other things, and told him her side of the story—about her search, the birds on the tree, the sandals that helped her cross the river, and the bird's excrement that helped her cure him.

The prince of course could not believe his ears, but his joy knew no bounds to learn that it was to his own sweet princess that he owed his life. He hugged her and kissed her and thanked her for everything she had undergone for his sake.

A few days later he took her to his native country and introduced her to his parents as the wandering *vaid* who had given him back his life and them their only son. They were happy to find that the so-called *vaid* was none other than a princess who loved their son. At once, they began to make grand preparations for their wedding. The old king sent invitations to all the neighboring kings and chieftains. Among those who accepted the invitation was, of course, the father of the princess. The sultan had been specially invited at Prince Sabar's request.

After the wedding, Prince Sabar's father held a grand *durbar* at which he introduced all the royal guests to the newlyweds. When the sultan's turn came, he was astonished to see that the bride was his own daughter whom he had banished for being ungrateful. The princess fell at his feet and asked him to forgive her. She also hoped she had proved to him that it was her own kismet that had brought her this happiness in spite of ill-treatment and exile.

The sultan was quite struck by the force of what had happened. He raised her up and embraced her. Then he told her, before the entire court, how much he regretted treating her so inhumanly and admitted he was now convinced that everyone has his or her own special destiny and it is to that kismet that one owes everything, both good and evil.

The Lord of Death

～ *Punjabi* ～ ～

There was a road, and everyone who traveled on it died. Some people said they were killed by a snake, others said by a scorpion, but somehow they all died.

Once a very old man was traveling along the road. When he got tired, he sat down on a stone, and suddenly he saw in front of him a huge scorpion. It was as big as a rooster, and even as he was looking at it, it changed into a snake and glided away. Wonderstruck, he decided to follow it at a little distance and find out what it really was.

The snake glided here and there, day and night, and behind it followed the old man like a shadow. Once it went into an inn and killed several travelers; another time it slid into the palace and killed the king himself. It crept up the waterspout to the queen's quarters and killed her youngest daughter. So it passed on, and wherever it went there was soon the sound of weeping and wailing, and the old man followed it, silent as a shadow.

The road suddenly turned into a broad, deep river, on the banks of which sat some poor travelers who longed to cross over but had no money to pay the ferryman. Then the snake changed into a handsome buffalo, with a brass necklace and bells around its neck, and stood by the brink of the stream. When the travelers saw this, they said, "This beast is going to swim to its home across the river. Let's get on its back and hold on to its tail, and we too can get to the other side."

So they climbed on its back, and the buffalo swam into the river. But when it reached the middle, where the river was deepest, it began to kick and roll until they all tumbled off, or let go, and were all drowned.

When the old man, who had crossed the river in a boat, reached the other side, the buffalo had disappeared, and in its stead stood a beautiful ox. Seeing this handsome creature wandering about, without any owner in sight, a peasant coveted it and lured it to his home. It was quite gentle, and allowed him to tie it up with his other cattle. But in the dead of night it changed into a snake, bit all the flocks and herds, killed all the sleeping folk, and crept away. But behind it, the old man still followed, silent as a shadow.

Soon they came to another river, where the snake changed itself into the likeness of a beautiful young woman covered with jewels. After a while, two brothers, both of them soldiers, came that way, and as they came towards her, she began to weep bitterly.

"What is the matter?" asked the brothers. "And why are you, a young and beautiful woman, sitting here alone?"

Then the snake woman answered, "My husband was taking me home. We were waiting for the ferry. He went to wash his face, slipped on a stone, fell into the river, and was drowned. Now I have no one. My relatives are far away."

"You've nothing to be afraid of," said the elder of the two brothers, who was much taken with her beauty. "Come with me and I will marry you and look after you."

"On two conditions," answered the woman. "You must never ask me to do any household work. And you must give me whatever I ask."

"I'll obey you like a slave!" said the young man.

"Then go to that well and get me a cup of water. Your brother will stay here with me," said the woman.

But as soon as the elder brother's back was turned, she said to the younger, "Let's leave before he comes back. I love you. I sent your brother away to get rid of him."

"No, no," said the young man. "You promised to be his wife. You are like a sister to me."

At this the woman was furious. She began to weep and wail when she saw the elder brother returning with the water. She cried out to him, "This brother of yours is an evil man. He asked me to run away with him and leave you here!"

Before the younger could say a word, the elder had drawn his sword and they began to fight. They fought all day long and by evening they lay dead on the banks of the river. Then the woman took the form of a snake once more, and the old man followed it, silent as a shadow.

At last the snake changed into an old white-bearded man. When the old man who was following it saw another ancient like himself, he took courage, went closer, and asked, "Who and what are you?"

Then the old white-bearded man smiled and answered, "Some people call me the Lord of Death, because I go about bringing death to the world."

"Give me death!" pleaded the other. "I've followed you for days and watched your ways. And I'm sick at heart."

But the Lord of Death shook his head and said, "Oh no, not yet. I give only to those whose time has come. You've sixty more years to go!"

Then the old white-bearded man vanished. But was he really the Lord of Death or a devil? Who can tell?

The Shepherd's Ghost

~ *Telugu* ~ ~

A shepherd and his wife lived in a village. Every day he went to graze his sheep. One day, he climbed a tree, sat on a branch facing the tree, and began cutting the branch where it joined the trunk.

A Brahman who was passing that way looked at him and said, "Hey, you! You'll fall down! You're cutting the branch you're sitting on."

The shepherd said, "How do you know I'll fall down, *sami?*"

The Brahman said, "Let me show you. Put your upper cloth on the branch, sit on the next branch, and cut the first one as you were doing. Then you'll see for yourself."

The shepherd did as he was told: he put his upper cloth on the branch and continued to cut it. When he was done, the garment fell to the ground with the branch.

The shepherd was greatly impressed. He thought, "*Abba!* This Brahman *sami* really knows a lot. He's a great man." Then he got off the tree in a hurry, fell at the feet of the Brahman, and asked him, "O *sami*, tell me, when am I going to die? You must tell me."

The Brahman said, "How do I know, you foolish man, about your birth and death? Just leave me alone."

The shepherd insisted: "I know you know everything. You really know. You must tell me. I'll give you a sheep." And he held on to his feet and refused to let go till the Brahman told him.

The Brahman didn't know what to do. So, just to get out of the situation, he said, "Look here. Before you die, your nose will get shorter. Your eyes will be sunken. That's when you'll die." Then he moved on.

The shepherd tended his sheep, thinking all the time of what the Brahman had said. Summer came. One day his wife didn't bring his food on time. He was thirsty. He was famished. He measured his nose with his finger and felt it was shorter than usual. He felt his eyes with his fingers. They felt sunken. "*Chhat!* I'm going to die!" he thought. He left his sheep then and there in the meadow and went home.

His wife was getting ready to leave home with his food basket. When he came home, she asked, "Where did you leave the sheep?" He didn't answer. "What's the use of talking? I'm dying anyway," he thought and was silent like a deaf-mute. His wife said, "Why don't you talk? What's happened to you?" He came into the house, held in his breath, and sat against the wall. He sat on his haunches, without breathing, I don't know how. His wife tried shaking him this way and that, but he wouldn't talk, nor would he breathe. He shut his eyes and wouldn't move. 'Oh, my husband's dead!' she cried, and ran out and told all her caste-people. They all came, pinched him, and slapped his cheek. But he made not a sound nor did he move. "Yes, he's dead," they said.

They brought a new cloth, made a bier, put him on it, and took him to the burial ground. There they made a pit this long and buried him in it. The idiot still held his breath. They kicked more earth into the pit, covered him with it, and were about to leave him there to go to the river to wash their feet and hands. The man, once he was stuck in the earth, wasn't able to let out his breath. So he pushed the earth this way and that and moved around in the pit. The loose earth gave way. He got up, with dirt all over his head, his mustache, and all over his body. He sat up and yelled, "Hey, you fellows! Where are you going, leaving me here?" When they heard him yelling, they turned and looked at the man they had just buried and saw him rise as if from the dead, covered from head to foot with dirt. They panicked and took to their heels, crying, "*Ayyo!* The shepherd's ghost is coming after us!"

When the other villagers asked them, they told them that the shepherd's ghost had risen and was coming after them. They all ran home, shut themselves in their houses, and bolted the doors. The shepherd walked to the village, went straight to his wife's place, and said, "Hey, woman, I didn't die. Open the door and let me in!"

She called out from behind the door, "O *sami*, please go away. I'll offer new clothes and break a coconut in your burial place. Leave me alone. Don't come to my house." He tried to explain, but she was too frightened to listen to what he said.

By now he was very hungry. Who would feed him now? He walked out of the village and found the temple of Hanuman, the Monkey God. He thought, "The priest will come with offerings of food to the god. I'll ask him to give me some." So thinking, he sat inside the temple. He sat there all night. Nobody came. Nobody opened a door in the whole village. The next morning, long

after sunrise, the villagers got up and opened their doors, started sweeping their front yards, and began going about their business. The priest cooked up some rice and lentils, poured some ghee on it, plucked some flowers and whatnot on the way, and came to the Monkey God's temple. There he poured ritual water on the image and was about to put flowers on the god's head. Just then, the shepherd, who was sitting behind the image, stood up and said, "Why, *sami*, you were late today. I was waiting for you." "Oh, the shepherd's ghost is here!" hollered the priest, threw everything down right there, and fled the place. People who were sweeping their front yards heard this hullabaloo and threw down their brooms and baskets. People untying the bullocks for the day's work left them there. They all ran in and bolted their doors.

The shepherd went again to his wife's house and tried to persuade her.

She wouldn't open the door even a chink. Then he went back to the temple and ate the food for a few days. But he had no clothes to wear—they had stripped him when they buried him. A thought occurred to him: "I must go to the washerman's ghat and get some clothes. When the washerman comes there, I'll ask him for a piece of cloth to cover my shame. I'll wrap it around me and come home." So he went to the ghat and hid in the *ubba*, the vat in which the washermen boil the dirty clothes.

A police inspector came around on his beat and saw that the villagers were all hiding in their houses behind bolted doors. He wondered: "The doors are shut at midday? Why, what's happening?" He knocked on people's doors and asked them what the matter was.

They said, "There's a shepherd's ghost abroad. We won't open the doors till it's gone." He said, "I don't see any ghost anywhere. What nonsense!"

He went to the village headman Reddy, who said the same thing. The police inspector said, "I'll protect you. Open the door." The Reddy took courage, opened the door, and came out. By and by, others also opened their doors and began going about their daily business.

Meanwhile, the policeman said to the washerman, "My clothes are dirty. I'll give them to you. Go to the river and wash them for me." The washerman said, "I can't. When I went there earlier, I saw the shepherd's ghost. He'll get me!"

"Oh, don't be such a coward. I'll come with you," said the policeman. So he mounted his horse and took the washerman with him to the ghat. There he asked the washerman to go and look into the vat while he held his horse. The washerman went to the *ubba* to put the dirty clothes in. There he saw the shepherd sitting in the vat—ashes and dirt all over his body, face, and mustache. When the washerman came near him, the shepherd called him by name: "Why, Subbanna! Why are you so late this morning? I've been waiting for you."

When the policeman heard this, he quickly mounted his horse and fled for his life. The washerman yelled and ran for his life. Again all the people in the village hurried home and bolted their doors.

Now the shepherd cursed them: "These motherfuckers!" He picked up a piece of cloth, wound it around his waist and draped another over his shoulder, and went home. Whatever he said to his wife, she just wouldn't hear him and didn't budge. Finally he cried, "No, I didn't die. A Brahman told me I'd die. I believed him. That's why I'm in all this trouble. Open the door and see for yourself."

When she opened the door a little and looked at him, he looked human all right. He had some clothes on. She took him in, poured water on him, washed off the dirt that was caked all over him, and gave him proper clothes. He put them on and went back to his sheep like every day.

This World and the Other

~ *Bengali* ~ ~

Two friends met on a street. They were going in opposite directions. One was going to see a woman and the other to a religious meeting where a great preacher and storyteller was featured that day.

The man who was on his way to the religious meeting said to the other, "Why do you want to go to that woman? Come with me to the religious meeting. The preacher is an inspiring speaker. He can dance, sing, and tell wonderful stories about saints and gods. Come with me."

The other man said, "Why don't you come with me? I'll find you a beautiful, sexy woman just like mine. Why do you want to waste your time on dull religious things?"

Neither could persuade the other. Each went his way.

But the man who went to the religious meeting couldn't concentrate on religious matters that day. He could only think of the wonderful time his friend was having in the arms of a lovely woman, and here he was wasting his life listening to a preacher.

And the man who was in the arms of the woman could not enjoy himself either. He could only think of his good friend who was earning merit and a place in heaven by listening to hymns and stories about saints and gods, while he was frittering away his life with a silly, frivolous woman.

That's why they say that man will neither give up this world for the other nor the other for this one.

If God Is Everywhere

~ Bengali ~ ~

A sage had a number of disciples. He taught them his deepest belief: "God is everywhere and dwells in everything. So you should treat all things as God and bow before them."

One day when a disciple was out on errands, a mad elephant was rushing through the marketplace, and the elephant driver was shouting, "Get out of the way! Get out of the way! This is a mad elephant!" The disciple remembered his guru's teachings and refused to run. "God is in this elephant as He is in me. How can God hurt God?" he thought, and just stood there full of love and devotion. The driver was frantic and shouted at him, "Get out of the way! You'll be hurt!" But the disciple did not move an inch. The mad elephant picked him up with its trunk, swung him around, and threw him in the gutter. The poor fellow lay there, bruised, bleeding, but more than all, disillusioned that God should do this to him. When his guru and the other disciples came to help him and take him home, he said, "You said God is in everything! Look what the elephant did to me!"

The guru said, "It's true that God is in everything. The elephant is certainly God. But so was the elephant driver, telling you to get out of the way. Why didn't you listen to him?"

A Tiger That Didn't Know
Who He Was

~ *Bengali* ~~

A pregnant tigress once jumped into the midst of a flock of sheep. As she did so, she went into labor, gave birth to a tiger cub, and died on the spot.

The kindhearted sheep nursed the cub, gave him suck, and brought him up among them. When they ate grass, the cub followed their example; when they bleated, he also learned to bleat, though his bleat sounded strange. The cub grew up looking like a tiger but had the character of a sheep.

One day a magnificent full-grown tiger watched with amazement this grass-eating tiger cub. As the big tiger came near, the flock of sheep scattered. The cub was left behind, and he bleated, terror-stricken. Then the big tiger came close to him, talked to him, made friends with him, and dragged him to a lake and said, "Look at yourself in the water. That is you. And look at me. You are exactly like me. You are not a sheep, but a tiger. Your food is not grass, but meat."

The grass-eating tiger couldn't believe it. The big tiger slowly convinced him he was no different from him. At first he wouldn't touch meat, and ate grass and bleated, till one day the big tiger forced him to eat a piece of flesh. He liked the taste of blood, stopped bleating and eating grass, and realized he was no sheep but a tiger. Then he went with the big tiger and lived like him.

Gandharva Sen Is Dead!

~ Bengali ~ ~

A king was holding court one day when his minister rushed in, lamenting and crying. The king asked him why he was crying so bitterly. The minister kissed the foot of the throne, bowed to the ground, and said, "My lord, *badshah*, Gandharva Sen is dead!" As he heard this, the king burst into tears and exclaimed, "O God, Gandharva Sen is dead!" The court broke up and everyone was ordered to observe forty-one days of mourning in memory of the dead. When the king went to his harem, he was still weeping. The begums of the harem, seeing the king in such grief, asked him the reason, and when he told them in a choked voice that Gandharva Sen was dead, they all began to cry and beat their breasts. The whole zenana was a scene of utter grief and confusion.

A servant girl of the senior begum who did not quite understand the reason for the pandemonium asked her mistress, "*Badshazadi!* Why is everyone crying?" The begum heaved a sigh and said, "Oh dear! Poor Gandharva Sen is dead!" The girl anxiously asked, "Who was Gandharva Sen to Your Majesty?" "Oh, I don't really know," said the begum, and she ran to the *badshah* and asked him who Gandharva Sen was that they were all lamenting his death. The *badshah* had no answer. Feeling a bit foolish, he went back to his court, summoned his minister, and asked him, "Minister, who was this Gandharva Sen that we are all mourning his death?" "Pardon me, Your Majesty," said the minister, "your slave doesn't know who Gandharva Sen was, but he saw the chief of police crying and saying that Gandharva Sen was dead, and he too cried for company." "You are a fool," thundered the monarch. "Go at once and find out who Gandharva Sen was." The minister bowed, and ran as fast as his legs would carry him till he met the chief of police at the gate of the palace and asked him who Gandharva Sen was. The man looked vacantly at the minister's face, and said that he didn't really know who the late Gandharva Sen was, but as the *jamadar* had come crying and saying that Gandharva Sen was dead, he had wept with him and informed the minister of it. Now the minister and the policeman both sought out the *jamadar* and asked him who Gandharva Sen was, for whom he had wept. The *jamadar* replied, "O sir, I can't say who or what he was, but as I saw my wife weeping over the death of Gandharva Sen, I felt pity for her and came weeping to you to report his death. You know, sir, crying and laughing excite sympathy and make us also cry and laugh. I cried because my wife was crying." The three men went then to the *jamadar*'s wife, who too denied any personal knowledge of the dead Gandharva Sen, and simply told them how she had gone to bathe in the tank and there had seen the village washerwoman crying bitterly and saying that her Gandharva Sen was dead.

Then the whole party rushed to the washerwoman's house and asked her who Gandharva Sen was to her that she had wept so piteously that morning for his death. "Oh, I'm so unlucky!" cried the washerwoman. "My heart still bleeds for him. He was my pet donkey. I loved him like my own son." She could hardly finish her sentence and burst once again into tears. The party felt thoroughly ashamed of themselves and quickly left the place.

The minister returned to the palace, fell at the feet of his king, and told him the truth—that the Gandharva Sen all of them had cried over was none other than a washerwoman's pet donkey. The *badshah* scolded him but pardoned him.

When the news reached the harem, the begums laughed loud and long at the *badshah* and his courtiers. They laughed and laughed till their sides ached.

Tenali Rama's Dream

~ *Telugu* ~ ~

One day the king announced that he had had a dream. "You know, Tenali Rama, you and I were walking in a strange place, just the two of us. We came to a path between two pits. One of them was filled with honey, and the other was a cesspool, filled with shit and piss and garbage. The path was narrow, but we had to cross it. As you and I tiptoed on this path, we both slipped. I fell into the pit of honey, and you fell into the cesspool filled with shit."

All the courtiers laughed and clapped. They were delighted that this pest, Tenali Rama, had got his due at least in a dream. The king said further, "I drank all the honey I could and somehow clambered back to the path. But you, poor fellow, were still struggling in all that shit. And just as you were about to climb onto the path, you slipped and fell back, head-first this time. Then I woke up."

The courtiers all laughed their heads off. Only Tenali Rama didn't.

But next morning he was back at the court, this time with a dream of his own. "Yesterday, Your Highness told us a dream. Last night I had a dream, and it continued where you left off. You climbed out of the honey pit, and I, after trying many times, got back to the path. But you and I couldn't really go back home in that state, could we? So I licked all the honey off your body with my tongue, and you then cleaned me off in the same way."

A Feast in a Dream

~ *Rajasthani* ~ ~

There were three brothers named Khan and a Meo, a man from a caste that follows both Hindu and Muslim customs. They set out to earn a living. They walked and walked till they reached a certain place where they could rest. The three brothers said, "We are three and this Meo is alone. We could control him." As they were all hungry, they gave the Meo some money and said, "Go and get something we can all eat."

The Meo went and bought a packet of *ladoos*. He thought, "These Khan brothers will not give me anything to eat. I should eat my share here." So he ate his share of the sweetmeats there and then and brought the rest to the brothers.

They looked at it and said, "Meo, you son of an owl, we are four and you brought so little. How did you eat so much?"

Then the Meo took another handful from the packet and ate it in a hurry, saying, "Brothers, just like this." So there was even less for the Khan brothers.

They thought, "If we ask him any more questions, he'll eat it all." So they distributed the *ladoos* equally and each ate his share. Some were satisfied, some were not. They ate anyhow, drank something, and set out to look for work.

They all got good jobs, better than they expected. Now they had money and were ready to return home. But the brothers said to each other, "Before we go home, we have something to do. This Meo ate most of our *ladoos*. We must take from him, make him penniless." Then they called him and said, "O brother, do one more thing for us before we go home. Make *khir* for us today."

They bought milk and sugar and spices, and the Meo made a very good rice pudding. They put it in a cauldron. It was night already, and they said, "The man who has the best dream of all will eat this *khir*. Agreed?"

"Yes, brothers, very well. He who has the best dream will eat the *khir*."

"We'll get up in the morning and tell each other our dreams. He who had the best dream will eat, and he who had a poor dream will not eat."

"Yes, brothers, very well."

Then they covered the cauldron with a piece of cloth and tied it up. They put it near their heads and prepared for sleep. The Meo thought, "These three are scoundrels. They will cheat me out of my share, though all of us spent equally."

The Khan brothers waited for the Meo to sleep, and the Meo waited for them to sleep. The Meo pretended to fall asleep and began to snore. The Khans watched him closely for a while and were convinced that he was fast asleep, so they unfolded their bedding and went to sleep. As soon as they did so, the Meo got up quietly, tiptoed to the cauldron, and without a sound, ate the whole cauldron of *khir*. He left nothing in the vessel. Then he came back to his bed, wrapped himself in a shawl, and straightaway went to sleep. He felt a kind of intoxication from having eaten so much.

In the morning, the three brothers woke up and began to talk. The Meo was still fast asleep. For what should he wake up? They began asking each other, "What dream did you have? What dream did you have?"

"O brothers, I dreamed that I reached Ajmer and I was in the court and it was beautiful," said one and asked the second man to tell them what he had seen.

The second man said, "I went to the court in Jaipur and saw the king."

The Meo had waked up meanwhile and was listening. The third man told his dream: "Brothers, what can I say? I went all the way to Mecca and saw the Prophet!"

Now the three men's dreams had been told. The Meo groaned, "Ah, ah, ah!" and yawned. He turned from side to side and moaned as if in sleep.

"O Meo, you son of an owl, are you getting up or not?"

"Oh, don't bother me," he said, moaning and turning aside.

"Tell us, tell us what you dreamed. What happened?"

"Brothers, this is what happened. A big man came to me and beat me up very badly. My whole body is hurting—ah, ah, ah! He said to me, 'Eat this *khir*, eat all this *khir*.' And when I'd eaten all of it, he beat me some more, and my whole body hurts. Ah, ah!"

"You fool, you son of an owl, we were sleeping near you. Why didn't you wake us? We could have saved you. Why didn't you wake us?"

The Meo said, "O brothers, how could I wake you? One was in Ajmer, one in Jaipur, and one had gone as far away as Mecca to see the Prophet. I cried out for you loudly so many times, but how could you hear?"

In Search of a Dream

~ Santali ~ ~

A raja had no children by his first wife. So he married a second wife, who bore him two sons, and they were all very happy that the raja now had heirs. But as it often happens, after the two sons had been born, the elder queen also gave birth to a son. This led to endless quarrels, for the younger queen had counted on her sons succeeding to the kingdom, but now feared the raja might prefer the son of his elder queen. She used all her wiles to persuade him to send away the elder queen and her son. The raja listened to her, gave the first wife a separate estate and house, and sent her away.

One night the raja had a dream, the meaning of which he could not understand. He dreamed that he saw a golden leopard and a golden snake and a golden monkey dancing together. The raja could not rest till he had found out the meaning of the dream, so he sent for his younger wife and her two sons and consulted them. They could give him no explanation, but the younger son said that he had a feeling that his half brother, the son of the elder queen, could interpret the dream. So that son was sent for, and when he heard the story of the dream, he said, "This is the interpretation: The three golden animals represent us three brothers, for we are like gold to you. God has sent this dream to you that we may not fight hereafter. We cannot all three succeed to the kingdom, and we shall surely fight if one is chosen as the heir. The dream means to say that whichever of us can find a golden leopard, a golden snake, and a golden monkey and make them dance together before the people, he shall be your principal son and shall be your heir." The raja was pleased with this interpretation and told his three sons that he would give the kingdom to the one who could find the three animals by the same day of the coming year.

The sons of the younger queen went away and thought about it, and decided it was useless for them even to try to find those dream animals. Even if they got a goldsmith to make the animals, they would never be able to make them dance.

But the son of the elder queen went to his mother and told her all that had happened, and she told him not to lose heart and he would find the animals. If he went to a *gosain*, a Vaishnava ascetic who lived in the jungle, he would find out what to do.

So the raja's son set out, and after traveling for some days he found himself in a dense jungle when it was nightfall. Wandering about, he at last saw a fire burning in the distance. So he went to it, sat down by it, and began to smoke. Now, the *gosain* was sleeping nearby. The smell of the smoke woke him up, and he rose and asked who was there.

"Uncle, it's me, your nephew."

"Really, is it you, my nephew? Where have you come from so late at night?"

"From home, Uncle."

"What made you remember me now? You have never visited me before. I'm afraid something has happened."

"Oh, really nothing terrible. I've come to you because my mother tells me that you can help me find the golden leopard and the golden snake and the golden monkey."

At this the *gosain* promised to help the raja's son to find the animals, and then put a cooking pot on the fire to boil. In it he put only three grains of rice, but when it was cooked they found they had enough for two meals. When they had eaten, the *gosain* said, "Nephew, I cannot really tell you what you have to do. But farther on in the jungle lives my younger brother. Go to him and he will tell you."

So the next morning the raja's son set out, and in two days reached the second *gosain* and told him what he wanted. This *gosain* listened to his story and also put a cooking pot on to boil, and in it he threw just two grains of rice. When it was cooked, there was enough for both of them. After the meal, the *gosain* said that he could not tell him where the animals could be found, but that his younger brother would know. So the next morning the raja's son continued his journey, and in two days he came to the third *gosain* and there he learned what was to be done. This *gosain* also put a pot on to boil, but in the pot he only put one grain of rice. Yet, when cooked, it was enough for a meal for both of them.

In the morning, the *gosain* told the raja's son to go to a blacksmith and have a shield made of twelve *maunds* of iron, with an edge so sharp that a leaf falling on it would be cut in two. So he went to the blacksmith and had the shield made, and took it to the *gosain*. The *gosain* said that first they must test it, and he set it edgewise under a tree and told the raja's son to climb the tree and shake some leaves down. The raja's son climbed the tree and shook the branches, but not a leaf fell. Then the *gosain* climbed the tree and gave the tree the gentlest of shakes, and the leaves fell in showers and every leaf that touched the edge of the shield was cut in two. The *gosain* was satisfied that the shield was made exactly as he wanted it.

Then the *gosain* told the raja's son that farther on in the jungle he would find a pair of snakes living in a bamboo house, and that they had a daughter whom they never allowed to come out of the house. He must fix the sharp shield in the doorway of the house and hide himself in a tree. When the snakes came out, they would be cut into pieces. Then he should go to the daughter, and she would show him where to find the golden animals. So the raja's son set out and at about noon came to the house of the snakes. He set the shield in the doorway as the *gosain* had told him. That evening, when the snakes tried to come out of their house, they were cut to pieces. A little later, when the daughter peeped out to see what had happened to her parents, the prince saw her. She was not a snake, but a very beautiful woman. He quickly went to her and began to talk, and it did not take long for them to fall in love. He consoled her, and the snake maiden soon forgot her sorrow over her parents' deaths. She and the raja's son lived together in the bamboo house for many days.

The snake maiden had strictly forbidden him to go anywhere to the west or south of the house. But one day the raja's son disobeyed her and wandered away to the west. After going a short distance, he saw golden leopards dancing, and as soon as he set eyes on them, he himself was changed into a golden leopard and began to dance with them. The snake maiden soon knew what had happened, and she led him back and restored him to his own shape.

A few days later, the raja's son went towards the south, and there he found golden snakes dancing at the edge of a tank. As soon as he saw them, he was changed into a golden snake and joined the dance. Again the snake maiden fetched him and restored him to his own shape. But again the raja's son went out, this time to the southwest, and there he saw golden monkeys dancing together under a banyan tree. When he laid eyes on them, he too became a golden monkey. Again the snake maiden brought him back and restored him to human shape.

After this the raja's son said that it was time for him to go back home. The snake maiden asked him why he had come there at all, and then he told her all about the raja's dream. Now that he had found the golden animals, he could go home.

"What about me?" cried the snake maiden. "Kill me first. You have killed my parents and I cannot live here alone."

"No, I will not kill you. I'll take you home with me," said the raja's son, which delighted the snake maiden. Then the raja's son asked how he could take the golden animals with him. So far he had only seen them. The snake maiden said that if he faithfully promised never to desert her nor take another wife, she would produce the animals for him when the time came. So he swore he would never leave her, and they set out for his home.

When they reached the place where the third *gosain* lived, the raja's son said he had promised to visit him on his way home and show him the golden animals. Now he did not know what to do because he did not have the animals with him. Then the snake maiden tied three knots in his upper cloth and told him to untie them when the *gosain* asked to see the animals. So the raja's son went to see the *gosain*, and the *gosain* asked whether he had brought the golden leopard and snake and monkey.

"I'm not sure," answered the raja's son, "but I've something tied up in my cloth." But when he untied the three knots, he found in them a clod of earth, a potsherd, and a piece of charcoal. He threw them away in disgust, and went back to the snake maiden and asked her why she had put such worthless rubbish in his cloth.

"You had no faith," said she. "If you had believed, the animals would not have turned into the clod and the potsherd and the charcoal."

So they moved on till they came to the second *gosain*, who also asked to see the golden animals. This time, the raja's son set his mind hard to believe, and when he untied the knots, there appeared a golden leopard, a golden snake, and a golden monkey. Then they went on and showed the animals to the first *gosain*, and finally went to his mother's house.

When the appointed day came, the raja's son sent word to his father to have a number of booths and shelters erected on a large field, and to have a covered way made from his mother's house to the field. Then he would show the dancing animals. So the raja gave the necessary orders, and on the day fixed for the event people gathered to see the fun. Then the raja's son brought the three animals to the field, and his wife hid herself in the covered way and caused the animals to dance. The people stayed watching all day till evening and reluctantly went home. That night all the booths and shelters turned into houses of gold. When he saw this, the raja left his younger wife and her children and went to live with his first wife.

And the raja's son married the snake maiden, inherited the kingdom, and ruled it justly and happily.

The Princess Whose Father Wanted to Marry Her

≈ *Tulu* ≈≈

A king had a daughter. One day, when he returned from supervising the irrigation of his lands, he saw his daughter standing on the terrace of his palace. She was buttoning her blouse. He caught a glimpse of her breasts, and wanted her for himself. He went straight to his queen and asked her, "Would it be all right if I ate what I planted?" She answered, "Of course." He asked his ministers the same question. They all said he could certainly eat what he planted. The king started making arrangements for a wedding. He sent invitations to distant kingdoms, ordered the town crier to announce the event to his citizens, and invited neighboring families. The day of the wedding arrived. People from near and far crowded the city. The bridegroom was dressed in silks and covered with jewels. But no one knew who the bride was.

The king's daughter had her suspicions. She had sensed her father's desire. So she asked the carpenters to make a big box for her and had it placed in a corner of her bedroom. On the wedding day, she got in it, closed the lid on herself and locked it from inside. When the king was all dressed up and ready, he sent the maidservants to get his daughter ready for the wedding. When they came looking for her in the upper story, she was nowhere to be found. They searched and searched. The king was downcast. All the guests were given their dinner in the banquet hall, and they left shaking their heads at the strange wedding that never happened.

Four or five days later, the queen could not bear to look at her daughter's box because it reminded her of the missing girl. "What's the use of her box without her?" she said, and asked the servants to throw it into the river. It floated along the flowing river for many days, till it reached another kingdom. The king of the realm and his minister were playing a game on the sands of the riverbank when they saw the box floating by. The minister waded into the water to bring it to the bank, but it moved away from him. When the king entered the water, the box moved towards him. He called his servants and had it carried into his palace bedroom.

Every night his mother would bring her son a jug of milk and a bunch of bananas. Before he went to bed, he would drink the milk and eat the bananas. Now, ever since the box had come into his room, he found at bedtime only half a jug of milk and half a bunch of bananas. One day he complained to his mother, "Why are you bringing me only half a jug of milk and half a bunch of bananas these days?" The mother said, "No, my son, I bring you every night a full jug of milk and a full bunch of bananas, as always." That night, the king hid himself in his bedroom. Soon after his mother had brought the usual jug of milk and bunch of bananas, he saw a beautiful woman come out of the box, eat half the bananas, and drank half the milk. As she was about to return to the box, he leaped out of his hiding-place, took her by the hand, and asked her, "Who are you? What is your story?" The princess told him all about herself, and from then on the king began to spend most of his time in his bedroom, abandoning all his other women.

But war came to the kingdom, and the king had to go into battle. As he got ready to go, he called his mother and said, "I want you to continue to bring a jug of milk and a bunch of bananas every night to my room. Don't ever forget to do so."

Now, a maidservant had seen through a crack in the door that the king brought out a lovely woman from the box in his room every night. She told the secret to the king's former favorite concubine, who decided at once to get rid of her rival. She went to the queen and asked her for the box in the king's bedroom. The queen at first wouldn't agree to give it to her, but the concubine knew how to persuade her. She wheedled the box out of her and had it carried to her own house. There she pried open the box and found the lovely princess. At once, she proceeded to mutilate her. She cut off her hands and had them buried in the row of yams in her garden. She cut off her legs and had them buried in the manure pit. She cut off her breasts and had them buried in the bin of paddy husk. She plucked out her eyes and put them in the pickle jar. Then she threw the rest of the princess's body into a pit in the back yard, where, still half-alive, she lay moaning without a limb or an eye.

On that very day, an old woman was passing that way and heard the moans. She climbed into the pit, rescued what was left of the princess, and took her home. The next morning, the princess called the old woman and said, "My eyes are in the pickle jar in the concubine's house. Get them for me." The granny went to the concubine, whom she knew, and begged her for some pickles. The concubine said, "Go into the kitchen storeroom and take the pickles from the jar." The old woman carefully picked out the princess's eyes from among the pickles and brought them home. When she fixed them back in her eyesockets, the princess regained her sight. Next day she asked the old woman, "Granny, granny, my hands are in the concubine's garden, in the row of yams. Go bring them to me." The old woman went to the concubine and begged her for a yam. The concubine said, "If you want a yam, why don't you go to the garden and dig one for yourself?" The old woman went straight to the row of yams, rummaged in the earth under them, brought back the severed hands, and fixed them back on the princess. The princess now had hands as before. The next day, she said to the old woman, "My legs are in the manure pit. Please go and get them." The old woman went to the concubine and said, "I've planted some cucumber seeds. They've just sprouted, and I need some manure to make them grow well. May I take some from your pit?" "Oh, we've plenty of manure. Take as much as you need," said the concubine. The old woman sorted out the legs from the manure in the pit and took them home. When she joined them to the princess's thighs, she had legs as good as new.

The next morning, the princess said, "Granny, granny, bring me today my two breasts from the bin of paddy husk in the concubine's house." The old woman went again to the concubine and said, "I have some new clay pots. I need some paddy husk so I can rub ash on them and darken them. Will you give me some?" "Take all the husk you want. We have plenty," said the concubine. The old woman picked out the princess's breasts, brought them home, and joined them to her chest. The princess was now whole again and beautiful as ever.

The war came to an end and the king returned home. He went straight to his bedroom and found the box and the princess missing. He called his mother and asked her, "What did you do with the box in my room?" "Your concubine has borrowed it," said the queen mother. The king hastened to the concubine's house. "Where's my box?" he asked. She said, "Why, I threw it in the river." He knew he would never find it now. The swift current in the river would have carried it far away, maybe even to the sea. He came home dejected and sat with his head buried in his hands.

Some days later, when the princess had heard that the king was back from the wars, she asked the old woman to arrange a grand banquet. Everyone wondered how a poor old woman could arrange a big banquet, but everyone was curious. The king too wanted to see how she would manage it. When everyone was seated in the old woman's little hut, suddenly, without any warning, the princess appeared with her *tambura*, tuned the strings, and sang her entire story in the form of a song. The king knew now that this was none other than the princess in the box. He went forward and took her by the hand. The king and princess had a great big gala wedding. And the concubine was hanged by her neck on the outskirts of the capital.

Mother Marries Son

~ *Marathi* ~ ~

Everyone knows the goddess Satwai. She is the one who has to write the future of every child on its forehead the night of the fifth day after its birth. And what she writes must happen.

Now, Satwai had a daughter. Every night she was left alone when her mother went out to write some baby's fate on its forehead. She asked her mother one day, "Mother, why do you go out every night and leave me alone?"

Satwai answered, "Daughter, I have to perform the task for which I'm appointed by God. I must therefore go and write the fate of newborn babies."

"Can anyone read what you write?"

"No, not even the gods know what I have written out for them."

"Did you write on my forehead also when I was born?"

"Of course."

"Then, Mother, tell me what you have written for me."

Satwai refused to tell her anything and went out as usual. But her daughter gave her no peace, pestered her, and threatened to leave the house if her mother didn't tell her what she had written on her forehead. At last, Satwai told her, "Daughter, it's your fate to marry your own son."

Shocked at this revelation, the daughter asked her, "Can't you change it for your own daughter?"

"No, I told you, what I write cannot be reversed. It must happen as I have told you."

The daughter was furious. "You did this to your own daughter?" she screamed. And she made up her mind to cheat her fate. She resolved never to marry, never even to see a man. So she went into a deep forest, built a hut there, and lived all alone for some years till she grew up to be a young woman.

Now it happened that a king, who was out hunting, passed through that forest He came to a lovely lake filled with clear, sweet water. He was thirsty—his mouth was parched. So he took some water in his cupped hands and drank it, gargled with a mouthful, spat it back into the lake, and then rode away.

The young woman came to the same lake a little later. She had been gathering fruit and roots all morning and she was tired and thirsty. She stopped at the lake, took some water in her cupped hands, and drank it. That water contained the mouthful spat out by the king, and as soon as it reached her belly she became pregnant. At first she didn't know that anything had happened to her, but soon realized she had a baby growing inside her. She was scared and didn't know what to do. In a few months, she gave birth to a handsome boy. As she knew the prophecy, she decided to destroy the baby. So she tore a piece from her sari, wrapped it around the child, and threw him from a steep mountainside.

Below the cliff lived a gardener and his wife, who had a beautiful grove of closely planted banana trees. The bundle of cloth with the child wrapped in it alighted on top of some thick, stout banana leaves and lay there till the gardener's eye fell on it. He took it down gently and brought it home to his wife. The couple, who were childless, were delighted and full of gratitude for this gift of the gods. The baby grew and thrived in their care and grew up to be a handsome young man.

Satwai's daughter lived on in the forest for years until she grew tired of her lonely life. She thought that she could now go back to the world; after all, she had killed her son and there was no danger of the prophecy coming true. She walked to the end of the forest, rounded the great cliff, came down into the valley, and arrived at the homestead of the old couple. They were very hospitable. When they found she had nowhere to go, they asked her to stay with them. She lived and worked in their house. They all liked her; she was lovely, and she worked hard.

In a few months, the old couple thought that God, who had sent them the boy, had now sent them this woman as a daughter-in-law. So they married their son to her. The woman became the mistress of the household, and her chores took her into every nook and corner of that house. One day, she was looking for some old pots in the loft and came across the torn piece of a sari. It didn't take her long to recognize it as her own. To make sure, she went down in a hurry and asked her mother-in-law about the old piece of cloth. Her mother-in-law told her the whole story of how they had found her husband as a baby wrapped in that cloth on top of a banana tree.

She knew at once that what Satwai had written had come true. She did not tell anybody what she knew, and lived on with her husband happily, blessed by her old parents-in-law, to whom she was always kind and dutiful.

A Cure

~ *Bengali* ~ ~

A young king was stricken with impotence. He was bitter and unhappy that he would never have a son and heir. The sight of the many beautiful women in his harem only made him sick with grief. No doctor could cure him; no system of medicine, Hindu, Muslim, or foreign, could restore to him the pleasures of potency, available even to the poorest man in his realm but not to him.

One day, word reached him that a dervish had just arrived in his kingdom and that he had cures for every disease imaginable and even for the incurable. Hoping against hope, the young king made his way secretly to the dervish. When the dervish heard what ailed the king, he took out a small vial that contained a glowing elixir, drank three-fourths of it himself, and gave what was left in the vial to the king with instructions to drink no more than a drop of it each morning for three days and watch for results. The king gratefully took it home, and the very first dose made a difference. The second drop of the elixir gave him the potency of a normal man. The third fully roused his sleeping passions, inflamed his desires, and made him a tiger in bed.

The young king was beside himself with joy. But as he became used to his newfound powers, he became more peaceful and now had time to think of other things and people. He thought of the dervish and his extraordinary powers, how he had freely drunk three-fourths of the elixir in one gulp, three drops of which taken in three days had made the king mad with desire. He became anxious to learn the secret and went to the dervish. After the usual courtesies, he asked the holy man, "Master, I do not know how to thank you for making me a man. Your elixir worked magic. I came here not only to thank you but to clear a doubt in my mind. I know how it worked on me, and I wonder how you, a holy man, a celibate, could drink so much of it and still remain calm. What's the secret?"

The dervish was silent for a while and then replied solemnly: "Your Highness, I will satisfy your curiosity tomorrow, if you live that long. Right now, my first duty is to try and save your life, which is about to be snuffed out. I can read people's faces. I know who you are and how long you'll live. Tomorrow, before sunrise, you are fated to die. But I shall try and see if I cannot save you. Here, open your mouth," he said, taking out another vial of his elixir, which he emptied to the very last drop down the king's throat. The king mechanically gulped it down. A mortal terror took hold of him and shook his whole being. He gasped for breath and tried to ask more questions, but couldn't. The dervish asked the king to go home and then disappeared into his hut.

The king could hardly walk to the palanquin that waited to take him home. His legs seemed to give way under him. When he entered his seraglio, beautiful women smiled at him and came forward to embrace him, but he waved them aside. Their beauty only made the pang in his heart unbearable. He had only one thought, the thought of his imminent death. Without a word, he went to his bedchamber, ordered that no one should visit him till summoned, shut the doors, and tried to put himself to sleep. But all he could do was toss and turn and roll all night. The silk and satin of his bed seemed to have thorns in them. Thoughts of death gnawed at him and filled his night with terrors. When the clock in the palace tower struck its hours and half-hours, he heard his own death knell. By morning, he was exhausted and lay moping in a stupor till the sun's rays woke him through the cracks in his shuttered windows. The sun was up, and he had lived to see it! His spirits perked up. He had a new lease on life. He hurried to the dervish, who had obviously saved his life.

The dervish, who sat smoking outside his hut, smiled to see the king approach and asked, "My lord, how did you enjoy your begums last night?"

"Enjoy the begums!" replied the king, shocked at the question. "I who had to die this morning?"

"I knew you would not die so soon, Your Highness," said the dervish quietly, "but I frightened you just to give you a practical demonstration. I wanted to answer your question why I was not upset by taking almost the whole of the elixir, a few drops of which maddened you. Now you know that when the specter of death is before your mind, it shuts its doors tight and close against all earthly desires. I made you drink a whole vial of the same elixir to rouse your lust, yet it failed to make the slightest impression on your mind while the terror of death held its sway there. Your Highness saw the phantom of death for only one night, but I see it dancing before my eyes every moment. How could I possibly have other thoughts? My life's aim is to prepare for death, and so I welcome and cherish it at all times in my mind. Now go home, and may you live long, but do not forget this lesson."

Saying this, the dervish bowed and disappeared.

A Tall Tale in Urdu

~ *Urdu* ~ ~

There were three tanks on the point of a thorn. Of these, two were dry and the third had no water. In the one that had no water, three potters settled down. Of these three potters, two had no hands and the third was handless. The handless potter made three pots. Of these, two were broken and the third had no bottom. In the last they cooked three grains of rice. Two turned out raw and the third was uncooked. They invited three guests to eat the one uncooked grain of rice. Of the three guests, two were angry and the third could not be calmed down. The third guest, who could not be calmed down, was given three blows with a shoe. Two blows missed him and the third did not hit him. To avoid getting beaten with a shoe, the guest fled. The host pursued him.

On his way, a wild elephant attacked the host. He struck the wild elephant with his fist and broke two ribs and a half of the elephant. The wounded elephant fled, and the host chased it. The elephant ran up a tree and crawled from branch to branch and from leaf to leaf. At last the elephant jumped down from the tree and saw a spouted cup, got into it by way of the mouth, and came out through the spout. The body of the elephant got through all right, but its tail got stuck. The man who was attacking it didn't want to kill such a helpless brute and went his way.

Then he saw a little girl lift the carcass of the elephant on a straw and ask her mother where she should throw it.

"It's only a little mouse," said the girl.

The man who was watching this said to himself, "How powerful must be the father of such a girl!" So he asked her where her father was.

She said, "He is away in the jungle grazing the oxen of seventy thousand treasure-carts, all tied up in a string that he carries around his waist."

The man went to the jungle and saw the girl's father, with seventy thousand treasure-carts tied around his waist. He went up to him and challenged him to combat.

"All right," said the father of the girl, "but we are alone here and we'll never agree who is the winner. Let us find a third man to act as umpire."

Just then they saw an old woman with a bent back passing by. She had some food in one hand and a pitcher of water in the other. They spoke to her and asked her to act as umpire.

"O my sons, an old woman like me is not fit for such a job. But I've a grown-up son, not very far from here. He would be a better person to judge because he carries about tied to his waist a string of seventy thousand camels."

The combatants agreed. The old woman put the bundle of food on top of the pitcher, which she placed on her head, and invited one of the men to sit on each of her hands. The man with the seventy thousand carts tied them carefully around his waist and sat on one of the old woman's hands; his opponent sat on the other.

Now, the old woman, when she was angry, used to threaten her son and say she would hand him over to the *qazi*'s bailiff. The son saw her coming from a distance, and saw two men perched on her hands. He concluded that these were the *qazi*'s men, so he spread his sheet on the ground and quickly tied his seventy thousand camels in it and took to his heels. The necks of some of the camels stuck out of the bundle, and one of them had its tongue out of its mouth. A kite, thinking it was a piece of meat, came swooping down and flew away with the bundle. It was too heavy, and by and by the bird had to drop it.

It so happened that the queen was walking on the roof of her palace and she chanced to look up just at that time and the bundle fell into her eye. She felt pain in her eye, so she called for the midwife. The midwife examined the queen's eye, and to her surprise, saw seventy thousand camels walking about inside. She seized the camels one by one and hid some of them in her pockets and some in the folds of her dress. The queen was no longer in distress, and the midwife hurried home in delight and counted all the camels, but found only sixty-nine thousand nine hundred and ninety-nine. The midwife was convinced that there had been seventy thousand camels and that she must have left one in the queen's eye. So she hurried back to the palace and examined the queen's eye, but couldn't find the missing camel. So she searched in the gram field through which she had passed, but could find no trace of the camel and gave up the search.

One day she made some *phulkis*, or small cakes of gram flour, and when she tore open the first one that was ready, she found the camel inside, but minus its head and neck.

"Where have you been all this time?" asked the midwife.

"I am here," said the camel, "but my neck and head are at Agra, and they will come to you in due time."

Now, the king of Agra had made a lovely garden, and for a time it was found that some animal ate up the plants every night. He ordered a search, but the animal could not be found. At last the king ordered the *wazir* himself to keep guard. The *wazir* did so, and he cut his little finger and put salt and pepper in the wound so that the pain would keep him awake.

At midnight he saw the neck of a camel appear and eat the plants. The *wazir* quickly ran up and caught the neck and asked who it was.

"Never mind who I am," said the camel's neck, "but take this and do as

I tell you." The neck gave him a seed and said, "Take this to the king. Sow it before him at the first *ghari*, the first half-hour of day. It will germinate in the second *ghari*, grow in the third, flower in the fourth, bear fruit in the fifth, ripen in the sixth, and the fruit will be eaten by the king in the seventh."

The *wazir* did as the camel's neck directed, and the seed was planted, and seven *gharis* later a ripe watermelon was placed before the king.

At that moment some astrologers were announced. They informed the king that a tremendous rainstorm was approaching, and that unless the king and his people took refuge in a safe place all of them would be killed. They were all alarmed, but the astrologers saw the watermelon and cried out in chorus:

"This is the very thing!"

So they advised that the insides be scooped out and everyone should enter it. So the king and his people and all their goods and cattle went into the watermelon, and the two halves shut together when all were in. Soon the rain came down in torrents, and it rained for days and all the land was flooded and the watermelon, with the king and his people, floated on the water.

After the storm was over, a big fish that was very hungry saw the melon and devoured it, but the melon was so big it stuck in the fish's throat. So the fish came out and lay gasping on the bank, when a crane that had eaten nothing for days ate the fish. But it would not go down, and the crane fell

down exhausted and was soon devoured by a cat, which too could not move and was eaten by a dog, which also lay down unable to leave the place.

Now, there was a *kanjar*, a wandering Gypsy, whose wife was pestering him to go and get something for the family to eat.

"Don't nag me," he used to say. "One of these days I'll find you food enough to last four days."

So he went out to hunt on the day the dog had swallowed the cat. He found the dog half dead and killed it with one blow of his bludgeon, and took it home in delight. His wife cut open the dog and cried out, "Why, husband dear, there's a cat inside the dog."

"Didn't I tell you I would bring four days' food? Keep the cat for tomorrow."

Next day she cut open the cat and found the crane, and she told her husband, who said, "Keep the crane for tomorrow."

Next day, she cut open the crane and found the fish, and the next day she cut open the fish and found the watermelon.

At the end of it all, when she cut open the watermelon, out came the king and his people and their cattle and horses and all their goods. And the king gave the Gypsy a piece of land rent-free and lots of money, and went back to his kingdom.

The Greatest

~ *Angami Naga (Assam)* ~ ~

One day a man was going to his field, and on the way he caught a rat. He brought it home and put it in a box, and when later he took it out, the rat miraculously turned into a beautiful girl. When he saw her he said to himself, "If I could marry this beautiful girl to a great man, then I would benefit from it." So he went to find the greatest man in the world, and he came to the chief of his clan. He said, "You are the greatest man in the world and I want you to marry my adopted daughter."

But the chief said, "I would like to marry her, but you say she should marry only the greatest man in the world. Now, Water is greater than me, because when I go into a river in flood it carries me away." The man went to Water, and spoke to it as he had spoken to the chief. Water said, "I'm not the strongest or the greatest, for when I am still, Wind comes and blows me into waves. Wind is greater than I am."

So the man went to Wind, but Wind said, "Mountain is stronger than I am. However hard I blow, I cannot move it even an inch." So he went to Mountain, which said, "Yes, I'm stronger than most things. Not even Wind can blow me away. But a rat can pierce my side whenever it pleases. I'm powerless before a rat."

The man didn't know where else to go. So he came home, and what did he find? He found that the girl had turned into a rat again, and he let her go.

A Story for Sundays
~ *Marathi* ~~

In a town called Atpat, there lived a poor Brahman. He would go every day to the woods to fetch firewood and grass. One day he saw a strange sight in the woods: forest spirits were worshipping the sun and performing a strange rite in honor of the sun god.

When he made bold to ask them, "What are you doing?" they said, "These are our rites for the sun god." "Tell me how to do them," he said. They replied, "No, it's a powerful ritual. If we teach the rites to you, you may become vain and you may not do them properly." But he promised, "No, I shall be humble and I shall observe the rites exactly as you teach me." Then they told him how to do it: when the month of Shravan came, he should draw a picture of the sun god with sandal paste on the very first Sunday and offer it flowers and fruit. He should make such offerings for six months. Then for the next six months, he should give alms to the poor.

The Brahman went home, waited for the first Sunday of the month of Shravan, and did exactly as he was told. The sun god was greatly pleased with his offerings. Riches poured into the Brahman's lap and he became famous. One day, the queen sent for him. When he arrived at the court, he was overcome with fear and trembling. But she set him at ease, spoke very kindly to him, and said, "There's nothing to fear. We've invited you here only to ask you to give your daughters in marriage to our house." The Brahman hesitated. "My daughters come from a poor family," he said. "They will be treated as servants in the royal household." "No, no," the queen reassured him. "We'll treat them royally. One will marry a king and the other a minister of the kingdom."

The Brahman happily agreed. The weddings took place and the Brahman's daughters went to their husbands' palaces. The Brahman did not see them for twelve whole years. He was busy with his own duties and rituals. At long last, when he visited the elder daughter who was married to a king, she gave him an ornamental seat, brought scented water to wash his hands and feet, and offered him sweet pudding. The Brahman said, "Before I drink or eat anything here, I must tell you my story." But his daughter said, "Father, I've no time to listen to your story. The king is getting ready for a hunt and I must look to his dinner at once." And she wouldn't listen to him. The Brahman found this behavior quite discourteous and left her palace in a rage.

He then went to the house of his second daughter, the minister's wife. She too welcomed her father, gave him a carved wooden seat, brought scented water to wash his hands and feet, and offered him sweet pudding. He said, "Daughter, before I eat or drink, I must tell you my story." She said, "Of course, Father, tell me the story. I'd love to hear it." Then she brought from her bedroom six pearls, gave him three to hold in his hand, and kept the other three in her own. The Brahman told her what he had never told anyone so far. He told her how he had met the spirits in the woods and how they had taught him to worship the sun god. She listened to all without missing a word. Then the Brahman happily ate and drank in her house and went home. When his wife asked him how their daughters were doing, he told her everything and said, "The elder one would not listen to my story. She will come to grief."

And so she did. The king, her husband, went with his army to another country and never came back. But the second daughter, who had listened to the story, lived well and prospered. Misfortune dogged the elder daughter's steps and she became very poor. One day she said to her eldest son, "We have nothing in the house. Go to my sister and ask her to give you a gift. Bring back anything she gives you." The next Sunday the boy went to his aunt's place, stood by the village tank, and called out to the women who had come there to wash and bathe, "Whose servants are you?" They answered, "We are the maidservants of the minister's wife." The boy said, "If that's so, go tell her that her sister's son has come to see her. Tell her that his clothes are in rags and ask her to let him come into her house through the back door." The women took him in through the back door. His aunt arranged for him to have a fragrant bath, gave him new clothes and a sumptuous feast. Then she gave him a pumpkin, which she had hollowed out and filled with gold coins. As he left, she called to him, "Don't drop it. Guard it and take it home carefully." But on his way home, the sun god came disguised as a gardener and stole the pumpkin filled with gold. When the boy reached home his mother asked him what his aunt had given him. He showed his empty hands and said, "What fortune gave, karma took away. I lost whatever my aunt gave me."

The next Sunday, she sent her second son. He too stood by the village tank and called out to the women washing and bathing there, "Whose servants are you?" They said, "We are the servants of the minister's wife." "Then tell her that her nephew is here to see her." He was let in through the back door, bathed and clothed and fed. When he was about to leave, his aunt gave him a hollow stick filled with gold coins and said, "Don't drop it. Guard it and take it home carefully." On his way home, the sun god came in the shape of a cowherd and stole the stick from him. When the boy got home, his mother asked him what his aunt had given him. He showed his empty hands and said, "What fortune gave, karma took away."

On the third Sunday, her third son went and stood by the village tank. His aunt received him like the others and had him bathed, clothed, and fed. And she gave him a parting gift of hollow coconut stuffed with gold coins and said, "Don't drop it. Guard it carefully and take it home." On the way, he rested on the edge of a well. When he put the coconut down, it rolled and fell into the water with a great splash. When he got home, his mother asked him what he had brought. He said, "What fortune gave, karma took away."

This happened one more time when she sent her fourth son. He was given an earthen pot full of gold, but it also was snatched away by the sun god, who swooped down on it in the guise of a kite.

On the fifth Sunday, the mother herself went and stood by the village tank. Her sister, the minister's wife, came there personally and took her home

through the back door and had her bathed, clothed, and fed. Then she told
her elder sister that her trouble had come because she had refused to listen
to their father's story, and she repeated the story to her. The king's wife
listened to it attentively and stayed with her sister until the following month
of Shravan, when they together worshipped the sun god.

Hardly had the king's wife finished her worship when her fortune turned.
She heard that her husband, after years of battle, had vanquished his enemies
and was returning home with cartloads of wealth. On his way to his capital,
he stopped in the town where the minister and his wife lived. When he
learned that his wife was with her sister, he sent a proper escort to fetch her.
"O Auntie, Auntie," cried all the queen's little nephews, "umbrellas have
come for you, and horses and elephants and soldiers." Everyone rushed out
to see, and the king and queen greeted each other after years of suffering and
separation. The sisters gave each other gifts and silks, and the royal couple
set out for home together.

At the first halting-place, the servants cooked the food. The queen filled
the king's plate and then her own, and she thought of the story her sister
had told her. She ordered her servants to go through the neighboring village
and bring back anyone who was hungry and too poor to buy food. They
found no one who was poor in that village, but on the way back they met a
starving woodcutter and brought him to the queen. The queen brought out
six pearls. She gave the woodcutter three of them and kept the other three
in her hand. Then she told him the story of her father and the forest spirits.
The woodcutter was all ears as he listened to the story, and even as he listened,
his bundle of sticks turned to gold. He was astonished and ecstatic, and vowed
that he would worship the sun in the way the forest spirits had taught the
Brahman.

The next day the king and the queen and his entourage reached the second
halting-place. When the food was ready, the queen filled the king's plate and
her own, and again asked her servants to bring from the neighboring villages
anyone who was hungry and too poor to buy food. They found a small farmer
whose crops had withered and whose well had dried up, and took him to the
camp. There the queen brought out six pearls, gave three to the farmer, and
kept three in her own hand. Then she told him the story of her father and
the forest spirits. And as he listened, before the tale was over, water began
to fill his well and his crops sprouted fresh and green. He went away delighted,

and took a vow that he would worship the sun in the same way the Brahman had learned from the forest spirits.

In the third halting-place, the queen told the story to a poor old woman. Her eldest son had been lost in the forest. Her second son had been drowned in a pond. Her third son had died of snakebite. And as she listened to the queen's story, the long-lost eldest son walked into the camp, and then the son who had been drowned in the pond, and last of all the son who had died of snakebite. The old woman went away shedding tears of joy, promising to worship the sun in the way the spirits had taught the Brahman.

When the cavalcade reached the fourth halting-place, the queen's servants found a man whose eyes were so crossed he could hardly see. He had no arms and legs. He didn't even have a name—people called him "Lump-of-Flesh." He was lying on his face when they found him. When they carried him into the camp, the queen had him turned over, then had him bathed and clothed. She brought out six pearls, put three of them on his belly, and kept three in her hand. Then she told him the story of her father and the forest spirits. He listened to it attentively, and as he listened arms and legs grew out of his body, and hands and feet appeared at the ends of them. His eyes were no longer crossed. He too went away grateful and delighted, and promised to worship the sun in the way the forest spirits had taught the Brahman.

At the end of the next day's march, the king and queen reached their capital. Food was cooked, and as they sat down to eat, the sun god himself appeared and joined them. The king had all the doors of the palace flung open, and ordered a fresh and far more splendid dinner to be prepared with any number of dishes, each dish displaying six separate flavors.

When it was served, the sun god and the king began to eat, but in the first mouthful the sun god found a long hair. He flew into a rage and shouted, "To what sinful woman does this hair belong?" Then the poor queen remembered that during her twelve years of poverty she had always sat under the eaves combing her hair, and knew that it must be one of her hairs which had wafted into the sun god's food. She fell at his feet, but the sun god would not forgive her until she had clothed herself in a rough black blanket, plucked a stick out of the eaves, and gone outside the town and thrown the stick and the hair over her left shoulder. Then he recovered his good humor and finished his dinner. And the Brahman, the king and queen, the minister's wife and her family, the woodcutter, the farmer whose well had dried up, the old woman who had lost her three children, and the man called Lump-of-Flesh with the crossed eyes, they all remained in the favor of the sun god and lived happily ever after.

Tenali Rama
and the Brahmans

~ Kannada; Tamil; Telugu ~ ~

The queen mother lay dying and she said, "I've one last wish. I'd love to taste a sweet mango before I die." But alas, it was not the mango season. The king sent messengers far and wide, and it was weeks before they could bring back one measly little mango. It was too late. The king's mother had died meanwhile. The king was heart-stricken that he could not satisfy a simple wish of his dying mother. Furthermore, he was afraid that she would haunt the palace as a discontented ghost. So he summoned the Brahmans in his court and asked them what he should do to appease his mother's spirit. The Brahmans had a solution: the king should make a gift of a gold mango each to one hundred Brahmans, and then the queen mother's soul would find peace. So the king ordered the palace goldsmiths to fashion a hundred mangoes of gold, picked a good day for the gift-giving ceremony, and arranged a royal feast.

On their way to the feast, the Brahmans had to pass Tenali Rama's house. He was standing at the door with iron rods and a stove full of red-hot embers next to him. He said to them, "Our king said to me yesterday: any Brahman who lets himself be branded with these irons will get two golden mangoes instead of one." The Brahmans were greedy and got themselves branded, some more than once. Then they went groaning with pain to the king's palace, but each of them got only one golden mango from him. They showed him their welts from the branding and asked for more mangoes. When the king got angry with them, they told him what his favorite, the jester Tenali Rama, had done. He was furious, summoned Tenali Rama, and asked for an explanation. The jester said, "Your Highness, when my mother died, she was racked by arthritis. The local doctors advised me that the real cure was to brand her joints with hot irons. But my mother, poor thing, she died before I could do it. When I heard that Your Highness was giving golden mangoes to these Brahmans to appease your dead mother's spirit, I thought I should do the same. I'm glad both our mothers are now at peace, thanks to these holy Brahmans."

A Hair's-Breadth Escape

~ *Tamil* ~~

A rich landlord was also a miser. As he was stingy and difficult, no tenant would work his lands. Soon his lands were untilled and his tanks and canals dried up. So he became poorer and poorer. Yet he never learned to be generous and was unwilling to pay his workmen. One day, a holy man visited him and heard about his troubles. He said, "I have a mantra. If you repeat it for three months day and night, a brahmarakshasa will appear before you. He will be your slave and obey all your orders. He will be equal to a hundred servants."

The landlord fell at his feet and begged to be instructed at once.

The holy man made him sit facing the west, and taught him the mantra. The landlord rewarded him handsomely, and the holy man moved on.

The landlord repeated the mantra night and day for three months, and on the first day of the fourth month, a huge brahmarakshasa stood before him. Fearsome though he was in size and appearance, the demon fell at the landlord's feet and asked him, "What do you want from me, master?"

The landlord was in shock. He was terrified by this huge monster and his thundering voice. Yet he said, "I want you to be my servant and obey my commands."

"That's what I'm here for. Tell me what you want me to do," said the demon very respectfully. "But," he continued, "I must always have work to do. When one job is done, you must give me another at once. I can't be idle even for one second. If you fail to give me work, I'll have to kill you and eat you. That's my nature."

The landlord smiled. He thought he had enough work to occupy several such *brahmarakshasas*. He took him at once to the large tank, which had been dry for years, and said, "Repair this tank and make it deep enough to drown two palmyra trees."

"Yes, my master," said the demon humbly and got to work.

The landlord thought this job would take months. The tank was two miles long and two miles wide. He went home happily, ate well, and had a good time with his wife, who hadn't seen him so jolly in years. But that evening, the demon suddenly appeared before him and said that he had finished his work on the tank. The landlord said, "What! Finished all that work in a few hours! Go then and take out all the weeds and stones in my lands. They are spread over twenty villages. Make it ready for cultivation. And don't come back till you've done everything."

"Yes, master," said the demon, and disappeared.

His lands were several hundred acres and spread all over the region. No one had worked on them for years, and they were all overgrown and covered with rubbish. That should take the demon months, if not years, thought the landlord.

As he was preparing himself for bed that night, the demon appeared before him and said, "It's done, master. Your lands are ready."

The landlord, though astonished and a little afraid of the speed with which things were getting done, said in haste, "Then till it and sow rice. Then irrigate it properly, just as much as is needed, no more, from the tank."

The demon said, "Yes, master," again and vanished.

That should take him at least a week, thought the landlord and went to bed. But the demon woke him up soon after and asked for more work. The landlord began to panic. All night he gave him new tasks, inventing new ones. His house was washed, his cows milked and bathed. New houses were built. Fruit trees and flowering trees from faraway places all over the world were imported and planted in his garden. The demon, as he got used to his master's wishes, was doing the jobs faster and faster, taking less and less time with each new task. He was tireless. By morning, the landlord was dead tired and terror-stricken. "I can't think of anything more for him to do. What shall I do? He will kill me the moment I stop! What shall I do?" he cried in despair, and began to tear out his hair.

When his wife saw him panic-stricken like this, she consoled him and said, "Don't lose courage. Think of everything you've ever wanted done, and get it done by this demon of yours. When you really run out of jobs, send him to me."

The landlord asked the demon to take him on his back and show him all that he had done. For miles he surveyed the handiwork of his demonic and perfect servant. The tank was deep, clean, and full of water, miles of it. His lands in twenty villages had been weeded, tilled, and sown with rice. His garden had been put in order and filled with all sorts of exotic trees. New houses had been built, furnished, and decorated. His cows had been washed and milked. Everything had been done within a few hours. As the landlord began to rack his brains for new projects and was getting more and more frantic, the demon asked him urgently, "What else do you want me to do? Tell me, tell me, give me something to do. I'm getting restless."

The man remembered what his wife had said and told the *brahmarakshasa*, "You're the best servant I've ever had. Now, please go to my wife. She has a little job for you."

Having bought himself a little time, the landlord began to pray and think of his impending death at the hands of this restless demon.

Just then, his wife herself came that way, a long curly black hair in her hand. She had just pulled it out of her head. She said to the demon, "Look here, *brahmarakshasa*, I've a small job for you. Take this hair and make it straight, and bring it back to me."

The demon took it gladly from her hand and went and sat in a pipal tree to make it straight. He rolled it many times on his enormous thigh and lifted it to the light to see if it was straight. But no, no matter what he did, it was still curly. After many useless attempts to straighten this Tamil woman's curly hair, he thought of something. He had seen goldsmiths heat wires in the fire and beat them till they became straight. So he went to a goldsmith's forge, when he was asleep, and put the hair in it. At once it frizzled and went up in smoke, leaving behind a bad smell. He was horrified. "What will I do now? What will my master's wife say if I do not return the hair she gave me?"

Not knowing what to do next, he became desperate, and was so afraid of what his mistress would say that he ran away, never to be seen again.

Between Two Wives

~ Tamil ~ ~

A middle-aged man, not content with his first wife, took a young woman for his second. The two wives didn't get along and quarreled all the time. So he had two households set up in different parts of the city. After much nagging and back-and-forth talk, he made his wives agree that he should stay with each of them on alternate days.

Whenever he stayed with his young second wife, she would sit him down and, pretending to delouse him, would pluck out all the grey hair on his head. She wanted him to look young, with a head of black hair.

And whenever he visited his first wife, who felt unhappy at being the older wife, she plucked out all his black hair. She wanted him to look older than herself, not younger.

Thus, in course of time, he had no hair at all left on his head.

The Dead Prince
and the Talking Doll

~ Kannada ~ ~

The king had a daughter. One daughter, but no sons. Now and then a certain beggar would come to the palace. He was strange, for each time he begged he would say, "You'll get a dead man for a husband. Give me some alms." The girl used to wonder: "Why does he say such weird things to me?" And she would silently give him alms and go in. This *bava*, this holy man, came to the door every day for twelve years. And every day he said, "You'll get a dead man for a husband."

One day the king was standing on the balcony and heard him say, "You'll get a dead man for a husband. Give me some alms."

The king came down and asked his daughter, "What's this talk, Daughter?"

She replied, "This *bava* comes every day and says, 'You'll get a dead man for a husband. Give me some alms.' Then I give him something. He has been saying it for twelve years, ever since I was a little girl."

The king was disturbed when he heard this. He was afraid the prophecy would come true. He didn't wish his only daughter to have a dead man for a husband. He said unhappily, "It's no good staying in this kingdom. Let's leave and spend our time in travels." And he got his servants to pack everything, and left the palace with his entire family.

Around that time, the prince of the neighboring kingdom fell mysteriously ill and died. But his body looked as if he had only fallen asleep, and astrologers said he would return to life after twelve years. So, instead of burying him, his father the king built a bungalow outside the town, laid his son's body in it, mortared and whitewashed the house on all sides, and left the body there, fully clothed and adorned. He locked the main door and left a written message on it. The message said: "One day a chaste woman who has made offerings to the gods for her husband will come here. Only she can enter the place. When she touches the door, it will open. It will open to no one else."

It was soon after this sad event that the first king arrived there with his wife and daughter and his entourage. They were all hungry and began to cook a meal for themselves. The king's daughter went for a walk and saw the locked door. The lock was of exquisite design and gleamed from a distance.

She went near and laid her hand on it. As soon as she touched it, it sprang open, and the door opened. She went in. The door closed and locked itself behind her. Ahead of her were twelve doors, one behind another; they all opened at her touch, and each closed behind her as she went through it.

Right in the heart of the house she found a dead man on a cot. He looked as if he was fast asleep. Before she could wonder what was happening to her, why doors opened before her and shut behind her, she was in the presence of the dead man. His family had left provisions for twelve years in the house: vessels, dishes, clothes, grains, spices. The princess saw all these things around her.

She remembered the holy beggar's words and thought, "I didn't escape it: his words are coming true." She unveiled the face of the body. It was dead as dead could be, but calm as a face in deep slumber. "Well, what's to be done? It looks as if I am imprisoned here with this dead man. Let's do something," she said, and started massaging his legs.

For almost twelve years she tended and massaged his body. She would wake up in the morning in the locked house with twelve locked doors, and where could she go? She bathed and cooked, kept house, and looked after the dead body, and thought about all the things that had happened to her.

~ ~~

Meanwhile, in the forest, the mother had said, "The food is all ready. Where's our girl gone?" Her father had walked outside and called her. She was nowhere to be seen, but they could hear her cries from inside the house. They had called out, "Daughter, why are you in there? Come out!"

She had answered from within and told her father what had happened.

"I touched the locks, and they fell open. As soon as I came in, they locked themselves shut. I am alone here."

"What is in there?"

"There's a dead man lying here. Nothing else."

"My girl, your luck has caught up with you. What the *bava* said is coming true. The locks can't be opened."

They had tried to enter the house from the sides and from behind, but it was as if it had been sealed. They had tried and tried, and finally said, "What else can we do? We'll go, and leave you to work out your fate." They had left sorrowfully. Time passed, and they grew old.

Inside the locked house, night and day the princess massaged the dead man's legs, took ritual baths, worshipped the gods at the right times, and made offerings for her husband. Around the tenth year, an acrobat's daughter came that way. She looked all around the house, tried the doors, and at last climbed onto the roof.

The princess was lonely. She was dying to see another human face. "If there's a chink in the house, I could pull in at least a child. If only I could have a girl for a companion!" she thought. Just then, she saw a young woman looking in through a window.

"Hey, girl! Will you come inside?"

"Yes," said the acrobat girl.

"Do you have any father or mother? If you do, don't try to come in. You can't get out. If you don't have parents, come inside."

"Oh no, I have nobody."

The princess began to pull her in through the window. The acrobat girl was agile—she twisted and contorted her body and got in. The princess was happy; she had company now. With a companion inside, time went faster. Two more years rolled by.

The prince's twelve years were coming to an end. The time was near for his life to stir again.

One day, when the king's daughter was taking her bath, she heard the omen-bird speak from a branch at the window. It said, "The twelve years are coming to an end. If someone will pluck the leaves of this tree, grind them and press them into a silver cup, and pour the juice into the dead man's mouth, he will come to life again."

The king's daughter heard this. At once, she plucked some leaves and pressed out the juice into a silver cup. Just when she was about to take it to the dead man, it occurred to her that she should finish her bath, purify herself, and offer worship to the lord Siva properly before she gave the juice to the prince. So she put down the cup and went back to bathe and offer worship.

The acrobat girl asked her, "What's this stuff in the cup? Why is it here?"

The princess told her about the bird's message and what the cup contained. As soon as she heard all this, the acrobat girl thought this was her chance. While the princess sat in worship, the acrobat girl parted the dead prince's lips and poured in the juice from the silver cup. As the liquid went in, he woke up as if he had only been asleep. Exclaiming, "Siva, Siva," he sat up straight. He saw the woman next to him and asked, "Who are you?"

She said, "Your wife."

He was grateful to her. They became husband and wife, while the princess sat inside absorbed in prayer, the woman who had served him for twelve long years.

When she came out, she heard the two of them whispering intimacies to each other. "O Siva, I did penance for twelve years, and it has turned out like this. Obviously, happiness is not my lot," she thought. She began to work as their servant, while the prince and the acrobat woman sat back and enjoyed themselves.

Yet after all she was a princess, born to a queen, and the other girl was only an acrobat's daughter. The prince could see the difference between them in manners and speech, and he began to suspect something was wrong. So later that day he said to both of them, "I'm going out for a hunt and then I'll go to the city. Tell me what you want."

The acrobat girl, who had been longing for her Gypsy kind of food, asked for all sorts of greens and dry flat bread to eat. The prince was disgusted. A woman should ask for saris and silk blouses, but this one asks for wretched dry bread! Then he told the acrobat girl to ask the other woman in the house what she would like. The princess answered, "I don't want anything much. Just tell the master what I'd really like is a talking doll."

"This one is strange, too. All she wants is a talking doll," he thought.

After a good hunt in the jungle, he brought the acrobat girl the evil-smelling greens and leaves and dry bread from some Gypsies, and gave the princess her talking doll. The acrobat girl was overjoyed at the sight of the rough food; now she would begin to thrive and get some color in her cheeks.

That night, after everyone had eaten and gone to bed, the talking doll suddenly began to speak and said, "Tell me a story."

The princess answered, "What story can I tell you? My own life has become quite a story."

"Then tell me your life's story," the doll insisted.

So the princess told the doll her entire story, as I've told you so far. Just like that. The doll nodded and said, "Hmm, hmm," as the princess told her tale. The prince, lying awake in the next room, heard it all. Finally the princess said, "I left the silver cup there on that ledge, and that woman gave the juice to the prince before I got back from my prayers. Now she's the wife and I'm the servant. That's the way it turned out." So she ended the story.

As he listened from where he lay in the next room, the prince felt his anger mounting. When the story came to an end, he took a switch and lashed at the acrobat girl sleeping next to him and drove her out of the house.

"You're not my wife, you're an acrobat wench! Get out of my sight!" he shouted. Then he went in and consoled the princess who had served him so lovingly for twelve years, and they talked to each other all night happily.

In the world outside, his father and mother had counted up the days and years. They knew the twelve years were over, and were anxious to see what had happened to their son. They came, and all the town came with them. They found the doors unlocked, and found in the heart of the house the couple, prince and princess, whispering loving words to each other.

Gratefully, the father-in-law and mother-in-law fell at the feet of their young daughter-in-law and said, "By your good work of many past lives, and your prayers in this one, our son has come back to life. He looks as fresh as if he had just wakened from a long night's sleep. It's all your doing."

They took the couple to their palace, and celebrated the wedding with great pomp and many processions. For the grand occasion they sent for the bride's parents, who had grown weak and old. Their eyes had become like cottonseeds, and they were ready to lie down in the earth. But their spirits revived at the good news, and they too hurried to the reunion at their daughter's wedding.

The Serpent Mother

~ *Gujerati* ~ ~

An old couple had seven married sons. All the sons and their wives lived with their old parents. The six senior daughters-in-law were well regarded because they had rich relatives. But the seventh one was ignored and despised, for she had no relatives at her father's place. She was an orphan. Everyone in her father-in-law's house took to calling her "the one who has no one at her father's place."

Every day the whole family would eat their meals joyously. The youngest daughter-in-law had to wait till everyone else was finished and then collect the scraps of food left in the bottom of the earthen pots and eat them. Then she had to clean the whole heap of pots.

Things went on this way till the season came for offering food to dead ancestors. They made sweet *khir*, rice pudding, with the milk of buffaloes. The youngest wife was pregnant and had a craving for the *khir*, but who would give her any? The others ate it with relish and left her nothing but half-burned crusts at the bottom of the earthen pot. She looked at them and said, "Half-burned crusts of *khir*—well, that'll do for me." She carefully scraped the crusts into a piece of cloth and decided to eat them somewhere where no one would see her. It was time to fetch water from the well. The well site was overcrowded with the women of the village. The young daughter-in-law thought she would eat her *khir* crusts after everyone else was gone. When her turn came to fetch water, she put her little bundle of *khir* near a snake-hole. She drew her pitcher of water from the well. She thought she would eat her *khir* after a bath.

While she was bathing, a female serpent came out of the hole unseen. She too was pregnant, and the smell of *khir* drew her. She craved to eat it, and she ate it all up and went back to her hole. She had decided that she would bite the owner of the *khir* if he or she used abusive language and cursed the thief who had taken it.

The young daughter-in-law returned eagerly after her bath to pick up her bundle. She found that the cloth was there but all the crusts of *khir* were gone. Not even a crumb was left.

"Oh," she cried, almost aloud, "I didn't get to eat any *khir* in the house and I didn't get to eat it even here. Maybe there's another unhappy woman like me somewhere around, and she may have eaten it. Whoever she is, let her be satisfied, as I would have been."

On hearing this, the female serpent came out of the hole and asked her, "Who are you, young woman?"

"Mother, I'm just an unhappy woman. I'm pregnant, and I craved to eat *khir*. I had some crusts here, but when I went for my bath, someone ate them up. Well, she must be someone unhappy like myself and may have been hungry. I'm glad that someone was made happy by my *khir*."

"Oh, I was the one who ate your *khir*," said the serpent. "If you had cursed me and abused me, I'd have bitten you. But you have blessed me. Now tell me why you're so miserable."

"Mother, I've no one to call mine in my father's place. The ceremony for my first pregnancy will be due soon. My parental relatives are supposed to perform it, and there's no one to do it," she said. As she spoke, her eyes filled with tears.

The serpent said, "Daughter, do not worry. From today on, just think of me and my kin as your parental relatives. We all live in this hole. When it's time to celebrate your first pregnancy, just put an invitation near the hole. It's a happy, auspicious occasion and should not go uncelebrated." Thus she became the young woman's foster mother. The young daughter-in-law went home, astonished at the turn of events.

When the auspicious day for celebrating the first pregnancy was near, the mother-in-law said, "This last daughter-in-law of mine has no brothers, nobody. Who's going to celebrate her first pregnancy?" The young wife said, "Mother-in-law, give me a letter of invitation for the ceremony."

"You brotherless woman, whom do you have at your father's or mother's place? Nobody! To whom will you give the letter of invitation?"

"I have a distant relative. Please give me a letter for her."

"Look, everybody! Our brotherless lady is out of her mind. She has suddenly found a relative."

At that point, a neighbor woman spoke up: "Oh, come along! Give the poor thing a piece of paper. What do you have to lose?"

The young daughter-in-law went to the snake-hole at the outskirts of the village, put the letter near it, and came back home.

The day for celebrating the first pregnancy came. The wives of the elder brothers and the mother-in-law ganged up on the young woman and began to mock her: "Just wait. Our daughter-in-law's relatives will come now from her father's place, her mother's place, from everywhere. They'll bring her presents and trunks full of clothes. Put pots of water on the stove to boil and bring wheat to make *lapasi*. Hurry, they'll all be here any minute!"

Even as they were teasing her and making jokes, guests arrived wearing festive red turbans. They looked like Moghul grandees. A noblewoman, looking like a Rajput, was among them. The young daughter-in-law knew at once that the noblewoman was none other than the serpent mother. Her mother-in-law and sisters-in-law were all astonished at the sight and began to mutter, "Where did these people come from? She has no one, not even a father or a mother or a brother. Where did all these relatives come from? And so rich!"

Then they began to welcome the guests: "Welcome, make yourselves at home. We have been waiting all this time for our young daughter-in-law's relatives." The pots for cooking *lapasi* for the festive occasion were actually placed on the stoves and preparations began.

Now the serpent mother called the young woman aside and whispered in her ear, "Daughter, tell them not to cook anything. Just put pots of spiced and boiled milk in this room. We'll drink it after we shut the door. We belong to the serpent community, as you know, and we can't eat ordinary food."

The young woman went to her mother-in-law and told her not to cook

anything because her paternal relatives belonged to a caste that drank only spiced milk—that was their prescribed food.

It was time for the meal. Vessels full of milk boiled with spices were put in the room. As soon as the door was shut, the guests resumed their original form as snakes, put their mouths to the vessels, and drank up the milk in no time at all.

The first pregnancy of the daughter was celebrated with all due ceremony. The guests gave gold and silver and silk to the husband and his relatives, who were wonderstruck and said, "Oh, look how much they've brought! They've given her such a rich dowry!"

The guests said at the end of it all, "Now give all of us leave to go and take our sister to our house for the delivery."

"Oh surely, surely! Please. After all, this is the daughter of your house. How can we refuse?" said the mother-in-law.

"And you don't have to send anyone to bring her back. We will come and bring our sister back to you," said the guests.

All the husband's relatives came out to bid good-bye to the young daughter-in-law and her relatives. The guests said, with great courtesy, "Now please go back in. We'll find our way." When all of them had gone back into the house, the serpents led the young woman to the hole on the outskirts of the village. There they said to her, "Sister, don't be afraid. We'll now assume our original forms. And we'll take you into the hole." The girl said, "I'm not afraid." Then they all entered the hole, taking the young woman with them.

As they went inside, she found spacious rooms. They were as beautiful as the datura flower. There were beautiful beds and swings. The serpent mother, the matron of the family, sat on a swinging bed that made noises like *kikaduka, kikaduka.* The snake god had jewels on his head and a big mustache. He was sitting on a soft, satin-cushioned seat.

The snake god treated the young woman as his daughter and looked after her every need in that underground world. She enjoyed the swinging bed made of gold and silver. Her new parents and the entire clan treated her with love and care.

Now the serpent mother was also ready to deliver. She told the young daughter-in-law, "Look here, Daughter, I want to tell you something, and don't be shocked. We are a community of snakes. We know that if all our babies survived, then we would disturb the balance in the world. There would be no place for any other creature, no place for people to walk, even. Therefore we eat our babies as they are born, and only those that escape will live on. Don't be upset when you see me doing this."

When the time came, the young woman stood near the serpent mother with an earthen lamp in her hand. The serpent went on devouring the eggs as they were laid. Seeing this, the young mother-to-be was filled with disgust. Her hands shook and the lamp dropped from her hand. In the darkness two eggs hatched and escaped. The serpent mother could bite off only the tails of the two babies before they got away. So there were two tailless snakes.

When the young daughter-in-law was nine months pregnant, she went into labor and delivered a son, beautiful as the ring on the finger of a god. The son grew bigger day by day. When he began to crawl on his knees, she told her serpent mother, "Mother, you've done a lot for me. Now please take me to my house."

The serpent mother gave her mattresses, a cradle, necklaces, anklets, all sorts of ornaments, and overwhelmed her with gifts. Then she said, "Daughter, I want you to do something. Put your hand into the mouth of your grandfather sitting here. Don't be afraid. He won't bite you."

The young woman shook with fear but put her hand into the old snake's mouth. The hand and the whole arm went into his mouth, and when she took it out, shaking all the while, the arm was covered with bracelets of gold.

"Now put in the other hand, all the way," said the serpent mother. The young woman, less afraid this time, put her other arm all the way into the mouth of the snake, and when she withdrew it, it too was covered with bracelets of gold. Then two brothers in human form went with her and left her at the outskirts of her husband's village. When she arrived at her door, both mother and son, surrounded by all the relatives, shouted with joy, "The young daughter-in-law has come! The young daughter-in-law has come! She has brought a big dowry. But nobody knows where her relatives' village is."

The young woman said nothing.

Her son grew. One day the wife of the eldest son of the family was cleaning grain and getting it ready for grinding. The little boy picked up fistfuls of the grain and began scattering it. The eldest daughter-in-law shouted, "Son, don't do that. Why do you want to scatter the grain? We are poor people and can't afford to waste it." This was meant to taunt the young daughter-in-law about her dowry. She was hurt by the taunt. She went to the outskirts of the village, stood near the snake-hole, and wept. When she came back, a number of bulls arrived, carrying bags full of grain to her husband's house. The husband's relatives were put to shame.

Once her son spilled some milk. The eldest daughter-in-law threw him a taunt: "Son, don't do that. Your mother's relatives are rich. They will send you a herd of buffalo. But we are poor people. Don't spill our milk."

Again, the young daughter-in-law went to the snake-hole and wept there. The serpent mother came out and said to her, "We'll take care of it. Go home now, but when you go, do not look behind you. Do not give buttermilk to a juggler. Say *Nagel, nagel* and a herd of buffalo will come to your house." The woman returned to her house, saying *Nagel, nagel* all the way, and a herd of buffalo followed her. When she reached home, she called out to her in-laws and said, "We must clean the buffalo shed." All the relatives came out and were amazed to see countless buffalo with white marks on their foreheads.

Now what was happening in the snake-hole? The two young snakes without tails were unhappy because no one wanted to play with them. Their playmates said:

> *Go away, Tailless, I won't let you play!*
> *Go away, Minus-Tail, I won't let you play!*

The two young snakes went to their mother and asked her, "Mother, Mother, tell us. Who made us without tails?"

She said, "Sons, you have a sister who lives out there on the earth. When you were born, the earthen lamp accidentally fell from her hand. So, you have no tails."

"Then we'll both go and bite her for doing this to us."

"No, no! How can you bite your sister? She is a good girl. She'll bless you."

"If she blesses us, we'll give her a sari and a blouse for a gift and come back. But if she says nasty things about us, we'll bite her."

Before the mother could say anything, the two tailless snakes crept away and went to the sister's house. It was evening. One hid himself near the threshold, the other one lay hidden in the watershed. They thought, "If she comes here, we'll bite her."

When the sister came to the threshold, she stumbled and her foot struck something. She said, "I'm the one without a parent. May my paternal relatives be pleased to forgive me if I've struck something. The serpent god is my father and the serpent mother is my mother. They've given me silk and jewels for my dowry."

When he heard these words, the tailless snake thought, "Oh, this sister is blessing me. How can I bite her?"

The sister went then to the watershed. There also, she stumbled and her foot hit something. Again she said, "I'm the one without parents. May my paternal relatives be pleased to forgive me if I've struck something. The serpent god is my father and the serpent mother is my mother. They've given me silk and jewels for my dowry."

The second tailless snake also thought, "This sister is blessing me. How can I bite her?"

Then both the brothers assumed human form, met their sister, gave her a sari and a blouse, gave her son golden anklets, and went home to their hole.

May the Serpent Mother be good to us all as she was good to her!

Teja and Teji

~ *Assamese* ~ ~

A rich peasant had two wives. The elder wife had a daughter, and the younger had a son and a daughter called Teja and Teji. Their stepmother didn't like them nor did she like their mother, who was her husband's favorite. One day, the two wives went to the tank to have a bath. The younger wife asked the elder one to scrub her back. While doing so, the elder wife pushed her into the tank and said, "Change into a tortoise and stay there." The younger wife changed at once into a big tortoise.

When their stepmother came back, Teja and Teji asked her about their mother. She scolded them and said, "How should I know where she's gone?"

Next morning, when Teja and Teji went out with the cows to graze them near the tank, a tortoise came out of the water and surprised them by talking to them. It said, "Children, I'm your mother. Your stepmother pushed me into the water and turned me into a tortoise. I worry about you and wonder whether you have enough to eat." Then she put a little of her vomit on a leaf and asked her children to eat it. They ate it and found to their surprise that their hunger was gone. From that day, they visited their tortoise mother every morning. She brought up food for them from her stomach and fed them.

The elder wife now noticed that her stepchildren no longer complained of hunger. They actually looked lovely and well-fed. She would give her own daughter good things to eat, but she looked scrawny and thin. She suspected that something was going on. So she sent her daughter with Teja and Teji one day to see if her stepchildren were getting something to eat outside the house. Teja and Teji didn't want their stepsister with them when they went to see their mother, so they sent her after a stray cow and quickly went to see their mother. But just as they were eating their meal in a hurry, their stepsister returned and found them. She also wanted a share of what they were eating and found it delicious and satisfying. Teja and Teji begged her not to say anything to her mother about what they were doing.

That evening, when the children returned home, the elder wife noticed that her own daughter was looking quite well-fed. She grilled her with questions. "Did you all eat something during the day?" she asked. "No, no, we didn't touch a thing," said the girl, but her mother persisted. When the mother threatened to beat her, the girl confessed and reported everything—about the tortoise in the tank, its vomit that all three of them ate, and how good it was.

That night, the elder wife put some potsherds under her sleeping mat and lay on it. As she tossed and turned, the potsherds crackled. Her husband asked her, "What's the matter?"

She said, "Oh, oh, I'm aching all over. My joints ache. I feel so sick."

He asked, "What can I do for you?"

She groaned and said, "I know what will cure these pains."

"What will cure them?"

She said, "That big tortoise in the tank. Its flesh will be good for me."

The peasant ordered his servants to catch the tortoise. Teja and Teji heard of this and ran to the tank to tell their mother. She said, "Weeping will get us nowhere. Listen carefully to what I'm going to say. They can't catch me with their nets. But if you come to the tank to catch me, I'll let myself be caught. They will cut me up and cook me into a curry. When they invite you to eat with them, hide the meat under the leaf on which they serve it. Then find some way of burying it with the leaves near this tank. You'll soon see a tree of gold and silver growing there, and it will help you."

Next morning the men tried to catch the tortoise, but she escaped their nets every time. When they got tired of it, the children went there and caught her easily. And they did as she had told them to do. They did not eat her flesh, and buried it secretly near the tank.

The very next morning, a tree of gold and silver had grown up there. Crowds gathered to see the wonderful tree. When the king heard about it, he wanted to take it to his palace. But no one could uproot it. Teja was standing near the tree and he said to the king, "Your Majesty, I can pull it up for you, but you must promise to marry my sister." Teja said that because his mother had told him to. The king agreed, and Teja pulled up the tree. The king was amazed. He thanked the boy, but said, "Your sister is too young for me. Let her grow up. Then I'll marry her."

The boy gave the king a grackle and a pomegranate seedling and said, "Your Majesty, it's just possible that you may forget about my sister and this promise. Take these two things with you. When the bird begins to talk and the plant bears fruit, come and take Teji to your palace." The king promised to do so.

Time passed, and one day the grackle started talking and the pomegranate bore fruit. But the king had completely forgotten about his promise. While he was resting one evening, the bird sang:

Ezar nizar paril . . .

The pomegranate is ripe
And ready to drop.
How can the king forget?
Sister Teji is grown up now.

The king heard the song and looked around. The bird sang again:

Ezar nizar paril . . .

The pomegranate is ripe
And ready to drop.
How can the king forget?
Sister Teji is grown up now.

The king now remembered the scene under the wonderful tree and his promise to marry the girl. So without any further delay, he set out for Teji's village, married the girl, and started back with his new bride.

The king had seven wives he had married earlier, and they didn't like the addition of another wife to their number. When the king returned in a boat with Teji and the boatmen were about to moor the boat at the ghat, the landing place with its flight of steps, the eldest wife sang out:

> *Not here, Teji,*
> *Do not get off here.*
> *O evil Teji,*
> *This is my ghat.*

When the boatmen tried to moor at another ghat, another wife sang out:

> *Not here, Teji,*
> *Do not get off here.*
> *O evil Teji,*
> *This is my ghat.*

In this way the seven wives did not allow her to get off at seven landing places. So the boatmen had to moor the boat at still another ghat.

Teji was happy with the king. But her stepmother was unhappy that she should be so fortunate. She jealously plotted and bided her time. When Teji gave birth to a boy a year later, the stepmother got her chance. According to custom, Teji had to go visit her parents. The king gave her leave. When she arrived, her stepmother seemed very loving and attended to her and the baby's comforts. One morning she said to Teji, "Come, let me do up your hair." While pretending to comb her hair, she pushed a thorn into Teji's head and said, "Change into a mynah bird." Teji instantly changed into a mynah bird and flew to the roof of the house.

A few days later, the king sent a letter and men to bring back Teji. Her stepmother meanwhile dressed her own daughter in Teji's clothes and ornaments, and sent her away with Teji's child in her arms. The mynah bird followed the palanquin of the false wife.

The stepsister looked like Teji, especially in Teji's clothes. The king didn't seem to notice any difference, but the baby gave her no end of trouble; he missed his mother. When the stepsister tried to dandle and nurse the child, the mynah cried:

> *Whose child is it? Who dandles it?*
> *She makes it weep all the more.*

The king overheard the bird singing like that, and he wondered. Teji had been weaving a netlike cloth on her loom before she left for her mother's house. It lay on the loom unfinished. When the stepsister sat at the loom and made a show of weaving, the mynah cried:

> Whose cloth is it? Who weaves it?
> She breaks the threads and leaves them knotted.

The king's suspicions, which had been growing, now were fully roused. He had seen his wife Teji handle the child quite well, and she could weave expertly. He took two sweet-balls in his hands and addressed the bird: "O mynah, I have in my hand two sweet-balls. One is the ball of hunger and the other the ball of thirst. If you are indeed someone of my own, then eat the ball of hunger. If you are someone else, then eat the ball of thirst." The bird alighted on his hand and pecked at the sweet-ball of hunger. As the king caressed the bird his hand felt something sharp in its head. He pulled it out, and lo! there was Teji in the flesh.

He now got the entire story from her and was furious at the treachery of the stepmother and her daughter. At once, he ordered his executioners to kill the impostor, put her flesh and fat in a cask, her head and hands and feet in another cask, and her blood in a third cask. When his orders were carried out, he asked two men to take the casks to Teji's stepmother. He told them: "Give her first the cask of flesh and fat and say this is venison. Leave the other casks with her when you leave her place in the morning."

So they took the casks to the evil woman. When she received the first cask she said to herself, "Excellent. My daughter went to the palace only the other day, and she has already sent me presents. That other one had no such feelings and sent me nothing." So the happy mother cooked the flesh and served it to her household, ate some herself, and lighted lamps with the fat. The king's men said they were unwell and did not eat anything. When the feasting was over and the lamps were burning high, they began to sing:

> A relative cooked it, a relative served it,
> They all ate it together.
> With a relative's fat they lighted the lamps,
> And the floor was flooded with light.

The woman overheard them singing and asked, "What are you singing there, fellows?" They said, "Oh, we have a high fever and don't know what we sing." Next morning she found that the men had left early and there were other casks near her door. She eagerly opened them, and when she saw the head and hands and feet and the blood of her dear daughter, and realized what she had fed on the night before, her grief and rage knew no bounds. She rent the air with her cries.

The Dove's Egg: A Chain Tale

~ *Malayalam* ~ ~

A dove laid an egg in the hollow of a big tree in front of the blacksmith's house. When she flew away from her nest in search of food, the blacksmith's wife stole the egg.

The dove came back to her nest and found the egg missing. The dove knew at once that the blacksmith's wife must have taken it. So she went to the woman and pleaded, "Give me back my egg, please."

The blacksmith's wife pretended that she knew nothing about it and said, "What egg are you talking about? I didn't see any egg."

The dove was heartbroken and flew about looking for help. On the way she met a pig, who asked, "Why are you crying, little bird?"

She said, "O pig, can you help me? Will you dig up the yams of the blacksmith's wife who stole my egg?"

"No, not I," grunted the pig, walking away.

She then met a hunter, who asked, "Why are you in tears, little bird?"

The bird said, "Will you shoot an arrow at the pig who wouldn't dig up the yams of the blacksmith's wife who stole my egg?"

"Why should I? Leave me out of this," said the hunter, walking away.

The dove wept some more and flew on till she met a rat, who also asked why she was in tears. The dove said, "Will you gnaw and cut the bowstring of the hunter who wouldn't shoot the pig who wouldn't dig up the yams of the blacksmith's wife who stole my egg?"

The rat too said, "Not I," and went his own way.

Next she met a cat, who asked, "What's the matter, little bird?"

"Will you catch the rat who wouldn't cut the bowstring of the hunter who wouldn't shoot the pig who wouldn't dig up the yams of the blacksmith's wife who stole my egg?"

The cat would rather mind her own business.

The poor dove was beside herself with anger and grief. Her wails attracted the attention of a passing dog, who asked her what was bothering her. She said, "Will you bite the cat who wouldn't catch the rat who wouldn't cut the bowstring of the hunter who wouldn't shoot the pig who wouldn't dig up the yams of the blacksmith's wife who stole my egg?"

"No, not I," said the dog and ran away.

The dove's wails grew louder and louder.

An old man with a long white beard came that way and asked the crying bird what the matter was. She said, "Grandfather, will you beat the dog who wouldn't bite the cat who wouldn't catch the rat who wouldn't cut the bowstring of the hunter who wouldn't shoot the pig who wouldn't dig up the yams of the blacksmith's wife who stole my egg?"

The old man didn't want to do anything of the sort and shook his head and went his way.

The dove next went to the fire for help and asked it to burn the white beard of the old man, but the fire wouldn't do it. Next the dove went to the water and asked it to put out the fire which wouldn't burn the beard of the old man who refused to beat the dog who wouldn't bite the cat who wouldn't catch the rat who wouldn't cut the bowstring of the hunter who wouldn't shoot the pig who wouldn't dig up the yams of the blacksmith's wife who stole the egg. Water too was unwilling to help.

Not long afterwards, the dove met an elephant and asked if he would stir up the water which wouldn't put out the fire which refused to burn the beard of the old man who wouldn't . . .

The elephant said, "No, not I."

Then the dove looked about and found a black ant, who also asked her what was troubling her.

"O ant! I know you can help me. Will you go into the elephant's trunk and bite him for not stirring up the water which wouldn't put out the fire which wouldn't burn the beard of the old man who wouldn't beat the dog who wouldn't bite the cat who wouldn't catch the rat who wouldn't cut the bowstring of the hunter who wouldn't shoot the pig who wouldn't dig up the yams of the blacksmith's wife who stole my egg?"

"Why not? Here I go," said the ant and crawled inside the elephant's trunk and bit it in the softest place, very hard. This made the elephant dash into the pool of water and stir it up. The water splashed and began to put out the fire, which went mad and burned the white beard of the old man, who beat the dog, who ran after the cat and bit her. The cat caught the rat, who gnawed the bowstring of the hunter's bow. The hunter tied on a new one and shot an arrow at the pig, who went and dug up all the yams of the blacksmith's wife.

The blacksmith's wife knew at once what she had to do and carefully put the dove's egg back in the nest in the hollow of the big tree.

That's how the dove got her egg back.

A Drum

~ *Hindi* ~ ~

A poor woman had only one son. She worked hard cleaning houses and grinding grain for the well-to-do families in town. They gave her some grain in return and she lived on it. But she could never afford to buy nice clothes or toys for her son. Once, when she was going to the market with some grain to sell, she asked her son, "What can I get you from the market?" He promptly replied, "A drum, Mother, get me a drum."

The mother knew she would never have enough money to buy a drum for her son. She went to the market, sold the grain, and bought some gram flour and some salt. She felt sad that she was coming home empty-handed. So when she saw a nice piece of wood on the road, she picked it up and brought it home to her son. The son didn't know what to do with it.

Yet he carried it with him when he went out to play. An old woman was lighting her *chulha*, her woodstove, with some cow-dung patties. The fire was not catching and there was smoke all around and it made the old woman's eyes water. The boy stopped and asked why she was crying. She said that she couldn't light her fire and cook. The boy said, "I have a nice piece of wood and you can start your fire with it." The old woman was very pleased, lit the fire, made some bread, and gave a piece to the boy.

He took the bread and walked on till he came upon a potter's wife. Her child was crying and flailing his arms. The boy stopped and asked her why the child was crying. The potter's wife said the child was hungry and she had nothing in the house to give him. The boy gave the bread in his hand to the hungry child, who ate it eagerly and stopped crying. The potter's wife was grateful to the boy and gave him a pot.

When he walked on, he came to the river, where he saw a washerman and his wife quarreling. The boy stopped and asked the man why he was scolding and beating his wife. The washerman said, "This woman broke the only pot we had. Now I've nothing to boil my clothes in before I wash them." The boy said, "Here, don't quarrel, take this pot and use it." The washerman was very happy to get a large pot. He gave the boy a coat in return.

The boy walked on. He soon came to a bridge, where he saw a man shivering in the cold without so much as a shirt on him. He asked the man what had happened to his shirt, and the man said, "I was coming to the city on this horse. Robbers attacked me and took everything, even my shirt." The boy said, "Don't worry. You can have this coat." The man took the coat and said, "You're very kind, and I want to give you this horse."

The boy took the horse, and very soon he ran into a wedding party with the musicians, the bridegroom, and his family, but all of them were sitting under a tree with long faces. The boy stopped and asked why they looked so depressed. The bridegroom's father said, "We're all set to go in a wedding procession. But we need a horse for the bridegroom. The man who was supposed to bring it hasn't arrived. The bridegroom can't arrive on foot. It's getting late, and we'll miss the auspicious hour for the wedding." So the boy offered them his horse, and they were delighted. When the bridegroom asked him what he could do in return, the boy said, "You can give me something: that drum your musician is carrying." The bridegroom had no trouble persuading the drummer to give the drum to the boy. The drummer knew he could easily buy another with the money he was going to get.

The boy now rushed home to his mother, beating his new drum, and told her how he got it, beginning with a piece of wood from the roadside.

In the Kingdom of Fools

᷍ *Kannada* ᷍᷍

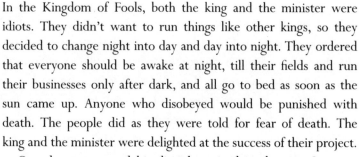

In the Kingdom of Fools, both the king and the minister were idiots. They didn't want to run things like other kings, so they decided to change night into day and day into night. They ordered that everyone should be awake at night, till their fields and run their businesses only after dark, and all go to bed as soon as the sun came up. Anyone who disobeyed would be punished with death. The people did as they were told for fear of death. The king and the minister were delighted at the success of their project.

One day a guru and his disciple arrived in the city. It was a beautiful city, it was broad daylight, but there was no one about. Everyone was asleep, not a mouse stirring. Even the cattle had been taught to sleep by day. The two strangers were amazed by what they saw around them and wandered around town till evening, when suddenly the whole town woke up and went about its nightly business.

The two men were hungry. Now that the shops were open, they went to buy some groceries. To their astonishment, they found that everything cost the same, a single *duddu*—whether they bought a measure of rice or a bunch of bananas, it cost a *duddu*. The guru and his disciple were delighted. They had never heard of anything like this. They could buy all the food they wanted for a rupee.

When they had cooked and eaten, the guru realized that this was a kingdom of fools and it wouldn't be a good idea for them to stay there. "This is no place for us. Let's go," he said to his disciple. But the disciple didn't want to leave the place. Everything was cheap here. All he wanted was good cheap food. The guru said, "They are all fools. This won't last very long, and you can't tell what they'll do to you next."

But the disciple wouldn't listen to the guru's wisdom. He wanted to stay. The guru finally gave up and said, "Do what you want. I'm going," and left. The disciple stayed on, ate his fill every day, bananas and ghee and rice and wheat, and grew fat as a streetside sacred bull.

One bright day, a thief broke into a rich merchant's house. He had made a hole in the wall and sneaked in, and as he was carrying out his loot, the wall of the old house collapsed on his head and killed him on the spot. His brother ran to the king and complained: "Your Highness, when my brother was pursuing his ancient trade, a wall fell on him and killed him. This merchant is to blame. He should have built a good strong wall. You must punish the wrongdoer and compensate the family for this injustice."

The king said, "Justice will be done. Don't worry," and at once summoned the owner of the house.

When the merchant arrived, the king asked him questions.

"What's your name?"

"Such and Such, Your Highness."

"Were you at home when the dead man burgled your house?"

"Yes, my lord. He broke in and the wall was weak. It fell on him."

"The accused pleads guilty. Your wall killed this man's brother. You have murdered a man. We have to punish you."

"Lord," said the helpless merchant, "I didn't put up the wall. It's really the fault of the man who built the wall. He didn't build it right. You should punish him."

"Who is that?"

"My lord, this wall was built in my father's time. I know the man. He's an old man now. He lives nearby."

The king sent out messengers to bring in the bricklayer who had built the wall. They brought him, tied hand and foot.

"You there, did you build this man's wall in his father's time?"

"Yes, my lord, I did."

"What kind of a wall is this that you built? It has fallen on a poor man and killed him. You've murdered him. We have to punish you by death."

Before the king could order the execution, the poor bricklayer pleaded, "Please listen to me before you give your orders. It's true I built this wall and it was no good. But that was because my mind was not on it. I remember very well a harlot who was going up and down that street all day with her anklets jingling, and I couldn't keep my eyes or my mind on the wall I was building. You must get that harlot. I know where she lives."

"You're right. The case deepens. We must look into it. It is not easy to judge such complicated cases. Let's get that harlot, wherever she is."

The harlot, now an old woman, came trembling to the court.

"Did you walk up and down that street many years ago, while this poor man was building a wall? Did you see him?"

"Yes, my lord. I remember it very well."

"So you did walk up and down, with your anklets jingling. You were young and you tempted him, so he built a bad wall. It has fallen on a poor burglar and killed him. You've killed an innocent man. You'll have to be punished."

She thought for a minute and said, "My lord, wait. I know now why I was walking up and down that street. I had given some gold to the goldsmith to make some jewelry for me. He was a lazy scoundrel. He made so many excuses, said he would give it now and he would give it then and so on all day. He made me walk up and down to his house a dozen times. That was when this bricklayer fellow saw me. It's not my fault, my lord, it's that damned goldsmith's."

"Poor thing, she's absolutely right," thought the king, weighing the evidence. "We've got the real culprit at last. Get the goldsmith, wherever he is hiding. At once!"

The king's bailiffs searched for the goldsmith, who was hiding in a corner of his shop. When he heard the accusation against him, he had his own story to tell.

"My lord," he said, "I'm a poor goldsmith. It's true I made this harlot woman come many times to my door. I gave her excuses because I couldn't finish making her jewelry before I finished the rich merchant's orders. They had a wedding coming, and they wouldn't wait. You know how impatient rich men are!"

"Who is this rich merchant who kept you from finishing this poor woman's jewelry, made her walk up and down, which distracted this bricklayer, which made a mess of his wall, which has now fallen on an innocent man and killed him? Can you name him?"

The goldsmith named the merchant, and he was none other than the original owner of the house where the wall had fallen. Now justice had come full circle, thought the king, back to the merchant. When he was rudely summoned back to the court, he arrived crying, "It wasn't me but my father who ordered the jewelry! He's dead! I'm innocent!"

But the king consulted his minister and ruled decisively: "It's true your father is the true murderer. He's dead, but somebody must be punished in his place. You've inherited everything from that criminal father of yours, his riches as well as his sins. I knew at once, even when I first set eyes on you, that you were at the root of this horrible crime. You must die."

And he ordered a new stake to be made ready for the execution. As the servants sharpened the stake and got it ready for the final impaling of the criminal, it occurred to the minister that the rich merchant was somehow too thin to be properly executed on the stake. He appealed to the king's common sense. The king too worried about it.

"What shall we do?" he said, when suddenly it struck him that all they needed to do was find a man fat enough to fit the stake. The servants were immediately all over town looking for a man who would fit the stake, and their eyes fell on the disciple who had fattened himself for months on bananas and rice and wheat and ghee.

"What have I done wrong? I'm innocent. I'm a *sannyasi!*" he cried.

"That may be true. But it's the royal decree that we should find a man fat enough to fit the stake," they said, and carried him to the place of execution. He remembered his wise guru's words: "This is a city of fools. You don't know what they will do next." While he was waiting for death, he prayed to his guru in his heart, asking him to hear his cry wherever he was. The guru saw everything in a vision; he had magic powers, he could see far, and he could see the future as he could see the present and the past. He arrived at once to save his disciple, who had got himself into such a scrape through love of food.

As soon as he arrived, he scolded the disciple and told him something in a whisper. Then he went to the king and addressed him: "O wisest of kings, who is greater? The guru or the disciple?"

"Of course, the guru. No doubt about it. Why do you ask?"

"Then put me to the stake first. Put my disciple to death after me."

When the disciple heard this, he caught on and began to clamor: "Me first! You brought me here first! Put me to death first, not him!"

The guru and the disciple now got into a fight about who should go first. The king was puzzled by this behavior. He asked the guru, "Why do you want to die? We chose him because we needed a fat man for the stake."

"You shouldn't ask me such questions. Put me to death first."

"Why? There's some mystery here. As a wise man you must make me understand."

"Will you promise to put me to death if I tell you?" said the guru. The king gave him his solemn word. The guru took him aside, out of the servants' earshot, and whispered to him: "Do you know why we want to die right now, the two of us? We've been all over the world but we've never found a city like this or a king like you. That stake is the stake of the god of justice. It's new, it has never had a criminal on it. Whoever dies on it first will be reborn as the king of this country. And whoever goes next will be the future minister of this country. We're sick of living the ascetic life. It would be nice to enjoy ourselves as king and minister for a while. Now keep your word, my lord, and put us to death. Me first, remember."

The king was now thrown into deep thought. He didn't want to lose the kingdom to someone else in the next round of life. He needed time. So he ordered the execution postponed to the next day and talked in secret with his minister. "It's not right for us to give over the kingdom to others in the next life. Let's go on the stake ourselves and we'll be reborn as king and minister again. Holy men do not tell lies," he said, and the minister agreed.

So he told the executioners: "We'll send the criminals tonight. When the first man comes to you, put him to death first. Then do the same to the second man. Those are orders. Don't make any mistakes."

That night, the king and his minister went secretly to the prison, released the guru and the disciple, disguised themselves as those two, and as arranged beforehand with their loyal servants, were taken to the stake and promptly executed.

When the bodies were taken down to be thrown to the crows and vultures, the people panicked. They saw before them the dead bodies of the king and the minister. The city was in confusion.

All night they mourned and discussed the future of the kingdom. Some people suddenly thought of the guru and the disciple and caught up with them as they were preparing to leave town unnoticed. "We people need a king and a minister," said someone. Others agreed. They begged the guru and the disciple to be their king and their minister. It didn't take many arguments to persuade the disciple, but it took longer to persuade the guru. They finally agreed to rule the kingdom of the foolish king and the silly minister, on the condition that they could change all the old laws. From then on, night would again be night and day would again be day, and you could get nothing for a *duddu*. It became like any other place.

Nonviolence

~ Bengali ~ ~

A particularly wicked snake infested a road and bit passers-by. A holy man happened to pass that way, and the snake rushed at him to bite him. He calmly looked at it and said, "You want to bite me, don't you? Go ahead."

The snake was subdued by this unusual response and was overpowered by the gentleness of the holy man. The holy man said, "Listen, dear friend, how about promising me that you won't bite anyone from now on?" The snake bowed and nodded assent. The holy man went his way, and the snake began its life of innocence and nonviolence.

Very soon, the neighborhood discovered that the snake was harmless and the boys began to tease it mercilessly. They pelted it with stones and dragged it around by its tail. Still it kept its promise to the holy man and suffered.

Fortunately, the holy man happened to come by to see his latest disciple and was touched by the bruised and battered condition of the snake. When he asked it what had happened, the snake said feebly, "O swami, you said I should not bite anyone. But people are so merciless!"

The holy man said, "I asked you not to bite anyone. But I didn't ask you not to hiss!"

The Barber's Secret

~ *Tamil* ~ ~

In Konkan there ruled a very good king. He seemed to have everything. He was handsome as the love god, sweet-spoken, just, and generous. A great and invincible warrior, he had even willingly given away parts of his kingdom to his enemies, after he had conquered them.

In addition to these wonderful virtues, he had another talent. People in court were in awe of him, for he could hear the slightest whisper. He really could hear a mosquito move or a pin drop. No one knew where or how he acquired this extraordinary power of hearing everything around him, and everyone wanted to know his secret.

One day, the king's personal barber saw something unusual under his long locks of hair. While he was shaving the royal face, he saw the king's ears. He thought he had seen ears like them somewhere else, but he couldn't remember where. He thought about it and thought about it. He even forgot he was in the middle of shaving the king's face, folded his razor, and stood there lost in thought, trying to remember where he had seen such ears. The king grumbled at first, asked him what the hell he was doing standing there like that, and then blew up in a fit of rage. But it didn't touch the barber, who heard nothing. The king got up and angrily said, "What's this you're doing? I'll chop off your head!"

The barber was startled from his trance, and cried out, "Ha!" But a moment later, he was lost in thought once more. Who can command or stop a man's thoughts? A king may try, but even he can't succeed. The barber's thoughts moved on their own, at their own speed. The half-shaven king shouted at the barber, who suddenly opened his eyes wide and let out a cry: "Ha, I've seen them on a donkey! I've seen them on a donkey!"

"What? What are you saying?" asked the king, exasperated by the fellow. As the king's voice grew louder with anger, the barber trembled and blurted out, "*Ayyo!* your . . . ears . . ."

Then he broke down and cried. The king asked him, "Why are you crying over my ears? What's wrong?"

The barber recovered, gathered courage, and said, "Your Majesty, I've seen your kind of ears on a donkey. A donkey's are a bit bigger, that's all."

The king was really angry now, but his good nature won over his rage. He ordered the barber never to talk about his ears to anyone. "They have been growing like this for a while," he said sadly. "But if you talk about it to anyone, I'll cut off your head."

The barber promised never to talk about it to anyone. Then he took out his razor and somehow managed to finish the shave he had interrupted. In order to buy the barber's silence, the king gave him a satchel of gold. Happy and burdened, the barber ran all the way home, taking back streets to avoid all his acquaintances. But all along the way, he shook with uncontrollable laughter; he neighed and grinned and cackled and showed all his thirty-two teeth. People who saw him thought he was crazy. They thought that a little lemon juice would cool his head and cure him of his madness.

When he reached home, his mother met him at the door. As soon as he saw her, he burst into peals of laughter. She wondered why he was laughing at her like that. When his wife came out, he was in fits of laughter, his voice moving up and down the scale. She asked him many questions, but she got no answer but this mad laughter. She got angry and spluttered at him. His laughter changed pace and he even began to sob with mirth. She was convinced that he had gone off his rocker and began to curse her fate. When people left him alone, his laughing fits seemed to leave him for a while. But when he went to take a bath, suddenly he remembered the donkey's ears and the laughter started up again. The cold water on his head controlled it a bit. His sides and chest, which had begun to hurt, now got a little rest.

As he didn't come out of the bathhouse for a long time, his mother came looking for him, which started him off again. He couldn't control himself. He was breathless. His mother gently led him to the kitchen and served him food. But as he took in a mouthful, his memory would reappear, making him splutter. His lungs ached, his stomach hurt, but he couldn't stop. The food went the wrong way. He sneezed, he choked, he almost fainted. But as soon as he recovered, the fit was on him again. In a lucid moment, his worried mother asked him, "What's happening? What's wrong?" How could he go against his king's orders and tell her? He was afraid of losing his head. After much questioning, he finally said, "How can I tell you?"

The mother asked again. "Why are you laughing like this? What did you see? Your eyes are red, your face is swollen. Why can't you tell us? Stop teasing us."

"How can I tell you? How can I disobey the king's orders? What shall I do?"

"Do you mean to say you have secrets you can't tell your own mother who gave you birth and wiped your bottom?"

"How can I disobey the king?" he said again, and another fit of laughter was upon him.

"*Ayyo!* listen, my son. Even if you can't tell me, can't you go tell it to a tree? A tree can't talk. So how can it tell anyone?"

The barber felt that was right. Suffering is relieved by the telling, goes the saying. So he went to the woods to talk to the trees, with the blessings of his mother.

There he addressed the trees:

> *O tree, O tree, tell no one*
> > *what I tell you now.*
> *O punga tree, tell no one*
> > *the secret I'll tell you.*
> *O padiri tree, tell no one*
> > *what I saw this morning.*
> *O iluppai tree, tell no one*
> > *my secret trouble.*
> *O tree of the forest, listen well:*
> *The great good king who rules our land*
> > *has a donkey's ears.*
> *O tree, O tree, tell no one*
> *I told you so. I told you this*
> *because I didn't want to die*
> > *of laughter.*
> *I've kept my word to my king*
> > *and I've listened to my mother.*
> *Laughter was killing me,*
> > *I've killed it now.*
> *I won't laugh any more,*
> > *night or day.*

He sang like this over and over till he felt he was rid of the secret that was bursting out of him. Then he returned home.

Soon after that, a musician well-versed in raga tunes and rhythms needed a new drum. He went to the woods looking for a suitable tree. He cut down one of the trees to which the barber had confided his secret, and carved a frame for his drum from it, stretched a skin on its sides, fine-tuned it, and went to the king's court to show his artistic skill.

There, the court singer sang the first part of a raga beautifully, and asked the drummer to play solo. The drummer played delicately, making, as they say, the drum speak. But to his and everyone else's astonishment, the drum sounded its rhythms like this:

> *Tlang Tak Taka Taka Tlang*
> *Tak Tlang Taka Tlang Taka Taka*
> *The ears of the king are the ears of a donkey.*
> *Tak Tlang Taka Taka Taka Tlang*
> *The ears of the king are the ears of a donkey.*

Everyone in the court could hear the words clearly, and they all looked at the king on the throne. Now they knew why their king could hear the slightest whisper in that hall.

Gopal Bhar Cures a Dreamer

~ *Bengali* ~~

Gopal Bhar lived next door to a poor couple who were incorrigible dreamers. One day, Gopal overheard them vying with each other about their daydreams. The husband said, "When I get some money, I'm going to buy a cow."

His wife added, "Then I'll milk the cow. We will need lots of pots. I'll have to go buy some."

Next day, she went out and bought pots. The husband asked her, "What did you buy?"

"Oh, pots. One for milk, one for buttermilk, one for butter, and one for ghee."

"That's great. But what about the fifth one?"

"That is for carrying some of our extra milk to my sister," said his wife.

"What! Carry milk to your sister? How long have you been doing that? Without even telling me or asking my permission?" shouted the husband. Flying into a rage, he grabbed the pots and smashed them all.

The wife retorted, "I'm the one who takes care of the cow and milks it. I'll do what I wish with the extra milk!"

"You slut! I work and sweat all day and buy a cow, and you give away the milk to your sister! I'll kill you first!" roared the husband and threw some more pots and pans at his wife.

Gopal thought this was going too far and walked over to his neighbors' house. He said innocently to the angry husband, "Now what's the matter? Why are you throwing things?"

"This woman is giving away the milk from our cow to her sister!"

Gopal asked, "Your cow?"

"Yes, the cow I'm going to buy when I have enough money."

"Oh, that one! You don't have a cow yet, do you?" said Gopal.

The man said, "Just wait, I'm going to get one."

"Oh really! Now I know what's happening to my vegetable garden!" said Gopal, picking up a stick and thrashing his neighbor.

"Stop! Stop! Why are you beating me?"

"Your cow! It's been eating all the beans and cucumbers in my garden and you're letting it!"

"What beans, what cucumbers? Where is your vegetable garden?"

"The one I'm going to plant! I've been planning it for months, and your cow has been destroying it!"

The neighbor suddenly saw the light, and they had a good laugh.

A Scavenger's Dream

~ Oriya ~ ~

The woman who used to clean the queen's latrine in the palace was sick one day, so she asked her husband, who was also a scavenger, to do the job for her. When he went to the palace, he was admitted through the back door so that he could remove the basket of night soil from under the queen's latrine-hole. When he went to the place under the latrine from where he could remove the basket, the queen was sitting on the seat. He looked up and caught a glimpse of her inner thigh. It was smooth as silk, fair and soft as a jasmine petal. With just one glimpse of it, the scavenger was infatuated with the queen. He began to imagine how beautiful the rest of her might be. Even while he trudged home, his mind was with that inch of the queen's thigh. He was so obsessed with her he could neither eat nor sleep. When his wife asked him what the matter was and why he was mooning that way, he slowly confessed to his obsession. He wanted the queen for himself.

"O God! How can you get the queen? You, a mere scavenger! If you had wanted any other woman, we might have tried. But the queen herself—forget it! Ordinary people can't even get a glimpse of her," said his wife, and tried to distract him from his obsessive vision of the queen's thigh. But she didn't succeed. His thoughts went round and round the same thing, and he was all wound up in them.

He began to act crazy, didn't change his clothes, didn't eat or sleep, and finally left home and became a wanderer. One day, when he was sitting under a banyan tree, thinking of nothing else but the queen's beauty, some villagers gathered around him. They had been watching him for days sitting in this meditative state, without food or sleep, without a word or even a movement. It fitted their idea of a sage, and they began to take care of him, brought him offerings, food, clothes, to most of which he was quite indifferent. His indifference only convinced them of his holiness. He didn't even seem to notice the crowds of devotees and disciples who gathered around him.

Within the month he had become a celebrity, and his fame spread all over the country. He couldn't care less. The queen too heard about him and wished to visit the holy man. She came with her retinue and stood before him. She prostrated herself before him, touched his feet, placed offerings in front of him. He didn't so much as look at her. He didn't know who she was and didn't even ask. It mattered not at all to him.

So intense was his desire that it had moved him to a state where he had no desire at all.

The Boy Who Sold Wisdom
～ *Gujerati* ～ ～

A poor Brahman boy was orphaned and found himself without a job. He was clever and he had learned many things by watching his father. One day, he had a brilliant idea.

He went into town and hired the smallest, cheapest place he could find and set up shop. He spent the few nickel coins he had on paper, ink, and a pen. Over his shop, he put up a placard that said "Wisdom for Sale." All around him were merchants who had large shops. They sold cloth, jewelry, fruits and vegetables, things that people bought every day. The Brahman boy called out all day long to passers-by at the top of his voice: "Wisdom! Wisdom of all kinds! Wisdom for sale! Reasonable prices!" Passers-by who had come to buy things they could see and smell and eat and hear thought he was weird. They crowded around and laughed at him. No one bought even one piece of wisdom from him. But he was patient.

One day, a merchant's son who was rich but stupid passed that way and heard the wisdom seller hawking his wares: "Wisdom! Wisdom of all kinds! Wisdom for sale!" He didn't know what was really being sold. He thought it was a vegetable or a thing he could hold in his hand. So he asked the Brahman boy what it would cost per *ser*. The Brahman said, "I do not sell wisdom by weight. I sell it by quality." The merchant's son put down a nickel and asked the Brahman boy to give him a nickel's worth of wisdom. The boy took out a piece of paper and wrote on it, "It is not wise to stand and watch two people fighting," and he asked the merchant's son to keep it tied in his turban cloth.

The merchant's son went home and showed his father what he had bought. He said, "I bought some wisdom for a nickel and I have it here, tied up inside this turban cloth." The father untied the knot, looked at the scrap of paper, and read what was written on it: "It is not wise to stand and watch two people fighting."

He was furious. He screamed at his son, "You fool, fancy paying a nickel for this nonsense! Everyone knows you should not stand and watch two people fighting." Then he went to the marketplace and stormed into the Brahman boy's shop and scolded him roundly: "You scoundrel! You've cheated my son. He is a fool and you are a cheat. Return the nickel or else I'll call the police."

The Brahman boy said, "If you don't want my goods, you can return it. Give me back my wisdom, and you can have your money back." The merchant threw the scrap of paper at the boy and said, "There! Now give me back my money." The boy said, "No, you've not given me back my wisdom. You've only returned the paper. If you want your money back, you'll have to sign a document saying that your son will never use my advice and that he will always stand and watch people fighting." The gathered passers-by took the side of the boy. So the merchant readily signed the document and took his money. He was happy it was so easy to undo his son's foolish bargain.

Now the king had two queens and they were rivals. The maids of the two queens also took part in the rivalry. They quarreled as bitterly as their mistresses. One day, each queen sent one of her maids to the market. They went to the same shop and both wanted to buy the same pumpkin. There was only one pumpkin, and each wanted it for her kitchen. They began to quarrel. Their abuse and gestures were so fierce that the grocer fled the place. The merchant's son, who happened to be nearby, remembered his father's contract with the Brahman boy and went there to watch the quarrel. The maids fought, tore at each other's hair, and came to blows. One of the maids noticed the merchant's son and said, "You be my witness. She struck me." The other maid cried, "You've seen with your own eyes who struck whom. You are my witness. She has hit me so many times." Then they remembered the time and other errands and went their ways.

The two maids went to their queens and told them about the quarrel, adding all sorts of colorful details. The queens were now furious and sent complaints to the king. Each also sent word to the merchant's son that he was the witness on *her* side. If he didn't speak in support of her, she would have his head chopped off. The merchant's son was in a panic. When his father heard of this, he too was in a panic. Finally the son said, "Let's go ask the Brahman boy. He has wisdom to sell. Let's see what he has to say to get me out of this scrape." So father and son went to the Brahman boy, who said he would help but the fee would be five hundred rupees. The merchant paid him the money and the boy said, "When they call you to court, pretend to be insane. Behave as if you understand nothing they say."

Next day, the king called the witness. He and his minister asked the merchant's son various questions, but he wouldn't answer any of them. He merely babbled and uttered nonsense syllables till the king lost his patience and drove him out of the courtroom. The merchant's son was delighted by the success of the ruse. He told everyone about the Brahman boy's great wisdom, which soon became a byword in the marketplace.

Now, the merchant was not pleased. He saw that his son would have to feign madness always or else the king would find out he had been tricked. He would certainly chop off the son's head if he found out. So back they went to the Brahman boy for more wisdom. For another five hundred, the boy advised them: "Go back to the king when he is in a good mood and tell him the whole story. He will find it amusing and will forgive you. But make sure he is in a mood for laughter." And so the merchant's son followed the advice, found the king in a merry mood, and told him the story. The king laughed a lot and forgave him.

Then the king was intrigued by what he had heard of the Brahman boy in the market, sent for him, and asked if he had any more wisdom to sell. The boy said, "Of course, I've plenty to sell, especially to a king. But my fee would be a *lakh*, a hundred thousand rupees." The king paid him the hundred thousand, and the boy gave him a piece of paper on which he had written, "Think deeply before you do anything."

The king was so delighted with the advice that he made it his motto. He had it embroidered on his pillows and engraved on his cups and plates, so that he would not forget it.

Some months later, the king fell ill. The minister and one of the queens had been conspiring to get rid of him. So they bribed the doctor and persuaded him to put poison in the king's medicine. When the medicine was brought to the king and he lifted the golden cup to his lips, he read the words engraved on it: "Think deeply before you do anything." Without suspecting anything, he thought about the words, lowered the cup, and looked at the medicine in it. The doctor, who was watching all this, felt nervous. His guilty conscience made him fear the king had guessed that his medicine had poison in it. While the king was thinking, the doctor threw himself at his feet and confessed to everything, praying to be forgiven. The king was amazed at first. But he soon recovered, called the guards, and had the doctor arrested. Then he sent for the minister and the queen and insisted they drink the poison in his cup. They too fell at his feet and begged for mercy. He had them hanged on the spot, and he banished the doctor from his kingdom. But he made the Brahman boy his minister and covered him with wealth and honors.

Two Jars of Persian

~ *Punjabi* ~ ~

A long time ago when the Durranis had conquered the Punjab, there was a small village where only weavers lived. The Durranis spoke Persian, and the weavers knew only Punjabi. So the villagers had a hard time. When the officers collected revenue, the villagers couldn't explain their accounts or present their complaints. They had to take everything lying down and pay up.

So the weavers called a meeting, and agreed that they would all contribute ten rupees each for a common fund to send two of their wisest men to Kabul or beyond to bring back a supply of the Persian language. No sooner said than done, two old greybeards whose wisdom was legendary among the weavers set out on a long journey. They trudged past the city of Peshawar and went through the dark Khyber Pass to get the precious commodity.

At every village, they stopped and anxiously asked, "Have you any Persian for sale?" In every village, they were laughed at or ignored, or hooted away. They finally arrived at the town of Jelalabad and met at the gates a rather

clever and heartless man. "We want to buy some Persian for our village," said the weavers. The man knew at once that they were great fools and he could gull them and take their money. So he said, "Of course. Come with me. If you're willing to pay the price, I'll get you two jars of the choicest Persian." Then he took them home for the night and gave them supper.

It was the time of year when wasps hang their nests from the beams. So this man put some sweet things into a couple of jars and filled them with black wasps, tied the mouths of the jars with cloth, and sold them to the travelers, saying, "Be careful not to open the jars on the way and let the Persian escape. Keep them safely sealed. They are full to the brim with Persian. When you get home, call everyone together on a Thursday, go into a dark room, close all the doors and windows, and take off all your clothes. Then open the jars. Everyone will get his share and be satisfied."

The two weavers then left for India with the precious jars. As soon as they arrived home, they called their neighbors together, told them the good news, and displayed the jars full of wonderful Persian. Then they couldn't wait to get into a dark chamber, take off their clothes, and open the jars. Once the imprisoned wasps were released, they flew all over the place and stung all the villagers as they groped around the walls, crying, "Where is the door? Where is the door?" At last the door was found, and they all escaped into the open air. They could hardly recognize each other, their features were so stung and swollen. One of them missed his mother and asked where she was. They said, "Your mother ran that way, with a great deal of Persian sticking to her." So they went in search of her and found the poor old thing stung so badly that she became quite ill and took to her bed.

After this experience, the weavers of the village decided never again to meddle with Persian and to leave that language to those who were cunning enough to master strange languages.

In Another Country

~ Punjabi ~ ~

A young man lost his father soon after he got married. The parents of his bride felt very sorry for him. The mother said, "He is alone now, the poor boy. He should take our daughter home with him. So let us send word to him. No friend like a good wife."

As soon as the message reached him, the young man dressed up for the visit, mounted his mare, and took off. On the way, he came to a jungle where he saw a mongoose and an enormous snake engaged in deadly combat. He reined his horse to watch the fight. The mongoose soon began to wear out its opponent and the snake's body was bloody with many wounds. Left to itself, the snake would soon be dead. The young man thought, "The snake is no match for the mongoose. It is an act of charity to separate them." So he tried to separate the two enemies. But every time he failed, the mongoose sprang again and again on the snake mercilessly. So the young man drew his sword and cut down the fierce mongoose with one stroke.

Then he went back to his horse, but before he could mount it, the snake rushed towards him and coiled itself around his body. The young man said, "I did you a good turn and saved your life. What are you doing?"

"It's true," said the snake, "you saved me from my enemy. But I shall not let you go. I shall eat you."

"Why?" said the young man, baffled and afraid and angry at the same time. "Doesn't one good turn deserve another? Will you kill me because I saved your life? In my country, we don't do such things."

"In these parts," said the snake, "the custom is very different. Everyone here follows the rule of returning evil for good."

The man began to argue with the snake as best as he could, but the snake wouldn't listen to anything he said. It had decided to eat him, being a python, and a hungry one at that. At last the young man said, "Very well, snake, you can eat me. But first give me eight days to go about my business and arrange my affairs. After that I'll come back and you can eat me."

The snake agreed and said, "You look like a good man. In eight days you must return to me."

Then the snake loosened its coils from around the man, released its hold, and let him go. He got back on his horse and rode on to his in-laws' place.

All his friends and in-laws were very glad to see the young bridegroom, and especially his little wife. He stayed with the in-laws for a few days. But he seemed depressed all the time, and they asked him, "Why, what's the matter? Are you still mourning your father's death? Can we do anything to help?" But he said nothing. On the seventh day, they spoke to their daughter: "Is he angry? What's the matter with him?" She tried to find out, but she didn't have much success, either.

The eighth day came, and he said, "Now let me go home." The father and mother gave the daughter her dowry, put the young couple in a bullock cart, and sent them off.

In a little while they had left the village behind them. The young man spoke suddenly to his wife and the servants: "Now, all of you go back home. I have come to know that I'm going to die on the way. Just go home."

The servants were alarmed, and they all left. But his young wife said, "Where you fall, I shall fall. What am I to do at my house?" So she stubbornly accompanied him.

When he arrived at the appointed spot, he got down and called the snake. "I have come," he said, "just as I promised. If you wish to eat me, come and eat me now!"

His wife heard these ominous words and followed him. Soon they heard a dreadful hiss and a huge snake crawled out of the jungle and came towards the young man, ready to devour him. The girl cried, "Stop! Why are you going to eat this poor man?" The snake then told her the whole story: how it was fighting with the mongoose and how her husband had interfered and killed its enemy. "And in this country," it continued, "our custom is to return evil for good."

The young wife now tried all the moral arguments she could think of to change the mind of this monstrous snake, but it was deaf to her pleadings and arguments. Then she said, "You say that in this country people do evil for good. That's really a strange custom, and so very unreasonable that I'd like to know the history of it. How did it all come about?"

"Do you see those five *talli* trees?" answered the snake. "Go to them and ask them in a loud voice so that they can hear you: 'What is the reason that, in this country, folks do evil in return for good?' and see what they say to you."

The wife went and did as she was told, addressing her question to the middle tree of the five. The tree answered her straightway: "Count us! We are now five, but once we were six—three pairs. The sixth was hollow, with a big cavity in its trunk." And it told her the story of the sixth tree:

Many years ago, a thief went and robbed a house in these parts, and the people followed him as he ran away. He ran and ran and ran, and at last he came here. It was night, but the moon was shining. He could see the cavity in the sixth talli *tree and he hid himself in it. As he heard the pursuers closing in on him, he begged the tree, "O tree, O tree, save me!" The* talli *tree heard his miserable cry and in sheer pity closed up its sides all around him and hid him in its safe embrace. The people walked all around us here and searched for him, but they didn't find him. So they went away. When the pursuit was over, the tree opened its sides and let the thief go. Now, when* talli *trees grow very old, they become very fragrant. Some people even think they grow sandalwood within them. So the thief, when he left the tree, had the scent of sandalwood all over him, and*

wherever he went he wafted a delightful fragrance. It had become a permanent part of him. So when he visited the city of a neighboring king, a man passed him on the road and suddenly stopped to ask him, "Where did you get that beautiful scent?"

"You must be dreaming," said the thief. "I have no scent."

"Oh, it's wonderful!" said the man, drawing in the surrounding air and the scent with it. "If you will give me this scent, I'll pay you for it."

Again the thief said, "Go away! I have no scent, nothing. It's all in your nose."

Then the man, who was a shrewd fellow, went to the king and told him, "A stranger has come to this city. He has a wonderful scent with him. He might be persuaded to give it to Your Highness."

The king then ordered his servants to bring the thief to his court, which they did, and the king said to him, "Where did you get that scent? Show it to me."

"I have no scent," said the thief.

"If you don't make any fuss and give it to me quietly, I'll reward you. If not, I'll put you to death and take the scent."

The thief was now terrified and said, "Don't kill me. I'll tell you the whole story." So he told the king how his life had been saved in the heart of the talli tree and how the scent of sandalwood had never left him since. Then the king said, "Come along and show me that wonderful tree. Where is it?"

Soon they arrived at this very spot, and the king gave orders to cut the tree down and carry it to his palace. When the talli tree heard his order, and when it understood the reason for it, it cried out aloud, "I saved the life of a man, and for this I lose my own life. From now on, therefore, let it be decreed in this jungle that whosoever dares to do good, to him it shall be repaid in evil!"

The young wife heard this sad story and returned to her husband's side.

"Well," said the snake, "did you consult the *talli* trees? Do you now believe that our custom here is just as I told you?"

She had to admit that it was so. But as the monstrous snake moved towards its victim, she wept and said, "What will become of me? If you must eat my husband, you must begin by eating me."

The snake found that entirely unreasonable. "You?" it cried. "But you have never done me the slightest good. You haven't even done me any harm. How then can I be expected to eat you?"

"But if you eat my husband," she said, "what's left for me? You yourself said that I've done you no good, and yet you want to hurt me and destroy my happiness. How can you?"

When the snake heard these words, it felt remorse, especially as she started weeping more than ever. It knew it had to eat the young man, but how could it console the bride? Doing her evil would not be right. It wanted to do something to comfort her. So it crept back into its hole and returned in a few minutes with two magic pills. "Here, you foolish girl," it said, "take these two pills and swallow them, and you'll soon have two lovely sons. You can devote yourself to them and they in turn will take good care of you. Now go!"

The girl accepted the pills, but with her natural cunning returning to her, she said, "If I take these two pills, I'm sure I'll get two sons. But what about my good name? Without my husband, my sons will be called bastards."

The snake had not thought of this complication. It was exasperated. "Women are preposterous beings!" it said, and crept back to its hole. This time it brought two more pills, gave them to the inconsolable woman, and said, "Revenge will bring you some satisfaction. When anyone maligns you and says ugly things about your sons, take one of these pills between your finger and your thumb, hold it over him, rub it gently so that the powder falls on him, and immediately you'll see him go up in smoke and ashes."

The young woman carefully tied the first two pills in her cloth, and looked at the other two pills doubtfully. Then with a sudden thought, she gently rubbed them over the snake, saying with an innocent air, "O snake, explain this mystery to me again! Is this the way I should rub them?"

The moment an atom of the magic powder touched the snake, it was on fire, and the next moment it was merely a long wavy line of grey dust lying on the ground.

Then with a happy face the little wife turned to her husband and said, "Whoever does good, in the end good will be done to him. Evil will be punished by evil. You did good, and see, you are rewarded. The snake did evil, and it was destroyed. God makes everything right at last."

After this they went home, where they lived happily for a long time.

One Man's Pleasure

~ *Urdu* ~~

A man from the city of Kabul in Afghanistan once visited India. Walking along an Indian street, he came to a sweetmeat shop where all sorts of sweets of different shapes and sizes were neatly displayed.

He knew only one or two words of Hindustani. He went up to the vendor of sweets and pointed at one particular kind that looked especially delicious. The man thought he was asking its name and said "*Khaja*." The word means both "sweets" and "eat it up." The man from Kabul knew only the second meaning and so he fell to, grabbing handfuls of sweets and gobbling them up with pleasure.

The vendor of sweets asked the stranger to pay for them. But the visitor didn't understand what he was saying and happily wandered away. The angry vendor complained to the police, who came and arrested the man from Kabul. The chief officer ordered that his head should be shaved clean and covered with tar, and that he should then be mounted on a donkey and run out of town in a procession to the sound of drums, so that everyone would know how a lawbreaker is punished in that part of the world. Though this is considered brutal punishment in India, the man from Kabul thought it was fun. He even felt charmed and honored by this treatment and the attention he got in the streets.

On his return, people asked him, "How was India?"

He answered, "Terrific! It's a charming country, and a rich country. You get everything for nothing there. You go to a shop and point to a pile of sweets you like, and they tell you to take all you want and eat it. Then the police come with drums and pipes, give you a shave, dye your head with hair-dye, and give you a nice donkey to ride through town to the accompaniment of lovely Indian music. And all for nothing! Lovely country, generous hosts, beautiful people!"

Raja Vikram and
the Princess of China

~ *Hindi* ~ ~

Vikramaditya, king of Ujjain, was a powerful and just sovereign. In the interests of justice, he often roamed alone and in disguise among his people to discover what was happening in his kingdom. In this way he came to know many strange and startling things and unraveled many mysteries.

A yogi once entered his dominions and began to live on the opposite bank of the river at the edge of the city. There he raised a small thatched hut, lighted a large *dhuni*, a sacred fire, in the center of it, and spent his days sitting in the middle of the burning fire. Soon the fame of his miraculous powers spread throughout the city, and many people came to see him. A band of disciples soon formed around him, and daily more and more people were converted to the new cult. The infection spread even to the palace of the raja, and Vikram soon began to suspect that all was not well with this seeming yogi and that some conspiracy against his life was being secretly hatched in that hut on the riverbank. So one night he slipped out of the palace in disguise, swam across the river, and hid himself in a corner of the yogi's hut.

What he saw in the hut sent a chill of horror through his body. The yogi was seated in the middle of a fire. In front of him lay a ghastly corpse, flat on its back. A man was sitting on the chest of the dead body. The raja recognized the man as one of his discontented former ministers, someone he had dismissed from his service. The man was repeating some mantras and now and then putting a flower dipped in red sandal paste into the mouth of the dead body. There was incense smoke all around. It was a ceremony to raise the dead. After an hour or so, the man cried out, "Speak, my son, speak." Then Vikram saw to his terror the lips of the corpse move, but he heard no sound. Again the man cried out, "Speak, my son, speak. I've sacrificed you to Mother Kali so that I may wreak vengeance on the ungrateful raja. Speak, my son, speak."

Then this murderer of his son put more flowers, sandal paste, and *bel* leaves into the dead son's mouth, and again the lips moved without a sound. The father cried out for a third time, but still nothing happened.

The yogi, seeing the man's disappointment, said, "Have patience. There must be some stranger in the room. That's why the goddess is silent." Then he raised his voice and said, "Whoever you are who's watching these sacred and secret rites, you'll change at once into a dog."

He said this three times, while Vikram tried to leave the hut. But the raja found himself rooted to the spot. At the end of the third repetition, he was changed into a dog and had to live in the hut.

When the raja was not in the palace the next morning, the ministers and other officers of state were afraid something dreadful had happened to him. But they didn't want any public panic, so they sent out bulletins that the raja was sick and would not hold a *durbar*, a court, for some days. Meanwhile, secret messengers were sent out in every direction to discover the whereabouts of the raja. Then the ministers and wise men of the court went to ask the advice of the old astrologer Varahamihira. The astrologer made his calculations and found by his art that the raja had been transformed into a dog by the yogi on the riverbank. He told the ministers, "This yogi is a terrible sorcerer. He is a mortal enemy of our raja. He would gladly have killed him off, but Vikram is protected by four *virs*, guardian spirits. In the coming new moon, the secret rites will end and then these four *virs* will lose their power before the superior power of Kali. Something must be done soon to save the raja." After saying this, he fell silent and sat for a long time in gloomy contemplation.

Then suddenly his face brightened, and he summoned his twin sons to his presence. He told them what had happened to the raja and said, "Children, we have long eaten the bread of the king. Now is the time to show our gratitude. We must save him even if it costs us our lives. Are you prepared?"

The twins, two very handsome lads, replied in one voice, "When have we refused to do your bidding and the king's service? Tell us what we can do."

The father then took them to the riverside, showed them the hut on the other bank, and said, "That is the hut of the sorcerer. At the door of the hut you'll see a black dog. That's really our raja. Now I'll change you into two deer. I want you to go there and entice the dog away to this bank. The river is not deep. The yogi's powers control that half of the river but not an inch beyond. So run as quickly as you can and bring the dog out of that limit. You're not safe as long as you're on the other side of the middle of this stream. Do you understand?" Then the old astrologer changed the twins into two beautiful deer, which swam the river towards the hut of the yogi.

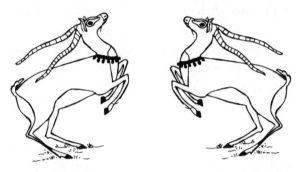

As soon as the deer got out of the water and came towards the door, the dog began to growl and ran after them. The deer at once plunged into the water with the black dog chasing them. The dog's howls roused the yogi from his trance, and he saw the dog chasing the deer. At first he suspected nothing, but as he stared at the deer his gaze pierced through their magic coats and he knew these were not animals but human beings. At once, the yogi changed himself into a kite and flew through the air after the deer, meaning to pluck out their eyes. The four *virs* who were protecting the raja saw what was happening and at once raised a dust storm. By this time the raja and the twins had almost reached the middle of the stream. Just then the kite pierced through the storm, swooped down at great speed, and plucked out one of the eyes of the deer in front. The next moment, the two deer and the dog had crossed the middle line and were beyond the reach of the yogi's power. The kite hovered high in the air but did not dare to cross the line.

The astrologer was waiting on the opposite bank. He restored all three of them to human shape. The raja was very grateful, as was the whole court, though their joy was dampened a little by the loss of one eye of the younger twin. They sent out the news that the raja had recovered from a dangerous illness with the help of the astrologer Varahamihira. Nothing was said about the adventures of the raja and the yogi.

But the yogi's disciples were increasing in numbers and strength. The protecting *virs* also told the raja that their powers would soon fail before the growing malignant power of the yogi. The raja asked the astrologer to advise him what to do in this pass. Varahamihira went back to his calculations and said, "O raja, I do not have the power to cope with the yogi. I know only three sciences, but he is the master of thirteen. In my trances I've searched throughout the world, but I've found no one superior to him in the magic arts except the daughter of the king of China. She knows fourteen sciences and can save you. If you can marry her, your life is safe."

The raja called all his ministers, gave them charge of the affairs of state, mounted his horse, and went alone towards the country of China. The councilors tried to dissuade him from the dangerous journey. But he wouldn't listen, and rode out of his city on his fabulous river-horse that moved swift as the wind over land and water.

He rode on and on for many days and then asked a passer-by, "Friend, whose dominion is this?" The man looked amazed and said, "Don't you know? All this country belongs to the good and great king Vikramaditya." Vikram rode on and on, and wherever he asked he found that it was his own kingdom. Never had he realized so vividly as now its extent and its riches. His desire to preserve it for his own dynasty became all the more intense as he rode through the land. After months of riding he crossed his frontier and entered the kingdom of China, and it took many weeks to reach the capital city. When he arrived there, it was late and dark, so he decided to stop in a garden outside it. Tying his horse to the trunk of a tree, he stretched himself out near it and soon fell into a deep sleep.

As luck would have it, a gang of thieves passed that way. When they saw the river-horse, they took it for a good omen. The gang leader said, "Whatever loot we get today, we'll divide among ourselves and this auspicious horse." They then entered the city and broke into the royal treasury. They took all the precious stones and jewelry, came out undetected, and went to the tree near where Raja Vikram was sleeping. There they divided their loot. A most precious necklace called the *nau lakha har*, a necklace worth nine *lakhs*, fell to the lot of the horse. The thieves put it around the animal's neck and went their way. Very soon after, the burglary was discovered, and the police ran in all directions to find the criminals. Some of them came to the spot where Vikram was sleeping and found the necklace on the neck of his horse. They rudely woke him up and hauled him, bound hand and foot, with his wonderful river-horse, before the emperor of China. The raja did not want to reveal his true identity, so he chose to say nothing and to suffer the punishment. The emperor thought he was one of the felons and unwilling to give him any information, and so ordered the executioner to cut off his hands and feet and throw him into the public square.

There he lay, mutilated and groaning in pain from the barbarous punishment. People mocked him and ill-treated him. He lay there all day, faint from the loss of blood, unpitied and uncared for. That night, an oilman happened to pass by. He took pity on the miserable raja, who was still young and handsome. He bound up his wounds and carried him gently to his poor hut. The oilman's wife was a vicious shrew, and when she saw what her husband had brought home, she cried, "O you blockhead, what have you done? Why have you brought this ugly *doond*, this cripple, here? Don't you know he's a criminal and the emperor has cut off his hands and feet to punish him? If the emperor hears that we have sheltered this villain, he will surely have us pressed to death in our own oil mill. Go back and leave him where you found him." But the kindhearted oilman wouldn't listen to this heartless woman and said to her, "Wife, I know what I'm doing. He's helpless. I've called him my son, and you should treat him as one. Don't try to talk me out of a good deed. Go and prepare some balsam and let me dress the wounds of this poor creature."

His wife obeyed and reluctantly helped him dress Vikram's wounds and nurse the patient. In course of time, the wounds healed and the raja began to regain his strength. Then the oilman put him on the seat of the oil press, and he was carried round and round the mill by the oxen. Thereafter the raja would sit there all day, and the oilman would bring him food and drink.

One day, the oilman noticed that his ward was very dirty and greasy and needed a bath badly. So he said to his wife, "We must wash our son today. He needs it."

The raja at once said, "Father, I don't want a bath unless you are willing to wash me in the tank in the princess's summer garden."

When she heard this, the shrew went into hysterics and cried, "Look at this *doond*, he won't have a bath except in the waters of the princess's tank! Don't you know that no male ever steps onto the golden pavements of that garden? Husband, don't you do anything so foolish and dangerous, just to satisfy an absurd whim of this ugly *doond!*"

The husband merely said, "But I will. He is my son and I must satisfy this simple wish, whatever it costs."

When it was dark, he took the raja on his shoulders and carried him to the summer garden of the princess of China. The garden was unguarded at that time, and the oilman took him to the edge of the tank. The raja then asked him to leave him there and come back at midnight to collect him. The oilman was at first afraid to leave his helpless adopted son alone, but Vikram persuaded him to do so. He left with a heart heavy with misgivings.

The raja now hobbled into the tank and bathed as best he could, came out of it, changed his clothes, and sat down to *puja*. After this act of worship, which took as long as three hours, he looked at the sky and saw that it was getting close to midnight. Then he sang out in a deep and beautiful voice a weird, soul-stirring air, the *Dipaka Ragini*, composed by him and known only to him. It was this music that had enslaved the invisible spirits of the air and fire and made them obedient instruments in his hand. The music had become another name for Vikram. As soon as he had sung the *Dipaka*, all the lamps in the city that had been put out for the night came alight by themselves, and people all over the city started up in amazement to see their lamps burning bright though they had just extinguished them. Such was the virtue of the *Dipaka*, the Illuminator.

As the music rose louder and higher, the lights burned brighter and more intensely. And as the music faded and died away, the lights also began to sink and go out, and the whole city was immersed in a darkness twice as deep as before.

The princess also was awakened when the lamps were lighted, and as she witnessed the strange miracle, she knew at once that it was the work of none other than Raja Vikram. Her heart was all aflutter as she thought of it, for it had been her ambition for a long time to see and to marry that great monarch of India, of worldwide fame. Through her knowledge of the secret sciences, she knew also that he had come in disguise and that he was staying with an oilman. Even her sciences could not tell her more than that.

When it was a minute past midnight, the oilman crept into the garden, carried the raja back in the dark to his hut, and put him in his bed. The sun was hardly up, and the oilman was still in bed trying to recover from the fatigue of his night watch, when he was roused by the king's men who came to summon him before the princess. The poor fellow was trembling all over and thought that his trespass into the garden had been detected. But when he was brought before the princess, he was relieved to see all the other oilmen of the city lined up next to him with joined hands.

The princess turned to the officers and said, "Are all the oilmen of this city present? You've omitted no one?"

The officers bowed and said that they had rounded up every last one of them. Then the princess addressed the oilmen:

"Look here, fellows, by six o'clock tomorrow morning, I want each one of you to supply me with a hundred maunds of oil. If you don't, you and your families will all be pressed to death in your oil mills. You can go now."

The oilmen returned home, weeping and crying and cursing the preposterous whims of the princess.

When our oilman returned from the palace of the princess of China, he was in despair. And as you can expect, he picked a quarrel with his wife. The vixen soon found out why her husband was feeling so bitter. She flew into a rage and said, "You ass, see now what you've done! Didn't I tell you not to shelter this *doond*, this bringer of ill-luck? Ever since he arrived, things have gone from bad to worse. Where will you get a hundred maunds of oil? We'll all die tomorrow morning in the oil mill, all because of your stupidity." And then she set up loud lamentations, and the poor man was beside himself. That day no fire was lit in his house and no food or drink was served. They sat there, their heads in their hands, in utter despair.

The helpless raja sat on the mill, hungry all day, and in the evening he called the oilman to ask him why no flour was kneaded and no oven was lit that day. The oilman reluctantly told him why. While he was weeping, his shrewish wife kept up her scolding and cursing him and his so-called son. Raja Vikram then said, "Father, if we must die, as we all must someday, let us at least die like men. Let us not die of starvation. Go and get some food prepared." After some reasoning of this sort, the couple got up and cooked their food. As they ate their meal, they firmly believed it was their very last. They were so oppressed by the sad fate awaiting them in the morning that they could hardly sleep, till at last sheer fatigue took over.

As soon as Vikram saw they were asleep, he sang in a low voice the *Bhairabi*

Ragini, and at once his four guardian spirits, the *virs*, appeared before him and spoke to him: "O great king, born in the family of Fire, why are you doing this? How long will you hide in this cripple's body? Tell us what you wish and we will do it."

The raja said, "You're my trusted friends. I'll soon be out of hiding. But you must help now as you've always done. Bring one hundred maunds of the best kind of oil." The *virs* vanished, and in an instant the hut of the oilman and the streets nearby were full of thousands of large black jars filled with oil.

The oilman's sleep was disturbed by bad dreams, and one was so horrible that he jumped out of bed with a fearful cry that roused the whole neighborhood. When he opened his eyes and saw the row of oil vessels, he thought they were soldiers, and he kept crying, "Oh help, help! They've come to murder me!" It took him some time to see that the so-called soldiers were not moving. When he went up close and examined them, his sorrow turned into joy. They were all jars of oil! And he didn't know how they had gotten there. With a happy heart, he ran to the palace early in the morning, before any other oilman, and told the princess that the oil was ready.

That was what the princess was waiting for. She knew that Raja Vikram was at his oilman's house, for no one but the raja's *virs* could have supplied so much oil at such short notice. She dismissed all the other oilmen, who by now had come trembling to the palace to report that they couldn't meet her demand. But she told our oilman to stay and not go home. When everyone else was gone, she asked him, "Now, oilman, tell me the truth. Whom are you sheltering in your house?"

The oilman stammered and replied, "I've no one with me, except my wife and a poor helpless creature, a *doond* I picked up from the public square. I've adopted him as my son. There's no one else, really."

The princess now knew that the *doond* was Vikram. So she told the oilman, "Two months from now, on full-moon day, my father the emperor will hold a great *durbar* and a *svayambara*, where I'll choose my husband. He will invite all the rajas and chieftains of the world. The whole city will be invited too. So you also come on that day and bring your *doond* with you. This is both an invitation and an order, do you hear?" With that, she dismissed him.

Two months passed in great bustle all over the city. Elaborate preparations were made in the Chinese capital, and soon the day of the *svayambara*, the bride-choice, arrived. Kings and princes thronged in from all quarters of the globe and pitched their tents around the imperial city. They all met in richly decorated pavilions. Every crowned head there was busy with the thought that it would receive the princess's garland. As they sat glittering in silk and jewels, in one corner of the multitude stood the oilman. He was carrying on his shoulders the mutilated Vikram. Both were dressed in their best, though their best came nowhere near what the servants of the royal guests wore on that festive day.

Suddenly the princess burst upon the assembly with two of her attendants, and everyone was dazzled by the blaze of her beauty. She had a garland of flowers in her hand and she looked all around, far and near, as if she were looking for someone in particular. At last, she caught sight of the oilman hidden in a corner. She at once walked there with unhesitating steps, and to the shock of everyone watching, she put the garland around the neck of the *doond*. The emperor of China himself was greatly humiliated, and the royal guests were horrified at this absurd choice.

But in a ceremony of *svayambara*, there was no way of getting out of a choice once made, so the emperor arranged for the oilman and the crippled bridegroom to be brought to the palace with pomp and procession. Knowing that the oilman had nothing at all to his name, he appointed the royal treasurer to manage it all. But when the officers came to make the necessary arrangements and the oilman and his wife got busy, Vikram forbade them to do anything. He practically drove away the king's men. When it was night, he asked his adopted father to carry him once again to the garden of the princess and put him at the edge of the tank. Once there, he said to the oilman, "Father, go home now and come back before dawn to fetch me."

When he was alone, Raja Vikram sang out the *Dipaka Ragini*. Again, as the strange, magical notes wafted on the air, the lamps burst forth into light, and again the princess woke up and saw the mysterious happening. But this time she quickly changed her shape and became an *apsaras*, a celestial damsel, and went to the garden. The raja did not recognize her in her new shape. The *apsaras* said, "O great raja, ask any boon. I'm greatly pleased with your song."

The raja said, "O beautiful woman from the world of Indra in heaven, make me whole. Heal my mutilated limbs."

As soon as she heard it, the princess vanished and returned with the cut-off parts, joined them to the stumps, and the raja was whole again. Then she vanished and returned to her palace.

The raja now invoked his four spirits, and they appeared at once and said, "We are ready. Command us."

"Friends," said the raja, "I won your service after years of penance and you've always served me well. The time for your release from thralldom is near. I gave you consciousness when you were aimlessly wandering through the air. Now, hurry home to my kingdom and bring together all my army. I want tents pitched for miles around the city. Let my elephants and horses in gold and silver trappings be ready at my command. Let my friend's hut be changed into a royal mansion full of jewels and gold, with servants in livery. Do everything befitting Vikram, the emperor of India, and do all this before dawn." The guardian spirits saluted him obediently and melted into thin air.

The poor oilman had witnessed all this from a hiding place. He now came forward trembling and fell at the raja's feet, crying, "Forgive me, O raja of India." Vikram quickly raised him from the ground and said in the kindest of tones, "Father, think of me always as your son. I can never repay the kindness you showed me in my time of trouble. Let's get home now. Dawn is already appearing in the east."

When they returned home, the oilman was amazed to find an imperial palace instead of his poor hut. His shrew of a wife came out to greet them, and she was dressed as a queen. She couldn't contain her joy. All her curses and scolding had now turned into bows and smiles.

The guardian spirits had done their work before dawn. The emperor of China soon heard that a mighty army had mysteriously surrounded the city during the night. He at once hurried out of the palace, bareheaded, barefooted, with a straw in his mouth as a sign of surrender and peace. But the raja came out of the tent and received his father-in-law with all due courtesy. Who can describe the happiness of the emperor when he found that the ugly *doond* whom his daughter had selected was really the glorious Raja Vikram? The news soon reached the rest of the city. All the rajas and chieftains who had been disgusted by the bride-choice and had planned to kill the *doond* now came in a group and threw themselves humbly before their successful rival —the great Vikram.

The wedding was a great gala affair. In the large pavilion magically con- structed by the *virs*, the bride and bridegroom sat on a raised dais in the evening and watched a superb dance performance with the assembly. While the dance was in progress, news was brought that a band of jugglers was waiting outside to show its talents before the noble assembly. The raja ordered them brought in. As soon as they entered, he recognized his enemy the yogi and his former minister among the chief performers. The raja turned pale, but the princess, when she found out what was happening, whispered, "Fear nothing. See how their own malice will turn against them."

The jugglers began with a performance called the raising of the dead. The former minister brought out from a long box the preserved body of his son, stretched it out on the ground, and sat on its chest. The yogi kindled a burning fire all around and sat in the middle. The other jugglers beat drums and tambourines. Slowly the corpse, with the man seated on its chest, rose into the air and vanished out of sight. Soon there was a clash of arms and the noise of a fight high up in the air. Then there fell to the ground now an arm, now a leg, then the trunk, and so on till all the body parts lay on the ground. Then the man came down and said, "O rajas, here you see the dismembered corpse. I'll now make it whole and give it life." He joined the various parts together, and the yogi gave him some ashes from his fire. As soon as the ashes were sprinkled on it, the dead body was whole and alive. It stood up and cried out, "Father, I'm hungry. Give me food." The former minister replied, "Change into a tiger and eat your enemy," pointing to Vikram.

At once the resurrected corpse changed into a tiger and sprang towards the raja. But the princess waved her hand, and the tiger jumped back with a tremendous roar as if struck by lightning. Furious with rage, it turned around, and before the yogi could intervene, the angry beast attacked the former minister, tore him to pieces, and rushed out of the pavilion. The yogi came out of the fiery circle and began to run away, but the princess again waved her hand and he stood rooted to the spot. She addressed him then in a voice of thunder: "You mean sorcerer, you have used divine powers for base ends. You'll be punished by them. So I have to do nothing. You'll wander, soulless and senseless, like a beast of the forest."

When she waved her hand, the sorcerer staggered out—an idiot, devoid of all human powers, as if a flame had been put out by a wave of that magical hand.

Vikram returned to his kingdom with his bride, to the great joy of all his subjects, and lived happily for a long time.

Walking on Water
~ *Bengali* ~~

A holy man was once meditating on the bank of a river, when another holy man wanted to impress him with the extraordinary powers he had achieved through his ascetic practices. So he came towards him, walking on the water.

When he reached the place where the first holy man was quietly sitting, he said, "Did you see what I just did?"

"Oh yes, I saw you come across the river, walking on the water. Where did you learn that?"

"I practiced yoga and penances for twelve years in the foothills of the Himalayas, standing on one leg, fasting six days of the week. And so I acquired this power."

"Really?" said the first holy man. "Why did you go to all that trouble to do this? Our ferryman here will ferry you across any day for two pennies."

The Guru and the Idiot
~ *Telugu* ~~

A rich guru had hundreds of disciples all over the country. He lived like a lord and traveled in a palanquin from town to town, visiting his followers and receiving gifts and donations. It took him twelve years to visit all of them even once.

While he was on one of these rounds, he was stopped on the road outside a certain town by a man who looked and acted like an idiot. He stood right in the middle of the road and would not let the palanquin pass till the guru had talked to him. The guru was impatient but agreed to talk to him for a minute. "What do you want?" he asked testily.

The man said, "I want to go to heaven. People tell me that you are a guru and know the way."

The guru laughed and said, "You want to go to heaven? That's easy. Just stand there with your hands lifted to the sky. You'll go to heaven." The man said, "That's all?" and before he could ask any more, the guru had ordered his palanquin bearers to move on and was gone.

Twelve years later, the guru had occasion to come that way again. As he reached the outskirts of the town, he saw a man standing there, looking at the sky, his hands lifted towards heaven. His hair and beard had turned grey, his nails had grown long and dirty, his clothes were in tatters. He didn't seem to mind. His eyes were riveted to the sky.

As the guru approached him, he saw an astonishing thing happen. He saw the man, the idiot, slowly rise towards heaven. The guru had a flash of understanding and knew what he should do. He at once got down from his palanquin, held on to the feet of the idiot, and rose with him to heaven. That was the only way he could have gone to heaven, and he knew it now.

Grateful Animals, Ungrateful Man

~ *Kumaoni, a Himalayan dialect of Hindi* ~ ~

Once a good man was passing through a forest. He looked for water and found a disused well. When he looked in, he heard voices calling out to him. A lion, a snake, a goldsmith, and a barber had fallen into it and couldn't get out. The lion said, "Please help me get out of this well and I'll not forget your good deed."

The man said, "Just the thought of a lion makes me shudder. If I take you out, you'll eat me up. You must be hungry."

The lion said, "Oh no, I promise not to do you any harm. Please help me."

With the help of some strong vines that were growing nearby, the good man pulled the lion out. The lion said, "Remember to visit me. I live in this forest. I'd like to give you something. Before I go, let me give you a piece of advice. Do not help these two men. They are evil."

Then the snake begged the man to take him out. When the good man said he was terrified of snakes, the snake too promised to do him no harm. He helped the snake out of the well. Before he went his way, he asked the man to think of him if he ever needed his help. The snake too warned him against helping the barber and the goldsmith.

But when the barber and the goldsmith begged him to help them also, he relented, thinking, "They are human beings, like me." And he let down some vines and pulled them out. They both thanked him over and over and asked him to visit them in the nearby city. They too promised to reward him for his good deed.

After his travels, the good man happened to visit the jungle again and found the lion. The lion was delighted to see him, took him around, and gave him a diamond ring as a present at parting.

Then the good man visited the city and looked for the goldsmith and the barber. They were all courtesy to him, but when he showed them the diamond ring on his finger, they secretly reported him to the king. The king had a daughter who had been killed by a lion during a journey in the forest. He had sent a town crier all over the kingdom to proclaim that anyone who had any clue to her death, anyone who found any of her ornaments, would get a reward. Now, the diamond ring did belong to the king's daughter.

The barber was now a *kotwal*, a bailiff in the king's service, and he promptly arrested the good man, threw him in jail, and tortured him. The man told them over and over again that he was innocent and that the ring was really a gift from a lion. Who would believe him? The king thought he had killed his daughter and stolen her ring. So he sentenced the good man to death by beheading.

In jail, feeling desperate, it occurred to him to think of the snake, who at once appeared before him and asked, "What can I do for you?" The good man told him everything that happened. The snake said, "I told you not to rescue those scoundrels. But I'll help you get out of here as you helped me once to get out of a tight spot. I'll go and bite the queen. You send word to the king that you can draw out the poison and save her life. I'll do the rest."

That very night, the queen lay senseless, bitten by a venomous snake. The king sent messengers everywhere for doctors and magicians. The queen was in agony, and everyone thought her last hour had come.

The next day, when the good man was about to be beheaded, as a last request he offered his services to cure the queen and save her life. He was immediately sent for, and as soon as he was in her chamber, his friend the snake appeared, put his mouth to the wound, and drew back his own poison. The queen was well again.

The king was pleased and grateful, but he was still angry with the man because he thought he had killed his daughter. The good man told his story again and again. He even called the barber and the goldsmith as his witnesses to tell the king how he had pulled them as well as the snake and the lion out of the well. But the goldsmith and the barber said they had never seen the man before. In despair, he wished the lion would come and confirm his story. As soon as he wished it, the lion arrived in the city with a great pride of lions, and the city was filled with their majestic roaring. The king and the citizens were amazed and terror-stricken. The king was now convinced that the good man was telling the truth, and the lions disappeared.

Although the barber and the goldsmith denied everything, the king ordered them to be beheaded in the good man's place.

When a Black Dog Dies

~ Urdu ~ ~

A *zamindar*, a rich landowner, was known for his short temper. He also had a weak heart. Therefore his household and his servants were under orders that they should be very careful about what they said to him and how they said it. Once, when he was visiting the city, a servant was dispatched to him with some news.

The master asked him, "You come from my house? How is everybody?"

"Very well, sir," said the servant. "Only the black dog is dead."

"Poor thing, why did it die? It seemed quite well when I left."

"It died of indigestion. How could it help dying when it eats so much horse meat?"

"Horse meat? Where did it get horse meat?"

"Where else but in our stables, sir."

"What, did our horses die?"

"How could they live when there were no grooms to feed them?"

"Why, what happened to the grooms?"

"Only what happens to people when they starve, sir, when there's no one to pay them."

"What are you saying? Why were they not paid? What happened to the steward, what happened to my wife?"

"How could they live when there's no cook to give them food?"

"Why, what happened to the cook?"

"How could he live, sir, when the kitchen caught fire and the fire spread to the whole house and killed everyone?"

The Village Rogue, the City Rogue, and the King of Rogues

~ *Oriya* ~~

One dark night, the village rogue and the city rogue, traveling in opposite directions, met under a tree. The village rogue had a bag of limestone on his head and the city rogue carried a big bag full of ashes. The village rogue said, "What are you carrying?" The city rogue answered, "I'm carrying a bag of camphor. What's that on your head?" The village rogue said, "Oh, that? It's a bagful of cowries. Are you interested?" The city rogue was interested and asked, "Will you take this camphor in return for your cowries?" The other man agreed and they exchanged bags.

The village rogue went home gleefully and said to his wife, "I did something terribly clever today. I exchanged a bag of worthless limestone for a bag of precious camphor." The city rogue went home to his wife and said, "Few men in this world are truly clever. I happen to be one of them. I've just cheated a fool out of his bag of cowries. I exchanged it for a bag of ashes. The fellow will have a heart attack when he opens the bag and the ashes fly in his face. Let him die, who cares for a fool's life?"

The children in both these families waited around anxiously for the bags to be opened. To their amazement and their parents' chagrin, one contained limestone, the other ashes. The faces of the rogues fell. The wife in each house scolded her spouse: "You braggart, don't you know any better? Silly man!" The biter was bit, the cheater cheated.

However, when they met again in the marketplace, they burst into laughter at each other. They became friends and thought of becoming partners. They even put *mahaprasad*, holy food from the temple, in each other's mouths by way of sealing their bond of friendship. The city rogue beamed and said, "When two people of our caliber get together, who can cheat us? We can cheat everyone else. We'll invade the fairs, the markets, the city streets, even the holy bathing-ghat and this sacred temple." The other one added, "We can steal not only gold and jewelry. That's too easy. We know how to steal even the sandalwood paste from the Brahman's forehead and the kohl from the eyes of pretty women."

They set forth and took for their first target the house of an old woman. She was rich but she was bent double with age. She walked around leaning on a stick. The two rogues gathered an account of her life from the villagers before they went to see the old woman. As soon as they met her, they fell at her feet and said, "Dear Auntie, you got married so long ago and never came to see your father's relatives. But we have not forgotten you. You played with us when we were babies. We've never forgotten you. Now the wedding of my son is getting arranged and you, as the eldest in our family, have to come and supervise it. Please get dressed and come with us."

It was true that the old lady had not visited her father's village in years. It was far away, and her own family had taken up all her time and energy. She shed tears recalling her childhood and early youth. She was comforted by these welcome guests. She wanted them to massage their bodies with warm oil and take a good warm bath. So she gave them oil in a golden cup and asked her son to take them to the nearby tank where they could bathe.

The rogues covered their bodies with oil, bathed in the tank, and hid the golden cup in the reeds. One of them suddenly raised a hue and cry that a crow had flown away with the glittering cup. "Crows are wicked," they said to the old woman later as they ate the meal she served. "They do such naughty things. We carelessly left the cup on the bank. We ran after the crow, but it flew away fast and disappeared. What shall we do?" The son of the old woman had watched everything but pretended he saw nothing. They thought he was an idiot.

The old woman felt unhappy at the loss of her cup and regretted not giving them oil in a copper, brass, or even a silver cup. She took the loss as a bad omen, and decided not to go to the wedding. She sent her son instead to attend the wedding. He accompanied the two rogues on his horse.

On the way the rogues said, "Brother, we are terribly hungry. You've lots of jewelry on you. If you pawned even one small piece, all three of us could have a terrific meal." The old woman's son said, "Why sell precious things? Only men without means do that. You don't know that I have good credit here. I'll get you a good meal, anything you wish. But you should not embarrass me. When I'm talking to these people here, you must do as I say. When anyone asks you, 'One? Or two?' you must always say 'Two.' Is that clear?"

The rogues agreed. Why not get two instead of one, whatever it is? The old woman's son went to a merchant in the village and said to him confidentially, "I've brought two laborers for you to hire. You can actually buy them. They will be yours for life. They are strong, and experts in farming. Pay me a decent sum and they're yours." The merchant looked them over and was satisfied. He asked them, "One? Or two?" They both said, "Two." "Done," said the merchant.

The young man took the money from him and left, before the two rogues could realize what was happening. The two men, now bought slaves, were taken to the garden to work there in spite of their protests. The merchant wouldn't hear any of it and threatened them with lashes. The two rogues now realized that the young son of the old woman was a bigger rogue than either of them. They fell at the merchant's feet, and begged, "Sir, we have never done a stroke of work in our lives. We always engage others to do the smallest thing for us. We are from good families and deserve to be treated like the decent people we are. The young man invited us here for a meal and to our surprise sold us to you body and soul."

The merchant, who was tough, said, "I don't care about your past history. I've paid good money for you. I can't be sentimental about such things."

The two men begged for mercy and said, "We have been cheated. So have you been cheated. If you send somebody with us, we'll find him and make him cough up the money and return it to you." The merchant was reluctantly persuaded that they were indeed innocent. He sent a servant with them to search for the offender.

Meanwhile, the young man rode his horse swiftly and reached the next village. He stopped at a sweetmeat shop and started gobbling up the sweets

with both hands. The boy who was minding the store was aghast at this unusual behavior and said, "If you like them so much, just pay for them and eat as much as you want." "Oh no," said the young man, "My name is Fly. Go in and tell your father that Fly is eating your sweets without paying for them. He'll understand. I'm a friend of his."

The young man ran and told his father about this strange "Fly." The father got angry and said, "You are a fool. How much can a fly eat? Who's minding the store? Go back at once and guard it."

Meanwhile the rogue filled a bag with sweets and rode away. On the way he saw an old woman with a charming young daughter. The young rogue was quite smitten with the young beauty, rode close to her, quickly picked her up, and carried her off on his horse before the old woman could realize what was happening. While she stood dazed by the speed of all this, and was about to scream, he shouted from the horse, "Don't worry about your daughter. My name is Son-in-Law."

The old woman screamed and howled till a crowd gathered. She told them all again and again, "My daughter! My daughter has been kidnapped! He's carrying her away! His name is Son-in-Law." People laughed at her and said, "What? Your daughter was swept off her feet and carried away by your son-in-law? Why are you making such a fuss, crying and carrying on like this? She's now grown up. Do you want her to stay with you forever? Your son-in-law was rightly impatient and carried her off. Good for him!"

The rogue rode on with the young woman into a forest and stopped to rest. The young woman liked him too and thought all this was quite exciting. When they stopped to rest awhile, they saw a bear nearby eating white ants. The bear soon saw the intruders and attacked the rogue head-on. The young man wrestled with the bear and with great skill pushed its nose to the ground and rubbed it in the dust. But he could not kill it without a weapon, nor could he let go. All the money from his pockets was scattered all around him. He fought with the animal for a long time, and just when he was getting tired and afraid that he wouldn't last much longer, a merchant arrived. He saw all the money scattered on the forest floor and began greedily to gather it. As he was doing so, he came upon the young man rubbing the bear's nose in the dust, and couldn't help asking, "What are you doing to that bear? How come all this money is scattered on the ground?"

The young rogue said, "Sir, this is not like any old wild bear. It drops money from its other end when I rub its nose in the dust. It loves to wrestle. I've now tamed it. It's quite harmless."

The merchant asked the rogue, "Will you sell it?"

The rogue replied, "If I get a good customer. But I'll not part with it for less than a *lakh* of rupees. You see, the bear gives ten thousand a day."

The merchant thought, "That's real cash flow. It's better than any business I've had. If I have this bear, I can retire on it. I'll have money without the worries of earning it." So he counted out a *lakh* of rupees. The rogue also demanded from him all the scattered rupees. He then told the merchant to hold the bear and rub its nose in the dust, and when the merchant relieved him of his charge, he rode away with the money and the young woman.

In the course of his onward journey, the rogue saw a washerman spreading out the week's laundered clothes to dry in the sun. The rogue began to chew the sweets he had brought in full view of the washerman till the washerman's mouth watered. When the rogue gave him a few, the washerman was enchanted by their taste. The rogue said, "I'm glad you like them. I love them. They are not ordinary sweets . . . these are from a special tree on that hill. It grows by the side of a lake. Just go there and pluck as many as you like. Eat them, drink the clear cool water from the lake, and if you collect enough you can even sell them and make some good money. They are really wonderful."

The washerman was taken with the idea and wanted to go right then to the hill. He left the rogue in charge of his clothes. They were costly garments, rich silks and satins. The rogue gathered them all, put the bundle on his horse, and rode to the next village. Once there, he tied the multicolored clothes to the branches of a tree and began to pray to it in a loud voice: "O my magic tree, O loom of the gods, bloom for me in silk and satin."

A merchant passing by heard these words and wondered, "How can a tree bear silk and satin as if they were many-colored flowers? This is strange, very strange. Such things may happen in heaven. But who ever heard of a silk-bearing tree on earth?" Then he approached the rogue and asked him, "What are you doing?"

The rogue said, "This is a strange tree. It bears silk and satin as other trees bear flowers. You climb it, sit on a branch, and say, 'Bloom, O magic tree, bloom for me in silk and satin!' and it'll do so. You'll find fully stitched clothes, dresses fit for kings and queens. Look, there's my sweet lady. She doesn't ever have to wear yesterday's clothes. She puts on new ones every day. She wears them for a single day and throws them away like yesterday's used flowers. Lucky, isn't she?"

The merchant was in textiles. He thought, "Why should I buy clothes for my shop from factories and pay dressmakers? Laborers are such a lot of trouble. This tree needs only a little tending and is no trouble. I'll make a lot of money in no time and be free of labor disputes. And these clothes are so beautifully made!"

So he struck a bargain with the rogue, paid him a lot of money, and became the proud owner of the magic tree. The rogue rode off with his young lady, who was having the time of her life.

The merchant eagerly climbed the tree and prayed it to bloom for him, repeating word for word the rogue's prayer. But nothing at all happened. It took him almost a day of trying and getting hoarse before he realized the tree was no magic tree, and that he had been had.

The first two rogues were still searching for the young rogue who had outwitted them. They came to the sweetmeat shop that had been plundered. They took the confectioner with them, and on their way met the old woman whose daughter had been carried off. All four of them walked on, and soon met the merchant who was still struggling with the bear and fast losing ground. The men hit the bear with a stick and killed it. They consoled the washerman who had lost all his laundry and was trying to figure out how he would face a townful of clients without their clothes.

They finally caught up with the young rogue in his place and took him to task. The rogue said, "I'm not a rogue. I'm not a thief. I'll return everything to you—everything but the sweets that I've already eaten, and I'll pay for those. I do these things for fun. I just wanted to show how easily people are led by their noses, especially if they want something very badly."

They were all pleased with his charm and courtesy. He ordered them a dinner of the daintiest dishes and asked servants to make soft beds for them. They ate their dinner happily and slept peacefully, assured that all their stuff would be returned to them.

Meanwhile the rogue had gone and bribed the watchman of the village, who came around to proclaim by beat of drum the king's order that anyone harboring any strangers in his house as guests must bring them to the king's court the next morning. The town crier said that these strangers were suspected of espionage. Anyone who didn't obey the order would be guilty of high treason and would be hanged at once.

The two rogues, the old woman, the two merchants, and the washerman heard this proclamation with fear and trembling in their hearts. They panicked and fled for their lives. After running till they felt quite safe, one of the rogues said to the other, "Brother, I'm the village rogue. You're the famous city rogue. But this fellow is the king of rogues. We are no match for him. We make a living by outwitting others, and here we are being outwitted, stripped of what we have, and run out of town."

The king of rogues lives happily now with his beautiful young lady. When I talked to him the other day, he said, "Mere cheating is no good. It adds color to life only when it's done with wit."

That's the end of my story.

A Qazi with a Long Beard

~ *Marathi* ~ ~

One evening, a *qazi* was reading an old book by the light of an oil lamp when he came across the sentence, "Men with long beards are usually quite stupid."

He had always wanted to be respected for his wisdom, and here he was with the longest beard in town! Everybody must think him utterly stupid. He couldn't bear the thought of it.

His eyes fell on the oil lamp. Without any further hesitation, he gathered his beard in his fist and lighted the end of it, so that he could have a shorter beard.

The beard was long, fine, and silky. It caught fire and burned in a blaze. When his fingers began to get burned, the *qazi* let go of his beard, and the flame leaped up and burned off his mustache and his eyebrows, and spread to the hair on his head and burned it all off.

Now he knew that men with long beards were really stupid.

The Priest Who
Could See as Far as Mecca

~ *Assamese* ~ ~

A Muslim priest was invited to a meal by a devout couple. As the *mulla* stepped over the threshold of the house, he suddenly cried, "Out, out!" as if he were chasing away an animal. His host asked him why he cried out the way he did. The priest explained, "I just saw a dog about to enter the holy Kaaba at Mecca. So I chased it away." The host was awestruck by the *mulla*'s spiritual powers that allowed him to see as far as Mecca, thousands of miles away.

But the woman of the house had her doubts. When she served the priest his meal, she hid the curry under the rice. When the *mulla* saw curry on the others' plates but not on his, he looked around. The woman asked him, "Do you want something?" The *mulla* said, "I don't see any curry on my plate." She replied, "You can see as far as Mecca. Can't you see what there is under the rice?"

Adventures of a Disobedient Son

~ *Kannada* ~ ~

A king had four wives and four sons, one son by each wife. He had no care in the world, and enjoyed every luxury and pleasure. He had many long titles; twenty-four other kings paid him tribute; and his kingdom was truly vast.

One day, as he sat on the swing under the full moon playing love-games with his queens, he was struck by a fancy. He summoned his four sons to his presence, and asked the eldest of them, "Son, you are my eldest, the future king of this country. What are your plans?"

The son obediently answered, "Father, I'll follow in your illustrious footsteps. I'll try to be a great king like you."

He asked the second son the same question: "Son, what are your plans?"

"Father, I'll be a statesman and help my brother rule the kingdom."

When the third one was asked, he answered, "I'll be a great commander and help my brother rule in peace."

When the fourth son's turn came, he answered differently: "Father, you are the king of kings. Twenty-four kings pay you tribute. I want to do better than you. I'll conquer kingdoms, marry four celestial wives, and build my own city."

"What!" the king exploded. "Do better than me? You beast on two feet! You'll marry celestial wives? And do better than me?"

In his rage, he called his servants and shouted, "Throw him out! Banish him to the jungle at once!"

His mother tried to pacify the old man, but he would not listen to her.

So she went in and prepared a bundle of rice for her banished son, and tearfully bade him good-bye.

The youngest son promptly left the palace, went out of the city, and walked straight on till he found himself in a forest where he heard nothing but the roar of tigers and lions on one side and the trumpetings of wild elephants and grunts of wild pigs on the other. He cautiously climbed a tall tree and spent the night among its branches. At dawn, in the light of day, he came down, bathed in a nearby lake, and prayed to the Bull, the vehicle of Siva and his family god, to protect him. As he was walking away, his eye fell on a cobra, its hood poised to fall upon a frog and gobble it up. He chased away the cobra with a stick and saved the frog's life. To his surprise, the frog spoke to him in gratitude and said, "Think of me if you are ever in need," and plonked into the water.

The young prince then ate from the bundle of rice his mother had given him, and walked on again through the wilderness till night fell. When it was dark, he saw a small lamp flickering in the distance, and he made for it like a bee to a flower. Soon he was standing at the door of a hut. When he called, "Anybody home?" a very old woman came out and took him in. She said, "You must be tired. Wash your feet and rest here tonight."

When she asked him why he was in this jungle, he briefly told her his story, and asked her in turn how she happened to live alone in this forest. She said, "My name is Sickle Granny. My story is a long one. Rest now. I'll tell you some other time."

But the young prince was curious and insisted on hearing the story right away. So she told him her story.

"I may not look like it, but I'm the daughter of a great sage. Though he was a sage famous for his austere way of life, one day he went mad with lust and bothered my mother no end. She didn't want to give in to his lust, for that would have canceled at once all his past history as a sage. She tried to save him from himself. But he wouldn't listen. He took her by force, had his way with her, and satisfied himself. So I was born, ugly as sin. Soon after I was born, he went into that same jungle you just came through, and while he was gathering fruit a tiger attacked him and tore him limb from limb. My mother died soon after, and I was orphaned. Because I knew I was very ugly, I stayed on in the forest and never went into town. I just prayed and worshipped every day, and I attained the powers one gets only by such penance. Many marvels have I seen then. I could tell you more, but it can wait. It's late and you must sleep."

The prince stayed with her and helped graze her cows. The old woman had only one rule for him: "When you take the cows out to pasture, never go towards the north." He had said, "Yes, I'll remember that." But one day his natural curiosity made him want to see what there was in the north that he shouldn't see, so he drove the herd in that direction. He came upon wonderful sights. He was particularly taken with a beautiful bathing tank, built with gold bricks and with steps set in crystal. Green, red, pink, blue, and yellow fish sported in the water. He had hardly sat down under the shade of the *jambu* tree that spread its branches over one side of it when four celestial women appeared, as if from the sky. He hid himself behind the tree and watched them take off their yellow silk *pitambara* saris, jump noisily into the well, and splash each other with the crystalline water, having a great time. On an impulse, the prince picked up one of the saris and fled. The sari belonged to none other than Indra's own daughter. She saw him run off with her sari, so she quickly got out of the water and ran after him, crying out, "O young man, you look like a hero. I'll marry you and no one else. Stop, turn around, and look at me."

Astonished, he stopped, and the celestial woman at once snatched the sari from his hands, changed him into cold stone, and vanished.

When the prince did not return home as usual by evening, the old woman became anxious. Wand and lantern in hand, she set out in search of him in the south, the east, and the west, but she found no trace of him. She guessed that he must have gone to the forbidden north, and when she went in search of him there she found him lying on the ground, a piece of rock. She struck it with her wand, and he returned to life and stood up in his own body. They hurried home to safety as she scolded him.

"Didn't I tell you never to go north? By 'never' I meant 'never.' "

"Yes, Granny, you did tell me. But I knew somehow that's where my life would be fulfilled. So I couldn't resist it—I went. In fact, I want to go there again."

"All right, go if you must. But take some precautions. Don't take the cows with you. And don't be beguiled by those celestial wenches, their looks and sweet words. This time, when you pick up the sari, run straight home. I'll be waiting for you, and I'll take care of the rest."

He followed her instructions. Next day, he ate his morning meal early and went back to the place of the beautiful tank and hid himself under the *jambu* tree. Today, too, the women arrived and unwrapped their saris before his unbelieving eyes. He gazed on them, his eyes moving from head to toe. What shapes! What complexions! Kohl-streaked eyes, faces like the moon, cascades of black hair flowing down to their buttocks, round breasts like perfect melons, and all of them young, virginal. They dived into the water, leaving their saris and pearls on the dry ground. The prince leaped out of his hiding-place, quickly snatched the same sari he had taken the previous day, and ran. Its celestial owner ran out of the water and followed him, weeping and calling to him. But he was not deceived. He ran straight to the hut and handed the heavenly sari to the old woman, who changed him at once into a small baby and put him in a cradle. She pretended to rock him and lull him to sleep with lullabies. With her magic, she had also placed the sari inside the baby's thigh and sewn it up without a seam showing. A few moments later, the celestial woman arrived at her door, panting, and asked her, "Did anyone come this way? A young man?"

"A young man? No, no one has come this way. I've been here for hours," said the old woman.

"He may be hiding here somewhere."

"Before you do anything, dear, you must hide your shame. It's not a good idea to go around naked. Take this piece of cotton cloth and wrap yourself up."

After a few minutes of this pretense and teasing, the old woman said to her, "I know where your sari is. You can have it back if you agree to marry him."

The celestial woman agreed. The old woman changed the prince back to his original form. They were married right there, in that hut, with the old woman as the wedding priest.

They lived there for a few days, and one day took leave of the old woman and moved on. He had yet to win three more wives for himself, hadn't he?

The prince and his celestial bride talked to each other endlessly on their journey and soon found themselves at the gates of a city. The townspeople were struck by their beauty; they thought he was like the lord Krishna and she like his consort Rukmini, the very dwelling-place of all that is lovely. A boy in the street who was eating a piece of sugar candy was so entranced watching them that he began to bite into his fist. A woodcutter missed his stroke and axed his own leg. People forgot themselves, looking at these splendid newcomers.

The prince rented a small house and found a job with the local king. A few days later, when the prince and his wife were sitting on a swing, gently swaying, two of the king's servants came there to give him his month's pay. They were so dumbstruck by his wife's beauty that they ran back to the king and, as soon as they found the words, stammered, "Your Highness, we've found you a most fitting prize in that new man's house. It's his wife. She looks so fantastic, she doesn't seem to be a mortal woman."

The king lost his reason and fell into a fantasy. The more vividly they described her, the more did he want her all for himself.

When the young man went to the court next day as usual, he found the king absent. He inquired where he was, and was told that the king was sick with a pain in his stomach. So he hurried to the king's quarters in the palace and greeted him, "Victory to the king!"

The king's voice was feeble: "I'm glad to see you. You're like a long-lost brother. I'm dying of a stomach ulcer. The only cure, my doctors tell me, is the poison of the snake Karkotaka. Who can get it for me?"

The prince did not see through the old man's guile. He volunteered and promised to get it if it would save the king's life. He came home thinking how he should go about getting the poison of Karkotaka, the most deadly of serpents. He sat down lost in thought, forgetting even to eat. His wife roused him from his deep reverie by asking what was troubling him. He told her about the king's illness and the remedy.

She had a way: "Go to the north beyond the Jambu Peak, and you'll reach the Seshadri Hills in a few miles. On those hills, under a *tamala* tree, you'll find a snake-mound. I'll give you a letter. Throw it in the snake-hole, and wait." And she gave him a letter to take.

He ate his dinner and slept happily. Early next morning he woke up and set out on his quest. On his way, he noticed a *bharani* worm writhing miserably in a spider's web on the twigs of a tree. He carefully released the worm from the filaments and saved its life. Then he walked on till he reached the snake-mound and slipped his wife's letter into the hole. Soon he heard noises from within. Several serpents came out to carry him magically into the netherworld, and set him before the king of snakes, who was intently reading the letter:

O Snake King of the Netherworld, this is a letter from Indra's daughter, who is like one of your own daughters. The bearer of this letter is my husband. As I am rather lonely in the earth-world, please marry your daughter to this fine man and send her with him. The two of us will be happy together, I assure you. Please grant his request, about which he will tell you.

Yours, etc.

The snake king liked his looks and proceeded to marry him to his daughter right away. Then he arranged for the newlyweds' journey. His personal retinue went with them for safe-conduct till they crossed the Jambu Peak. The prince was also given a sealed vial of Karkotaka's venom. When they reached home by evening, the two women, who were old friends, were ecstatic to see each other and gave each other many hugs.

The next day the prince took the vial of deadly venom to the king, who asked his servants to open it carefully in the palace courtyard. Even as they opened it a little, a tamarind tree in the yard began to smolder, caught fire, and became a heap of ashes. The king asked them to take the venom far away and bury it deep. So the king's first ruse didn't succeed. The prince hadn't been lost or killed, and he had managed to get the deadliest venom of all. The king was now even a little afraid of the young man.

A month later, on a holiday, the king's servants brought the prince his monthly pay at home as they had done before. This time they saw two beautiful women instead of one sporting with him, and they hurried back to the king with their drooling descriptions. The king was beside himself with desire for the young man's fabulous wives. He sent for the prince again and said he had one of his terrible headaches, for which the cure would be a crocodile's bile. Would the brave young man get it for him?

The prince came home lost in thought. Both his wives asked him in unison, "Lord and husband of our souls, what is troubling you?" And he told them what his king wanted from him. Where could he go for a crocodile's bile? For his wives, that seemed like nothing extraordinary. They both sat down at once, wrote letters, and asked him to throw them in the great ocean.

He felt confident again, ate and slept well that night, and set out early next morning in the direction his wives told him to go. On the way, he saw a young crocodile that was stranded on dry land and growing feebler by the hour. He carried it tenderly to the river, where it revived at once, finding its element. The grateful animal said, "O mortal, you saved my life. If you are ever in need, think of me," and glided into the depths.

He reached the seashore and as soon as he threw the letters into the waves, four crocodiles appeared and carried him safely to the presence of the King of All the Seas, who, after reading the letters, eagerly offered his daughter to him with a dower of the ocean's best diamonds—and of course, a supply of the best crocodile bile.

When the prince came home, the three unearthly beauties were happy together. Next day, when he brought the king the crocodile bile he had asked for, the king's heart sank. He knew his plans had failed again.

The next month when the servants brought the prince his pay, they were dazzled by the sight of three celestial damsels laughing mischievously with him on the swing after a sumptuous meal together. They rushed back to the king as they had done before and told him what they had seen—three women who were out of this world, beautiful beyond compare. The women's charms had made them eloquent. The king went almost mad with desire.

So he summoned the young prince again next day and praised him: "You are really a hero. You obviously can do anything. Do you think you can go to Indra's heaven and find out how my father, mother, and brothers are doing? Only you can bring me such news."

"As you wish, my king," said the prince and went home to consult his wives.

All three of them sat up all night and wrote letters—five hundred of them. He took the whole sackful, went to the king, and asked him to get ready a deep pit of fire. When the pit was filled with firewood and lit, the prince leaped into the flames. At once, the god of fire, who was waiting for him, transported him to his world, read the celestial women's letters addressed to him and other gods, and offered him his own shining daughter in marriage. Then he sent him back to the earth. On his way back home, the prince happened to notice a stream of water running towards an anthill, and he stopped to divert the stream away from the ants. He slept well that night, surrounded by four loving women.

Next morning, he took a letter to the king and another to the minister who was giving him advice. The letter to the king read as follows:

Dear Son,

Your messenger brought us all the news about you and made us very happy. We are comfortable here without a care. We eat, drink, and dress like gods. Why don't you come and see us here? You can stay with us forever. You can come the same way your messenger came. Really, there is no other way. Come soon. We will be waiting eagerly for your visit.

Yours, etc.

The king and his wicked minister were excited by these letters. They were filled with the desire to go bodily to heaven. The king ordered a great fire built before sunrise. The news spread and the whole town was ready to jump in. They all wanted to go to heaven and see their dead relatives. But the prince said, "Good people, be patient. Let His Royal Highness and the honorable minister go first." The king and the minister, resplendently dressed, entered the fire with their entire families and entourages, and were burned to ashes before everyone's eyes. The prince sent the townspeople home with the words: "Look, the wicked king and his villainous minister are dead, as you can see. This fire won't take you to heaven. It will only burn you. Go home now, and live your lives well."

When he went into the king's palace, he found in the king's chamber the name of a Brahman on a piece of paper. He at once searched for the Brahman, found him in a little hut, and crowned him king, though the Brahman protested: "I'm a poor man and I like it that way. What do I need a kingdom for? You rule it yourself."

But the prince persuaded him: "No, this is all yours. You can give me shelter when I come here next."

Then he left town and went with his four wives to the forest where, with their help, he cleared a large space, built a great new city, and lived there happily for a while.

Meanwhile, his father had fallen on bad times and lost his kingdom and wealth. He had become so poor that he was cutting and selling wood for a living. The whole royal family roamed from place to place in search of a pittance. One day, they arrived in the new city. The prince saw them from his balcony as they walked in the street down below. He brought them home and gave them every comfort and luxury.

One day soon after, before going on a hunt with his three elder brothers, the prince gave his first wife's sari to his mother for safekeeping, with strict warnings not to let it out of her sight and not to give it to anyone. At that time, the daughters-in-law were bathing. The first wife somehow found out about the sari and asked her mother-in-law most sweetly, "Mother, let me see that new yellow silk *pitambara* sari. It's beautiful. Please give it to me. Let me wear it today."

The mother-in-law replied, "No, no, I can't. My son asked me not to give it to anyone."

"What, not even to me?" said the first wife in a hurt tone. Then she used her wiles, spoke beguilingly, and won over the somewhat simple old woman. She wheedled the sari out of her, and before anyone could say a word, the four celestial women quickly wrapped themselves in it and flew straight to heaven. That very moment, the great new city that was their creation also vanished, and nothing was left but the primeval jungle in its place.

The old mother began to cry helplessly. The prince and his brothers, who were out hunting, seemed suddenly caught in an unknown fastness in the jungle as if it had thickened around them before they knew it. The brothers asked him, "What's happening?" He knew. "It's all our mother's doing," he said. They slashed all about them with their swords, somehow extricated themselves from the tangle of bushes and creepers, and came to where the mother was sitting distraught and in tears. The young prince brought them all to the kingdom now ruled by the Brahman, who was very happy to receive them. Then he went in search of his errant wives.

The celestial wives had spent a while in the world of the gods, but had soon begun to miss their husband. They remembered his pranks with longing, so they decided to come down to the earth. There they found him wandering aimlessly, and offered to take him with them to their world.

"Come meet my father," said the first wife, Indra's daughter, "and you'll be able to bring us all back with his permission. When you kidnapped me before, you didn't get his permission."

"Why not? I'll come and meet your father and get his permission this time. Let's go," said the prince, and they transported him to the world of the gods by changing him into a fish in a vessel of water for the duration of the journey. Once they were in the upper world, they vanished, abandoning him in a strange place. "Women!" muttered the prince to himself and started asking around for Indra's capital. He was soon taken there. Everyone was amazed at the presence of a live earthling. It was not long before he was in the presence of Indra, who heard his tale and said playfully, "If you want these girls, you'll have to prove yourself worthy of them. You must perform four tasks that I shall set you. If you succeed, I'll marry them all to you once more."

Indra scattered a basket of tiny sesame seeds in a vast field and said, "There! Pick them all up in three hours and you can have the fire god's daughter back."

The prince was baffled at first and thought hard. Suddenly he remembered the ants he had saved from being washed away. As soon as he thought of them, a whole swarm of them appeared, and according to his wish, picked up every sesame seed scattered in the field and left them in a neat heap. Thus he won back one wife, his youngest.

Indra then threw his signet ring into a deep well that looked bottomless, and asked him to retrieve it. In a flash, the prince remembered the frog, which appeared in an instant and darted into the well at his bidding. But it returned almost at once, looking mortally afraid because there was a coil of snakes guarding the bottom. It summoned its young tadpole son, took it down into the well, and threw it to the snakes, which came up to eat the tadpole. Then the old frog dived in and leaped up with Indra's ring. Thus the prince won back the princess of the water-world.

"Now," said Indra, taking the prince to a plantain tree, "I want you to cut this tree in three pieces with one stroke. Then you'll get back the snake princess."

The young prince at once thought of the crocodile he had saved on his way to the sea. The reptile appeared even as he thought of it, saluted him, and asked what he wanted done.

"Do you see this plantain tree? I want it cut in three pieces with one stroke of your sharp tail." Before he even finished saying that, the tree lay before him in three neat pieces. He had won the snake princess as well.

Now Indra set him his last test. With his magic, he made his daughter's three friends look exactly like his own daughter, and said, "Tell me who is your first wife."

The prince was completely at a loss. He was faced with four look-alikes that he could not tell apart, though he looked at them closely. Suddenly he remembered the *bharani* worm, which arrived from nowhere, now a winged insect. It touched the sari of Indra's daughter and flew in circles around her head. At once the prince said, "There, that's my first wife!" and seized her hand. He had won her too.

The gods were amazed at the way the humble animals of the earth-world had come to the help of this mortal man. Indra, who had hugely enjoyed the fun of it all, arranged a heavenly wedding ceremony for the young people and had them married according to celestial customs.

The prince descended to the earth with all four wives and went straight to his father's kingdom and original capital, which were now in the hands of foreign kings. He conquered them and all the minor kings around them, became king of the old kingdom, and brought back his parents and brothers to the capital.

One day, under the light of the full moon, as he sat on the palace swing with his four queens, he remembered another such day. He asked for his father, and when he arrived, the son said to him, "Father, did I do what I once said I would do?"

To which the father replied, "Yes, my son, you did. If one has sons, one should have sons like you."

Hanchi

~ Kannada ~ ~

An old woman had two children, a son and a daughter. The girl had golden hair, but the brother had not been struck by it till one day, when both of them were grown up and the girl was a lovely young woman, he suddenly saw her hair of gold as if he had never seen it before and at once fell in love with her.

He went to his mother and begged her to give him his sister in marriage. The poor old woman was shocked and knew at once that disaster was ahead. But she hid her feelings and sent him to the nearby town to buy rice and flour and lentils for the wedding feast. As soon as he left the house, she went to her daughter and said to her, "Daughter, the time has come for you to leave me. You're as good as dead to me after this day. You're too beautiful to live here in safety. You have hair of gold; no one can look at it without desire. So I shall have a mask made for you; it will hide your face and hair and save you from future danger."

Then she ran to the potter and gave him a gold vessel to make a clay mask to fit her daughter's face. That very night she gave her daughter a bundle of food and sent her away with the parting words: "Never remove the mask from your face till your situation is better." When her daughter was gone, the poor woman poisoned herself in her grief. The son came home next day and found his sister gone and his mother dead. Searching in vain for his sister everywhere, he lost his mind and became a wandering madman.

The girl in the clay mask wandered from place to place as long as her mother's bundle of bread and rice lasted. Because her mask looked so much like a clay tile—*hanchu*—she changed her name to Hanchi. At noon and again by moonlight, she would stop by wayside brooks, untie her bundle of food, and eat. At last she came to a place very far from her hometown and struck up acquaintance with an old woman, who gave her food and shelter. One day the old woman came home and said that a *saukar*, a rich man, who lived nearby needed a maidservant and that she had arranged to send Hanchi to his place. Hanchi agreed and went to the big house to work. She was an expert cook, and no one could equal her in making sweet rice dishes.

One day the *saukar* arranged for a banquet in his orchard and ordered Hanchi to make her special dishes of sweet rice. That day, everyone in the household went to the orchard for a grand meal—everyone, that is, except Hanchi and a younger son of the *saukar*, who had gone out somewhere. Hanchi thought she was alone, so she heated water for an oil bath. She wished to finish her bath before they all returned. She took off her mask, undid her splendid golden hair, applied oil all over her parched body, and started bathing. Meanwhile the young man who had gone out came back home, and shouted for the maid. Hanchi did not hear him in the bathhouse. Impatiently, he came in search of her, heard sounds in the bathhouse, and peeped in and saw her

in all her beauty. He sneaked away before she saw him, but he had fallen deeply in love with the glowing beauty of her body and the glory that was her hair, and decided at once to make her his wife.

As soon as the family returned from the orchard, the son took his mother aside and told her of his desire. She was quite puzzled by her son's fascination with a black-faced maidservant. She asked him not to make a fool of himself over a dark lowborn wench, and promised to get him a really good-looking bride from a rich family if he would wait a little. But he would not hear of it. He was stubborn and¹ they had a heated argument, at the end of which he dragged his mother to where Hanchi was, put his hand to the girl's face, snatched off her mask, and dashed it to the ground. There stood Hanchi in all her natural loveliness, crowned by her splendid tresses of gold. The mother was struck dumb by this extraordinary beauty and now found her son's infatuation quite understandable. Moreover, she had always liked the modest, good-natured Hanchi. She took the bashful young woman with her to an inner chamber and asked her a few questions, listened to her strange story, and liked her all the better for it. At the first auspicious moment, Hanchi was married to the young man.

The newlyweds were happy as doves, but their happiness didn't last long. There was a holy man whom everyone called Guruswami in the *saukar's* house. He was the rich man's chief counselor, and had a reputation for secret lore and black arts of many kinds. This man had long been casting lecherous glances at Hanchi and wanted her for himself. When Hanchi's mother-in-law told him one day of her eagerness to see a grandson by Hanchi, he had his plan ready. He told her that he could make Hanchi conceive with the help of his magic arts, and asked her to send the young woman to him. But first he asked for some plantains, almonds, betel leaves, and betel nuts to use in his magical rites.

On an auspicious day, Guruswami summoned Hanchi. He had before him all the fruits and nuts over which he had chanted his magical formulas. If she ate them, his love-magic would work on her and she would be irresistibly attracted to him. When she came in, he was chanting secret spells and praying that Hanchi would be his. But Hanchi was a clever girl and knew all about these wicked magicians. When he gave her a plantain, she secretly dropped the enchanted fruit into a trough and ate another she had brought with her. Guruswami went to his room that night, trusting that his magic would draw her to him and bring her into his arms. While he lay waiting for her, a she-buffalo ate the enchanted plantain in the trough and fell in love with Guruswami. She was in heat and came running to Guruswami's chamber and butted at his door with her horns. Thinking that Hanchi had come, he hastily opened the door and was badly mauled by the amorous buffalo.

But he did not give up. On several days he asked Hanchi's gullible mother-in-law to send her to him for certain rites. When she came, he gave her enchanted almonds and betel leaves. But clever Hanchi played the same old trick and ate the harmless almonds and leaves she had carefully brought with her. She palmed away Guruswami's gifts and put them into various measures and bowls on her way back to her quarters. As Guruswami lay waiting for her that night, the measures and vessels came rolling towards his bedroom and knocked against the door. He hastily opened his door for the long-awaited Hanchi, and instead of her caresses, received hard blows from the inanimate vessels, which were irresistibly drawn to him. After the third visit, Hanchi threw the magic betel nuts at a broomstick that stood in a corner. When Guruswami opened his door and received a thorny broomstick into his greedy arms, he had to accept failure. He changed his tactics.

He went to his old friend, Hanchi's father-in-law, and suggested they have another of his famous picnics in the orchard. The old man agreed. As before, Hanchi prepared her fine sweet rice dishes, and like a good daughter-in-law, stayed behind to look after the house while everyone else was away.

When the family were at the orchard picnic, Guruswami found an excuse to go home. He told everyone he had left something behind, and hurried back. On the way, he collected pieces of men's clothing such as coats and turbans. Then, while Hanchi was in the kitchen, he stole into her room and planted a man's coat and turban there, and threw bits of chewed betel and stubs of smoked cheroots under the bed and on the floor.

After planting all this false evidence in Hanchi's room, he ran breathlessly to the orchard where the family were enjoying themselves and cried, "Your daughter-in-law is a whore! I surprised her with a lover. She has forgotten the dignity of her family, her womanhood. This is sinful. It will bring misfortune to the whole clan! The slut!"

At these shocking words from their trusted family friend, they all ran to the house. With righteous indignation, Guruswami showed them the man's clothing, the tell-tale cheroot stubs and pieces of betel, as unquestionable evidence of Hanchi's adultery. Hanchi was as surprised as the rest of them, but her protests were just not heard. She accused Guruswami himself of being a bad man and told them of his black magic, but they all were so angry and suspicious that they beat her till she had blue welts. When she found that everyone was against her, she became silent and gave herself over to her fate. They shut her up in a room and starved her for three days, but they got no confession out of her. Her stubborn silence sent her husband and his father into fits of rage. Then Guruswami, finding that his plot was going well, suggested, "All this will not work with this wretched woman. We must punish her properly for her sin. Put her into a big box and give the box to me. I'll have it thrown into the river. You are too good to this sinner. We must punish her as she deserves!"

Anger and shame had made them blind, and they listened to him. Hanchi was dragged out, shut up in a box, and handed over to Guruswami. He had her carried out of the house, happy that his plot had succeeded.

Then he had to think of a way to get rid of the servants. He asked them to carry the box to an old woman's house outside town and leave it there till morning, as the river was still a long way off. Unknown to Guruswami, this old woman was none other than Hanchi's good friend who had helped her get a job and settle in the town. Guruswami told her there were ferocious mad dogs in the box; he was taking them to the river to drown them next day. He asked her to be very, very careful with it, not to meddle with it or open it lest the dogs should be let loose. When he left her, he had scared her more than he intended to. He promised he would soon come back to take the dangerous dogs away.

After he left, the old woman heard peculiar noises coming from the box and thought at first it was the dogs. But then she heard her own name being spoken: Hanchi in the box had recognized her old friend's voice and was calling for help. The old woman cautiously pried open the lid and found, to her great astonishment, Hanchi crouching inside the box! She helped the miserable girl out of her prison and gave her food and drink. Hanchi had eaten nothing for days and she was ravenous. She told her old friend all about her misfortunes and the villain Guruswami's plot to get her. The old woman listened carefully, and her mother wit soon found a way out. She hid Hanchi in an inner room, went into town, and found someone who was about to get rid of a mad dog. She had it muzzled, brought it home, and locked it up in the box. She took care to loosen the muzzle before she locked up the dog.

Guruswami was back very soon, eager to taste his new power over Hanchi. He came in perfumed and singing. When he examined the locks, the old woman assured him in a frightened voice that she was too scared even to touch the box. He asked her now to leave him alone in the room for his evening prayers.

He closed the door carefully and bolted it from the inside. Then, calling Hanchi's name lovingly, he threw open the lid of the box. His heart leaped to his mouth when he saw a hideous dog, foaming at the mouth, which sprang

upon him and mangled him horribly with its bites. He cursed his own wicked-
ness and cried that he was served right by all-seeing God, who had transformed
a woman into a dog. Full of remorse, he called for mercy as he sank down
under the dog's teeth. Neighbors, drawn by the cries of the wretched man,
soon gathered and killed the dog. But they could not save Guruswami. He
had been fatally infected with rabies.

Hanchi's husband and his family were shocked by what had happened to
their friend Guruswami. Months later, the old woman invited them one day
to her house. The good woman could not rest till she had seen justice done
to Hanchi. When Hanchi's in-laws came, the old woman served them a
delicious meal, with wonderful sweet rice dishes that no one could have
prepared but Hanchi. Everyone who tasted them was reminded of her and
felt sad. They naturally asked who this excellent cook was who equaled Hanchi.
Instead of replying, the old woman presented Hanchi herself in the flesh. Her
in-laws were amazed—they had believed Hanchi was dead and gone, drowned
beyond return in the river. Guruswami had got rid of her for them, and the
poor fellow had gone hopelessly mad soon after. The old woman cleared up
the mystery of Hanchi's reappearance by telling them the true story about
her and the villain Guruswami.

The husband and his family were full of remorse for what they had done
to Hanchi and ashamed they had been taken in by such a viper as Guruswami.
They cursed him at length and asked Hanchi to pardon them.

Hanchi's good days had begun. Her luck had turned, and brought her every
kind of happiness from that day forward.

Buffalo into Rooster

~ *Marathi* ~ ~

Patil was a poor man, but he had a wife who loved him and they
had two buffaloes to their name. As they grew older and poorer,
the woman said to her husband, "Why don't you take one of our
buffaloes and sell it in the market? We could do with some extra
money."

 Next morning, when Patil was on his way to the market in the next village, he met a man who was leading his horse to the same place. Patil told him that he was taking the old buffalo to sell it. The stranger seemed to take a fancy to the buffalo. He said, "Why do you want to take it that far? Give it to me and I'll give you my horse."

Patil thought, "Why not? A horse is less trouble, and what's more, fun for the children." So he said, "All right, give me the horse."

When he tried to ride the horse to the market, he found that it was blind. Soon he met a man with a cow.

"Where are you going, old man, with that horse?"

"I was on my way to the market to sell my old buffalo. But I exchanged it for this horse, and it's blind."

"Is that what happened? This cow of mine is a fine animal. Why don't you take it and give me the horse? I can use a horse."

Patil looked at the cow and liked the looks of it. Moreover, a cow is less work than a horse. So he changed the cow for the horse, but it didn't take him long to find out that the cow was lame in one leg.

He then met a man with a she-goat. When the man asked where he was going, Patil told him: "I wanted to sell my old buffalo in the market. On the way, I exchanged it for a blind horse. Now I have this lame cow in place of the horse. I'll have to sell it."

"Oh, why do you want to sell it? I can use a cow. Take my she-goat and give me the cow," said the stranger.

When Patil started to walk the she-goat, he found it was quite sick. Just as he reached the market, he met a man with a rooster under his arm, and managed to exchange the goat for the rooster.

It was noon. He was hungry and he didn't have a penny on him. All he had was a rooster in his hand. He took it to the market and all he could get for it was a single rupee. With it he bought some food, washed his hands and feet in a pond, and sat down under a pipal tree with his food on a leaf. Just as he was about to put a morsel in his mouth, a beggarman in tatters appeared from nowhere and said, "I haven't eaten for days. Give me some food." Patil couldn't bear to see the beggar starve while he ate his fill, so he gave him the whole leaf full of food and left for home.

His wife was waiting for him. She had cooked and cleaned and fed the children by the time he arrived. She asked him how the day went and why he looked so beaten.

He said, "I'll tell you everything. Give me a glass of water first."

After cooling himself off with a drink of water, he began to tell her what had happened.

"I did not sell the buffalo. I exchanged it for a horse."

"Oh, fine!" said his wife. "Where is it? Children, Daddy has brought a horse!"

"Wait. I don't have the horse. I exchanged it for a cow."

"Oh, lovely! I always wanted a cow. The children can have some cow's milk at last. Children, go look outside. Daddy has brought a cow," said the wife.

"Wait, wait. I wanted to bring the cow home, but I exchanged it for a she-goat."

"A she-goat is even better. Goat's milk makes children strong. And a goat takes care of itself. Children, go see the new goat!"

"Don't be in such a hurry. I exchanged the goat for a rooster," said the poor man.

"That's fine. It'll wake us up every morning. Where is it? Let's all go see it," said the eager wife.

"Listen, I don't have the rooster. I got hungry, so I sold the rooster for a rupee and bought something to eat."

"That's all right. What could we have done with a rooster? I'm glad you ate something for lunch. You shouldn't go hungry after all that work you did," said the good wife.

"Wait till I tell you everything, please. I was about to eat when a starving beggar appeared. So I gave him all the food and walked home."

"And you went hungry? Poor man! But what you did was right. You should never turn away a beggar at mealtime. Now, if you'll wash up, I'll get you something to eat. You must be famished," said the wife, and served him a proper meal.

Next morning, when Patil woke up and opened the door of his hut, he was amazed by what he saw. He called his wife to come quickly. Right in front of their door stood a collection of animals: a buffalo that was not old, a horse that was not blind, a cow that was not lame, a she-goat that was well and frisky, and a splendid rooster. Right next to them was a leaf, with a shining rupee on it. As they wondered at what they saw, the wife whispered in awe, "Who in the world could have done this? That beggar you fed yesterday?"

The man said, "Yes, that beggar! He must have been God, who else?"

The Prince Who Married His Own Left Half

~ *Kannada* ~ ~

There was a king who had a son. When the prince came of age, the king wished to have him married, but the young man didn't want to get married; he would listen to no one's advice, not even to his elders'. The father became rather desperate and threatened to hang himself if the prince didn't get married. The son then said, "All right. Split my body in two and bury my left half in flowers. A woman will be born out of it. I'll marry her. I won't marry anyone else."

The king was terrified that his son would die in the process of cutting him in half. He asked him, "Is there no other way, a simpler way?" The prince said, "There's no other way. Other women are uncontrollable. It's hard to keep them in line."

The king finally agreed. He had the prince's body cut into halves and buried the left half in flowers. In a few days, a woman was born among the flowers. The king married her to his son according to the proper rites.

The prince had a wonderful palace built in a deserted place for his wife, and visited her there. The king also was very fond of his daughter-in-law. He too would visit her now and then and see that everything was right for her.

One day a wizard came to that place on his way to some far-off country. He saw this wonderful palace in a deserted area and started walking around it. The king's daughter-in-law, who was standing at her window, saw him and smiled at him.

The wizard took shelter in an old woman's house in the nearby village.

The old woman made garlands for the king's daughter-in-law every day. One day the wizard made a fantastic garland, gave it to the old woman, and said, "Take this to the king's daughter-in-law and tell me what she says."

The old woman took the garland to the king's daughter-in-law, who looked at it closely and got the message. Though she felt happy inside, she pretended to be angry; she pressed her hand in vermilion and slapped the old woman's cheek. The old woman came home weeping and showed the man her cheek. He consoled her by saying, "Don't worry about it. It's nothing. She just wants to let me know she is having her period."

A few days later, he made another garland for the palace and gave it to the old woman. This time, when she received the garland, the king's daughter-in-law dipped her hand in white lime and slapped the old woman's breasts. The old woman came home weeping. When the man saw the white marks, he said, "Don't worry. She wants to tell me that it's full-moon time."

In a few days, he sent the palace a third garland. This time the king's daughter-in-law dipped her hand in black ink and hit the old woman on her backside. She came home crying and told him what had happened. The man said, "You must read these things right, old woman. She wants me to come to the back of the palace on a dark new-moon night."

When he went there on the dark new-moon night, he saw a rope hanging from the balcony of the palace. He gripped it and hauled himself up, and went in through a window. The king's daughter-in-law was waiting for him; she was happy to see him, and they made love. She said to him tenderly, "If you come in your natural shape, the guards at the gate will not let you in. So disguise yourself, and you can come here often." The wizard said, "That's easy," and after that he visited her in the guise of a snake. He would enter the palace through the drainpipes. As soon as he came into her room he would change into a man, and they would make love. Many days passed in this way.

One day when the king came to see his daughter-in-law, he saw a snake slithering in through the drainpipe. He at once called his servants and had them kill it. He asked them to throw the dead snake outside the palace, and went to his daughter-in-law's chambers. He said, "You know, I saw a snake coming into the house. Your luck was good. I saw it and got it killed and thrown outside." The daughter-in-law cried out, "*Ayyo!* What a terrible thing!" and fainted.

When she came to, after much first aid, she was grief-stricken inside that her lover had been caught and killed; but outwardly she pretended to be terrified of the snake and her narrow escape. Before he left, the king tried to comfort her by saying, "Why are you scared? The snake is really dead and gone." From that day on, she was in mourning; she gave up food and sleep.

One day a *dasayya*, a holy mendicant, came to her door asking for alms. She called him in and asked him a favor: "Look here, *dasayya*, I'll give you a rupee. It seems there was a dead snake lying outside. Will you go check if it's still there?" He went out and checked, and came back to report that it was still there. She said to him, "Go take the dead snake to a cemetery, cremate it, and bring me the ashes. I'll give you two rupees for your trouble." The *dasayya* agreed, took it to a cemetery, cremated it according to proper funeral rites, and brought her back the ashes. She gave him two rupees first, then added three more. "Go now to a goldsmith and buy me a talisman" she ordered. The *dasayya* went out again and came back with a talisman.

She placed her dead lover's ashes in the talisman and tied it around her shoulder. Mourning her lover's death, she grew thinner day by day. The prince heard about her emaciated state and thought, "My wife has some secret sorrow. I must go to her and console her. She's growing thinner each day."

He came to the palace and asked her why she looked so thin and sick. He tried in any number of ways to get her to tell him what was happening. But she didn't part her lips once; she didn't tell him a thing. He made her sit on his lap and used all the arts he knew to persuade her. Finally she said, "What else can I do? You've kept me here in a prison. I get to see your face once on full-moon day and once on new-moon day. How can my heart be happy or content?" The king's son felt very contrite when he heard her sorrows. "Then I'll stay here all the time, every day," he said to console her.

She then said, "I'm going to tell you a riddle. If you can answer it, I'll throw myself in the fire and die. If you can't answer it, you must throw yourself in the fire and die. If anyone asks afterwards why this happened, neither of us should tell them why. If you agree to these conditions, I'll tell you the riddle. Otherwise, let's quit." The foolish prince agreed. He placed his hand in hers and gave her his word. Then she said:

> *One for seeing it,*
> *Two for burning it,*
> *Three for wearing it on the shoulder—*
> > *A husband for the thigh,*
> > *A lover for the shoulder.*
> *Tell me what it means.*

The prince struggled and groaned as he tried to solve the riddle. He could not for the life of him find any answer, so according to his word, he threw himself into the fire and died. His wife took another lover and lived happily.

A Buffalo Made of Lac

~ *Tamil* ~ ~

A very poor Brahman was sick of his poverty and thought of going to Banaras, where pilgrims gather from all over India. They would certainly offer him bigger fees and charities than he would ever see in his miserable Tamil small town. So, when his wife nagged him, compared herself with all her richer neighbors, wanted ornaments and silk saris, and pointed to his little daughter going about in rags, he decided to leave town and try his luck in the holy city.

He spent two years on the banks of the Ganges and accepted all sorts of gifts—even gifts that were considered inauspicious, such as oil and buffaloes. He accepted such gifts especially because the pilgrims had to pay large fees to the Brahmans to receive them. All this Brahman wanted now was money. He didn't care how he made it. In a couple of years he had made several thousand rupees and the thought of how much it would please his wife made him want to return at once. On his return journey, he stopped in Poona. He knew it would please his wife no end if he took her a hefty piece of jewelry. So he went to a goldsmith and spent most of his money on two heavy gold necklaces, each with a hundred beads.

The jeweler looked very honest but was not really honest. He was very courteous and obliging in his services. He even gave the Brahman the necklaces a day before they were actually due. Everything was exactly as the Brahman had ordered: there were a hundred beads in each. The weight was right, and the touchstone showed the gold to be of high quality. And the design was elegant indeed.

The Brahman was more than satisfied. He was pleased, and he told the goldsmith, "You're most honest and punctual, unlike the other goldsmiths I've known. I wish I had more money to give you a proper tip." The goldsmith thanked him for his compliment and waived the tip, which pleased the Brahman even more.

He reached home, and his wife and daughter were happy to see him after such a long absence. They were even happier when he presented them with the shining hundred-bead necklaces. While the little girl went out to show off her lovely new present, his wife went into the kitchen to cook. As she sat before the fire, the happy woman took off her necklace and weighed it in her hand. As she fingered it and felt its weight, she began to feel something was not quite right about it. She thought it might not be a bad idea to test the gold. She slipped off one of the beads and put it in the fire. At once, there was a fizzle and a wisp of smoke, and it began to burn like lighted lac. She was horrified to see that her good husband had been deceived by a wily goldsmith. She took some time to recover, and then went to her husband and told him as coolly as she could about the way he had been tricked. The Brahman nearly went out of his mind when he heard this. He couldn't bear to think of all the hard-earned money he had thrown away for a few beads of lac. Ever afterwards, he had only one thought, one fixed idea in his head: that goldsmiths were never to be trusted.

Two or three days later, it occurred to him to ask how his wife had managed to live while he was away at Banaras. She said, "I bought a splendid milch buffalo from Ponnasari, the goldsmith here. You know, he lives near the temple."

"What!" exclaimed the Brahman. "You bought a milch buffalo from that goldsmith, that scoundrel?"

"Yes, from the goldsmith. It gives a lot of milk every day. I make butter from the milk and sell some of it. That gives me money enough to live comfortably. It gives two pails of milk twice a day."

"You poor thing! You've not looked at it carefully. It's not a real buffalo. It's a buffalo made of lac!"

"No, no, how can it be? It gives us milk. Therefore, it cannot be made of lac."

"That's why I say women are fools! What if it gives you milk? It's still made of lac. Don't tell me it isn't. You don't know anything about goldsmiths."

"No, I swear, it grazes and eats grass. So it cannot be made of lac."

"O my good wife, you don't have the brains to see through the tricks of goldsmiths. I still say it's made of lac. Don't argue with me."

"No, no, how can that be? Since I bought it, the buffalo has given birth to two calves. You can see them there in the yard. How can it be a buffalo made of lac?"

By now the Brahman was quite angry. "You stupid woman! You don't know the ways of goldsmiths. You are a simpleton. So you believe that the animal is an ordinary living thing? No, it isn't. Whatever you may say, I'm still certain it's made of lac. Now hold your tongue and go about your business."

The poor wife could only pity her husband and the state he was in. She couldn't for the life of her convince him by anything she said or did. He had one fixed idea and only one. Finally, in desperation, she went into the yard, dragged the poor buffalo into the house, made a small cut in one of its ears, and showed him the flowing blood as evidence that it was a living animal. When he saw the red blood, her husband shouted at her, "You foolish woman, you continue to think the buffalo you bought from that goldsmith Ponnasari is a real one and not made of lac? You think you are showing me blood? Is it not the color of lac and isn't the buffalo made of lac? Do you also want to deceive me?"

Some of the most sensible men of his town came to convince the Brahman that the buffalo in his house was really a living animal. But he would not be shaken in his belief that it was not. It was bought from Ponnasari the goldsmith. How could it be anything other than a buffalo made of lac?

They tell this story to account for a well-known Sanskrit verse:

Foolish woman, what if it gives us milk,
What if it grazes on grass,
What if it brings forth calves?
You do not know the tricks of goldsmiths.
For all that, it is a buffalo made of lac.

A Contest of Lies

~ *Hindi* ~ ~

In a village, a Bania kept a grocery shop where he sold rice, salt, oil, and such. One day, on his way to a neighboring town, he met a Jat, a peasant, who was also going to the town to pay his monthly installment of a loan to the *mahajan*, the banker. It was a loan his great-grandfather had taken out to pay for the funeral of *his* great-grandfather. In half a century, the compound interest had swelled the small loan of a hundred rupees into a thousand. The poor fellow was wondering anxiously how he could save his ancestral lands from the clutches of this moneylender, when he heard the Bania say to him, "Hey, Chowdhuri! I see you're on your way to the *mahajan* to pay your installment. Can't you do anything to save your lands?"

The poor Jat said, "Ah, Shahjee! It's a sad story, as you know. My great-grandfather borrowed a hundred rupees and it has swelled to a thousand. How can my few acres of land pay for it?"

"Don't worry too much about it. What's written on your forehead must happen. So let's forget it and amuse ourselves with stories. It'll make our journey more pleasant. What do you say?"

"Shahjee, that's a great idea. There's no use weeping and wailing over what's written on our foreheads. So let's tell stories and pass the time. But on one condition: however untrue or absurd the story may be, neither one of us must call it a lie. If one of us calls the other's story a lie, he must pay the other a thousand rupees."

"Agreed," said the Bania. "Let me begin." Then he proceeded to tell the following story:

"You know my great-grandfather was the greatest man among the Banias and was terribly rich."

"True, Shahjee, true!" said the Jat.

"Now this great ancestor of mine once equipped forty ships, sailed to China, and traded there in rich jewels."

"True, Shahjee, true!" said the Jat.

"He stayed there long enough to amass a large fortune. When he returned home, he brought back many curiosities from that country. Among them was a speaking statue of pure gold. It was so cunningly made that it could answer any questions put to it."

"True, Shahjee, true!"

"When he returned home, many people came to have their fortunes told by that wonderful statue and went away supremely satisfied by its replies. One day, your great-grandfather came to my ancestor to ask some questions of the speaking statue. He asked, 'What caste of men is the wisest?' The statue replied, 'The Bania.' He next asked, 'What caste is the most foolish on earth?' It replied, 'The Jat.' The last question your great-grandfather asked was, 'Who will be the greatest blockhead in my family?' The statue replied at once, 'Chowdhuri Lahri Singh.' (That was the name of the Jat now listening to the Bania.)

"True, Shahjee, quite true!" said the Jat, though the Bania's taunt pierced his heart. But he inwardly decided to repay the Bania in his own coin and in such a way that he would remember for a long time.

"Well, then," the Bania continued, "the fame of the statue spread far and wide, and reached the king, who summoned my great-grandfather and made him his prime minister, in exchange for the statue."

"True, Shahjee, true," said the Jat.

"After a long time my great-grandfather retired as the favorite counselor of the king, and my grandfather succeeded him. He lived in great style and

neglected his ministerial duties somewhat. So the king was displeased and
ordered that he should be trampled to death by an elephant. He was thrown
in front of a mad elephant, but as soon as the brute saw him, it became calm,
bowed humbly before my grandfather, and lifted him gently with its trunk
onto its back."

"True, Shahjee, true," said the Jat.

"The king was so impressed by this incident that he recalled my grandfather
and conferred great honors on him. After the death of my grandfather, my
father became prime minister, but he didn't like the job. He resigned and
went abroad. In his travels he saw many wonders, as for instance, men with
one leg who hung head down from trees, one-eyed giants, green monkeys,
and so on. One day my father saw a mosquito hovering near his ear to bite
him. He didn't know what to do: as you know, we Banias are forbidden to
kill any living creature."

"True, Shahjee, true," said the Jat.

"So then, my father fell on his knees and begged the insect to be merciful.
The mosquito was pleased and said, 'Most noble Shahjee, you are the greatest
man I've seen. I would like to do something for you.' Saying this, the mosquito
opened its mouth, and my father saw within it a great big palace of burning
gold, with many windows, gables, gates, and so on. At one of the windows
sat the most beautiful woman he had ever seen. Right behind her, he also
saw a peasant about to attack the princess. My father, who was famous for
his chivalry, at once jumped into the mouth of the mosquito and entered its
belly. It was all dark there, and he found himself groping in the belly of the
insect."

"True, Shahjee, quite true," said the Jat.

"After some time, the darkness melted away and my father again saw the
palace, the princess, and the ugly peasant. My father, who was a courageous
man, fell upon the peasant, who was none other than your father. They fought
for a year in the stomach of the mosquito, at the end of which your father
fell at my father's feet and begged for mercy. So my father, who was very
merciful, let him go. Then he married the princess and lived in that palace,

and I was born there. Your father remained in the service of my father as a doorkeeper and used to sit day and night at the door keeping watch. When I was fifteen, a rain of boiling water fell on our palace, which melted entirely, and we were thrown into a burning sea. After much trouble, the four of us reached the shore, your father, my father, the princess, and myself. When we jumped onto the shore, suddenly we found ourselves in a kitchen, and the cook was terrified when she saw us. We assured her that we were people and not ghosts. The woman said, 'You are nice fellows to spoil my broth! What business did you have to enter that pot of boiling water in which I was cooking my fish and frighten me like this?' We all apologized to her and said, 'If we were in that pot, we didn't know better. For the last fifteen years we have been living in a palace in the belly of a mosquito.' 'Ah, I remember now,' said the cook, 'just fifteen minutes ago I saw a mosquito, which bit me on my arm. Here is the bite mark of that wretched insect. I'm afraid you must have been injected into my arm by the bite. I did feel a lot of pain. I squeezed out the poison, a black drop as large as this mustard seed, and it fell into this boiling water. I never imagined that you were in it.' I knew then that I was only fifteen minutes old though I looked and acted like a boy of fifteen years. We were all surprised that we had been in the belly of the mosquito for only fifteen minutes. In that short space of time, I was born and had grown big, and your father and mine had grown older by fifteen years. Though I look like an older man, I am really a child of ten years. I just grew up quickly when I lived for fifteen minutes in the burning belly of that mosquito."

"True, Shahjee, true," said the Jat.

"When we came out, we found we had come to another country. In fact, we were in this village. My father, who was once the prime minister, took to shopkeeping and I took it up after him. The princess, my mother, died the other day, as you know. This is my story."

"True, Shahjee, true," said the Jat. "Your story is very true. My story is also true, but it is not as wonderful as yours. Here it is:

"My great-grandfather was the richest Jat in the village. He was handsome, noble, wise, distinguished. Everyone praised him. He was the headman of the village and he protected the weak and the poor. In the village meetings, he was always on their side. He would lend his oxen to others who didn't have any and send his own men to help others reap their harvests, and anyone was welcome to the grain in his store and the milk in his dairy. He settled all the disputes of all the villages around, and his word was more respected than any emperor's or judge's. And he was a terror to the wicked, as he was stronger than Bhimsen."

"True, Chowdhuri, true," said the Bania.

"Well, once there was a great famine in our village. No rain fell. The rivers and wells dried up and the trees withered away. The cattle starved, birds and beasts died on all sides. When my great-grandfather saw that the stores were getting low and the people would soon die of hunger if nothing was done, he called together all the Jats and said to them, 'Brothers, surely the god of rain is angry. If we don't do something soon, we'll all die of hunger. If you'll give up your fields to me for six months, I'll make sure that they are all fruitful.'

"All the Jats agreed. Then my great-grandfather girded up his loins and with one strong pull lifted up the whole village of a thousand acres of land and placed it on his head."

"True, Chowdhuri, true," said the Bania, smiling to himself at this tissue of preposterous nonsense.

"Well, then my ancestor carried the whole village on his head and went about in search of rain. He went wherever it rained and collected all the rainwater on the fields and in the reservoirs. Then he asked the Jats to plow the land and sow seed. For six months he went from country to country like this, collecting rain, while the Jats plowed and sowed. The crops had never been so splendid. The corn and wheat stalks rose to the sky."

"True, Chowdhuri, true," said the Bania.

"After this tour around the world with the entire village and all the villagers on his head, he returned to his country and placed the village where it originally stood. My great-grandfather reaped a great harvest that year, and the whole village belonged to him. Every grain of corn and wheat was as big as your head."

"True, Chowdhuri, true," said the Bania.

"Well, then all the grain was collected, but it was so plentiful that there was not room enough to store it. People from all parts of the country heard of our wonderful harvest and came from faraway places to buy the grain. My ancestor made a great profit, but he distributed thousands of rupees among the poor and gave away grain to the hungry."

By the time the story reached this point, the two fellows had entered the town and the Jat continued his story:

"At that time, your great-grandfather was a very poor man, and my great-grandfather out of sheer pity employed him as a servant to weigh and measure the grain."

"True, Chowdhuri, true," said the Bania.

"Night and day, your poor ancestor worked at weighing and measuring the grain and he was very pitiable. He also was a blockhead and made many mistakes, for which he would get good thrashings from my great-grandfather. Poor fellow!"

"True, Chowdhuri, true," said the Bania.

By this time, they had entered the shop of the *mahajan* to whom the Jat owed money. The moneylender was at his till and greeted his customers with the words "*Ram, Ram,*" and then sat down on the floor. But the Jat ignored the *mahajan* and went on with his story:

"Well, Shahjee, when my great-grandfather had sold off all his harvest, there was nothing more to weigh and measure. So your great-grandfather lost his job. Before going away, he asked my ancestor for a loan of a hundred rupees. My ancestor generously gave it to him."

"True, Chowdhuri, true," said the Bania.

"Very good," said the Jat, raising his voice so that the moneylender might also hear. "Your ancestor did not repay the debt."

"True, Chowdhuri, true," said the Bania.

"Neither did your grandfather nor your father pay off that debt, nor have you paid it till now."

"True, Chowdhuri, true," said the Bania.

"Now that sum of one hundred rupees with interest and compound interest at the usual rate makes exactly one thousand rupees, which is what you owe me now," said the Jat.

"True, Chowdhuri, true," said the Bania helplessly.

"So, as you have admitted to the debt before our *mahajan* and other witnesses, will you please pay the thousand rupees you owe me to him? Then I can have my lands released," said the Jat.

This came down like a thunderbolt on the Bania's head. He had admitted the debt before witnesses. He was on the horns of a dilemma. If he said it was merely a story and was false, he must pay a thousand rupees according to the terms of his bet. If he said it was true, he must pay according to his own admission. So, willy-nilly, he paid his forfeit of a thousand rupees and regretted it bitterly for the rest of his life.

It's Done with Mirrors

~ Telugu ~ ~

A harlot once dreamed that a certain Brahman visited her and made love to her. When she woke up, she called her servants, described the Brahman to them, and asked them to demand payment for her services. They seized the Brahman as he was walking along the road, told him of the affair, and demanded payment. He was aghast. He said he didn't know anything about it as he was safely in bed with his own wife the previous night; he was also penniless, besides. But the servants wouldn't let go of him. He begged and argued and pleaded. A crowd gathered to see the fun, and someone told the king about the incident. He summoned both the harlot and the Brahman to his court.

The harlot said, "My customers always pay me for my services. This man visited me in my dream last night and enjoyed himself. Even I am embarrassed to tell you the things he did to me. He must pay me for it."

The king said, "All right, you deserve payment. But you'll have to wait a little."

Then he ordered a pole to be planted in the street, hung a bag of silver coins from the top, and arranged a mirror under it.

"Now," he said to the harlot, "you can put your hand into the mirror and take your money. It's all yours."

The woman was baffled and said, "How can I put my hand into the mirror and take my money? Give me the real money in that bag."

"No, no," said the king, "that money is not yours. The Brahman visited you in your dream. The proper payment for it is the money you see in the mirror."

The Kurumba
in the Parrot's Body

~ *Kota* ~ ~

Years ago, a sorcerer of the Kurumba tribe used to come daily to the villages of the Kotas, kill the Kota men, and sleep with all the beautiful women. The Kotas talked about it to each other a lot and wanted to find a way of killing him off. As he had done similar things to the neighboring Toda tribesmen, the Kotas and the Todas also talked to each other and came to a decision. "Let's hide near the path at the edge of the forest, waylay that black Kurumba, and cut him to pieces," they said. And so they did.

When the Kurumba came walking that way, they jumped on him, cut off his arms and legs, and threw them in all directions. But as they were happily returning, telling each other how good it was to kill the evil sorcerer, the arms and legs they had thrown about suddenly came together and that black Kurumba was right there in front of them, standing in their path, laughing his head off. He said, "Hey, you Kotas, you Todas, so you killed me, did you? Look, I've come back. You useless fellows, you think you can kill me like that?" The Kotas and the Todas were dumbstruck at this miracle and said, "Look at this wonder! What can we do against such a man?" Then in great fear they went home to their villages.

Within weeks, many good men among the Kotas and the Todas died and their wives became wailing widows. The villages were filled with the sound of lamentation.

The Kurumba was pleased with himself. "I took my revenge, a head for a head!" he said to himself and laughed with great satisfaction. He came every day to the village, pronounced his charms from a distant field, and whatever woman he thought of would come to him of her own accord, alone, and give herself to him.

But, as they say, the sorcerer's wife knows more than the sorcerer. So it was with that black Kurumba's wife. She changed herself into a kite and came flying over all the seven villages of the Kotas. She too had her charms, which she would utter: then all the strong handsome men would come by themselves, sleep with her, and go home by evening. She took the men, and her husband, the black Kurumba, took the women. The villagers said, "One day his downfall will come." And it did.

One day, he was sitting under a hill-guava tree, eating his fill of the fruit. A parrot sat on one of the branches, lamenting and screaming in great sorrow. The Kurumba understood the language of birds. So he asked, "Hey, parrot, why are you crying so much?"

The parrot said, "What can I say? My husband, who was life of my life, died today. I'm heartbroken and I can't stop crying. Who will end my grief?"

The black Kurumba's heart melted with pity for her and he wanted to comfort her somehow. So he himself entered into the body of the parrot that had died. In an instant, the parrot came alive and flew with a whirr to his wife.

The parrot wife was happy and kissed the male parrot and said, "You tricked me. You wanted to test me. You pretended to be dead and made me cry and watched me, didn't you? You males cannot be trusted. You don't have hearts like us." Then they flew around each other, and the female suddenly saw the Kurumba's body lying dead under the tree. The dead man's mouth was open; his arms and legs were stretched straight out.

She said, "Poor man. Only a few minutes ago, he was talking to me. He took pity on my grief. I must do something in return." Then she took a leaf of the tree and prayed to God, saying, "If I'm a true parrot, please grant me a boon. Just as I wept for my mate, this man's wife must be weeping her heart out for him somewhere. Till she comes and finds him, please grant that no dog, jackal, bear, tiger, or any other wild beast shall touch his body. May it lie here just as it is now." With that prayer, she threw the leaf on the body of the Kurumba, and the two birds flew away with a whirr of wings to the next forest. There were a thousand parrots in that forest, singing and laughing. It was like God's world.

This forest was near a pear orchard next to one of the Kota villages. All the parrots used to go there and eat the fruit merrily. The owner of the orchard was angry with the birds and planned one day to spread a net and catch them. He made a net with cords from a fibrous tree, spread it out, and scattered a lot of fruit on it.

Next morning, the entire flock of a thousand parrots were caught in that net. They were screaming and crying, "We're caught! We've fallen into the hunter's hands!" All except the Kurumba parrot—remember, he was a man and he knew many tricks.

He said in parrot-words to all the other parrots, "If you fly up and down like that, you'll be snared even more. He will pick us up one by one and kill us all. If you want to save your life, listen to me." They said, "What, what? Tell us."

He said, "It's very simple. When the hunter comes here and touches you, shut your eyes and play dead. Then he'll think, 'These birds are dead,' and throw us down one by one and say, 'One, two, three . . .' When he counts up to a thousand, we shall all fly up together in the air with a big whirr and fly high and escape." They all came to an agreement before the hunter arrived.

When he came, all the birds looked as if they were dead. "Strange," he said to himself, "I didn't put out any poison or anything, and they're all dead!" He felt bad about it. "If I cook them and eat them, I may get sick. Let's see how many there are." Then he began to pick them up one by one, throw them down, and count: one, two, three . . .

When he had almost reached the end, he said, "Nine hundred and ninety nine!" and the knife in his left hand came down with a thud. The Kurumba parrot that had taught the other nine hundred and ninety-nine parrots the trick said aloud, "One thousand!" and all the parrots who heard it and the thud of the knife suddenly flew up together in a great whirr of wings and escaped into the sky. But the Kurumba parrot that had taught them the trick was caught in the hunter's hand.

The hunter was angry: "Those naughty parrots have tricked me. I'll cook this one and eat it and crunch its bones. I'll twist its neck, kill it, pluck all its feathers, dress it well, and make a broth of it." But when he seized its neck, it spoke: "Hey, hunter! Don't kill me. Take me home. I'll bring you prosperity if you take care of me. If you cook me into a broth, you'll hardly have a mouthful."

The hunter was amazed and said, "This is a wonder. In all my born days, I never heard a parrot like this. It speaks our language and talks so well. Even if someone gave me a thousand rupees, I wouldn't kill it." Then he kissed it and smoothed its feathers, took it home, and showed it to his wife and children and mother. When the parrot spoke, it was so wise that none of the elderly men and women were equal to it.

The news soon spread to all the seven Kota villages that the hunter had found a parrot that could talk of life and death and all the affairs of men. People came to see the magic bird. And anyone who came brought a measure of grain and gave it to the man. Soon his house overflowed with grain and he became very prosperous.

It is a Kota custom to have a dancing-day during a funeral. On that day they eat opium poppy, get high, and laugh and sport day and night. On one such day, the village headman's wife got high on opium and went to see the parrot. As she stood there, one leg on a step, she exposed her thighs, and the parrot rebuked her: "Are you a prostitute or a wife for your husband? Are you a man or a woman?" The headman's wife was humiliated and left the place without a word, walking away slowly.

That night, she went and lay on the mat next to her husband, who was also high on opium. When he turned to her, she turned away, saying, "If you can't end my sorrow, go to sleep." When he asked her what her sorrow was, she told him, "Bring me that parrot that talks. If you don't, I'll die!" She even took an oath. So the headman said, "Even if it costs a thousand rupees, I'll bring it to you. Now turn around and put your arms around me." She hugged him and kissed him all over, lifted him over her body, and they made love.

Just as he was about to come, she held him tight between her thighs. He could not finish. He was willing to give her anything she asked for. She said, "Touch my eyes and take an oath that you'll bring me the parrot. Then I'll release you." He was unable to bear it any longer. He said, "I'll bring you that parrot, even if it costs me many buffaloes. Now release me and let me finish." He then touched her eyes, and she released him happily.

She didn't sleep that night, and woke up her husband early and sent him off to the owner of the parrot. The headman said to him, "Touch my head and give me a promise." The hunter didn't want to offend him, so he touched his head according to custom and promised him. Then he asked him what he wanted. The man said, "Take my buffaloes and give me your parrot. How many buffaloes do you want?"

"I didn't know what you were going to ask," the hunter said. "I can't give you my parrot."

The headman said, "But you touched my head and promised!"

So they began to quarrel, till the village elder called them. The headman said, "He touched my head and made me a promise. Now he's going back on it." The hunter said, "I touched his head and promised, not knowing what he was about to ask." The elder said, "That matters little. You touched his head and made a promise. Keep it. In this caste we say, 'When we have promised with our mouths, we must be willing to sell even our mothers!' So give him your parrot."

The hunter was afraid of the judgment that would fall on him, so he took five milch buffaloes and gave the headman the parrot. But just as he was about to give it away, the parrot said to the hunter, "That woman was showing her thighs without any care for propriety, so I rebuked her. That's why she wants me. She's going to kill me. So before you give me away, pluck one of my feathers and put it in the pocket of your cloak. Then I won't die. I'll come alive in your pocket."

The hunter did just that and hid a feather in his pocket before he gave the parrot to the headman, who was very pleased with the wisdom of the talking bird. He took it home and said to his wife, "I paid five milch buffaloes for it, and it is a wise bird. Take good care of it." She said she certainly would and asked him to make a cage for it, which he did.

She put the parrot in the cage and hung it in front of her and said, "You stupid parrot! You insulted me. You abused me. I'm going to prick you with this needle every day."

The woman gave it seed and treated it well in her husband's presence. Then when he left the house, she would prick it with her long sewing needle and make it scream.

When he came home that evening, the parrot complained to the headman, "Father, your wife pricked me with a sewing needle and hurt me in my behind." When he called her and asked her about it, she said, "How can you listen to this foolish bird?" The bird said, "She came the other day, all drunk with opium, and showed her thighs, so I rebuked her. That's why she's doing this to me." The husband didn't fully understand it. So he said, "Give it some seed and look after it carefully," and went away on his business.

The woman stabbed the bird with her long needle between its ribs. The bird died at once, but its life returned to the feather in the hunter's pocket.

Soon the bird's body began to smell. When the woman told her husband that the bird was dead and was stinking, he took it and threw it on the rubbish heap. He thought, "I lost five milch buffaloes by listening to this woman." She thought, "Even if it cost five buffaloes, it doesn't matter. I'm glad I'm rid of it."

Meanwhile, the feather in the hunter's pocket said to him, "Father, there's a corpse under a tree on the little hill. You'll see some fun if you rub this feather on the face of that corpse."

The man thought this was a wonder and that he would go to the hill and look for the corpse. But it was late, so he decided to set out in the morning.

That night, in the Kota village, a grandfather had a dream. This is what it said: "We've had a quiet time these five or six months. We haven't been troubled by the black Kurumba. His life is in a feather in the pocket of a hunter. The hunter will come today and rub the feather on the dead Kurumba's face. Then the Kurumba will come to life and he will trouble you just as he troubled you before. Get up. Go at once and take that feather from the hunter's pocket and burn it with ten bundles of fuel on your dancing-ground. Otherwise you'll have no peace in the streets of your village. You'll suffer again as you suffered before."

The old man got up at once and asked his wife to light the lamp. If anyone dreams, it's the custom of the Kotas to light the lamp and tell others the dream. That's what the old man did. Then he gathered some people and sent them to find the hunter with the feather in his pocket. They knew who he was; they found him sleeping, woke him up, and asked him to come with them to the hill where the corpse lay. But first they ordered him, "Show us the feather," and he did. The feather said, "There's a corpse under a tree on the little hill. If you carry me there and rub me on its face, I'll show you some fun."

When they heard it speak, the men said, "Our elder's dream was a true dream. Our god spoke in that dream. It also said, 'Gather ten bundles of fuel! twirl the fire-sticks! light a fire, and burn the feather!'" And the young men did just that.

When the flames were high and the feather was burning in the middle, it cried, "Father, Mother, I'm dying!" Then it hissed like a burning corpse and died. They all danced round and round the fire. The next day, when they went to the little hill, they found the dead body at the foot of the tree. The corpse was as fresh as if the man had died just that day.

They said to one another, "That bad Kurumba is dead. We won't be troubled by him any more." Then they carried off the body and threw it into a big gully. From that day on, the village prospered and lived without fear.

After a few months, they heard the news that the black Kurumba's wife had waited and waited for his return. When he had not come back even after six months, she grieved over him, became thin, thin as a stick, and she too died.

The people began to say, "That hunter was a good man. That's why God did this. He saw to it that the black Kurumba would become a parrot, and that through him grain and buffaloes would come to the hunter." Then they lived and ate well and prospered.

That's the story of the parrot.

The Eighth Key

~ *Sindhi* ~ ~

A wise king of Sind grew old and was at death's door. He called his chief minister, handed him eight keys, and said to him, "I'm not going to live very much longer. I want you to guard the throne for my young son till he comes of age. When he is ready to rule by himself, give him seven of these eight keys. Do not give him the eighth till he has ruled for five years." The chief minister promised to do exactly as he had been told, and the old king died in peace.

The chief minister took charge. He watched the young prince grow up as if he had been his own son. He ruled the kingdom justly till the young man came of age and then, on an auspicious day, handed over a rich and well-run kingdom and the seven keys. After the coronation, the prince eagerly opened the seven vaults for which the seven keys were meant, and there he found gold and silver and precious stones of every kind. He was delighted and grateful to the faithful minister who had guarded everything for him and crowned him king when the time was right. For a time all went well, till an evil talebearer, envious of the minister, whispered in the king's ear that there were really eight vaults in the palace and the minister had given him only seven keys.

The young king was furious. He suspected the minister of treachery, of keeping the eighth treasure-vault for himself. He demanded that the eighth key be given to him at once or else he would put the old minister to death on the spot. The old man fell at his feet and told him how he had promised the king's father that he would hand over the eighth key only when five years had passed after the coronation. The young king was too excited to wait. He insisted on getting the key, and when he had it in his hand he rushed to the eighth vault, turned the key in the lock, and threw the door open. He was amazed when he saw that the whole vault had nothing in it. Even the walls seemed bare. As he looked around the empty vault, he saw that one of the walls was different: it held the portrait of a beautiful young woman. The king's eyes were riveted to the picture, and as he gazed and gazed, he was enchanted. He fell in love with the woman in the picture. He was so overcome that he fainted and fell to the floor. The minister, who was right behind him, held him, sprinkled rosewater on his brow, and revived him. As soon as he came to, the young king's eyes returned to the woman in the picture, and he told the minister that he should bring her to him as soon as he could, or else he would give up his kingdom and fast unto death.

The old minister was unhappy to see the king's present state of infatuation with someone he had never seen in life. He comforted him and promised to go at once in search of the beautiful woman in the picture. He set sail that very week in a vessel loaded with merchandise of all kinds and with some trusty servants. They touched every port they could find and showed the elders and courts of each kingdom the portrait found in the eighth chamber. But no one had seen the woman nor heard of anyone of that description. After a whole year of such wanderings, they reached a distant kingdom, and there they displayed the picture in the harbor. The people standing by at once clapped their hands and exclaimed, "That's our own princess!" The minister was soon ushered into the king's presence, and one look at the princess in the palace convinced him that this was the right princess. The minister told the king that he was a merchant, gave him fabulous gifts, and received permission to stay in the country till he sold all his merchandise. What he really did was to gather information about the character of the princess and her family. He heard nothing but good things. Having satisfied himself, he set sail again homeward and many months later he landed in his own capital. When he told the king that he had found the woman in the picture and that she was even more beautiful in life, the king could not wait to go and see her himself.

Filling the vessel again with merchandise, the king, the minister, and the same band of trusty servants set sail once more. After many months and storms and hardships, they reached the land of the princess. The minister again presented himself to the father of the princess as the merchant who had visited them the previous year. He had heard that the princess was fond of toys, and as his countrymen were expert toymakers, he had brought her special ones that could walk and talk, toy lions and tigers that could roar, and mechanical birds that flew up slantwise into the air. The princess was enchanted, and then the minister said, "These are nothing compared to what you will see in our ship. My master, who is on the ship, would let me bring only the commonest toys of our country. Why don't you come visit our ship?" The princess was wild with excitement, and she set out at once with six of her maids. Once she was aboard, the young king received her with great courtesy and showed her toys more fabulous than the ones she had seen so far. While she was jumping with excitement as she looked at each new toy, the crew cut the anchor cable and set sail for the open sea. They did it so quietly that the princess and her maids did not realize what was happening till they were far away from land.

When the princess and her maids discovered that they were being kidnapped, they were terrified and angry, and they broke down and cried. The young king comforted the princess by telling her how he had fallen in love with her picture and had sailed across the seven seas to find her. He so wooed her and charmed her that she soon returned his love and promised to become his queen once they reached land. It took months, but the young couple were in love and very happy.

When they were almost in sight of land, the king and his bride were promenading on the deck, gazing into each other's eyes. The old minister was seated in the prow, squinting his eyes as he watched the progress of the ship. Now, among other things he had learned in life, he had learned to understand the speech of birds. As he was peering towards the land, he saw a mynah bird and a parrot fly to the ship and perch in the rigging. The minister waited to hear them talk. After they had sat on the ropes for a while, the mynah said, "I'm a bit bored on this ship. Tell me a story." The parrot, after a little hesitation, said, "There is a story right here, going on before our very eyes. Do you see the young king and his bride and how happy they look? Well, the king has only three more days to live. When he lands three days from now, he will be welcomed by his troops, his horses, and his elephants. His palace guard will bring him his royal horse, the most beautiful of all. But that horse is not what it seems; it is a demon in the shape of a horse. As soon as he mounts the horse, it will carry him high into the air and drop him into the sea."

The mynah was almost in tears. "The princess will be widowed even before she is married! And they look such a perfect couple. She will be plunged into grief. Can anyone do anything to save the king?" asked the mynah anxiously. "Yes, my dear, something can be done. If someone cuts off the head of the horse before the king even touches it, the king will be saved. But tell no one what I've just told you. For if anyone repeats what I've said, one third of his or her body will be turned to stone." Then the parrot and the mynah flew away. The minister, who had heard it all and understood it all, was now anxious again about his master, who was happily strolling on the deck with his equally happy bride, unconscious of what awaited them.

Next day, the two birds flew back to the ship and sat in the same place in the rigging. The minister saw them and went back to sit close to them. He didn't want to miss a word. The mynah saw the king and his bride again on the deck and asked the parrot, "Tell me, will the king be safe once he escapes from the demon horse? Will they marry and live happily ever after?" "No, no, not so fast, my dear," said the parrot, "the king and the princess may never be happy. He has other dangers waiting for him. If he is saved from the horse, he will arrange a gala wedding for himself and his bride. At the wedding, the king will see a gorgeous plate made of pure gold. He will be so taken with it that he will pick it up and try to pass it around to the courtiers to make a collection for the Brahmans who are conducting the wedding ceremony. But as soon as he touches the plate, he will fall dead. You see, the plate is smeared with a potent poison, and it will enter his skin and kill him in minutes." The mynah was as upset at this prospect as it had been before. "Can't someone save the king somehow?" "Yes, if someone snatches the gold plate with gloved hands and throws it away, he will be saved. But remember, don't tell this to anyone, for if you do, a third of your body will be turned to stone." As the minister sadly pondered what he had just heard, the two birds took wing and flew away.

The next day was the last day of the voyage. The minister, whose heart was heavy with secrets, sat again in the prow of the ship expecting the birds to return, which they did. The mynah asked the parrot, "If the king is saved from the poisoned plate, will he then marry the princess and live happily ever after?" "No, no, my love. The king will not live long, and the princess is fated to suffer. After the wedding, the couple will sleep in the royal bedchamber. When they are tired and fast asleep, a snake in the roof of the bridal chamber will drop poison on the bride's cheek. When the king wakes up and kisses the cheek of his bride, he will fall down dead," said the parrot. The mynah, full of pity for the newlyweds, asked again, "Is there no way the king can escape this dreadful end on his wedding day?" "Yes, my love," said the parrot, "there is only one chance, but it is so remote that the king will surely die of this snake's poison. If someone hides himself in the bridal chamber and kisses the poison off the bride's cheek as soon as the snake drops it, the king will be saved. And the person who does this will not die if he drinks a full glass of milk at once. But who can hide in the privacy of a bridal chamber? Now don't tell anyone about this, for if you do, a third of your body will be turned to stone." After this conversation, the two birds flew away.

Now the minister had sworn to serve his master loyally even at the cost of his own life. Anxious as he was, he decided never to let his king out of his sight. When the king landed and tried to mount the demon horse, the minister quickly drew his sword and cut off its head with one stroke. This made the king very angry. He was even angrier when the minister would give him no explanation for what he had done. The minister knew that a third of his body would turn to stone if he so much as breathed a word about what he knew. The king was bewildered by his minister's behavior. But he knew that the man had always served him and his father before him loyally, so he forgave him.

Arrangements were made for a gorgeous wedding, and while it was being celebrated among guests from a hundred countries, the king's eyes fell on a beautiful golden plate. He had just stretched out his hand to pick it up when the minister snatched it with his gloved hands and ran with it to throw it into a running stream. The king could not understand his minister's mad behavior. He asked him for an explanation, but the minister said nothing for fear that a third of his body would be turned to stone. The king was furious, but it was a great public occasion, so he let his minister's misbehavior pass one more time.

After the wedding ceremonies were over, the tired royal couple went to bed and fell asleep. They did not know that the minister had hidden himself behind a curtain near their bed. While he watched over them, a snake descended from the roof and dropped venom on the face of the sleeping bride. At once, he stepped up to the bed and kissed the drop of venom off her face, and drained a glass of milk he had brought with him as an antidote. The bride's sleep was disturbed by all this and she woke up. She had felt the minister's kiss on her cheek. She screamed and woke the king at once. In his fury at seeing the minister in his most private bedchamber, the king summoned the guards and ordered them to seize the man and hang him at dawn from the battlements.

The guards seized the old minister and took him to prison. There the old man asked, as a last favor, to see the king before he died. The king did not have the heart to refuse it. The minister was taken in chains to the royal chamber, and there he poured out the whole truth. As he narrated how the parrot had warned its listener about the demon horse, his feet and legs turned to marble. Then as he told the king about the poisoned plate, his body turned to marble as far as his armpits. Lastly, when he finished his tale of the poison dropped by the snake in the roof, his head and shoulders became marble too.

The king was too astonished to react at first, but as soon as he recovered from the shock, he broke down and wept bitter tears at what had happened to his most faithful minister. He put the petrified body in a separate room, hung garlands upon it, and worshipped it in great sorrow.

In course of time, the queen gave birth to a son. Every day his father brought him to the room where he kept his minister's image in stone and talked to him about the loyalty and goodness of the dead man. One day, when the boy was three years old, the very same mynah and parrot that had perched on the ship's rigging and prophesied the later events happened to fly into the room and began a conversation. The king could now understand their speech because he was standing close to the minister's image. The parrot said to the mynah, "Look, the king is very sad at what happened to his minister. If he wants to, he can bring him back to life." The mynah asked, "How, how can he do it?" The parrot answered, "He will have to kill his son and sprinkle his blood all over the stone image. The minister will become flesh and blood once again."

The king thought long and hard about what he should do and what would be right. He came to the conclusion that he owed everything to his minister, who had saved his life not once but three times. He drew his sword and cut

off his son's head in a flash, before he could waver. Then he sprinkled the
boy's blood over the marble image. The minister at once came to life. And
as soon as he learned how he had been restored to human form, he prayed
so intensely to God that God granted his prayer. The boy's head was returned
to his body, life returned to him, and he woke up as if from a deep sleep.
The king then called his queen and told her everything that had happened.
Though she shuddered at the thought of her son's head being cut off by his
own father, she agreed the king could not have done anything else. Anyway,
the minister's prayers and God's mercy had brought the boy back to life.
Then the king, the queen, and their son, guided by the minister's wisdom,
lived long and happily and well.

How the Weaver
Went to Heaven

~ Urdu ~ ~

There was once a weaver whose field used to be visited every night
by an elephant of Indra, the king of heaven. It would come down
from the sky and graze in his field, leaving it devastated. He asked
his weaver friends what animal could be doing this to his field.
"Perhaps it's the village grindstones. Maybe they get up in the
night and visit your field," they said. So he had every grindstone
in the village tied up, but the damage went on as before. He again
consulted his friends and they said, "Maybe it's the village rice-
pounders. Maybe they get up in the night and visit your field,
when everybody is fast asleep." So he had all the rice-pounders
tied up, but the damage continued. In fact, it got worse.

Then he went one night and lay in wait in the field. And what did he see?
He saw an elephant fly down and graze on the crop. As it was about to fly
away, he caught hold of its tail and went with it to Indra's court in heaven.
There he sat in a corner and saw the celestial dancers dance and heard them
sing. Nobody there seemed to take any notice of him, and he even had his

fill of divine dishes in the gods' kitchen. Next night, when the elephant was flying back to earth, he held on to its tail and came home.

As soon as he landed, he told his friends of all the wonders he had seen and said, "What's the use of living in this wretched place? Let's all go to Indra's heaven." They agreed, and when the elephant was flying back after its nightly meal of earthly crops, first the weaver clung to its tail, his wife clung on to her husband's legs, and so all his kinsfolk held on too, in a long human chain. The elephant didn't seem to notice the human baggage it was carrying, and it flew away with them through the air. When they had got very high, the weaver began to think to himself, "What a fool I was not to bring my loom with me!" And with this thought, he felt like wringing his hands, and so he let go his hold and they all came tumbling down to earth again.

That's why they say a weaver has never made it to heaven.

The Tiger-Makers

~ Kannada ~ ~

Once four Brahmans went all over India and amassed every kind of knowledge. They wanted to show each other what each could do with his various skills and secret arts.

So they met in a forest, and one of them found a bone. It happened to be a tiger's thighbone. The Brahman who found it said, "I can create the whole skeleton of this animal," and he did so.

The second Brahman said, "I can give it skin, flesh, and blood," and so he did. There in front of them stood a lifelike tiger, stripes and all.

The third Brahman said, "You know what I can do? I know how to give it life."

The fourth Brahman, who was not half as learned as the others, said, "Wait, don't give it life. We believe you."

But the third Brahman said, "What's the use of having the power to do something and not doing it? I've never been able to exercise this art of mine. I'm going to give life to this thing. Just watch."

The fourth Brahman said, "If you insist. But please wait till I climb this tree." And he quickly scampered up the nearest tree.

Then the third Brahman, with his mantras and magic skills, breathed life into the tiger. As soon as it came to life, it was hungry and looked around for something to eat. And it pounced on the three Brahmans, who stood there huddled in terror, unable even to run away. It killed them all and devoured them at leisure, leaving only their bones on the forest floor.

All that the fourth Brahman could do was to watch this carnage from his perch, petrified by shock and horror. When the tiger had finished its meal and walked away purring into the forest, he slowly and sadly climbed down and went home to make arrangements for the funerals of his learned friends.

When a Tale Is Finished

~ *Oriya* ~ ~

In Orissa, I've heard, they sing this song when a tale is finished:

My story is done.
The flowering tree is dead.

O flowering tree, why did you die?
The black cow ate me up.

O black cow, why did you eat the tree?
The cowherd didn't look after me.

O cowherd, why didn't you look after the cow?
The daughter-in-law didn't give me food.

O daughter-in-law, why didn't you give food to the cowherd?
My little baby was crying.

O baby, why did you cry?
The black ant bit me.

O black ant, why did you bite the baby?
I live in the dirt
And when I find soft flesh, I bite.

And Then, Bhurrah!

~ *Marathi* ~~

A storyteller was tired of telling stories, but the children and the grown people who were around him were not yet tired of listening to them. They asked for more.

So he began to describe how a vast number of birds were sitting on a tree. People asked as usual at a pause, "And then?"

He said, "One bird flew from the tree with a sound like *bhurrah!*"

"And then?"

"*Bhurrah!* went another bird, flying from the tree."

"And then?"

"Another bird went *bhurrah!*"

"And then?"

"*Bhurrah!*"

This went on until nothing was heard but "And then?" and "*Bhurrah!*"

Finally someone asked, "How long is this going to go on?"

The storyteller answered, "Till all the birds are gone."

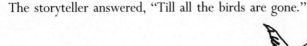

Notes

In these brief notes, I shall mention the source of each tale, suggest the type as indexed by the international indexes of folktales, list some of the languages in which parallel tales have been reported, and add a few cultural glosses where necessary.

By looking up the type in these indexes, the curious reader, if so inclined, will be able to find the general summary of the tale type and in what regions of India or of the world variants of such a tale are told. For instance, the last tale in this book, "And Then, *Bhurrah!*" is identified as AT 2300, Endless Tales. If one looks it up in Stith Thompson and Warren Roberts' *Types of Indic Oral Tales* (Helsinki: Suomalainen Tiedeakatemia, FF Communications No. 80, 1960), one will see that similar tales have been collected in Marathi by Manwaring (our tale), in Hindi by Crooke in *North Indian Notes and Queries*, vol. 4, no. 420 (February 1985), and in Telugu by Ramaswami Raju in *Indian Fables* (London: S. Sonnenschien, 1887). The world index, *The Types of the Folktale*, by Antti Aarne, translated and enlarged by Stith Thompson (Helsinki: Suomalainen Tiedeakatemia, FF Communications No. 184, 1964), henceforth AT, lists examples from over a dozen languages of the world (German, Lithuanian, Icelandic, Scottish, etc.), with bibliographic references. These type numbers will then help the reader to find similar tales from different regions of India and from different parts of the world. We should mention also the *Motif Index of Folk Literature*, by Stith Thompson (Bloomington: Indiana University Press, 1955); the misleadingly titled motif index for India, *The Oral Tales of India*, by Stith Thompson and Jonas Balys (Bloomington: Indiana University Press, 1958); *Indian Animal Tales*, by Laurits Bødker (Helsinki: Suomalainen Tiedeakatemia, FF Communications No. 170, 1957); and *Types of Indic Oral Tales: Supplement*, by Heda Jason (Helsinki: Suomalainen Tiedeakatemia, FF Communications No. 242, 1989).

These indexes, however useful, were made in the 1950s and 1960s and are based on outdated theories. The Indian index was made without access to collections in the regional languages, though it is surprising how many of the major tale types were already gathered and translated by the beginning of this century. The collection of folktales in some of the mother tongues of India has begun again only in the last few decades. So many of the tales in this book do not find any mention in the indexes, though there are many parallels—for folktales, like a language, are an infinite use of finite means. The individual telling of a tale often combines motifs and types that occur independently. Where several tale types come together in a tale, I shall note it this way: AT 306A + 465A, for example, in the long and complex tale "Adventures of a Disobedient Son." For some, I suggest only approximate tale types and motifs. Some Indian guru tales, jester tales, stories about stories, and ritual (*vrata*) tales need to be freshly surveyed and indexed.

As this is a book for the general reader, these notes will be minimal. For some of the remarks about the spread of the tales, I rely on information gathered in the indexes and from Stith Thompson's *The Folktale* (New York: Holt, Rinehart and Winston, 1946). A large number of these tales have been reported only from Indian languages.

I have avoided the need for a glossary of Indian words by glossing less familiar terms either where they occur in the text or in these notes.

Tell It to the Walls From field notes. Told by Kanakkamal in Srirangam.

This collection of tales is punctuated with tales about tales that tell us the ways the tellers think about tales. This one speaks of the cathartic function of telling one's story (and by implication, of all narrative), even to a wall. It also carries a psychosomatic insight, the relation of obesity to keeping one's sorrows to oneself.

Untold Stories Adapted from Verrier Elwin, *Folk-Tales of Mahakoshal* (London: Oxford University Press, 1944), pp. 302–3.

This Indian variant of AT 516 is reported also from Kannada. For another, very different telling of the same plot, see "The Eighth Key," from Sindhi. In Europe and England, it is known as the story of Faithful John. This Indian variant highlights not the faithful servant but the revenge of the untold stories. The earliest literary version occurs in the *Kathasaritsagara* (The Ocean of Story), an eleventh-century Sanskrit anthology of tales. See also "Brother's Day."

Stories cry out to be told, passed on, and so kept alive. If they are not told, they take other forms and exact revenge on the one who hoards them and suffocates them. Here is a theory of repression in the cultural realm. Traditions depend on being circulated, communicated to others and to future generations.

Gopal Bhar the Star-Counter Adapted from Edward C. Dimock, Jr., ed. and trans., *The Thief of Love* (Chicago: University of Chicago Press, 1963), pp. 183–85.

Motif J1124, Clever Court Jester. Also collected in Hindi, Kannada, Tamil, and Telugu. Also Motif H702.1, How Many Stars in the Heavens? Also reported in Hindi and Tamil.

Of the famous court jesters of Indian folklore, Gopal Bhar of Bengal, Tenali Rama(krishna) of Vijayanagara in South India, and Birbal at Akbar's Delhi court are noteworthy. All three appear in this book. Often the same stories are told about different jesters. For a recent and excellent work on the comic tradition in Indian literature and folklore, see Lee Siegel, *Laughing Matters* (Chicago: University of Chicago Press, 1987).

In this tale, the Nawab is the Muslim overlord of the Hindu Maharaja.

Bopoluchi Retold from Flora Annie Steel, *Tales of the Punjab*, 1st ed. (London: Macmillan, 1894), pp. 48–51.

AT 956B, The Clever Maiden at Home Alone Kills or Outwits the Robbers. Also collected in Bengali, Gondi, Hindi, Konkani, Tamil, and Sinhalese.

See Introduction on women-centered tales. The active, often heroic, role of the women in many of these tales contrasts with the stereotype of the submissive Indian woman, based on classical heroines like Sita in the *Ramayana*. On this point too, folk traditions counterpoint classical ones.

The Jasmine Prince Adapted from Natesa Sastri, *Indian Folk-Tales* (Madras: Guardian Press, 1908), pp. 277–80; published also as *Folklore in Southern India*, 3 vols. (Bombay: Education Society Press, 1884–88).

AT 1511, The Faithless Queen, especially The Queen and the Loathsome Paramour (Motif T232), + 1355B, Adulteress Tells Her Lover "I Can See the Whole World" (Motif K1271.4). AT 1511 is also reported Bengali, Gondi, Hindi, and Kota; 1355B has international variants in Hungarian, Lithuanian, and Italian.

Fourteen worlds: In Hindu cosmology, Earth is the middle world among fourteen—six above, seven below.

Sona and Rupa Retold from Shyam Parmar, *Folklore of Madhya Pradesh* (New Delhi: National Book Trust of India, 1972), pp. 171–74.

AT 722, The Sister in the Underground Kingdom.

The next three tales are about siblings. The first, "Sona and Rupa," deals with a brother's incestuous desire for his sisters. Wishes and acts forbidden in the culture are made explicit and confronted in such tales. See also "Hanchi," "The Princess Whose Father Wished to Marry Her," and "Mother Marries Son."

Told in more than one region (Gondi, Hindi, Kannada, Tulu), this tale speaks of the way incest destroys the ordered world of family and kinship, where relatives by birth and relatives by marriage ("in-laws") are set apart. A kinship system depends on the distinction between sisters and wives. The sisters have to climb higher and higher, away from the corrupt world below, as their kith and kin try to coerce them into breaking the incest taboo. In some Kannada versions, the pursuing brother and the fleeing sister both fall into a well and become two different kinds of fish—two kinds that are never caught together nor cooked together. They keep the brother and sister apart even after death.

Brother's Day Adapted from Ann Grodzins Gold's translation in *Village Families in Story and Song*, The Indiakit Series, Outreach Educational Project, South Asia Center, University of Chicago.

A variant of AT 516. See note on "Untold Stories."

The close brother-sister bond may lead to forbidden incestuous desires as in the previous story, as well as to protective and generous feelings as in this one. Special rituals celebrate this bond.

Sisters depend on brothers for many things. Brothers are their link with their parental home. They escort their married sisters home for visits, bring gifts of clothing on special days like Brother's Day, called "Brother Second" in Hindi. Brother Second takes place twice a year, on the second day following the spring holiday of Holi and on the second day following Divali, the fall festival of lights. For this day, daughters, fetched by their brothers, return to their parents' villages. If a wife is unable to attend, her brother comes to visit her with gifts, as in this story. Versions of "Brother's Day" are common not only in Rajasthan but all over North India.

Note that although the sister almost harms her brother, unintentionally, several times, she ultimately saves him, first from the perils on the road and finally from the dreaded snake enemy. To save him, she has first to curse him and then identify herself totally with him, giving up her own life, in a sense, to buffer him against danger.

The story and rituals of Brother Second are performed near an outside wall, with cow-dung figures of brother, sister, bride, and snake as well as of the inside of a house with a cooking hearth. The figures are made before the story is told. Offerings of food are made and left to be eaten by stray animals (dogs, goats, birds). At the end of the story, all the women present whose brothers are alive stretch their hands up on the wall as far as they can reach, repeating the curses from the story as well as the blessing: "May he live long!" The ritual is said to promote long life for all brothers of the women who participate in it.

I'm indebted to Ann Gold for this note.

The Brahman Who Swallowed a God Retold from Rev. William McCulloch, *Bengali Household Tales* (London: Hodder and Stoughton, 1912), pp. 23–29.

Motif 2371.2, Gods Tricked into Help in Escaping One's Fate. Also collected in Hindi and Tamil.

The poor hungry, gluttonous Brahman is a stock character in Indian tales, frequently comic and satirical. In this kind of tale, one sees that folklore is not always reverential towards the higher powers, be they kings, gods, or fate. It domesticates the divine, depicts the gods perspiring, defecating, catching colds, and so on. See "How Tenali Rama Became a Jester."

Thakur: A respectful form of address to gods, masters, Brahmans, and other figures of authority.

One Man's Virtue Retold from an oral telling by D. P. Pattanayak.
Motif J211, Choice Between Wealth and Virtue. Also reported in Punjabi.

A Crow's Revenge Heard by the author in childhood in Mysore.
Bødker 24, Murder by Strategy.
An oral tale widely told to children, this often appears as a lesson in children's primers. The earliest version is in the fifth-century Sanskrit compilation *The Pancatantra*. As in many tales told to small children, a small bird or animal triumphs over a terrifying predator by mother wit.

A Story in Search of an Audience Retold from a Telugu telling by K. Katyayini in Hyderabad, July 5, 1988, and an oral translation by V. Narayana Rao.
Motif M311, Prophecy: Future Greatness of Unborn Child. Also collected in Gondi, Hindi, Kannada, and Punjabi. *Vratakathas* like these are yet to be classified and indexed.
This is a ritual tale, or *vratakatha*, told as part of a women's ritual: the telling and the hearing of this tale (about a similarly magical tale) bring about magical results. As the old woman tells the unborn girl who hears the story, deserts will bloom, the lame will walk, the blind will regain their sight. The first part of the story is about a story begging to be heard, a teller in search of a listener. The teller begins with her family—sons, daughters-in-law, grandchildren—and moves into the town's streets, almost from caste to caste, traversing the spaces of the town and the whole society till she finds a captive yet willing audience in the unborn child in a low-caste woman's womb. The Marathi "Story for Sundays" elaborates further some of these aspects of the ritual tale.
These stories are named for a weekday in certain months. For example, this one is a story for Sundays in the month of Magha (November–December). Such story rituals are performed to bring prosperity to the family. For a description of another of these rituals, see note on "Brother's Day."

The Clay Mother-in-Law Adapted from A. K. Ramanujan, "The Clay Mother-in-Law," *Southern Folklore Quarterly*, vol. 20, no. 2 (June 1956), pp. 130–35.
AT 1653, The Robbers Under the Tree, + Motif J2415, Foolish Imitation of Lucky Man or Woman.
The next two stories are mother-in-law and daughter-in-law tales. The first speaks of a somewhat stupid but devoted daughter-in-law and the second of a feisty one who gets the better of the mean mother-in-law. Mother-in-law tales are plentiful in India—it is significant that no fathers-in-law appear in these tales. Two women, mother and wife, vie for power over the single male in the household.

Given the dependence of women on men (whether they be sons or husbands) for both money and status in the society, conflict is inevitable, and prominently featured in women's tales.

The section AT 1653, The Robbers Under the Tree, occurs independently and combines with other tales as well, in Bengali, Gondi, Kannada, Konkani, Naga, Punjabi, Tamil, and Santali.

The Clever Daughter-in-Law Translated from H. J. Lakkappa Gowda, *Janapada Kathavali* (Bangalore: Karnataka Co-op Publishing, 1971).

AT 1535, The Rich and the Poor Peasant, + 956B, The Clever Maiden at Home Alone Kills or Outwits the Robbers.

What elsewhere (in Bengali, Gondi, Hindi, Konkani, Kota, Naga, Tamil, and Santali) is told as a story of rivalry between a rich and a poor peasant or brothers, as in Hans Christian Andersen's literary version, "Big Klaus and Little Klaus," is told here as the tussle between a mother-in-law and a daughter-in-law, the latter (younger and powerless) outwitting the former. See also note on the previous story.

The Barber and the Brahman Demon Retold from Ram Satya Mukharji, *Indian Folklore* (Calcutta: Sanyal, 1904), pp. 100–103.

AT 1168A, The Demon and the Mirror. Also collected in Gondi, Hindi, and Santali.

See Introduction on comic tales. For other tales about demons outwitted, see "A Hair's-Breadth Escape" and "A Musical Demon."

Why the Fish Laughed Retold from Rev. J. Hinton Knowles, *Folk-Tales of Kashmir* (London: Kegan Paul, Trench, Trubner, 1893), pp. 484–90.

AT 875D, The Clever Girl at the End of the Journey. Also reported in Santali and Hindi. See note on "Akbar and Birbal."

A Parrot Called Hiraman Retold from Lal Behari Day, *Folk-Tales of Bengal* (London: Macmillan, 1883), pp. 209–19.

AT 546, The Clever Parrot. Also collected in Hindi, Punjabi, and Kashmiri.

What Puss-in-Boots or a helpful fox does in Grimms' and other European tales—helping a man or a woman find a spouse—a parrot does here. In some Indian variants, a swan or a goose plays the parrot's role as matchmaker.

A Plague Story Retold from Mukharji, *Indian Folklore*, p. 52.

The Monkey and the Crocodile Heard by the author in childhood.

AT 91, The Monkey Who Left His Heart at Home. Also reported from Punjabi, Rajasthani, and Tibetan, among other languages.

This widely told ancient Indian tale is first recorded in the *Pancatantra* (fifth

century) in Sanskrit, although it probably dates back as early as the third century
B.C. (See Introduction.)

What Happens When You Really Listen Retold from V. Narayana Rao's oral
translation of a Telugu story collected in Hyderabad in the summer of 1988.

Motif J2495, Religious Words Interpreted Literally. Also collected in Kannada
and Tamil.

Many tales are woven around our major Indian texts and authors. These are
yet to be classified and studied. The *Ramayana* epic in its many written and oral
forms is a special focus for folk elaborations. Many of these illustrate the magical
properties of the Rama story and how it enthralls the listener. In this tale, a
stupid, uncultured man becomes part of the action of the *Ramayana* when he
finally gives ear (and heart) to it, breaking through the barrier between fiction
and reality—not unlike a Woody Allen character in *The Purple Rose of Cairo*.

Tenali Rama Heard by the author in childhood.

Tenali Rama was a jester at the court of Krishnadevaraya, king of Vijayanagara
in South India in the sixteenth century, just as Gopal Bhar was the jester of
Bengal and Birbal the jester of Moghul North India. Scores of stories are told
about him all over South India in Kannada, Tamil, and Telugu. Children's books,
comics, and even a television serial have been created around this legendary jester,
who is known variously as Tenali Ramakrishna, Ramalingudu, and Tenali Raman.

For an excellent essay on Tenali Rama, see David Shulman, *The King and the
Clown in South Indian Myth and History* (Princeton: Princeton University Press, 1985),
chap. 4.

How Tenali Rama Became a Jester

One variant of this story says that the goddess appeared before Tenali Rama
with a pot in each hand, one containing wisdom and the other wit. She asked
him to choose one, but he grabbed both and drank the contents. The goddess
was furious and condemned him to become a *vikatakavi*. Most Indian scripts are
syllabaries—i.e., each letter denotes a consonant and the following vowel. Hence
the five letters of the word *vi-ka-ta-ka-vi* make a perfect palindrome—which the
jester, cleverer than the goddess, sees when she does not.

Tenali Rama's *Ramayana*
AT 1693, The Literal Fool.

The court jester plays many pranks on the *Ramayana* theme. They tend to
literalize the fiction or the metaphor, to show what happens when you break the
barrier between imagined fiction and lived reality. For another view of the same
issue, see "What Happens When You Really Listen."

The Burning of Lanka (Motif J2062.7) is often part of a series of disastrous pranks played by the "literal fool," in stories told in Assamese, Bengali, Hindi, Telugu, and other languages.

Two Sisters Retold from an oral telling by Sitakant Mahapatra.

AT 780A, The Cannibalistic Brothers. Also collected in Assamese and Bengali.

This story is often told in the "Singing Bones" form. A girl is murdered by her near kin (brothers, stepmother) and is transformed into a bird or a tree (Motif E631); sometimes a musical instrument (E632) is made from the tree, and she comes out of it at night, cleans house (N831.1), and performs other tasks till she is discovered. The present version does not include the episode of the cannibalistic brothers.

Sukhu and Dukhu Retold from Arun K. Ray's translation of the Bengali tale in Ramanath Das, *Thakurmar Galpa* (Calcutta: Satish Chandra Seal, 1911–12); cited in Ralph Troger, *A Comparative Study of a Bengali Folktale* (Calcutta: Indian Publications Folklore Series, 1966), pp. 81–87.

AT 480A, The Kind and Unkind Girls: The Pursuit of Blowing Cotton. Over a thousand variants of this type have been collected the world over. It is also a favorite in India—in Bengali, Hindi, Kannada, Konkani, Punjabi, and Tamil. Eighteen Indian variants are reported in the AT index. In Europe (e.g., Grimms' tales) it is known as the story of Frau Holle. See Warren E. Roberts, *The Tale of the Kind and the Unkind Girls* (Berlin: *Fabula*, Supplement B, 1958), and Ralph Troger, *A Bengali Folktale*.

Note how the image of a "good girl" is constructed through the tests she passes: helping a cow, a tree, and a horse, in some cases cleaning house for an old woman, doing exactly as she is told by dipping only twice in the pond, and not being greedy in choosing the smallest of the offered caskets. The unkind sister refuses to do all the above and gets punished many times over.

The motif of a hero or heroine choosing among caskets appears most famously in Shakespeare's *Merchant of Venice*.

One, Two, Three Retold from C. H. Bompas, *Folklore of the Santal Parganas* (London: David Nutt, 1909), pp. 192–94.

AT 1704, Sign Language Misunderstood. Also collected in Hindi, Kannada, Tamil, and Telugu.

The Wife Who Refused to Be Beaten Retold from Knowles, *Folk-Tales of Kashmir*, pp. 144–51.

AT 888A. Reported also from Punjabi, Santali, Tamil, and Telugu.

Another woman-centered tale about a feisty wife who rescues her stupid husband.

The Ogress Queen Retold from Knowles, *Folk-Tales of Kashmir*, pp. 42–50.

AT 462, The Outcast Queens and the Ogress Queen. Also collected in Bengali, Gondi, Hindi, Kannada, Punjabi, and Telugu. The "Ogress Queen" tale usually includes AT 302A, The Youth Sent to the Land of the Ogres, which also occurs independently.

Note the motif of the External Soul (E710). The life of the ogre is in an iconic object—a spinning wheel, a bird, or a bee in a distant place. The young man's quest is also for these. When he captures one of these and breaks, mutilates, or kills it, the ogre suffers analogous injury and death. Voodoo involves just such a notion of the external soul.

Killed by a Tiger Retold from an oral telling by Sitakant Mahapatra.

AT 934B, The Youth to Die on His Wedding Day.

This tale and the next express opposite attitudes to fate and prophecy. In this tale, the fate of being killed by a tiger is inexorable. This tale type has international variants, in Catalan, Czech, Finnish, Greek, Hungarian, Irish, and Swedish.

Outwitting Fate Retold from Pandit Natesa Sastri, *The Indian Antiquary*, September 1888, pp. 259–64.

AT 934D, Outwitting Fate.

In this tale, a clever man outwits fate, or rather fulfills the letter of fate's commands but makes the outcome happy. This tale has been reported only for Indian languages so far (Bengali, Gujerati, Tamil), contradicting the usual stereotype of Indians and other "Orientals" as fatalists.

Four Girls and a King Retold from Charles Swynnerton, *Indian Nights' Entertainments; or, Folk-Tales from the Upper Indus* (London: E. Stock, 1892), pp. 56–62.

Motif H630, Riddles of the Superlative, + K445.1, God to Reveal Self to Those of Legitimate Birth. Also told in Kannada.

See note on "Akbar and Birbal."

If It Isn't You, It Must Be Your Father

Bødker 1256; Motif U31, Rights of the Strong. Also told in Hindi.

Heard by the author in childhood, this little dialogue tale is an effective political parable. It certainly captures the logic of racist demagoguery whereby ancestors and history are cited to justify persecution and genocide.

Why Audiences Laugh or Cry Retold from Swynnerton, *Indian Nights' Entertainments*, p. 8.

AT 1834, The Clergyman with the Fine Voice. Also collected in Gondi and Hindi.

Akbar and Birbal Adapted from Frances Pritchett's translations from Mha-narayan, *Lata'if-e Akbar, Hissah Pahla: Birbal Namah* (Delhi: Matba Jauhar-e Hind, 1888).

See note on "Gopal Bhar the Star-Counter."

Many of these tales belong to type AT 921, where a shrewd person (jester, peasant, frequently his daughter) gives clever answers to the king's questions, which are often riddles. These are Indic examples of a worldwide genre of stories.

The Night-Blind Son-in-Law Translated from a tale collected by Do. Na. Ramegowda, in *Nammurina Janapada Kathegalu* (Mysore: Ta. Vem. Smaraka Gran-thamale, 1875), pp. 76–79.

AT 1685, The Foolish Bridegroom, + 1685A, The Stupid Son-in-Law. Also collected in Assamese, Bengali, Gondi, Kashmiri, Punjabi, Tamil, and Telugu.

Stories of the foolish bridegroom are told all over the world and appear in Renaissance jestbooks in Europe and in oral tales. The theme of the stupid son-in-law is a great and ancient Indian favorite. Given the power a husband has over a wife, it is not surprising that there should be recourse for the bride's family to deflate him. After a wedding ceremony is safely over, women sing songs insulting the bridegroom and his relatives, who in many communities have to be treated like gods. Tales of the stupid son-in-law fulfill similar purposes. See also "Shall I Show You My Real Face?"

Shall I Show You my Real Face? Heard by the author in childhood from his grandmother. A somewhat bowdlerized version appears in H. Kingscote and Natesa Sastri, *Tales of the Sun; or, Folklore in Southern India* (1890), pp. 119–30.

AT 1152, The Ogre Overawed by Displaying Objects (also told in Assamese, Bengali, Hindi, Kannada, and Kota) + AT 312A, The Brother Rescues His Sister from the Tiger (also collected in Kannada, Lhota Nagas, Oriya, Santali, and Telugu).

The man who comes from elsewhere and marries the daughter of the household is suspect, especially in endogamous and closely knit communities. In such communities, marriages are arranged after careful inquiries regarding the family and history of the proposed bride or groom. Also, suspicion and hostility regarding a brother-in-law, fears that he may ill-treat the daughter of the house, inform this tale. It may also express a brother's jealousy of the stranger who has carried off his sister and a sister's trust in a rescuing brother when she is in trouble with her husband.

A female counterpart to this tale is "The Ogress Queen," where an unknown woman who marries a king turns out to be a cannibal.

A Malcontent Cured Adapted from Knowles, *Folk-Tales of Kashmir*, p. 321.

AT 1689, "Thank God They Weren't Peaches." Told also in Punjabi, and in Swedish, Spanish, Hungarian, and English.

The Kite's Daughter Retold from J. Borooah, *Folk-Tales of Assam* (Gauhati: Lawyers' Bookstall, 1st ed. 1915; rev. by Praphulladatta Goswami, 1963), pp. 103–16.

AT 709A + 897, The Orphan Girl and Her Cruel Sisters-in-Law.

The first part of this story, where an abandoned girl is raised by a bird, is told separately in Kannada, Konkani, Tamil, and Telugu. The rest of the story follows a widely told tale of an orphan girl and her cruel sisters-in-law who set her difficult tasks in which she is helped by animals. In "The Kite's Daughter," the animals' role is played by her kite mother and the sisters-in-law are replaced by co-wives. Both these stories are reported only from Indian languages such as Gujerati, Hindi, Kannada, Oriya, and Santali.

In Indian tales various formulas end the tales: e.g., in Assamese, "Our clothes had to be sent to the washerman and so we came back," or "The jack-fruit tree bore fruit and then I returned." Such formulas bring the listener back to the real world from the fantasy world of the tale. See Introduction for other examples.

Chait Bihu: a festival in the month of Chaitra (March–April), the first month of the Hindu calendar; a New Year festival in some parts of India.

A Flowering Tree Translated by A. K. Ramanujan; a version published in Brenda E. F. Beck et al., eds., *Folktales of India* (Chicago: University of Chicago Press, 1985).

AT 706, The Maiden Without Hands. Variants have been collected in Hindi and Kashmiri.

Superficially this story resembles a widely told European tale in which the heroine marries a king, has her hands cut off, is banished and finally restored. This Indian tale (for which no variants have been reported yet from languages other than Kannada) has some special features: the girl becoming a tree becoming a girl is the central unit of the tale, repeated explicitly five times. The first time she does it for money; thereafter she is coerced into becoming a tree by her mother, her husband, and her insensitive teen-age sister-in-law. It is also a progressive series of violations till she becomes a mere thing without speech or movement, something betwixt and between, neither tree nor woman. She is restored to full womanhood only when her husband, chastened and changed by loss and grief, lovingly restores the broken branches of the tree-woman. There is a lesson for ecology here: to hurt a tree is to hurt a human. The metaphoric links between a tree and a woman are multiple and ancient, well attested in poetry, myth, and art. In languages such as Sanskrit and Tamil, the word for flowering is also the word for menstruation.

Amma: Term of address for a mother, also used as a respectful term for an older woman, a superior, etc.

Surahonne: Alexandrian laurel, a flowering tree.

A Musical Demon Adapted from Sastri, *Indian Folk-Tales*, pp. 173–88.

AT 1164D, The Demon and the Man Join Forces. Also collected in Assamese, Bengali, Hindi, and Punjabi.

Some variants (e.g., the Punjabi) have a shrewish wife routing both her husband and the demon. The husband later exorcises the demon from the body of a queen by telling her that his wife is waiting outside with her broom.

Other Lives Adapted from Knowles, *Folk-tales of Kashmir*.

Motif E605, Reincarnation in Another Human Form. Also told in Bengali and Tamil.

Reincarnation, or a person having many lives, is one of the cornerstones of the theory of karma in Indian religions. This tale is unusual in that folktales do not usually concern themselves with previous lives or with karma, as do other genres of Indian literature (epic, myth, etc.). See Introduction.

Living Like a Pig Retold from an oral telling by B. V. L. Narayana Row, in Hyderabad, 1988.

Motif E611.3, Man Reincarnated as Swine. Also told in Assamese and Tamil.

This tale is a comic comment on the previous one. A story is told about Vishnu incarnating himself as a wild boar and saving the world. However, he so enjoyed living a pig's life with a sow and a family of piglets that he refused to return to his divine form. When Siva could not persuade him to do so, he had to dispatch the wild boar with his trident and release the god from the life of a hog.

A Heron in the Mouth Retold from Pandit Shyama Shankar, *Wit and Wisdom of India* (London: Routledge, 1924), pp. 134–36.

AT 1381D, The Wife Multiplies the Secret. Reported also in Hindi, Gondi, and Santali.

A number of tales depict how a stupid son or spouse is unable to keep a secret and multiplies it. It is a comment on rumor and gossip, as well as on the way tales are made.

Tenali Rama's Art Heard by the author in childhood.

In "Tenali Rama's *Ramayana*," Tenali Rama makes fun of the literal-minded need for realism. In this tale, he takes on artists and connoisseurs who call for imagination on the part of viewers.

One More Use for Artists Retold from Putlibai D. H. Wadia, *The Indian Antiquary*, vol. 17, no. 206 (March 1888).

Heron Boy Adapted from Peter Claus's translation from the Tulu telling by Kargi.

Motif T5543, Woman Gives Birth to Crane. Also told in Konkani (Goa).

Abba: An exclamation of astonishment.

Mami: Term of address for a mother-in-law or aunt.

The Tiger's Adopted Son Collected by K. Mahapatra and Norman Zide.

AT 535, The Boy Adopted by Tigers. Also told in Gondi.

How to Live on Half a Pice Retold from Geo F. D'Penha, *The Indian Antiquary*, December 1897, pp. 337–41.

Motif H915, Task Assigned Because of Girl's Own Foolish Boast. Also collected in Hindi, Tamil, and Telugu.

The Magic Bowls Retold from A. K. Ramanujan's translation in *Southern Folklore Quarterly*, vol. 20, no. 3 (September 1956), pp. 155–58.

AT 503, The Gifts of the Little People. Also collected in Telugu.

The Four Jogis Adapted from Bompas, *Folklore of the Santal Parganas*, pp. 181–83.

AT 915, The Misunderstood Precepts. Also collected in Kashmiri.

This tale parodies scores of tales wherein a king buys precepts that save his life. See "The Boy Who Sold Wisdom."

A Friend in Need Retold from an oral telling by M. G. Shashibhooshan.

AT 122G, "Wash Me" ("Soak Me") Before Eating (Motif K553.5); Bødker 638. Variants of this tale occur early in the Buddhist Jatakas.

Winning a Princess Adapted and translated from Paltadi Ramakrishna Achar, *Tuluvara Janapada Kategalu* (Madavu: Supriya Prakashana, 1987).

AT 559* (in Jason's *Types of Indic Oral Tales: Supplement*), The Dumb Princess. Also collected in Gujerati, Marathi, and Punjabi. See also AT 852, The Hero Forces the Princess to Say "No."

Here is a story that uses stories to seduce and win a difficult woman, as Scheherazade barters stories to keep off death. The stories that are told are called dilemma tales, popular in India and Africa. They all end with a question, and turn around the definition of a social role or relationship: what makes a husband, who is the truly noble person, etc. The most famous of such riddle tales in India occur in the *Vetalapancavimsati* (Twenty-five Tales of the Vampire), in the eleventh-century *Kathasaritsagara*. Heinrich Zimmer wrote an interesting Jungian essay on these tales, *The King and the Corpse* (New York: Bollingen Books, 1957). See also William Bascom's *African Dilemma Tales* (The Hague: Mouton Publishers, 1975), with 142 examples.

AT 653 and its subtypes cover many of these tales. Some of these are very popular, e.g., The Four Skillful Brothers: over 270 examples are reported from

Europe and Asia, 22 from the Americas, 6 from Africa. In India, variants are found in Bengali, Gondi, Hindi, Kannada, Tamil, and Telugu.

Flat rice (*avalakki*): rice scalded, dried, fried, and flattened in a mortar.

Crossing a River, Losing a Self Heard by the author in childhood.

AT 1287, Numskulls Unable to Count Their Own Number. Also collected in Bengali, Hindi, Gondi, Kashmiri, and Punjabi. A tale also told all over Europe: in Dutch, English, Finnish, French, Irish, German, Russian, and other languages.

In South India, this story is part of a hilarious cycle about Guru Paramartha (Paramananda in Telugu) and his disciples. It was recorded very early in Tamil by Fr. Beschi, an Italian priest who wrote in Tamil under the name Viramamunivar (1680–1746). Whether he brought these tales from Europe or gathered them in Tamil Nadu, these stories are certainly part of oral repertoires in South Indian languages. The present version closely resembles his telling, reprinted in a compilation of literary and folk materials, *Vinotaracamancari*, by Viracami Cettiyar (1876).

Prince Sabar Retold from Putlibai D. H. Wadia, *The Indian Antiquary*, vol. 16, no. 202 (November 1887), pp. 322–27.

AT 923B, The Princess Who Was Responsible for Her Own Fortune, + AT 432, The Prince as Bird. AT 923B reported exclusively from India (so far), in 25 variants: Bengali, Gondi, Hindi, Kannada, Kashmiri, and Tamil, among others; 432 has over 8 Indian variants: e.g., Bengali, Hindi, and Kannada.

The story opens with a King Lear motif: a father asks his daughters to tell their love for him, is disappointed by the words of the youngest, and banishes her. Then the tale moves on to a woman's search for her lost husband. See also note on "Adventures of a Disobedient Son," in which a father asks a similar question of his sons.

The Lord of Death Adapted from Steel, *Tales of the Punjab*, pp. 207–10.

The Shepherd's Ghost Adapted from an oral translation by V. Narayana Rao of a tale reported on pp. 308–16 of *Anantapuram Jilla Janapada Kathalu*, a Ph.D. dissertation by C. Peddi Reddy.

AT 1313A, The Man Takes Seriously the Prediction of Death. Fifteen Indian variants so far, reported from Bengali, Hindi, Punjabi, and other languages. Told also in French, Hungarian, Lithuanian, and Turkish.

This World and the Other

This story and the following one are attributed to Sri Ramakrishna; see note on "A Tiger That Didn't Know Who He Was." This tale is also reported from Oriya and Telugu.

If God Is Everywhere

Motif 2499.5. Also reported from Marathi.

A Tiger That Didn't Know Who He Was Adapted from *The Gospel of Ramakrishna* (New York: The Vedanta Society, 1907), pp. 203–4.

Many kinds of oral tales are part of the repertoire of Indian religious teachers. Sri Ramakrishna, the great nineteenth-century Bengali saint, told many parables which have become part of the oral tradition. The book cited above records his conversations, songs, and tales.

Gandharva Sen Is Dead! Retold from Mukharji, *Indian Folklore*, pp. 15–17.

AT 2023, Mourning for the Dead Ass (Motif Z32.2). Also collected in Hindi and Urdu.

Tenali Rama's Dream Retold from David Shulman's translation from Telugu, in *The King and the Clown in South Indian Myth and History*.

Motif J1527, Dream Answered by Dream. Variants in Hindi, Kannada, and Tamil.

A Feast in a Dream Adapted from Erin Moore's translation from Rajasthani, in "Dream Bread: An Exemplum in a Rajasthani Panchayat," *Journal of American Folklore*, vol. 103, no. 409 (July–September, 1990), pp. 312–13.

AT 1626, Dream Bread. Also reported in Hindi, Kashmiri, and Punjabi.

An international tale, collected in Japan, Europe, Iceland, Canada, the United States, Puerto Rico, and Brazil. The tale has usually three male companions, one of whom is considered stupid or of a lesser status. In a thirteenth-century Persian tale, a Jew outsmarts a Muslim and a Christian to win a Muslim. In a Kashmiri version, a Parsi outsmarts a Muslim and a Christian. In the Rajasthani tale collected by Moore, a Meo tells the tale about a Meo outdoing two Muslims of higher status (*khanzada*), and uses it to show the cleverness of his own community. Meos are a minority caste, often scorned by others. The story was told during a village council (*pancayat*) as a retort to a Muslim who accused the Meo of not attending to the needs of the villagers. For details, see the Moore article cited above.

In Search of a Dream From Bompas, *Folklore of the Santal Parganas*, pp. 196–201.

AT 550, Search for the Golden Bird, + AT 551, The Sons on a Quest for a Wonderful Remedy for Their Father. (This Indian variant does not have the motif of the treacherous brothers, K2211.) Also Motif H1217, Quest Assigned Because of a Dream. Reported also from Assamese, Bengali, Gondi, Hindi, Kannada, Kashmiri, Oriya, and Tamil, among other languages.

Maund: A unit of weight, equal to 82 pounds.

The Princess Whose Father Wanted to Marry Her Translated and adapted from Achar, *Tuluvara Janapada Kategalu*.

AT 706, The Maiden Without Hands. Also Motifs T411.1, Lecherous Father, and S160, Mutilation. Also collected in Hindi and Kannada.

See "A Flowering Tree" for a very different variant of the theme of the mutilated heroine.

Mother Marries Son Adapted from Irawati Karve, "A Marathi Version of the Oedipus Story," *Man*, June 1950, pp. 71–72.

AT 931, Oedipus. Variants are also found in Kannada, Konkani, and Tamil.

Here, the Oedipus story is told from a mother's point of view, and that makes it a woman-centered story. The son is merely a pawn in her fate. And the Marathi tale does not end with the mother's suicide as the Greek myth does, nor does the son blind himself. Many Indian narratives (including the *Ramayana*) have two or more endings, the one tragic, the other happy, or at least resigned. This tale too has another ending: in the Kannada versions, the mother has a son by her own son, then discovers the truth about her marriage, and sings a lullaby that truly expresses the horrible way in which incest destroys well-ordered family structures:

> Sleep, my son,
> my grandson,
> husband's brother,
> sleep well!

Then she hangs herself with her own sari. In a third ending, she runs to the goddess in her confusion and grief, and says, "O goddess, what have you done to me? You've made me marry my own son!" The goddess smiles and says, "Such things happen. Accept them. It's not your fault. Go home and serve your parents-in-law and take care of your husband and your baby." Entirely unacceptable as such an ending may seem, these stories do not flinch from exploring different possible solutions—those of resignation, defiance, suicide, absolution by a goddess, even outwitting fate. Irawati Karve, the anthropologist, who overheard this story told by her servant woman to her daughter, notes that both teller and listener laughed out loud at the end of the story, amused by the queer happenings! For a detailed discussion of the significance of such tales, see my paper "The Indian Oedipus," in Lowell Edmunds and Alan Dundes, eds., *Oedipus: A Folklore Casebook* (New York: Garland Press, 1983), pp. 234–66.

A Cure Retold from Mukharji, *Indian Folklore*, pp. 70–73.

Qazi: A Muslim priest and judge.

A Tall Tale in Urdu Adapted from Mirza Mahmud Beg, *North Indian Notes and Queries*, November 1894, pp. 134–37.

AT 1962N, The Great Wrestlers + 1960D, The Great Vegetable. Also collected in Bengali, Hindi, Punjabi, and Telugu.

For another use of tall tales, see "A Contest of Lying."

The Greatest Adapted from J. H. Hutton, "Folktales of the Angami Nagas of Assam," *Folk-Lore*, vol. 25 (1914), pp. 494–95.

AT 2031C, The Man Seeks the Greatest Being as a Husband for His Daughter. Also reported in Bengali, Gondi, and Hindi.

A Story for Sundays Retold from C. A. Kincaid, *Deccan Nursery Tales* (London: Macmillan, 1914), pp. 1–13.

Another ritual tale about the efficacy of ritual tales. See "A Story in Search of an Audience."

Atpat(nagar): Many Marathi folktales are set in this legendary town.

Shravan: A month in the Hindu calendar, roughly the month of August.

Tenali Rama and the Brahmans See note on "Tenali Rama."

Motif J1527, Dream Answered by Dream. Also told in Hindi.

A Hair's-Breadth Escape Retold from Natesa Sastri, "The Brahmarakshasa and the Hair," *The Indian Antiquary*, October 1887, pp. 293–94.

AT 1175, Straightening Curly Hair. Also collected in Hindi and Telugu.

Between Two Wives From field notes.

The Dead Prince and the Talking Doll From A. K. Ramanujan, "Telling Tales," *Daedalus*, Fall 1989, pp. 239–62.

AT 437, The Supplanted Bride (The Needle Prince). Also collected in Bengali, Hindi, and Marathi.

The Serpent Mother Adapted from "The Mother Serpent," collected by Praphulladatta Goswami, in Richard Dorson's *Folktales Told Around the World* (Chicago: University of Chicago Press, 1978), pp. 181–87.

476-A, The Serpent Relatives (in Jason's *Types of Indic Oral Tales: Supplement*). Also collected in Marathi and Telugu.

Teja and Teji Adapted from "Teja and Teji," collected by Praphulladatta Goswami, in Dorson, *Folktales Told Around the World*, pp. 177–81.

AT 511, One Eye, Two Eyes, Three Eyes, + 403, The Black and the White Bride. AT 511 collected also in Hindi, Kannada, Kashmiri, and Punjabi, among others; 403 in Bengali, Gondi, Hindi, Kannada, Kashmiri, Konkani, Tamil, and Telugu.

The Dove's Egg: A Chain Tale Adapted from a translation by M. G. Shashi-bhooshan of Palghat.

AT 248A, The Elephant and the Lark. Also collected in Assamese and Kannada.

A Drum Adapted from Usha Nilsson's translation.

AT 170A, The Clever Animal and the Fortunate Exchanges. Also collected in Bengali, Gondi, Kannada, Marathi, Punjabi, and Tamil.

This story of fortunate exchanges is often told about an animal (monkey, jackal). In the Tamil version, the monkey ends up with the drum and beats it, chanting the whole list of exchanges.

In the Kingdom of Fools From A. K. Ramanujan, *Who Needs Folklore? The Relevance of Oral Traditions to South Asian Studies*, South Asia Occasional Papers Series, no. 1, Center for South Asian Studies, University of Hawaii at Manoa, 1990, pp. 21–27.

AT 1534A, The Innocent Man Chosen to Fit the Stake. Also collected in Assamese, Bengali, Hindi, Kashmiri, Marathi, Punjabi, Tamil, Telugu, and Urdu.

This complex tale parodies governments' attempts at economic reform and the legal system, as well as the Hindu notion of karma.

Nonviolence Retold from the records of Sri Ramakrishna's oral teachings, *The Gospel of Ramakrishna*, p. 40.

See note on "A Tiger That Didn't Know Who He Was."

The Barber's Secret Translated and retold from *Vivekapotini* 99, reprinted in *Tamilnattu palankataikal*, compiled by Vai. Kovintan (Madras: New Century Book House, 1965).

AT 782, Midas and the Ass's Ears. Also reported in Gondi, Hindi, Kannada, and Santali.

Gopal Bhar Cures a Dreamer Retold from Edward C. Dimock's oral translation.

AT 1430, The Man and His Wife Build Air Castles. Variants found in Gondi, Hindi, Punjabi, Tamil, and Telugu.

A Scavenger's Dream Retold from a story told by D. P. Pattanayak.

The Boy Who Sold Wisdom Retold from C. A. Kincaid, *Folktales of Sind and Guzerat* (1925; reprint ed., Ahmedabad: New Order Book Company, 1976).

AT 910, The Good Precepts. Also reported in Hindi, Kannada, Kashmiri, Punjabi, Tamil, and Telugu. Hundreds of tales are current about a father's or a wise man's good counsel ("Never plant a thorn tree," "Test the chair before sitting down," etc.) that saves the hero from rash acts or untimely death.

Two Jars of Persian Retold from Swynnerton, *Indian Nights' Entertainments*, pp. 85–86.

AT 1296A, Fools Go to Buy Good Weather. Also collected in Kashmiri.

In Another Country Retold from Swynnerton, *Indian Nights' Entertainments*, pp. 133–38.

AT 813B, Wife Rescues Husband from Snake (Devil, etc.).

One Man's Pleasure Retold from Shankar, *Wit and Wisdom of India*, pp. 92–93.

AT 1699, Misunderstanding Because of Lack of Knowledge of a Foreign Language.

Raja Vikram and the Princess of China Retold from Shaikh Chilli, *Folk-Tales of Hindustan*, 2nd ed. (Allahabad: Panini Office, 1913), pp. 108–29.

I have included this long romantic quest tale, even novella, as an example of bardic narrative, though such tales are told also now and then by domestic tellers. See "Adventures of a Disobedient Son." They use scores of motifs, mix many plots, and appeal to our sense of suspense and the marvelous—an older analogue of Superman stories.

Raja Vikramaditya is the legendary king of Ujjain, the hero of many adventure tales in Indian languages. He is also the hero of the *Vetalapancavimsati* (Twenty-five Tales of the Vampire), in which he carries a vampire on his back and has to answer the latter's riddle-tales on peril of death. See note on "Winning a Princess."

One may assign to this long, complex tale a number like AT 425R, Marvelous Being Woos Princess.

Walking on Water Also told in Oriya, this story is attributed to Ramakrishna. See note on "A Tiger That Didn't Know Who He Was." Scores of such irreverent Indian religious tales are yet to be collected and indexed.

Various esoteric cults such as Tantra aim at achieving supernatural powers: flying through the air, being invisible, or walking on water. Saints like Ramakrishna pooh-pooh such accomplishments as unspiritual and trivial.

The Guru and the Idiot From field notes. A *bhakti* story that places faith, even an idiot's, above worldly success as a guru.

Grateful Animals, Ungrateful Man Adapted from G. D. Upreti, *Proverbs of Kumaon and Garhwal* (Lodiana, 1894), pp. 322–23.

AT 160, Grateful Animals, Ungrateful Man. Also collected in Bengali, Gondi, Kannada, Santali, and Tamil.

The first literary occurrence of this oral tale is in the *Pancatantra* in the fifth century.

When a Black Dog Dies Retold from Shankar, *Wit and Wisdom of India*.

AT 2040, The Climax of Horrors. This tale has been reported from Gujerati and Kannada. It is also told in English, Spanish, Hungarian, Russian, and other languages.

The Village Rogue, the City Rogue, and the King of Rogues Retold from K. B. Das and L. K. Mahapatra, *Folklore of Orissa* (New Delhi: National Book Trust, 1876), pp. 141–48.

AT 1525, The Master Thief, and variants. Scores of stories are told all over the world about thieves, their tricks and contests. The AT index lists 32 subtypes. The ones about how one thug is outdone by another are Indian favorites, exclusively reported for Indian languages, e.g., Assamese, Bengali, Punjabi, Kannada, Tamil, and Telugu.

Obviously, people delight in seeing rogues who cheat everyone else get cheated themselves. The present story is a string of these: first one rogue outwits another and then a third outwits both in a series of episodes that are often told as independent tales.

A Qazi with a Long Beard Retold from Wilfred E. Dexter, *Marathi Folk Tales* (London: Harrap, 1938), p. 35.

The Priest Who Could See as Far as Mecca Retold from Praphulladatta Goswami, "Assamese Tales of Priests and Priesthood," *Journal of Indian Folkloristics*, vol. 4, nos. 7–8 (1981).

Adventures of a Disobedient Son Collected from a *gondaliga* performance in Kittur by B. T. Patil, translated by A. K. Ramanujan.

AT 923, Love Like Salt, + 413, Marriage by Stealing Clothing, + 465A, The Man Resented Because of His Beautiful Wife, + 554, The Grateful Animals. This worldwide tale has over 23 Indian variants, in Assamese, Bengali, Gondi, Hindi, Kota, Punjabi, Santali, and Tamil.

A long tale commonly told by public storytellers, but told also in households, this example was collected for me from a Kannada bard (*gondaliga*), who is often part of a small group of performers with musical instruments, etc. Other adventure stories in their repertoire are tales such as "Raja Vikram and the Princess of China." These are usually quest stories, with lots of magic objects, weddings, conquests of demons, and long journeys to other worlds.

Note how this tale opens with a King Lear motif but, like *Ran*, Kurosawa's movie based on *Lear*, explores the rivalry of father and son in a patriarchal system. The story is one continuous battle with father figures to whom the young man has to prove himself—the banishing father, the king who covets his wife and sends him on dangerous missions, and Indra, the king of heaven, who puts him through tests before he gives him his daughter.

Hanchi Earlier versions of this translation appeared in *Southern Folklore Quarterly* in 1956, and in a paper, "Hanchi: A Kannada Cinderella," in Alan Dundes, ed., *Cinderella: A Folklore Casebook* (New York: Garland Publishing, 1983).

AT 510B, The Dress of Gold, of Silver, and of Stars, + 896, The Lecherous Holy Man and the Maiden in a Box. AT 510B has been reported from Bengali, Gondi, Hindi, and Tamil; 896 (which occurs early in the *Kathasaritsagara*) from Hindi, Konkani, Tamil, and Telugu.

Tales of the Cinderella cycle are told all over the world, from Alaska to South Africa, from Indonesia to South America. The earliest known example is Chinese, from the ninth century. Yet they do not all mean the same thing. If Charles Perrault's Cinderella story, made to order for the French court, represents a kitchenmaid making it to the throne, the Indian tale of Hanchi depicts the making of an ideal wife. The story continues even after she is unmasked and married to the rich man's son. She has to face the unwelcome attentions of a family guru, to withstand his mantras and passes, and to be discovered all over again and reunited with the family.

But the central structure of the Cinderella tale type has two parts to it: she is found and lost and found again. (Because of this structure, some fanciful scholars have even thought that Cinderella symbolizes the sun, lost and found each day!) The Indian tale, however, begins with a brother desiring his sister—as some European Cinderellas begin with a father's incestuous pursuit. The sister flees her brother, finds a kind old woman (who plays the role of the fairy godmother), and meets the rich family. The second part describes her struggle to escape the adulterous designs of the guru. Thus the two parts describe two temptations: incest and adultery, both of which she resists.

The French Cinderella is known by her glass slipper; the Indian Hanchi, for her special kind of rice dishes. In the Hindu world, food symbolism is embedded in caste, class, and rituals of every kind. The Sanskrit words for eating and sexual enjoyment have the same root, *bhuj*. Just as the glass slipper in the French tale may represent both female sexuality and social class, a special dish of milk and rice becomes the sign of Hanchi's womanhood, of her place in the family as the provider of food, and of her unsullied sexual purity that withstands temptations both within the kin group and outside it. Thus the Cinderella tale type finds a different context and meaning in the Indian tellings.

Buffalo into Rooster Indumati Sheorey, *Folktales of Maharashtra* (New Delhi: Sterling Publishers, 1973), pp. 63–67.

AT 1415A, The Foolish Trader. Also collected in Hindi, Konkani, and Santali.

The Prince Who Married His Own Left Half From A. K. Ramanujan, "The Prince Who Married His Own Left Half," in Margaret Case and Gerald Barrier, eds., *Aspects of India: Essays in Honor of Edward C. Dimock, Jr.* (Delhi: Manohar, 1985). The paper contains a detailed analysis of the tale.

AT 851A, Turandot, Princess Who Sets Riddles, + 516A, The Sign Language of the Princess, + Motif H805, Riddle of the Murdered Lover. Variants reported from Kashmiri and Newasi (Nepal).

A Buffalo Made of Lac Retold from S. M. Natesa Sastri, *The Indian Antiquary*, March 1887, pp. 80–83.

Motif J2214, Absurd Generalization from a Particular Incident.

Though Sanskrit is a classical language, in India it too has oral traditions. Scores of tales are told in what might be called "folk Sanskrit," or told in our mother tongues with Sanskrit tags or proverbs like this one about a man's obsessive generalization of his betrayal. The proverb is often quoted first in a context that fits it, and then the story is told as an explanation. See "Shall I Show You My Real Face?"

A Contest of Lies Retold from Chilli, *Folk-Tales of Hindustan*, pp. 11–20.

AT 1920F, He Who Says "That's a Lie" Must Pay a Fine. Also collected from Kashmiri and Punjabi.

This story of two people telling tall tales has an interesting structure. The tale within the tale is told to humiliate the listener and his clan; when he protests it is a lie, he has to pay a forfeit. The tale within the tale brings closure to the frame tale. It also relates the characters in the inner tale to the teller and the listener in the outer tale—which is how tales (and also proverbs) function. The characters within a tale become analogues to the characters outside it; the situation within the tale becomes a metaphor for the situation outside it. See Introduction.

It's Done with Mirrors Retold from C. V. Subramiah Pantulu, "Folklore of the Telugus," *The Indian Antiquary*, January 1897, pp. 27–28.

AT 1804B, Payment with the Clink of Money, + Motif J1172, Judgment as Rebuke to Unjust Plaintiff.

The Kurumba in the Parrot's Body Retold from M. B. Emeneau, *Kota Texts*, vol. 2 (Berkeley and Los Angeles: University of California Press, 1946), pp. 270–89.

AT 233A, Birds Escape by Shamming Death, + 243, The Parrot Pretends to Be God. Both types occur early in the *Pancatantra* and are part of oral traditions in Hindi, Kannada, and other languages.

The Kurumbas, Kotas, and Todas are neighboring tribes in the Nilgiri or

Ootacamund Hills. In this Kota tale of sorcery, a man enters the body of a parrot, and several parrot tales are attached to this motif.

Parrots are central characters in many tale cycles such as the Sanskrit *Sukasaptati*, the Persian *Tutinameh* (thirteenth century), and the Hindi *Totakahani*. In the first, a man leaves his wife with a parrot to guard her chastity. When she tries to leave home to meet a lover, the parrot begins a story and keeps her engaged all night. It tells stories night after night till the man comes back and finds his wife still faithful—seventy-five tales later.

Maybe because parrots and mynahs can imitate human speech, they are also usually the birds that prophesy the future of heroes and heroines, as in "The Eighth Key." See also "The Parrot Called *Hiraman*."

The Eighth Key Retold from Kincaid, *Folktales of Sind and Guzerat*, pp. 45–54.

AT 516, told in Europe as the story of Faithful John. Also collected in Bengali, Gondi, Hindi, Kannada, Marathi, Punjabi, Rajasthani, and Tamil.

Told from Portugal to India and often considered to be of Indian origin, this tale appears in the eleventh century in the *Kathasaritsagara*. The motif cluster of the three perils (e.g., a tree or bridge falling on the prince, poisoned food, a snake coming into the bedchamber) and the faithful servant or relative overhearing a conversation between two birds (or Fate muttering to herself) and thereby averting the dangers occurs in different tales. In "Untold Stories," the emphasis is on the need of the stories to be told; in "The Eighth Key," on the fidelity of the minister and the romance; in "Brother's Day," on the love between brother and sister and how a sister protects her brother. ("Brother's Day" is also a ritual tale.) Thus motifs and plots are enlisted for different meanings and contexts. The same plot tells different stories.

How the Weaver Went to Heaven Adapted from *North Indian Notes and Queries*, vol. 4 (February 1895), p. 193.

AT 1250B, The Fool Dangling from the Elephant's Tail (Motif J2133.5.2). Also collected in Bengali, Punjabi, and Santali.

The Tiger-Makers Heard by the author in childhood, in Kannada.

Motif J1705.3, Foolish Pundits, + J2130, Foolish Disregard of Personal Danger. Also collected in Tamil and Telugu.

This old Indian analogue of a man-made Frankenstein monster that kills its makers appears early in the *Pancatantra*, where three learned Brahmans make a lion. I've always heard it told about a tiger, not a lion.

When a Tale Is Finished Adapted from Das and Mahapatra, *Folklore of Orissa*, pp. 148–49.

Similar verses end tales in Assamese and Bengali. Sometimes the content of this verse is told as a full-fledged tale. For other kinds of endings, see note on "The Kite's Daughter."

And Then, Bhurrah! Retold from Rev. A. Manwaring, *Marathi Proverbs* (Oxford: Clarendon Press, 1899), p. 37.

AT 2300, Endless Tales. Also collected in Hindi and Telugu.

Permissions Acknowledgments

~ Grateful acknowledgment is made to the following for permission to reprint previously published material:

American Folklore Society: "A Feast in a Dream" from "Dream Bread: An Exemplum in a Rajasthani Panchayat" by Erin Moore. Reprinted by permission of the American Folklore Society from the *Journal of American Folklore*, vol. 103, no. 409 (July–September 1990). Reprinted by permission.

Center for South Asian Studies, University of Hawaii at Manoa: "In the Kingdom of Fools" from *Who Needs Folklore? The Relevance of Oral Traditions to South Asian Studies*, 1990, originally published as South Asia Occasional Papers Series, no.1. Reprinted by permission.

Daedalus: "The Dead Prince and the Talking Doll," from "Another India," reprinted from *Daedalus*, Journal of the American Academy of Arts and Sciences, vol. 118, no. 4 (Fall 1989). Reprinted by permission.

Garland Publishing Inc.: "Hanchi: A Kannada Cinderella" from *Cinderella: A Folklore Casebook*, edited by Alan Dundes. Reprinted by permission.

Manohar Book Service: "The Prince Who Married His Own Left Half" from *Aspects of India: Essays in Honor of Edward C. Dimock, Jr.*, edited by Margaret Case and Gerald Barrier. Reprinted by permission.

National Book Trust, India: "Sona and Rupa" from *Folklore of Madhyra Pradesh* by Shyam Parmar, and "The Village Rogue, the City Rogue, and the King of Rogues" from *Folklore of Orissa*, edited by K. B. Das and L. K. Mahapatra. Reprinted by permission.

Oxford University Press: "Untold Stories" from *Folk-Tales of Mahakoshal* by Verrier Elwin. Reprinted by permission.

Princeton University Press: "Tenali Rama's Dream" from *The King and the Clown in South Indian Myth and History* by David Shulman.

Sterling Publishers Pvt. Ltd.: "Buffalo into Rooster" from *Folktales of Maharashtra* by Indumati Sheorey. Reprinted by permission.

University of California Press: "The Kurumba in the Parrot's Body" from *Kota Texts* (vol. 2, no. 2, 1946) by M. B. Emeneau. Reprinted by permission.

University of Chicago Press: "Gopal Bhar the Star-Counter" from *The Thief of Love*, edited and translated by Edward C. Dimock, Jr. "The Serpent Mother" and "Teja and Teji" from *Folktales Told Around the World*, edited by Richard M. Dorson. "A Flowering Tree" from *Folktales of India*, edited by E. F. Beck et al. Reprinted by permission.

University Press of Kentucky: "The Magic Bowls" from "Some Folktales from India," from *Southern Folklore Quarterly*, September 1956. Reprinted by permission.

∼ *About the Editor* ∼ ∼

A. K. RAMANUJAN was born in Mysore, India. He was educated at Mysore University, at Deccan College in Poona, and at Indiana University, where he received a Ph.D. in linguistics. As scholar, translator, and poet, he has received numerous grants and fellowships, among them two grants from the National Endowment for the Humanities, a MacArthur fellowship, and a Fulbright scholarship. He is the author of several volumes of poetry, including *The Striders*, *Relations*, and *Selected Poems*; his translations from the languages of India include *Speaking of Siva*, *Some Kannada Poems*, *Samskara*, *Hymns for the Drowning*, and *Poems of Love and War*. His translations, poetry, and essays have appeared widely in journals and anthologies. Ramanujan is currently William E. Colvin Professor of South Asian Languages and Civilizations and a member of the Committee on Social Thought at the University of Chicago.